Withdrawn

Standard Catalogue of British Coins

COINS OF ENGLAND

AND

THE UNITED KINGDOM

22nd Edition

Edited by

Stephen Mitchell and Brian Reeds

adapted, with additional material, from catalogues originally
compiled by H. A. and P. J. Seaby

London

A Catalogue of the Coins of Great Britain
and Ireland
first published 1929

Standard Catalogue of British Coins
Volume 1. Coins of England and the United Kingdom

22nd edition, 1986

© B.A. Seaby Ltd.
8 Cavendish Square
London W1M 0AJ

Distributed by

B. T. Batsford Ltd.

P.O. Box 4, Braintree, Essex CM7 7QY, England

Typeset by Pardy & Son (Printers) Ltd., Ringwood, Hampshire.

Printed by Butler & Tanner Ltd., Frome, Somerset.

ISBN 0 900652 88 8

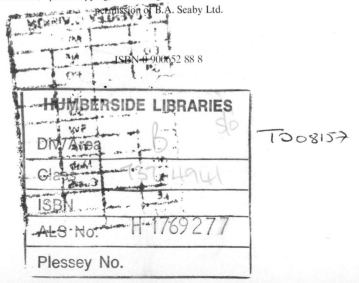

CONTENTS

PREFACE

Over twenty years ago we prepared the text for the first issue of *Coins of England and the United Kingdom* as the first volume of Seaby's 'Standard Catalogue of British Coins', which itself had been an adaptation and improvement upon our *Standard Catalogue of the Coins of Great Britain and Ireland*, first published in 1945. Over the years the text has been subject to considerable change, the most important being in 1978 when the first of the current series of revised editions was published in a format consistent with our other catalogues on Greek, Roman and Byzantine coins.

For the collector the principal improvements may be seen in the steady increase of detailed information; in values being stated in more than one grade of preservation; in the constant improvement and revision of the text to take into account new coins found each year, and to keep abreast of current numismatic research.

We do not try to lead the market or to consciously anticipate demand for any particular series of coins; we try to reflect the market, taking note of fixed and auction prices during the year. As only a very few of the coins herein actually turn up in any one year, our aim, as far as possible, is to present to the collector our opinion of what he may reasonably expect to pay for a particular coin.

This catalogue, then, is primarily intended for the collector, but it will also be found to be a compact general handbook for the archaeologist, museum curator and amateur coin finder and, for that matter, any person who has a coin to identify and who wishes to know its approximate value.

We would like to acknowledge the help we have received from a number of collectors and specialists in certain series, and we have particularly valued the comments and suggestions of those who have used previous editions of the catalogue. Those who have been engaged in the revision of this edition, apart from the Editors, are Gavin Manton (Roman coins), Peter Seaby and Frank Purvey.

THE BRITISH COIN MARKET 1985–6

During the last twelve months, the market for British coins has continued in a somewhat depressed state. There have, of course, been exceptions and we have noticed that at auctions some rare and choice pieces have brought some really quite strong prices.

It is also noticeable, that items in the London auction houses have been selling in some quantity, albeit at below catalogue prices, This, we suspect, represents a reasonable strong trade market at the 'right price', or more significantly a realistic view on behalf of the seller, who a year or two ago may well have been holding out for a return to prices realised in the 1980–1981 peak.

The editors' task in the compilation of the prices, has this year been made easier by the sale of part of the extensive collection formed by the late Mrs. Norweb by Spink & Son. This contained many rare and beautiful pieces and has enabled us to state prices which have hitherto been non existant or based on old and comparative records or general expertise. In most of these cases we have entered the 'hammer' price, condition and date of sale This year for the first time we have included EF prices for the early George III gold coins.

In our own first public auction on 23 April:

Portrait Offa penny. S.905.	realised	£3200
Portrait Alfred the Great penny. S.1061.	realised	£2050
Edward I groat. S.1379.	realised	£2100
George I crown 1726. Roses & plumes. S.3639.	realised	£2000
George II crown 1741. Roses. S.3687.	realised	£1100
George V Pattern crown 1910. E.S.C.384.	realised	£5000

The auction itself was very well attended by collectors and dealers alike, bidding was brisk throughout the day and with hundreds of postal bids to negotiate, buying was well spread and active. Despite a few inconsistencies in both directions, prices were generally around estimate and only six percent remained unsold. .

One noticeable feature of prices, confirmed by trends in this catalogue, was that high value coins (over £1000 approx) were relatively weak, whereas an area of some optimism seemed to be the late hammered and especially early milled silver in average to choice condition, where there was much bidding and prices were buoyant.

THIS CATALOGUE

Arrangement

The arrangement of this catalogue is not completely uniform, but generally it is divided into metals (gold, silver, copper, etc.) under each reign, then into coinages, denominations and varieties. In the Celtic section the uninscribed coins are listed before the dynastic coins; under Charles II all the hammered coins precede the milled coinage; the reign of George III is divided into coins issued up to 1816 and the new coinage from 1816 to the end of the reign; and under Elizabeth II the decimal issues are separated from the £.s.d. coinages.

Every major coin type is listed though not every variety. We have endeavoured to give rather more coverage to the varieties of relatively common coins, such as the pence of Edward I, II and III, than to the very much rarer coins of, for instance, King Offa of Mercia.

Values

The values given represent the scale of **retail prices** at which Seaby's are offering coins **for sale** at the time of going to press, and *not* the price that Seaby's pay. These prices are based on our knowledge of the numismatic market, the current demand for particular coins, recent auction sale prices and, in those cases where certain coins have not appeared for sale for some years, our estimation of what they would be likely to sell at today, bearing in mind their rarity and appeal in relation to somewhat similar coins where a current value *is* known. Values are given for two grades of preservation from the end of the 10th century and for three grades of preservation for most coins of the 19th and early 20th centuries (except for Ancient British where the price is for the condition in which the coin usually appears).

Seaby's endeavour to be reasonably conservative in grading the state of preservation of coins, as our clients well know. Collectors normally require coins in the best condition they can afford and, except in the case of a really rare coin, a piece that is considerably worn is not wanted and has little value. The values given in the catalogue are for the exact state of preservation stated at the head of each column; and bearing in mind that a score of identical coins in varying states of wear could be lined up in descending order from mint condition (FDC, *fleur de coin*), through *very fine* (VF) to *poor* state, it will be realized that only in certain instances will the values given apply to particular coins. A 'fine' (F) coin may be worth anything between one quarter and a half of the price quoted for a 'very fine' (VF), on the other hand a piece in really mint condition will be valued substantially higher than the price quoted for 'extremely fine' (EF).

We emphasize again that the purpose of this catalogue is to give a general value for a particular class of coin in a specified state of preservation, and also to give the collector an idea of the range and value of coins in the English series. The value of any particular piece depends on three things:

Its exact design, legend, mintmark or date.
Its exact state of preservation; this is of prime importance.
The demand for it in the market at any given time.

Some minor varieties are much scarcer than others, and, as the number of coins issued varies considerably from year to year, coins of certain dates and mintmarks are rarer and of more value than other pieces of similar type. The prices given for any type are for the commonest variety, mintmark or date of that type.

Ordering coins from this catalogue

We obviously do not have every coin in stock that is listed in this catalogue. A large selection is, however, always available for viewing by personal callers and coins may be ordered by post on seven days approval from time of delivery by known clients who have a credit account with us.

When making enquiries please ensure that the number of the coin is quoted correctly and that the reference is to the 22nd edition.

A BEGINNER'S GUIDE TO COIN COLLECTING

The Scope

Coin collecting is a fascinating recreation. It requires little physical exertion and only as much mental effort as one wishes to give at any one time. Numismatics has vast scope and boundless ramifications and byways, and it encompasses not only things historical and geographical, but it also touches on economics, metallurgy, heraldry, literature, the fine arts, politics, military history and many other disciplines. This catalogue is solely concerned with British coinage, but from the start the beginner should appreciate that the coinage of our own nation may be seen as a small, but important part of the whole gamut of world currency.

The first coins, made of electrum, a natural alloy of gold and silver, were issued in western Asia Minor about the middle of the seventh century B.C. Over the next century or so coinage of gold and silver spread across the Aegean to mainland Greece, southwards to the eastern Mediterranean lands and eventually westward to the Adriatic cities and the Greek colonies in southern Italy, Sicily and beyond. The coins of the Greeks are noted for their beautiful, sometimes exquisite craftsmanship, with many of the coin types depicting the patron deities of their cities. Coins of Philip II of Macedon (359–336 B.C.), father of Alexander the Great, circulated amongst the Celtic peoples of the Danubian basin and were widely copied through central Europe and by the Gauls in France. Gold Gaulish staters were reaching Britain around the beginning of the first century B.C. and the earliest gold to be struck in the island must have been produced shortly afterwards.

The coins of the Romans cover some seven centuries and comprise an enormous number of different types current throughout a major part of the civilized world from Spain to further Syria and from the Rhine in the north to the Sudan in the south. The Roman province of Britain was part of this vast empire for four hundred years and innumerable Roman coins have been recovered from sites in this country, most being made of brass or bronze and many being quite inexpensive.

Following the revival of commerce after the Dark Ages coinage in Western Europe was virtually restricted to silver until the thirteenth century, though gold was still being minted at Byzantium and in the Islamic world. In the Middle Ages many European cities had their own distinctive coinage, and money was issued not only by the kings, but also by many lesser nobles, bishops and abbots. From the time of the later Crusades gold returned to the west; and the artistic developments of the Renaissance brought improved portraiture and new minting techniques.

Large silver crown-size thalers were first minted at Joachimsthal in Bohemia early in the sixteenth century. With substantial shipments of silver coming to Europe from the mines of Spanish America over the next couple of centuries a fine series of larger coins was issued by the European states and cities.

Both Germany and Italy became unified nation states during the nineteenth century but balancing the reduction in European minting authorities were the new coins of the independent states of South and Central America. Over the past quarter century many new nations have established their independence and their coinage provides a large field for the collector of modern coins.

It can be seen that the scope for the collector is truly vast, but besides the general run of official coinage there is also the large series of token coins—small change unofficially produced to supplement the inadequate supply of authorized currency. These tokens were issued by merchants, innkeepers and manufacturers in many towns and villages in the 17th, 18th and 19th centuries and many collectors specialize in their local issues.

Some coins have designs of a commemorative nature; an example being the recent Royal Wedding crown, but there are also large numbers of commemorative medals which, though never intended for use as coinage, are sometimes confused with coins, being metal objects of a similar shape and sometimes a similar size to coins. This is another interesting field for collectors as these medals may have excellent portraits of famous men or women, or they may commemorate important events or scientific discoveries. Other metallic objects of coin-like appearance may be reckoning counters, advertising tickets, various other tickets and passes, and items such as brass coin weights.

Minting processes

From the time of the earliest Greek coins to about the middle of the 16th century coins were made by hand.

The method of manufacture was simple. The obverse and reverse designs were engraved or punched into the prepared ends of two bars of iron, shaped or tapered to the diameter of the required coin. The obverse die, known as the *pile*, was usually spiked to facilitate its being anchored firmly into a block of wood or metal. The reverse die, the *trussel*, was held by hand or grasped by tongs.

The coin was struck by placing a metal blank between the two dies and striking the trussel with a hammer. Thus, all coinage struck by this method is known as 'hammered' money. Some dies are known to have been hinged to ensure exact register between the upper and lower die. Usually a 'pair of dies' consisted of one obverse die (normally the more difficult to make) and two reverse dies. This was because the shaft of iron bearing the reverse design eventually split under the constant hammering; two reverse dies usually being needed to last out the life of the obverse die.

Sometime toward the middle of the 16th century experiments, first in Germany and later in France, resulted in the manufacture of coins by machinery.

The term 'milled' which is applied to all machine-made coins comes from the type of machinery used, the mill and screw press. With this machinery the obverse die was fixed and the reverse die brought into contact with the blank by heavy vertical pressure applied by a screw or worm-drive connected to a cross bar with heavy weights at each end. These weights usually had long leather thongs attached which allowed a more powerful force to be applied by the operators who revolved the arms of the press. New blanks were placed on the lower die and struck coins were removed by hand. The screw press brought more pressure to bear on the blanks and this pressure was evenly applied.

Various attempts were made during the reigns of Elizabeth I and Charles I to introduce this type of machinery with its vastly superior products. Unfortunately problems associated with the manufacture of blanks to a uniform weight greatly reduced the rate of striking and the hand manufacture of coins until the Restoration, when Charles II brought to London from Holland the Roettiers brothers and their improved screw press.

The first English coins made for circulation by this new method were the silver crowns of 1662, which bore an inscription on the edge, DECVS ET TVTAMEN, 'an ornament and a safeguard', a reference to the fact that the new coins could not be clipped, a crime made easier by the thin and often badly struck hammered coins.

The mill and screw press was used until new steam powered machinery made by Boulton and Watt was installed in the new mint on Tower Hill. This machinery had been used most successfully by Boulton to strike the 'cartwheel' two- and one-penny pieces of 1797 and many other coins, including 'overstriking' Spanish eight real pieces into Bank of England 'dollars', the old Mint presses not being able to exert sufficient power to do this. This new machinery was first used at the Mint to strike the 'new coinage' halfcrowns of 1816, and it operated at a far greater speed than the old type of mill and screw presses and achieved a greater sharpness of design.

The modern coining presses by Hordern, Mason and Edwards, now operating at the new mint at Llantrisant are capable of striking at a rate of up to 300 coins a minute.

Condition

One of the more difficult problems for the beginner is accurately to assess the condition of a coin. A common fault among collectors is to overgrade and, consequently, overvalue their coins.

Most dealers will gladly spare a few minutes to help new collectors. Dealers, such as ourselves, who issue price lists with illustrations enable collectors to see exactly what the coins look like and how they have been graded.

Coins cannot always be graded according to precise rules. Hammered coins often look weak or worn on the high parts of the portrait and the tops of the letters; this can be due to weak striking or worn dies and is not always attributable to wear through long use in circulation. Milled coins usually leave the mint sharply struck so that genuine wear is easier to detect. However a ×8 or ×16 magnifying glass is essential, especially when grading coins of Edward VII and George V where the relief is very low on the portraits and some skill is required to distinguish between an uncirculated coin and one in EF condition.

The condition or grade of preservation of a coin is usually of greater importance than its rarity. By this we mean that a common coin in superb condition is often more desirable and more highly priced than a rarity in poor condition. Few coins that have been pierced or mounted as a piece of jewellery have an interest to collectors.

One must also be on the lookout for coins that have been 'plugged', i.e. that have been pierced at some time and have had the hole filled in, sometimes with the missing design or letters re-engraved.

Badly cleaned coins will often display a complexity of fine interlaced lines and such coins have a greatly reduced value. It is also known for coins to be tooled or re-engraved on the high parts of the hair, in order to 'increase' the grade of the coin and its value. In general it is better to have a slightly more worn coin than a better example with the aforementioned damage.

Cleaning coins

Speaking generally, *don't* clean coins. More coins are ruined by injudicious cleaning than through any other cause, and a badly cleaned coin loses much of its value. A nicely toned piece is usually considered desirable. Really dirty gold and silver can, however, be carefully washed in soap and water. Copper coins should never be cleaned or washed, they may be lightly brushed with a brush that is not too harsh.

Buying and selling coins

Swopping coins at school or with other collectors, searching around the antique shops, telling your relatives and friends that you are interested in coins, or even trying to find your own with a metal detector, are all ways of adding to your collection. However, the time will come for the serious collector when he wants to acquire specific coins or requires advice on the authenticity or value of a coin.

At this point an expert is needed, and generally the services of a reputable coin dealer will be sought. There are now a large number of coin dealers in the U.K., many of whom belong to the B.N.T.A. or the I.A.P.N. (the national and international trade associations) and a glance through the 'yellow pages' under 'coin dealer' or 'numismatist' will often provide local information.

We at Seaby's have been buying and selling coins for over fifty years, and have been publishing a priced catalogue since 1929. In addition to our books on English, Greek, Roman and Byzantine coins and on British tokens, we also publish 'Seaby's Coin and Medal Bulletin', a magazine containing articles, and lists of coins for sale.

Our stock of coins for sale represents every period from Greek and Roman times to the present day, and individual prices of coins range from a pound or so to several thousands. Callers at our premises are always made very welcome.

When buying coins Seaby's reckon to pay a fair proportion of the retail value; this ranges from a half or less for inexpensive common or low grade coins to three quarters or more for particularly choice and expensive items.

Useful suggestions

Security and insurance.   The careful collector should not keep valuable coins at home unless they are insured and have adequate protection. Local police and insurance companies will give advice on what precautions may be necessary.

Most insurance companies will accept a valuation based on the Standard Catalogue. It is usually possible to have the amount added to a householder's contents policy. A 'Fire, Burglary and Theft' policy will only cover loss from the assured's address, but an 'All Risks' policy will usually cover accidental damage and loss anywhere within the U.K. We can recommend a Lloyd's broker, if requested.

Coins deposited with a bank or placed in a safe-deposit box will usually attract a lower insurance premium.

Keeping a record.   All collectors are advised to have an up-to-date record of their collection, and, if possible, photographs of the more important and more easily identifiable coins. This should be kept in a separate place from the collection, so that a list and photographs can be given to the police should loss occur. Note the price paid, from whom purchased, the date of acquisition and the condition.

Storage and handling.   New collectors should get into the habit of handling coins by the edge. This is especially important as far as highly polished proof coins are concerned.

Collectors may initially keep their coins in paper or plastic envelopes housed in boxes, albums or special containers. Many collectors will eventually wish to own a hardwood coin cabinet in which the collection can be properly arranged and displayed. If a home-made cabinet is being constructed avoid oak and cedar wood; mahogany, walnut and rosewood are ideal. It is important that coins are not kept in a humid atmosphere; especial care must be taken with copper and bronze coins which are very susceptible to damp or condensation which may result in a green verdigris forming on the coins.

From beginner to numismatist

The new collector will feel that he has much to learn. He can best advance from tyro to experienced numismatist by examining as many coins as possible, noting their distinctive features and by learning to use the many books of reference that are available. It will be an advantage if there is a local numismatic society to join as this will provide an opportunity for meeting other enthusiasts and obtaining advice from more knowledgeable collectors. Most societies have a varied programme of lectures, exhibitions and occasional auctions of members' duplicates.

Those who become members of one or both of the national societies, the Royal Numismatic Society and the British Numismatic Society, can be sure of receiving an annual journal containing authoritative papers.

Many museums have coin collections available for study and a number of museum curators are qualified numismatists.

SOME COIN DENOMINATIONS

Gold

Angel	Eighty pence (6s. 8d.) from 1464; later 7s. 6d., 10s. and 11s.
Aureus	Roman currency unit (originally $\frac{1}{40}$th lb), discontinued A.D. 324.
Britain Crown	Five shillings, 1604–12; 5s. 6d. (66d.) 1612–19.
Broad	Twenty shillings, Cromwell, 1656.
Crown	Five shillings, from 1544 (and see below and Britain crown above).
Crown of the Rose	Four shillings and 6 pence, 1526.
Crown of the Double Rose	Five shillings, 1526–44.
Florin (Double Leopard)	Six shillings, Edward III.
George Noble	Eighty pence (6s. 8d.) 1526.
Gold 'Penny'	Twenty to twenty-four pence, Henry III.
Guinea	Pound (20s.) in 1663, then rising to 30s. in 1694 before falling to 21s. 6d., 1698–1717; 21s., 1717–1813.
Halfcrown	Thirty pence, 1526 intermittently to 1612; 2s. 9d. (33d.), 1612–19.
Helm (Quarter Florin)	Eighteen pence, Edward III.
Laurel	Twenty shillings, 1619–25.
Leopard (Half florin)	Three shillings, Edward III.
Noble	Eighty pence (6s. 8d., or half mark), 1344–1464.
Pound	Twenty shillings, 1592–1600 (see also Unite, Laurel, Broad, Guinea and Sovereign).
Quarter Angel	1s. 10$\frac{1}{2}$d., 1544–7 and 1558–1600.
Rose-Noble (or Ryal)	Ten shillings, 1464–70.
Rose-Ryal	Thirty shillings, 1604–24.
Ryal	Ten shillings, Edward IV and Henry VII; fifteen shillings under Mary and Elizabeth I (see also Spur Ryal).
Solidus	Roman currency unit ($\frac{1}{72}$nd lb) from A.D. 312: the 's' of the £.s.d.
Sovereign	Twenty shillings or pound, 1489–1526 (22s. 6d., 1526–44), 1544–53, 1603–04 and from 1817 (see also Pound, Unite, Laurel, Broad and Guinea, and Fine Sovereign below).
'Fine' Sovereign	Thirty shillings, 1550–96 (see also Rose-Ryal)
Spur-Ryal	Fifteen shillings, 1605–12; 16s. 6d., 1612–25.
Stater	Name commonly given to the standard Celtic gold coin.
Third guinea	Seven shillings, 1797–1813.
Thistle Crown	Four shillings, 1604–12; 4s. 5d., 1612–19.
Thrymsa	Early Anglo-Saxon version of the late Roman tremissis (one-third solidus).
Triple Unite	Three pounds, Charles I (Shrewsbury and Oxford only, 1642–4).
Unite	Twenty shillings, 1604–12 and 1625–62; 22s., 1612–19.

Silver (and Cupro-Nickel)

Antoninianus	Roman, originally 1$\frac{1}{2}$ denarii in A.D. 214 (later debased to bronze).
Argenteus	Roman, a revived denarius.
Crown	Five shillings, 1551–1965.
Denarius	Roman, originally 10 then 16 asses (25 to the aureus), later debased: the 'd' of the £.s.d.
Farthing	Quarter penny, 1279–1553.
Florin	Two shillings, from 1849–1967.

Groat	Four pence, 1279–c. 1305 and 1351–1662 (Halfgroat from 1351). 'Britannia' groat, 1836–55 (and 1888 for Colonial use only). See also Maundy.
Halfcrown	Thirty pence (2s. 6d.),1551–1967.
Halfpenny	Intermittently, c. 890–c. 970, c. 1108 and, more generally, 1279–1660.
Maundy money	Four, three, two and one penny, from 1660.
New pence	Decimal coinage: 50p. from 1969, 25p. (crown) 1972 and 1977, 80, 81, 10p. and 5p. from 1968. 'New' removed in 1982.
Quinarius	Roman, half denarius or 8 asses; later debased.
Penny (pl. pence)	Standard unit of currency from c. 775/780 A.D.
Sceat	Early Anglo-Saxon, small, thick penny.
Shilling	Twelve pence, 1548–1966.
Siliqua	Roman, $\frac{1}{24}$th solidus.
Sixpence	From 1551–1967.
Testern (Portcullis money)	One, two, four and eight testerns for use in the Indies (and equal to the Spanish 1, 2, 4 and 8 reales); 1600 only.
Testoon	Shilling, Henry VII and VIII.
Threefarthings	Elizabeth I, 1561–82.
Threehalfpence	Elizabeth I, 1561–82, and for Colonial use, 1834–62.
Threepence	From 1551–1944 (then see Maundy).
Twenty pence	Decimal coinage from 1982.

Copper, Bronze, Tin, Nickel-Brass, etc.

As	Roman, an early unit of currency; reduced in size and equal to $\frac{1}{16}$th denarius in Imperial times.
Centenionalis	Roman, replaced the depleted follis in A.D. 346.
Dupondius	Roman, brass two asses or one-eighth of a denarius.
Farthing	Quarter penny: Harrington, Lennox, Richmond, Maltravers and 'rose' farthings, 1613–49; regal issues, 1672–1956 (tin, 1684–92).
Follis	Roman, silver-washed bronze coin, $\frac{1}{8}$th argenteus, introduced c. A.D. 290, later debased.
Half Farthing	Victoria, 1839–56 (and for Colonial use 1828–37).
Halfpenny	From 1672 to 1967 (tin, 1685–92).
New Pence	Decimal coinage; 2p., 1p. and $\frac{1}{2}$p. from 1971. 'New' removed from 1982.
Penny	From 1797 to 1967 (previously a silver coin).
Pound	Decimal coin from 1983.
Quadrans	Roman, quarter as or $\frac{1}{64}$th denarius.
Quarter Farthing	For Colonial use only, 1839–53.
Semis	Roman, half as or $\frac{1}{32}$nd denarius.
Sestertius	Roman, brass four asses or quarter denarius.
Third Farthing	For Colonial use only, 1827–1913.
Threepence	Nickel-brass, 1937–67.
Twopence	George III, 'Cartwheel' issue, 1797 only.

SOME NUMISMATIC TERMS EXPLAINED

Obverse	That side of the coin which normally shows the monarch's head or name.
Reverse	The side opposite to the obverse.
Blank	The coin as a blank piece of metal, i.e. before it is struck.
Flan	The whole piece of metal after striking.
Type	The main, central design.
Legend	The inscription.
Field	That flat part of the coin between the main design and the inscription or edge.
Exergue	That part of the coin below the main design, usually separated by a horizontal line, and normally occupied by the date.
Die	The block of metal, with design cut into it, which actually impresses the coin blank with the design.

Die variety	Coin showing slight variation of design.
Mule	A coin with the current type on one side and the previous (and usually obsolete) type on the other side, or a piece struck from two dies that are not normally used together.
Graining	The crenellations around the edge of the coin, commonly known as 'milling'.
Proof	Carefully struck coin from special dies with a mirror-like or matt surface. (In this country 'Proof' is *not* a term used to describe the state of preservation, but the method of striking.)
Hammered	Refers to the old craft method of striking a coin between dies hammered by hand.
Milled	Coins struck by dies worked in a coining press.

ABBREVIATIONS

Archb.	Archbishop	*mm.*	mintmark
Bp.	Bishop	mon.	monogram
cuir.	cuirassed	*O., obv.*	obverse
d.	penny, pence	p.	new penny, pence
diad.	diademed	pl.	plume
dr.	draped	quat.	quatrefoil
ex.	exergue	qtr.	quarter
grs.	grains	rad.	radiate
hd.	head	℞., *rev.*	reverse
i.c.	inner circle	s.	shillings
illus.	illustration	var.	variety
l.	left	wt.	weight
laur.	laureate		

CONDITIONS OF A COIN

(i.e. grade of preservation) in order of merit as generally used in England.

Proof. See above.

FDC = *Fleur-de-coin.* Flawless, unused, without any wear, scratches or marks. Usually only applied to proofs.

Unc. = *Uncirculated.* A coin in new condition as issued by the Mint, but, owing to modern mass-production methods of manufacture and storage, not necessarily perfect.

EF = *Extremely Fine.* A coin that shows little sign of having been in circulation, but which may exhibit slight surface marks or faint wear on very close inspection.

VF = *Very Fine.* Some wear on the raised surfaces; a coin that has had only limited circulation.

F = *Fine.* Considerable signs of wear on the raised surfaces, or design weak through faulty striking.

Fair. A coin that is worn, but which has the inscriptions and main features of the design still distinguishable, or a piece that is very weakly struck.

Poor. A very worn coin, of no value as a collector's piece unless extremely rare.

EXAMPLES OF CONDITION GRADING

EXTREMELY FINE

VERY FINE

FINE

FAIR

Edward III groat   *George II halfcrown*   *Victoria halfcrown*

BRITISH MINTS

LEGEND

Anglo Saxon and Norman, including Angevin mints.(to 1279)	●
Edwardian and later mints.(after 1279)	○
Mints operating in both periods.	◉
Charles I and Civil War mints.	✳

Map drawn by Alan

CELTIC COINAGE
PERIOD OF BELGIC MIGRATION

The earliest uninscribed coins found in Britain were made in Gaul and brought to this country by trade and by the migration of Belgic peoples from the continent (Gallo-Belgic issues A to F). The earliest may date from sometime late in the second century B.C., coinciding with Germanic tribes pushing westward across the Rhine and ending with refugees fleeing from the Roman legions of Julius Caesar. Certain of these coins became the prototypes for the first gold staters struck in Britain, their designs being ultimately derived from the gold staters (M) of Philip II, King of Macedonia (359–336 B.C.).

The following list is based on the 1975 edition of R. P. Mack, *The Coinage of Ancient Britain*, which now incorporates the classification for the uninscribed coins published by D. F. Allen, *The Origins of Coinage in Britain; A Reappraisal*, and from information kindly supplied by H. R. Mossop, Esq.

M   1   3   5   7

Gold Gallo-Belgic Issues   *

1	Gallo-Belgic A. (Ambiani), *c.* 125–100 B.C. *Stater.* Good copy of Macedonian stater, large flan. Laureate hd. of Apollo to l. or r. ℞. Horse to l. or r. *M. 1, 3*	£750
2	— *Quarter stater.* As last. *M. 2, 4*	£300
3	— B. (Ambiani), *c.* 115 B.C. *Stater.* Somewhat similar to 1, but small flan and "defaced" *obv.* die, some with lyre shape between horse's legs on *rev. M. 5, 7*	£450
4	— — *Quarter stater.* As last. *M. 6, 8*	£250
5	— C. (Ambiani), *c.* 100–70 B.C. *Stater.* Disintegrated face and horse. *M. 26*	£350
6	— D. *c.* 80 B.C. *Quarter stater.* Portions of Apollo head. ℞. Unintelligible mixture of stars, crescents, pellets, zig-zag lines; often referred to as "Geometric" types. (See also British 'O', *S. 49*) *M. 37, 39, 41, 41a, 42*	£175
7	— E. (Ambiani), *c.* 57–45 B.C. *Stater.* Blank *obv.* ℞. Disjointed curved horse, pellet below. *M. 27*	£200
8	— F. (Suessiones), *c.* 50 B.C. *Stater.* Disintegrated head and horse to r. *M. 34a*	£250
9	— Xc. *c.* 80 B.C. *Stater.* Blank except for VE monogram at edge of coin. ℞. S below horse to r. *M. 82a*	£400
10	— — *Quarter stater.* Similar, but horse to l. *M. 83*	£250
11	— Xd. *c.* 50 B.C. *Quarter stater.* Head l. of good style, horned serpent behind ear. ℞. Horse l. *M. —*	£500

* The price in this section is for the condition in which the coin usually appears.

13   18

Armorican (Channel Isles and N.W. Gaul), *c.* 75–50 B.C.   *

12	*Stater.* Class I. Head r. ℞. Horse, boar below, remains of driver with Victory above, lash ends in one or two loops, or "gate"	£45
13	Class II. Head r. ℞. Horse, boar below, remains of Victory only, lash ends in small cross of four pellets	£40
14	Class III. Head r., anchor-shaped nose. ℞. Somewhat similar to Class I	£45
15	Class IV. Head r. ℞. Horse with reins, lyre shape below, driver holds vertical pole, lash ends in three prongs	£50
16	Class V. Head r. ℞. Similar to last, lash ends in long cross with four pellets	£50
17	Class VI. Head r. ℞. Horse, boar below, lash ends in "ladder"	£60
18	*Quarter stater.* Similar types to above ....*from*	£85

Celtic Coins Struck In Britain
Uninscribed gold staters

19   20   21   22

19	A. Westerham type, *c.* 95–65 B.C. As 5, but horse more disjointed. *M. 28, 29*	£325
20	B. Chute type, *c.* 85–55 B.C. Similar but crab-like figure below horse. *M. 32*	£250
21	C. Yarmouth (I.O.W.) type, *c.* 80–70 B.C. Crude variety of 5. *M. 31*	£450
22	D. Cheriton type, *c.* 80–70 B.C. Variety of 20 with large crescent face. *M. 33*	£600
23	E. Waldingfield type, *c.* 90–70 B.C. Annulet and pellet below horse. *M. 48*	*Extremely rare*
24	F. Clacton type 1, *c.* 90–70 B.C. Similar to Westerham type but rosette below horse to l. *M. 47*	£425

* The price in this section is for the condition in which the coin usually appears.

25 28

*

25 G. Clacton type 2. Similar, but horse r., with pellet, or pellet with two
curved lines below. *M. 46, 46a* £350

26 H. North East Coast type, *c.* 75–30 B.C. Variety of 5, pellet or rosette
below horse to r. *M. 50, 50a, 51, 51a* £400

27 I. — — Similar, horse l., pellet, rosette or star with curved rays below.
M. 52–57 . . . . £450

28 J. Norfolk wolf type, *c.* 65–45 B.C. ℞. Crude wolf to r. or l. *M. 49, 49a,*
49b £750

30 31

29 Ka. Coritani, South Ferriby type, *c.* 30 B.C.–A.D. 10. Crude wreath. ℞.
Disjointed horse l., rectangular compartment enclosing four pellets above.
M. 447–448 . . . . £450

30 Kb. — — Similar, but star or rosette below horse. *M. 449–450a* £400

30A — — — Trefoil with central rosette of seven pellets. ℞. Similar to last.
M. 450a. In auction 1985 £5500. (this coin) . . . . *Unique*

30B — — — Similar, but horse r. *M. —* . . . . *Unique*

31 L. Whaddon Chase type, *c.* 45–20 B.C. ℞. Spirited horse r. of new style,
various symbols below. *M. 133–138a, 139a* £350

32 — — *O.* Plain. ℞. Horse r., with ring ornament below or behind.
M. 140–143 . . . . £325

33 Lx. North Thames group, *c.* 40–20 B.C. *O.* Blank apart from reversed SS.
℞. Similar to last. *M. 146* . . . . *Extremely rare*

34 Ly. North Kent group, *c.* 45–20 B.C. *O.* Blank. ℞. Horse l. or r., numerous
ring ornaments in field. *M. 293, 294* £350

35 37

35 Lz. Weald group, *c.* 35–20 B.C. *O.* Blank. ℞. Horse l., panel below. *M. 84,*
292 . . . . £600

* The price in this section is for the condition in which the coin usually appears.

Uninscribed gold staters *continued*   *

36   Lz. *O*. Blank with some traces of Apollo head. ℞. Horse r., large wheel ornament below. *M. 144–145* £400

37   M. Wonersh type, *c.* 35–20 B.C. Crossed wreath design with crescents back to back in centre. ℞. Spiral above horse, wheel below. *M. 148* £375

38   39

38   NA. Iceni, *c.* 30 B.C.–A.D. 10. Double crescent design. ℞. Horse r. *M. 397, 399* £600

39   NB. — Trefoil on cross design. ℞. Similar to last. *M. 401–403a* £600

40   NC. — Cross of pellets. ℞. Similar to last. *M. 400* £625

41   43

41   QA. British "Remic" type, *c.* 45–25 B.C. Crude laureate head. ℞. Triple-tailed horse, wheel below. *M. 58, 60, 61* £350

42   QB. — Similar, but *obv.* blank. *M. 59, 62* £300

43   R. Dobunni, *c.* 30 B.C.–A.D. 10. Similar, but branch emblem or ear of corn on *obv. M. 374* £600

Uninscribed Quarter Staters

44   45   46

43A F. Clacton type. *O*. Plain, traces of pattern. ℞. Ornamental cross with pellets. *M. 35* £375

44   LX. N. Thames group, *c.* 40–20 B.C. Floral pattern on wreath. ℞. Horse l. or r. *M. 76, 151, 270–271* £250

45   LY. N. Kent group, *c.* 45–20 B.C. *O*. Blank. ℞. Horse r. *M. 78, 284–285* . £250

46   LZ. Weald group, *c.* 35–20 B.C. Spiral design on wreath. ℞. Horse l. or r. *M. 77, 80–81* £250

47   — — *O*. Blank. ℞. Horse l., panel below. *M. 85* £300

48   N. Iceni, *c.* 30 B.C.–A.D. 10. Floral pattern. ℞. Horse r. *M. 404* £250

* The price in this section is for the condition in which the coin usually appears.

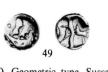

49   50   51

49 O. Geometric type, Sussex group, *c.* 80–60 B.C. Unintelligible patterns
   (some blank on *obv.*). *M. 40, 43–45* . . . .   *
                                                                                          £125
50 P. — Kentish group, *c.* 65–45 B.C. O. Blank. ℞. Trophy design. *M. 36, 38*   £200
51 QC. British "Remic" type, *c.* 40–20 B.C. Head or wreath pattern. ℞.
   Triple-tailed horse, l. or r. *M. 63–67, 69–75* £200
52 R. Dobunni, *c.* 30 B.C.–A.D. 10. O. Blank. ℞. Somewhat as last. *M. 68* . .   £325

Uninscribed Silver

53   55   56   58

52A(L) North Thames group. Head r. with headband (or diadem) and flowing
   hair. ℞. New style horse of Whaddon Chase type (See *S.* 31a). *M.* — . . .   *Unique*
52B — — Similar. ℞. Pegasos. *M.* — £250
53 LX. Head l. or r. ℞. Horse l. or r. *M. 280, 435, 436, 438, 441* £175
54 — — Head l. ℞. Goat r., with long horns. *M. 437* £225
55 — — Two horses or two beasts. *M. 442, 443, 445* £200
56 — — Star of four rays or wreath pattern. ℞. Horse or uncertain animal r.
   M. 67, 272a, 414, 439, 440 . . . .   £175
56A— — Hd. r. with corded hair and headband. ℞. Horse l., leaf (?) below,
   ornaments in field. (Somewhat similar to *S.* 77.) *M.* — . . . .   *Extremely rare*
56E — — *Half unit.* Cruciform pattern with ornaments in angles. ℞. Horse l.,
   ear of corn between legs, crescent and pellets above. *M.* — . . . .   *Extremely rare*
57 LZ. South Thames group. Wreath or head of serpent. ℞. Horse. *M.* —
   (*Allen L 28-10*) £275
58 — — Helmeted head r. ℞. Horse. *M. 89* £250
58A — — Facing hd. of Celtic god with horns, wheel between. ℞. Triple-tailed
   horse l., ornaments in field. *M.* — . . . .   *Extremely rare*
58B— — Two swans (or cranes), boar and eel (?) below. ℞. Reindeer l., boar
   on hindquarters. *M.* — . . . .   *Unique*
59 — —*Quarter unit* (3½–4 grains). Similar to 58. *M. 90–91* £200

60   63   64

60 Durotriges, *c.* 60 B.C.–A.D. 20. Size and type of Westerham staters (nos.
   19 and 81 above). *M. 317.* Quality of Ꝛ varies, price for good Ꝛ £175
61 — Size and type of Sussex Geometric type (no. 49 above). *M. 319* £125
61A— 'Starfish' design. ℞. 'Geometric' pattern. *M. 320* £175
62 — Very thin flans, *c.* 55 B.C. Crude hd. of lines and pellets. ℞. Horse similar.
   M. 321 . . . .   £300
63 Dobunni, *c.* 30 B.C.–A.D. 10. Head r., with recognisable face. ℞. Triple-
   tailed horse l. or r. *M. 374a, b, 375, 376, 378* £150
64 — Very crude head. ℞. Similar to last. *M. 378a–384d* £90
65 — *Quarter unit.* As last. *M. 384c* . . . .   *Extremely rare*

* The price in this section is for the condition in which the coin usually appears.

6 CELTIC COINAGE

Uninscribed silver *continued*

66   69   72

                                                                     *

66 Coritani, *c.* 50 B.C.–A.D. 10. I. Prototype issue of good style and execution. Boar r., with rosette and ring ornaments. ℞. Horse. *M. 405, 405a, b, 406, 451* £250
67 — — *Half unit.* Similar. *M. 406a, 451a* £135
68 — II. South Ferriby type. Vestiges of boar on *obv.* ℞. Horse. *M. 410, 452, 453* £175
69 — — *O.* Plain. ℞. Horse. *M. 453a, 454* £175
70 — — *Half unit.* Similar. *M. 455–456* £150
71 — — *Quarter unit.* Similar. *M. 456a* £150

    74   77   82

72 Iceni, *c.* 10 B.C.–A.D. 60. Boar r. ℞. Horse r. *M. 407–409* £75
73 — *Half unit.* Similar. *M. 411* £75
73A — — Antlered deer. ℞. Horse r. *M.* — . . . . *Unique*
73B — Quarter unit. Similar to 73. *M.* — . . . . *Unique*
74 — Head r. ℞. Horse. *M. 412–413e* £50
74A — Large bust of good style. ℞. Horse r. . . . . *Extremely rare*
74B — Similar, but inverted ear of corn between legs of horse on *rev. M.* — *(413 variety)* . . . . *Extremely rare*
75 — Double crescent and wreath pattern. ℞. Horse. *M. 414–415, 440* £40
76 — *Half unit.* Similar. *M. 417a* £135
76a — — Three crescents back to back. ℞. Horse r. *M. 417* £175

Uninscribed Bronze

77 LX. North Thames group. Head l. with braided hair. ℞. Horse l. *M. 273, 274,* see also *M.281* £90
78 — — Horned pegasus l. ℞. Pegasus l. *M. 446* . . . . *Extremely rare*
79 — — Other types . . . . *.from* £225
80 LY. North Kent group. Boar. ℞. Horse. *M. 295–296* £150
81 Durotriges, *c.* A.D. 20–50. Debased form of Æ stater (no. 60). *M. 318* . . £50
82 — Cast coins, *c.* A.D. 50–70. As illustration. *M. 322–370* £75

          83   84

Potin (bronze with a high tin content)

83 Thames and South, *c.* 1st century B.C. Cast. Class I. Crude head. ℞. Lines representing bull. (*Allen,* types A–L). *M. 1–22a* £35
84 Kent and N. Thames, *c.* mid. 1st century A.D. Cast. Class II. Smaller flan, large central pellet. (*Allen,* types M–P). *M. 23–25* £80

* The price in this section is for the condition in which the coin usually appears.

CELTIC DYNASTIC ISSUES

The Celtic dynastic issues are among the most interesting and varied of all British coins. A great deal is known about some of the issuers from Julius Caesar's *Commentaries* and other sources—chiefly the kings of the Atrebates, Regni and Catuvellauni—while many are issues of kings quite unknown to history bearing legends which defy interpretation.

Roman influence in coinage design is particularly noticeable in the reign of Cunobelin (*c.* A.D. 10–40), but the Icenian revolt of A.D. 61 in which Colchester and London were sacked with the massacre of over 70,000 Romans resulted in the termination of British Celtic coinage which previously had been allowed to circulate along with Roman coins.

The dates given for the various rulers are, in most cases, very approximate. Staters and quarter staters are gold coins of varying quality.

N.B. Bronze coins in poor condition are worth very much less than the values given for 'Fine' coins. All coins, even good specimens, are worth less if they lack clear legends, are struck off-centre or have striking cracks.

SOUTHERN BRITAIN

Atrebates and Regni. *Berks., Hants., Surrey and Sussex* *

85 **Commius,** *c.* 35–20 B.C. *Stater.* Portions of laureate hd. r. ℞. COMMIOS
around triple tailed horse r. *M. 92* £2500
Copied from the "Remic" type QA (no. 41), this is the first inscribed British coin.

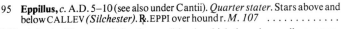

85   86   88

86 **Tincommius,** *c.* 20 B.C.–A.D. 5. Celtic style. *Stater.* Similar, but TINC
COMMI F, or TIN DV around horse. *M. 93, 94* £850
87 — *Quarter stater.* TINCOM, zig-zag ornament below. ℞. Horse l. *M. 95* . £500
88 Classical style. *Stater.* TINC or COM · F on tablet. ℞. Horseman with
javelin. *M. 96, 98, 100* £900
89 — *Quarter stater.* TINC on a tablet, C above, A or B below. ℞. Medusa hd.
facing. *M. 97* £450
90 — — *O.* As 88. ℞. Horse l. or r. *M. 99, 101–104* £400
91 — *Silver.* Head r., TINCOM. ℞. Eagle facing. *M. 105* £700
92 — — Head l. ℞. Bull charging l., TINC. *M. 106* £600
92* — — Facing hd. with ornate hair. ℞. As last. *M.* — £350
92A — — Laureate head l. ℞. Boar standing r., pentagram, TINCO in ex. ... *Extremely rare*
92B — — Similar, but head r., C (?) behind. ℞. Bull charging r. *M.* — .... *Extremely rare*
92C — — — TINCOMMIVS. ℞. Horse l. *M. 131b.* (Listed in Mack under
Verica.) .... *Extremely rare*
93 — — TINC. ℞. Animal prancing l. *M. 106a* .... *Extremely rare*
93A — Victory r., TIN. ℞. CO. F. within wreath. *M.* — £300
93B — — TINC in angles of four rays, pellet in centre. ℞. Lion on hippo-
camp l. *M.* — £350
93C — — Five pointed star, pellet in centre. ℞. Boy on a dolphin r., TIN
below. *M.* — £250
94 — *Silver quarter unit.* C F within two interlinked squares. ℞. Dog to r.,
TINC. *M. 118* .... *Extremely rare*
94A — — Eagle r., TINC. ℞. Two handled krater, REX above. *M.* — £350

89   95

95 **Eppillus,** *c.* A.D. 5–10 (see also under Cantii). *Quarter stater.* Stars above and
below CALLEV *(Silchester).* ℞. EPPI over hound r. *M. 107* £350

* The price in this section is for the condition in which the coin usually appears.

Atrebates and Regni *continued*

<table>
<tr><td>96</td><td>98</td><td>99</td></tr>
</table>

*

95A — EPPILLV · COMM · F · around crescent. ℞. Horse r., star above and below. *M.* — .... *Extremely rare*

96 *Silver.* EPP over eagle. ℞. REX crescent CALLE. *M. 108* £275

96A — Bearded hd. r. in wreath, no legend. ℞. Boar r., EPPI COM or EPPI F CO. *M.* —.. £275

96C — Quarter unit. Crook-ended cross, pellets in angles. ℞. Horse r., EPP *Extremely rare*

96D — — Ram (?) r., dividing EPPI CO. ℞. Bull's hd. facing. *M.* — ... £300

96E *Bronze.* Floral design of 8 petals surrounded by 4 crescents and 4 annulets. ℞. Hound r., EPPI above, COM F below .... *Extremely rare*

97 **Verica,** *c.* A.D. 10–40. *Stater.* Group I. COM · F on tablet. ℞. VIR below horseman r. *M. 109, 110* £700

98 — II. Similar but title REX added. *M. 121* £650

99 — III. Vineleaf between VI – RI. ℞. Horseman r. *M. 125* £750

100 *Quarter stater.* I. COM · F etc. ℞. Horse VIR etc. *M. 111–114* £400

101 — II. VERIC COM · F in two lines. ℞. Horse r., REX below. *M. 122* £400

102 — III. Vineleaf, VERI below. ℞. Horseman as no. 97. *M. 124* £400

103 — — Head or seated figure. ℞. Horseman r. *M. 126–127* £425

104 *Silver.* I. Crescents, COM · F. ℞. Boar. *M. 115* £150

104A — — — ℞. Eagle l. VIR. *M.*— £350

104B — — VIRIC across field, ornaments above and below. ℞. Pegasus r., star design below (12.2 grs.) .... *Extremely rare*

<table>
<tr><td>105</td><td>107</td><td>110</td><td>113</td></tr>
</table>

105 — II. Name around circles. ℞. Lion r. *M. 123* £225

106 — III. Horseman with spear. ℞. Horseman with shield. *M. 128* £225

107 — — Seated figure. ℞. Two cornucopiae. *M. 129* £250

107A — — Bird l. ℞. As last. *M.* — .... *Extremely rare*

108 — — Head r. ℞. Seated or standing figure. *M. 130–131* £275

108A — — Head r. ℞. Eagle. *M. 131a* .... *Extremely rare*

108B — — Bull butting r. ℞. Figure standing l. *M.* — .... *Extremely rare*

108C — — Bull dividing VERICA REX. ℞. Stg. fig. with head on a standard, COMMI F. *M.* — £250

109 *Silver quarter unit.* I. *O.* Various. ℞. Animal. *M. 116–117; 119–120e* ... £175

109A — — Eagle l., VE. ℞. Boar's hd. r., CF. *M.* — .... *Extremely rare*

109B — Sphinx C.F. ℞. Dog or wolf curled head to tail. VERI. .... *Extremely rare*

109C Eagle r. VERCA COMMI F. ℞. Wine krater. *M.* — .... *Extremely rare*

110 — III. C · F in wreath. ℞ Head r., VERI. *M. 132* £175

111A — IV. VIR/VAR on tablet. ℞. Pegasus r., CO below. *M.* — .... *Extremely rare*

* The price in this section is for the condition in which the coin usually appears.

*

11B — — VERICA around bucranium. ℞. Tomb, or altar, C.F. *M.* —	*Extremely rare*
11C — — 'Maltese cross' design, pellets in angles. ℞. Hand grasping trident, VER REX.	*Unique*
11D— Two corpucupiae. ℞. Eagle. *M.*—	*Extremely rare*
11E Acorn pattern r. ℞. RVER CA, seahorse?	*Extremely rare*
11F Interlinked C's or crescents, standard between dividing CR at top. ℞. Hippocamp, VERICA. *M.* —.	£250
11G Human headed Sphinx, VERIC. ℞. Hd. r., SCF(?). *M.* —	£250
11H Helmeted bust r. in Roman style. ℞. Horse r., CF between legs. *M.* —	£250
112 **Epaticcus,** *c.* A.D. 25–35. *Stater.* TASCI · F, ear of wheat. ℞. EPATICCV, horseman r. *M. 262*	£1250
113 *Silver.* Head of Hercules r., EPATI. ℞. Eagle stg. on snake. *M. 263* . .	£125
114 — Victory seated r. ℞. Boar. *M. 263a*	£150
114A — EPATI in panel. ℞. Lion r. *M.* —	*Extremely rare*
115 *Silver quarter unit. O.* EPATI. ℞. Lion's head (?), TA below. *M. 264*	£325
115A — Lion (?) r., EPA. ℞. TΛ in centre of double lozenge. *M.* —	*Rare*
116 *Bronze.* Head r. ℞ Horseman charging r., EPA. *M.* —	*Unique*
Only known from P. W. P. Carlyon-Britton, sale, 1913, lot 65.	
117 **Caratacus,** *c.* A.D. 35–40. *Silver.* As 113, CARA. *M. 265*	£1000
The above two rulers were brother and son of Cunoblin, (see Catuvellauni), but their coins appear in the same area as Verica's.	
117A *Silver quarter unit.* CARA around pellet in circle. ℞. Pegasus r., no legend. *M.* —	£1000

Cantii *Kent*

118 **Dubnovellaunus,** *c.* 15–1 B.C. *(See also under Trinovantes). Stater. O.* Blank. ℞. Horse r., DVBNOVELLAVNOS or DVBNOVI. *M. 283–283*	£450
119 *Silver.* Griffin r. or horned animal. ℞. Horse l. or seated figure. *M. 286–287*	£250
120 — Head l. ℞. Pegasus. *M. 288*	£250
121 *Bronze.* Boar. ℞. Eagle, horseman or horse. *M. 289, 291, 291a*	£175
122 — Animal. ℞. Horse or lion l., DVBN on tablet below. *M. 290*	£175

117    117A    118    124

123 **Vosenios,** *c.* A.D. 5. *Stater. O.* Blank. ℞. Serpent below horse. *M. 297* . . .	*Extremely rare*
124 *Quarter stater.* Similar, VOSII below horse. *M. 298*	£450
125 *Silver.* Griffin and horse. ℞. Horse, retrograde legend. *M. 299a*	£350
126 *Bronze.* Boar l. ℞. Horse l., SA below. *M. 299*	£250

128 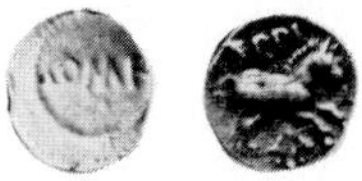   130    131

127 **Eppillus,** *c.* A.D. 10–25. *(See also under Atrebates.) Stater.* COM · F in wreath. ℞. Horseman l., EPPILLVS. *M. 300*	£900
128 — Victory in wreath. ℞. Horseman r. Illustrated above. *M. 301*	£1100

* The price in this section is for the condition in which the coin usually appears.

*

129   *Quarter stater.* EPPIL / COM · F. ℞. Pegasus. *M. 302* £300
130   — EPPI around wreath, or COM · F. ℞. Horse. *M. 303–304* £300
131   *Silver.* Head r. or l. ℞. Lion or horseman. *M. 305–306* £300
132   — Diademed head l. or r., IOVIR. ℞. Victory or capricorn. *M. 307–308a* .   £300
133   *Bronze.* Head l. ℞. Victory holding wreath. *M. 311* £250
134   — Cruciform ornament or bull. ℞. Eagle. *M. 309–310* £250
135   — Bearded head l. ℞. Horse r. *M. 312* £250

136

136   **Amminus,** *c.* A.D. 15? *Silver.* Plant. ℞. Pegasus r. *M. 313* £650
137   — A within wreath. ℞. Capricorn r. *M. 314* £500
138   *Silver quarter unit.* A within curved lines. ℞. Bird. *M. 316* £250
139   *Bronze.* Head r. ℞. Capricorn r. *M. 315* £250

Unattributed coins of the Cantii

140   *Silver quarter unit.* Horseman. ℞. Seated figure wearing belt and holding
       spear or staff. *M. 316e* . . . .   *Extremely rare*
141   *Bronze.* Boar or head. ℞. Lion to r. or l. *M. 316a, c* £150
142   — Animal r. ℞. Horse l. *M. 316b* £150
143   — *O.* Uncertain. ℞. Ring ornaments. *M. 316d* . . . .   *Extremely rare*
144   *Bronze quarter unit.* Quatrefoil pattern. ℞. Horse r. *M. 316f* £150

145   148

Durotriges   *W. Hants., Dorset, Somerset and S. Wilts*

145   **Crab.** *Silver.* CRAB in angles of cross. ℞. Eagle. *M. 371* £750
146   *Silver quarter unit.* CRAB on tablet. ℞. Star shape. *M. 372* £500
147   **Uncertain.** *Silver.* Two boars back to back. ℞. Ring ornaments etc. in field.
       M. 373 . . . .   *Unique*

NORTH THAMES

Trinovantes   *Essex and counties to the West*

150   152   154

148   **Addedomaros,** *c.* 15–1 B.C. *Stater.* Crossed wreath or spiral. ℞. Horse,
       wheel or cornucopiae below. *M. 266–267* £500
149   — Double crescent ornament. ℞. Horse, branch below. *M. 268* £700
150   *Quarter stater.* Similar, but rectangle or wheel below horse. *M. 269* £300
       *[Note. For uninscribed bronze, sometimes attributed to Addedomaros,
       see S. 77 (M. 273/274).]*
151   **Diras?,** *c.* A.D. 1? *Stater. O.* Blank. ℞. DIRAS and snake (?) over horse,
       wheel below. *M. 279* . . . .   *Extremely rare*

* The price in this section is for the condition in which the coin usually appears.

*

152	**Dubnoveḷḷaunus,** *c.* A.D. 1–10. *(See also under Cantii.) Stater.* Wreath design. ℞. Horse l., branch below. *M. 275*	£500
153	*Quarter stater.* Similar. *M. 276*	£275
154	*Bronze.* Head r. or l. ℞. Horse l. or r. *M. 277–278,* see also *M. 281*	£75
155	— Without legend but associated with the Trinovantes. Head or boar. ℞. Horse or horseman. *M. 280a, b, d*	£120

Catuvellauni   *N. Thames, Herts., Beds., spreading East and South*

157   163

Tasciovanus, *c.* 20 B.C.–A.D. 10, and associated coins

157	*Stater.* Crescents in wreath. ℞. TASCIAV and bucranium over horse. *M. 149–150*	£750
158	— Similar, sometimes with VER *(Verulamium).* ℞. Horseman r., TASC. *M. 154–156*	£700
159	— Similar, but T, or V and T. ℞. Similar to last. *M. 157*	*Extremely rare*
160	— As 157. ℞. Horse, CAMV monogram *(Camulodunum).* M. 186	£800
161	— TASCIOV / RICON in panel. ℞. Horseman l. *M. 184*	£900
162	— TASCIO in panel. ℞. Horseman r., SEGO. *M. 194*	£900
163	*Quarter stater.* Wreath, TASCI or VERO. ℞. Horse, TAS or TASC. *M. 152–153*	£350
164	— *O.* As 160. ℞. CAMVL mon. over horse. *M. 187*	£350
165	— *O.* As 161, omitting RICON. ℞. Pegasus l. *M. 185*	£350
166	— *O.* As 162. ℞. Horse l. omitting SEGO. *M. 195*	£350
167	*Silver.* Bearded head l. ℞. Horseman r., TASCIO. *M. 158*	£200
168	— Pegasus l., TAS. ℞. Griffin r., within circle of pellets. *M. 159*	£200
169	— Eagle stg. l., TASCIA. ℞. Griffin r. *M. 160*	£200
170	— VER in beaded circle. ℞. Horse r., TASCIA. *M. 161*	£150
171	— — ℞. Naked horseman, no legend. *M. 162*	£150

172   175   178

172	— Laureate hd. r., TASCIA. ℞. Bull butting l. *M. 163*	£150
173	— Cruciform ornament, VERL. ℞. Boar, r. TAS. *M. 164*	£150
173A	— Saltire over cross within square, serpentine design around. ℞. Similar to last. *M. —*	*Extremely rare*
174	— TASC in panel. ℞. Pegasus l. *M. 165*	£150
175	— — ℞. Horseman l. carrying a long shield. *M. 166*	£150
176	— SEGO on panel. ℞. Horseman. *M. 196*	£250
177	— DIAS / C / O. ℞. Horse, VIR (?) below. *M. 188*	£250
178	*Bronze.* Two heads in profile, one bearded. ℞. Ram l., TASC. *M. 167*	£75
179	— Bearded head r. ℞. Horse l., VIIR, VER or TAS. *M. 168–169*	£75
180	— Head r., TASC. ℞. Pegasus l., VER. *M. 170*	£75
181	— — TAS ANDO. ℞. Horse r. *M. 170a*	*Unique*
182	— Head r., TAS. ℞. Horseman r., VER. *M. 171*	£75
183	— VERLAMIO between rays of star-shaped ornament. ℞. Bull l. *M. 172*	£75

* The price in this section is for the condition in which the coin usually appears.

Tasciovanus *continued*

185   190   191

*

184	*Bronze.* Similar, without legend. ℞. Sphinx l., legend SEGO? *M. 173*	£75
185	— Similar. ℞. Bull r. *M. 174*	£75
186	— Similar. ℞. Horse l., TASCI. *M. 175*	£75
187	— Head r., TASC . . . ℞. Horse r. in double circle. *M. 175*	*Extremely rare*
188	— Laureate hd. r., TASCIO. ℞. Lion r., TASCIO. *M. 176*	£75
189	— Head r. ℞. Figure std. l., VER below. *M. 177*	£85
190	— — TASCIAVA. ℞. Pegasus l., TAS. *M. 178 (double bronze denomination)*	*Extremely rare*
191	— Cruciform ornament of crescents and scrolls. ℞. Boar r., VER. *M. 179* .	£100
192	— Laureate head r. ℞. Horse l., VIR. *M. 180*	£80
193	— Raised band across centre, VER or VERL below, uncertain objects above. ℞. Horse grazing r. *M. 183a*	£100
194	— RVII above lion r. within wide beaded circle. ℞. Eagle looking l., sometimes reading RVE. *M. 189*	£100
195	— Bearded head r., RVIIS. ℞. Horseman r., VIR. *M. 190*	£90
196	— RVIIS on panel. ℞. Animal l. *M. 191*	£100
197	— Head r., TASC DIAS. ℞. Centaur r. playing double pipe, or sometimes horses, *M. 192*	£100
198	*Bronze half denomination.* Lion? r. ℞. Sphinx l. *M. 181*	*Extremely rare*
199	— Bearded head l. or r., VER. ℞. Goat or boar r. *M. 182–183*	£100
200	— Head l. ℞. Animal l. with curved tail. *M. 183b, c*	£100
201	— Annulet within square with curved sides. ℞. Eagle l., RVII. *M. 193* . . .	£100

202   203   205

202	**Andoco,** *c.* A.D. 5–15. *Stater.* Crossed wreath design. ℞. Horse r., AND. *M. 197*	£1000
203	*Quarter stater.* Crossed wreaths, ANDO. ℞. Horse l. *M. 198*	£325
204	*Silver.* Bearded head l. in looped circle. ℞. Pegasus l., ANDOC. *M. 199* . .	£400
205	*Bronze.* Head r., ANDOCO. ℞. Horse r., AND. *M. 200*	£150
206	*Bronze half denomination.* Head l. ℞. Horse r., A between legs, branch in exergue. *M. —*	£175

* The price in this section is for the condition in which the coin usually appears.

207 208

| | *|

207 **Cunobelin** *(Shakespeare's Cymbeline), c.* A.D. 10–40. *Stater.* CAMVL on panel. ℞. Leaf above two horses galloping l., CVNOBELIN on curved panel below. *M. 201* £800

208 — Ear of corn dividing CA MV. ℞. Horse prancing r., CVNO below. *M. 203, 206, 210–213.* Varying in style, from— £600

209 — Similar, but horse l. *M. 208* . . . . *Extremely rare*

210 *Quarter stater.* Similar to 207. *M. 202* £350

211 — Similar to 208. *M. 204, 209* £350

212 — Similar to 208 but CAM CVN on *obv. M. 205* £450

213 *Silver.* Two bull headed snakes intertwined. ℞. Horse l., CVNO. *M. 214* . . £250

214 — Head l., CAMVL before. ℞. CVNO beneath Victory std. r. *M. 215* £175

215 — CVNO BELI in two panels. ℞. CVN below horseman galloping r. (legends sometimes retrograde). *M. 216, 217* £225

216 — Two leaves dividing CVN. ℞. CAM below horseman galloping r. *M. 218* £250

217 — Flower dividing CA MV. ℞. CVNO below horse r. *M. 219* £250

218 — CVNO on panel. ℞. CAMV on panel below griffin. *M. 234* £225

219 — CAMVL on panel. ℞. CVNO below centaur l. carrying palm. *M. 234a* . £225

219A CAMVL on panel. ℞. Figure seated l. holding wine amphora, CVNOBE. *M. —* £250

219B — Plant, CVNOBELINVS (see no. 136 Amminus). ℞. Hercules stg. r. holding club and thunderbolt, dividing CA MV. *M. —* . . . . *Extremely rare*

219C — Laur. hd. r., CVNOBELINVS. ℞. Pegasus springing l., CAMV below. *M. —* . . . . *Extremely rare*

220 — CVNO on panel. ℞. TASC F below Pegasus r. *M. 235* £250

221 225

221 — Head r., CVNOBELINI. ℞. TASCIO below horse r. *M. 236* £350

222 — Winged bust r., CVNO. ℞. Sphinx std. l., TASCIO. *M. 237* £150

223 — Draped female figure r., TASCIIOVAN. ℞. Figure std. r. playing lyre, tree behind. *M. 238* £250

224 — Male figure stg. dividing CV NO. ℞. Female std. side saddle on animal, TASCIIOVA. *M. 239* £250

224A — Laur. hd. r., CVNOBELINVS. ℞. Victory r., TASCIO[VAN . . .]. . . . . *Extremely rare*

225 — Figure r. carrying dead animal, CVNOBELINVS. ℞. Figure stg. holding bow, dog at side, TASCIIOVANI. *M. 240* £275

226 — CVNO on panel, horn above, two dolphins below. ℞. Figure stg. r., altar behind. *M. 241a* £300

* The price in this section is for the condition in which the coin usually appears.

Cunobelin *continued* *

227 *Silver.* CVNO on panel. ℞. Fig. walking r., CV N. *M. 254* £225
228 — — ℞. Animal springing l. *M. 255* £285
229 — CVN in centre of wreath. ℞. CAM below dog or she-wolf stg. r. *M. 256* . £285
230 — CVNO, animal l. ℞. CA below figure std. r. holding caduceus. *M. 258* . . £425
231 — SOLIDV in centre of looped circle. ℞. Standing figure l., CVNO. *M. 259* £450
232 *Bronze.* Head l., CVNO. ℞. Boar l., branch above. *M. 220* £65
233 — CVNOB ELINI in two panels. ℞. Victory std. l., TASC · F. *M. 221* £65
234 — Winged animal l., CAM below. ℞. CVN before Victory stg. l. *M. 222a* . £65
235 — Bearded head facing. ℞. Similar to no. 232. *M. 223* £100
236 — Ram-headed animal coiled up within double ornamental circle. ℞. CAM below animal l. *M. 224* £125
237 — Winged animal r., CAMV. ℞. CVN below horse galloping r. *M. 225* . . . £80
238 — Bearded head l., CAMV. ℞. CVN or CVNO below horse l. *M. 226, 229* . £75
239 — Laureate head r., CVNO. ℞. CVN below bull butting l. *M. 227* £100
240 — Crude head r., CVN. ℞. Figure stg. l., CVN. *M. 228* £75
241 — CAMVL / ODVNO in two panels. ℞. CVNO beneath sphinx crouching l. *M. 230* £80

242 247 251

242 — Winged beast springing l., CAMV. ℞. Victory stg. r. divides CV NO. *M. 231* £80
243 — Victory walking r. ℞. CVN below, horseman r. *M. 232* £80
244 — Beardless head l., CAM. ℞. CVNO below eagle. *M. 233* £80
245 — Laureate head l., CVNOBELINI. ℞. Centaur r., TASCIOVANI · F. *M. 242* £75
246 — Helmeted bust r. ℞. TASCIIOVANII above, sow stg. r., F below. *M. 243* £75
247 — Horseman galloping r. holding dart and shield, CVNOB. ℞. Warrior stg. l., TASCIIOVANTIS. *M. 244* £60
248 — Helmeted bust l., CVNOBII. ℞. TASC . FIL below boar l. std. on haunches. *M. 245* £125
249 — Bare head r., CVNOBELINVS REX. ℞. TASC below bull butting r. *M. 246* £75
250 — Bare head l., CVNO. ℞. TASC below bull stg. r. *M. 247* £100
251 — Winged head l., CVNOBELIN. ℞. Metal worker std. r. holding hammer, working on a vase, TASCIO behind. *M. 248* £75
252 — Pegasus springing r., CVNO. ℞. Victory r., sacrificing bull, TASCI. *M. 249* £75
253 — CVNO on panel within wreath. ℞. CAMV below horse, full faced, prancing r. *M. 250* £95

* The price in this section is for the condition in which the coin usually appears.

254

		*
254	*Bronze.* Bearded head of Jupiter Ammon l., CVNOBELIN. ℞. CAM below horseman galloping r. *M. 251*	£90
255	— Janus head, CVNO below. ℞. CAMV on panel below, sow std. r. beneath a tree. *M. 252*	£150
256	— Bearded head of Jupiter Ammon r., CVNOB. ℞. CAM on panel below lion crouched r. *M. 253*	£90
257	— Sphinx r., CVNO. ℞. Fig. stg. l. divides CA M. *M. 260*	£175
258	— Animal stg. r. ℞. CVN below horseman r. *M. 261*	£175
259	*Half bronze denomination.* Animal l. looking back. ℞. CVN below horse l. *M. 233a*	£200

S.W. MIDLANDS

Dobunni *Glos., Here., Mon., Oxon., Som., Wilts. and Worcs.*

260   267

260	**Anted.** *Stater.* Ear of corn. ℞. ANTED or ANTEDRIG over triple tailed horse r. *M. 385–386*	£750
261	*Silver.* Crude head r., as 64. ℞. AN TED over horse l. *M. 387*	£250
262	**Eisu.** *Stater.* Similar to 260 but EISV or EISVRIG. *M. 388*	£1400
262A	*Quarter stater.* EISV across field. ℞. Horse, no legend. *M.* —	£750
263	*Silver.* Similar to 261 but EISV. *M. 389*	£350
264	**Inam.** (or Inara). *Stater.* Similar to 260 but INAM (or INARA). *M. 390*	*Extremely rare*
265	**Catti.** *Stater.* Similar to 260 but CATTI. *M. 391*	£1300
266	**Comux.** *Stater.* Similar to 260 but COMVX outwardly. *M. 392*	£1400
267	**Corio.** *Stater.* Similar to 260 but CORIO. *M. 393*	£1100
268	*Quarter stater.* COR in centre. ℞. Horse r. without legend. *M. 394*	£1500

269   270

269	**Bodvoc.** *Stater.* BODVOC across field. ℞. As last. *M. 395*	£1200
270	*Silver.* Head l., BODVOC. ℞. As last. *M. 396*	£600

* The price in this section is for the condition in which the coin usually appears.

EASTERN ENGLAND

Iceni   *Cambs., Norfolk and Suffolk*   *c.* A.D. 10–61

272   273   279

*

271	**Duro.** *Silver.* Boar. ℞. Horse r., CAN(S) above, DVRO below. *M. 434* . . .	£500
272	**Anted.** *Stater.* Triple crescent design. ℞. ANTED in two monograms below horse. *M. 418*	*Extremely rare*
273	*Silver.* Two crescents back to back. ℞. ANTED as last. *M. 419–421*	£40
274	*Silver half unit.* Similar to last. *M. 422*	£80
275	**Ecen.** *Silver.* As 273. ℞. Open headed horse r., ECEN below. *M. 424*	£40
276	*Silver half unit.* Similar, but legends read ECE, EC, or ECN. *M. 431*	£85
277	**Ed.** *Silver.* Similar to 275 but ED (also E, EI and EDN) below horse. *M. 423, 425b*	£150
278	**Ece.** *Silver.* As 273. ℞. Stepping horse r., ECE below. *M. 425a*	£80
279	— Similar, but "Y" headed horse r., ECE below. *M. 426–427*	£75
280	— Similar, but horse l. *M. 428*	£75
281	**Saemu.** *Silver.* As 273. ℞. "Y" headed horse r., SAEMV below. *M. 433* . .	£300
282	**Aesu.** *Silver.* As 273. ℞. As last, AESV. *M. 432*	£300

283

283	**Prasutagus,** Client King of the Iceni under Claudius; husband of Boudicca. *Silver.* Head of good style l. SUB RII PRASTO. ℞. Rearing horse r., ESICO FECIT. *M. 434a*	£1500
	The attribution by H. Mossop of these rare coins to King Prasutagus has been made after a study of the legends on the ten known specimens and is published in "Britannia", X, 1979.	
284	**Iat Iso.** *Silver.* IAT ISO (retrograde) on tablet, rosettes above and below. ℞. Horse r., E above. *M. 416*	£500
285	**Ale Sca.** *Silver.* Boar r., ALE below. ℞. Horse, SCA below. *M. 469*	*Extremely rare*

* The price in this section is for the condition in which the coin usually appears.

Coritani *Lincs., Yorks. and E. Midlands* *c.* A.D. 10–61

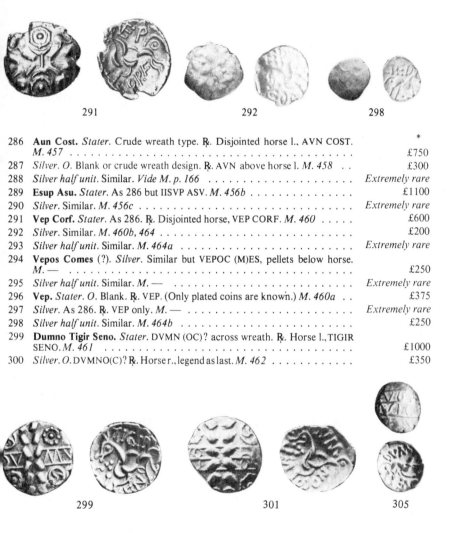

291   292   298

286	**Aun Cost.** *Stater.* Crude wreath type. ℞. Disjointed horse l., AVN COST. *M. 457*	*
		£750
287	*Silver. O.* Blank or crude wreath design. ℞. AVN above horse l. *M. 458*	£300
288	*Silver half unit.* Similar. *Vide M. p. 166*	*Extremely rare*
289	**Esup Asu.** *Stater.* As 286 but IISVP ASV. *M. 456b*	£1100
290	*Silver.* Similar. *M. 456c*	*Extremely rare*
291	**Vep Corf.** *Stater.* As 286. ℞. Disjointed horse, VEP CORF. *M. 460*	£600
292	*Silver.* Similar. *M. 460b, 464*	£200
293	*Silver half unit.* Similar. *M. 464a*	*Extremely rare*
294	**Vepos Comes** (?). *Silver.* Similar but VEPOC (M)ES, pellets below horse. *M.* —	£250
295	*Silver half unit.* Similar. *M.* —	*Extremely rare*
296	**Vep.** *Stater. O.* Blank. ℞. VEP. (Only plated coins are known.) *M. 460a*	£375
297	*Silver.* As 286. ℞. VEP only. *M.* —	*Extremely rare*
298	*Silver half unit.* Similar. *M. 464b*	£250
299	**Dumno Tigir Seno.** *Stater.* DVMN (OC)? across wreath. ℞. Horse l., TIGIR SENO. *M. 461*	£1000
300	*Silver. O.* DVMNO(C)? ℞. Horse r., legend as last. *M. 462*	£350

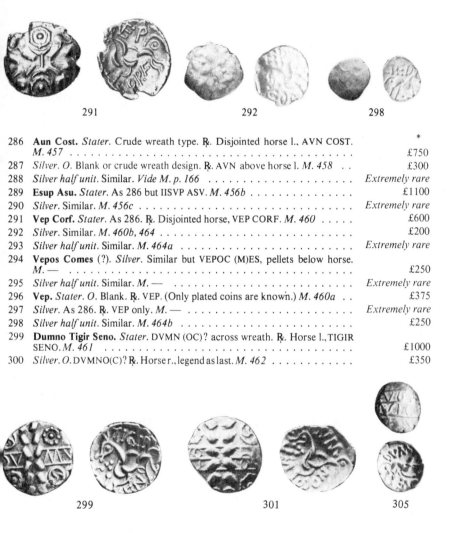

299   301   305

301	**Volisios Dumnocoveros.** *Stater.* VOLI / SIOS in two lines. ℞. Horse, DVMNOCOVEROS across crude wreath. *M. 463*	£700
302	*Silver.* As last. *M. 463a*	£350
303	*Silver half unit.* As last but DVMNOCO. *M. 465*	£350
304	**Volisios Dumnovellaunos.** *Stater.* As 301. ℞. Horse, DVMNOVELLAVNOS. *M. 466*	£750
305	*Silver half unit.* As last but DVMNOVE. *M. 467*	£250
306	**Volisios Cartivel.** *Silver half unit.* As 301. ℞. Horse, CARTIVEL. *M. 468*	*Extremely rare*

* The price in this section is for the condition in which the coin usually appears.

ROMAN BRITAIN

From the middle of the first century A.D. until the early part of the fifth century, Britannia was a province of the vast Roman Empire—a single state encompassing the whole of the Mediterranean basin. In common with other western provinces, no local coinage was officially produced in Britain during this period (unlike the Eastern part of the Empire where hundreds of towns were permitted to issue municipal currency) until the latter part of the third century. It was, therefore, the regular Imperial coinage produced mainly at Rome until the mid-third century, that supplied the currency requirements of the province, and no representative collection of British coins is complete without some examples of these important issues.

Although Britain was on the fringe of the Roman World, and never entirely subdued by the legions, a surprisingly large number of coin types allude to events in the province—usually frontier wars in the north. In the closing years of the third century, the usurper Carausius established two mints in Britain; one in London, the other not yet certainly identified (either Camulodunum: Colchester or Clausentum: Bitterne, Southampton). After the defeat of the rebellion London became an official Roman mint, with a substantial output of bronze coinage until its closure, by Constantine the Great, in A.D. 325. Other coins were produced unofficially in Britain at various times: soon after the conquest (copies of bronze coins of Claudius, etc.), in the troubled times of the early 270s (copies of Claudius II and the Tetrici, i.e., "Barbarous radiates") and the final years of the occupation (mostly imitated from the bronze coinage of Constantius II—"soldier spearing fallen horseman" type).

The Roman legions were withdrawn to the continent by Honorius in A.D. 411, but a Romano-British civil administration continued to operate for some time afterward until disrupted by the Teutonic invasions.

For general information on Roman coinage see *Roman Coins and their Values* by D. R. Sear and *Roman Coins* by J. P. C. Kent; for more detailed works consult *Roman Imperial Coinage*, the British Museum Catalogues of Roman coins, *Roman Silver Coins* (4 vols.) by H. A. Seaby and *The Coinage of Roman Britain* by G. Askew (2nd Edition).

An invaluable companion volume for anyone studying Roman coinage is S. W. Stevenson's *A Dictionary of Roman Coins*.

THE REPUBLIC

Only a few representative examples are listed. Many Republican coins circulated well into the Imperial period and found their way to Britain.

		F	VF
451	C. Naevius Balbus, moneyer, 79 B.C. Æ *denarius*. Diad. hd. of Juno r. ℞. Victory in triga r.	£10	£25

452   454

452	C. Calpurnius Piso, moneyer, 67 B.C. Æ *denarius*. Head of Apollo r. ℞. Horseman galloping r.	£12	£35
453	**Julius Caesar,** dictator, †44 B.C. Made two expeditions to Britain in 55 and 54 B.C. Æ *denarius*. Laur. head r. ℞. Venus stg. l.	£120	£300
454	Æ *denarius*. Elephant stg. r. ℞. Sacrificial implements	£30	£80
455	**Mark Antony,** triumvir, †30 B.C. Æ *denarius*. Galley r. ℞. Legionary eagle between two standards	£22	£65

Known for all Legions from I (PRImus) to XXIII, though only the following are known to have served in Britain during the Roman occupation—II Augusta, VI Victrix, IX Hispania, XIV Gemina Martia Victrix and XX Valeria Victrix.

THE EMPIRE

456   461

		F	VF
456	**Augustus,** 27 B.C.–A.D. 14. *R denarius.* ℞. Caius and Lucius Caesars ..	£22	£65
457	*Æ as.* ℞. The Altar of Lugdunum	£30	£90
458	**Divus Augustus Pater,** commemorative issue. *Æ as.* ℞. PROVIDENT S . C. Altar	£30	£90
459	**Livia,** wife of Augustus. *Æ dupondius.* ℞. Legend around S . C.	£80	£250
460	**Agrippa,** general and statesman, †12 B.C. *Æ as.* ℞. Neptune stg. l.	£35	£100
461	**Tiberius,** A.D. 14–37. *R denarius.* ℞. Livia seated r.	£45	£120
	This coin is often referred to as the "Tribute Penny" of the Bible.		
462	**Drusus,** son of Tiberius, †A.D. 23. *Æ as.* ℞. Legend around S . C.	£45	£125
463	**Nero Claudius Drusus,** father of Claudius, †9 B.C. *Æ sestertius.* ℞. Claudius seated amidst arms	£140	£400
464	**Antonia,** mother of Claudius, †A.D. 37. *Æ dupondius.* ℞. Claudius stg. l. .	£65	£185
465	**Germanicus,** father of Caligula, †A.D. 19. *Æ as.* ℞. Legend around S . C. .	£40	£120
466	**Agrippina Senior,** wife of Germanicus, †A.D. 33. *Æ sestertius.* ℞. Two mules drawing covered carriage	£250	£750
467	**Caligula,** 37–41. *Æ as.* ℞. VESTA. Vesta seated l.	£45	£125

468   474

468	**Claudius,** 41–54. Invaded Britain A.D. 43. *N aureus.* ℞. DE BRITANN on triumphal arch	£650	£1800
469	*R denarius.* Similar	£120	£350
470	*R didrachm* of Caesarea. ℞. DE BRITANNIS below Emperor in quadriga r.	£95	£300
471	*Æ sestertius.* ℞. SPES AVGVSTA S . C. Spes walking l., of barbarous style, struck in Britain	£90	£275
472	*Æ dupondius.* ℞. CERES AVGVSTA S . C. Ceres seated l., of barbarous style, struck in Britain	£40	£120
473	*Æ as.* ℞. S . C. Minerva brandishing javelin	£30	£90
474	**Nero,** 54–68. *R denarius.* ℞. SALVS. Salus seated l.	£55	£150
475	*Æ as.* ℞. S . C. Victory flying l.	£30	£95
476	**Galba,** 68–69. *R denarius.* ℞. DIVA AVGVSTA. Livia stg. l.	£60	£175
477	**Otho,** 69. *R denarius.* ℞. SECVRITAS P . R. Securitas stg. l.	£100	£300
478	**Vitellius,** 69. *R denarius.* ℞. XV . VIR SACR . FAC. Tripod with dolphin ..	£55	£150

479   483

	F	VF
479 **Vespasian,** 69–79. Commanded one of the legions in the Claudian invasion of Britain. Ⱥ *denarius.* ℞. ANNONA AVG. Annona seated l.	£15	£40
480 Æ *as.* ℞. PROVIDENT. S . C. Large altar	£24	£75
481 **Titus,** 79–81. Ⱥ *denarius.* ℞. FORTVNA AVGVST. Fortuna stg. l.	£25	£75
482 **Domitian,** 81–96. Ⱥ *denarius.* ℞. IMP . XI. COS . XI . CENS . P . P . P. Minerva fighting	£12	£35
483 Æ *dupondius.* ℞. VIRTVTI AVGVSTI. S . C. Virtus stg. r.	£18	£55
484 **Nerva,** 96–98. Ⱥ *denarius.* ℞. CONCORDIA EXERCITVVM. Clasped hands	£25	£75

485   489

	F	VF
485 **Trajan,** 98–117. Ⱥ *denarius.* ℞. P . M . TR . P . COS . IIII . P . P. Victory standing r. on prow	£12	£35
486 Æ *sestertius.* ℞. S . P . Q . R . OPTIMO PRINCIPI. S . C. Fortuna stg. l.	£40	£135
487 **Hadrian,** 117–138. Visited Britain *c.* A.D. 122 and constructed his famous wall from the Tyne to the Solway. Ⱥ *denarius.* ℞. FIDES PVBLICA. Fides stg. r.	£12	£35
488 Æ *sestertius.* ℞. ADVENTVI AVG . BRITANNIAE. S . C. Emperor and Britannia sacrificing over altar	*Extremely rare*	
489 — ℞. BRITANNIA. S . C. Britannia seated l.	*Extremely rare*	
490 — ℞. EXERC . BRITANNI. S.C. Emperor on horseback addressing soldiers	*Extremely rare*	
491 Æ *as.* ℞. PONT . MAX . TR . POT . COS . III . BRITANNIA. S . C. Britannia seated l.	£100	£350
492 **Sabina,** wife of Hadrian, Ⱥ *denarius.* ℞. CONCORDIA AVG. Concordia seated l.	£20	£55
493 **Aelius Caesar,** 136–138. Æ *as.* ℞. TR . POT . COS . II . S . C. Fortuna stg. l.	£30	£100
494 **Antoninus Pius,** 138–161. His generals in Britain pushed the Roman frontier forward to the Forth–Clyde line (the Antonine Wall). Ν *aureus.* ℞. IMPERATOR II . BRITAN. Victory stg. on globe	£450	£1200
495 Ⱥ *denarius.* ℞. AEQVITAS AVG. Aequitas stg. l.	£10	£30

496   499

				F	VF
496	Æ *sestertius*. ℞. BRITANNIA. S . C. Britannia seated l. on rocks			£350	£1000
497	— ℞. IMPERATOR II . BRITAN. S . C. Victory stg. on globe			£150	£450
498	Æ *as*. ℞. Victory l. holding shield inscribed BRI · TAN			£75	£225
499	— ℞. BRITANNIA COS . IIII. S . C. Britannia seated l. in attitude of sadness			£45	£135

This coin was very possibly struck at a temporary travelling mint in Britain.

				F	VF
500	**Faustina Senior,** wife of Antoninus Pius, *R denarius.* ℞. AVGVSTA. Ceres stg. r.			£10	£30
501	Æ *sestertius*. ℞. IVNO S . C. Juno stg. l.			£32	£100
502	**Marcus Aurelius,** 161–180. *R denarius*. ℞. COS III. Jupiter seated l.			£12	£35
503	Æ *sestertius*. ℞. IMP . VI . COS . III. S . C. Roma seated l.			£35	£100

504   510   515

				F	VF
504	**Faustina Junior,** wife of Marcus Aurelius. *R denarius*. ℞. IVNONI REGINAE. Juno and peacock			£12	£35
505	Æ *as*. ℞. DIANA LVCIF . S . C. Diana stg. l.			£12	£35
506	**Lucius Verus,** 161–169. *R denarius*. ℞. CONCORD . AVG . COS . II. Concordia seated l.			£15	£45
507	**Lucilla,** wife of Lucius Verus. Æ *dupondius*. ℞. SALVS S . C. Salus stg. l. . . .			£6	£15
508	**Commodus,** 177–192. There was considerable military activity in northern Britain in the early part of his reign. *R denarius*. ℞. MARTI VLTORI AVG. Mars stg. l.			£15	£45
509	Æ *sestertius*. ℞. BRITT . etc. Britannia stg., holding sword and wreath . .			*Extremely rare*	
510	— ℞. VICT . BRIT . etc. Victory seated r., inscribing shield			£75	£225
511	**Crispina,** wife of Commodus, Æ *as*. ℞. IVNO LVCINA S . C. Juno stg. l. . .			£22	£65

		F	VF
512	**Pertinax,** 193. One time governor of Britain, under Commodus. Æ *denarius*. ℞. LAETITIA TEMPOR COS . II. Laetitia stg. l.	£175	£500
513	**Didius Julianus,** 193. Æ *sestertius*. ℞. CONCORD MILIT S . C. Concordia stg. l.	£200	£600
514	**Clodius Albinus,** 195–197. Proclaimed emperor while governor of Britain. Æ *denarius*. ℞. MINER . PACIF . COS . II. Minerva stg. l.	£45	£120
515	**Septimius Severus,** 193–211. Campaigned in Britain with his sons Caracalla and Geta; died at York. N *aureus*. ℞. VICTORIAE BRIT. Victory l., holding wreath and palm	£850	£2500
516	Æ *denarius*. ℞. Similar	£20	£60
517	— ℞. Similar, but Victory seated l.	£20	£65
518	— ℞. Similar, but Victory stg. beside palm tree	£24	£70
519	— ℞. VIRT . AVG. Roma stg. l.	£9	£25

520   528

		F	VF
520	Æ *sestertius*. ℞. VICTORIAE BRITANNICAE S.C. Two Victories affixing shield to palm tree, two captives below	£175	£500
521	Æ *dupondius*. ℞. Similar, but Victory inscribing shield on palm tree	£85	£250
522	Æ *as*. ℞. Similar, Victory stg. r. holding vexillum	£85	£250
524	**Julia Domna,** wife of Septimius Severus. Æ *denarius*. ℞. PIETAS PVBLICA. Pietas stg. l	£9	£25
525	**Caracalla,** 198–217. Personally led the campaign of A.D. 210. N *aureus*. ℞. VICTORIAE BRIT. Victory seated l., holding shield	£850	£2500
526	N *quinarius*. ℞. VICTORIAE BRIT. Victory advancing l., holding wreath and palm	£1100	£3000
527	Æ *denarius*. ℞. MARTI PACATORI. Mars stg. l.	£9	£25
528	— ℞. VICTORIAE BRIT. Victory advancing l., holding wreath and palm .	£22	£65
529	— ℞. VICTORIAE BRIT. Victory advancing r., holding trophy	£22	£65
530	Æ *sestertius*. ℞. VICT . BRIT . P . M . TR . P . XIIII . COS . III . P . P . S . C. Victory stg. r., erecting trophy	£175	£500
531	— ℞. VICT . BRIT . etc. Victory inscribing shield on tree	£150	£450
532	— ℞. VICTORIAE BRITANNICAE. S . C. Two Victories erecting shield on tree	£200	£600
533	Æ *dupondius*. ℞. VICTORIAE BRITANNICAE. S . C. Victory seated l., on shields	£28	£80
534	**Plautilla,** wife of Caracalla. Æ *denarius*. ℞. PIETAS AVGG. Pietas stg. r. .	£16	£45
535	**Geta,** 209–212. Æ *denarius*. ℞. PONTIF . COS . II. Genius stg. l.	£18	£50
536	— ℞. VICTORIAE BRIT. Victory advancing r., holding wreath and palm .	£28	£75
537	Æ *sestertius*. ℞. VICTORIAE BRITANNICAE. S . C. Victory seated r., inscribing shield	£200	£600

537   541

		F	VF
538	— ℞. VICTORIAE BRITANNICAE. S . C. Victory standing r., erecting trophy; Britannia stg. facing with hands tied	£200	£600
538A	**Geta,** 209–212. Billon *tetradrachm* of Alexandria, Egypt. ℞. NEIKH . KATA . BPET. Victory flying l.	£250	£750
539	**Macrinus,** 217–218. *R denarius.* ℞. SALVS PVBLICA. Salus seated l., feeding snake	£28	£80
540	**Diadumenian,** *as Caesar,* 217–218. *R denarius.* ℞. PRINC IVVENTVTIS. Diadumenian holding sceptre	£70	£200
541	**Elagabalus,** 218–222, *R denarius.* ℞. FIDES MILITVM. Fides stg. r., holding standards	£22	£60
542	**Julia Paula,** wife of Elagabalus. *R denarius.* ℞. CONCORDIA. Concordia seated l.	£30	£85
543	**Aquilia Severa,** wife of Elagabalus. *R denarius.* ℞. CONCORDIA. Concordia stg. l.	£65	£160
544	**Julia Soaemias,** mother of Elagabalus. *R denarius.* ℞. VENVS CAELESTIS. Venus stg. l.	£25	£65
545	**Julia Maesa,** grandmother of Elagabalus. *R denarius.* ℞. IVNO. Juno stg. l.	£16	£45

546   550

		F	VF
546	**Severus Alexander,** 222–235. *R denarius.* ℞. PAX AVG. Pax advancing l.	£9	£25
547	Æ *sestertius.* ℞. FIDES MILITVM. S . C. Fides stg. l.	£20	£60
548	**Orbiana,** wife of Severus Alexander. *R denarius.* ℞. CONCORDIA AVGG. Concordia seated l.	£70	£200
549	**Julia Mamaea,** mother of Severus Alexander. *R denarius.* ℞. VENVS VICTRIX. Venus stg. l.	£12	£35
550	**Maximinus I,** 235–238. *R denarius.* ℞. PAX AVGVSTI. Pax stg. l.	£9	£25
551	Æ *sestertius.* ℞. VICTORIA AVG. S . C. Victory advancing r.	£25	£75
552	**Maximus Caesar,** 235–238. Æ *sestertius.* ℞. PRINCIPI IVVENTVTIS. S . C. Maximus stg. l.	£45	£135
553	**Balbinus,** 238. *R denarius.* ℞. VICTORIA AVGG. Victory stg. l.	£60	£175
554	**Pupienus,** 238. *R denarius.* ℞. PAX PVBLICA. Pax seated l.	£60	£175

	F	*VF*
555 **Gordian III,** 238–244. Æ *denarius*. ℞. SALVS AVGVSTI. Salus stg. r. feeding serpent	£9	£25
556 Æ *antoninianus*. ℞. ORIENS AVG. Sol stg. l.	£6	£15
557 Æ *sestertius*. ℞. AEQVITAS AVG. S . C. Aequitas stg. l.	£18	£55

558    563

	F	*VF*
558 **Philip I,** 244–249. Æ *antoninianus*. ℞. ROMAE AETERNAE. Roma seated l.	£6	£16
559 Æ *sestertius*. ℞. SECVRIT. ORBIS S . C. Securitas seated l.	£22	£70
560 **Otacilia Severa,** wife of Philip I. Æ *antoninianus*. ℞. PIETAS AVGVSTAE. Pietas stg. l.	£8	£22
561 **Philip II,** 247–249. Æ *antoninianus*. ℞. AETERNIT . IMPER. Sol advancing l.	£8	£22
562 **Trajan Decius,** 249–251. Æ *antoninianus*. ℞. DACIA. Dacia stg. l.	£9	£25
563 **Herennia Etruscilla,** wife of Trajan Decius. Æ *antoninianus*. ℞. PVDICITIA AVG. Pudicitia stg. l.	£9	£24
564 **Herennius Etruscus Caesar,** 251. Æ *antoninianus*. ℞. SPES PVBLICA. Spes advancing l.	£16	£45
565 **Hostilian Caesar,** 251. Æ *antoninianus*. ℞. PIETAS AVGVSTORVM. Sacrificial implements	£22	£65
566 **Trebonianus Gallus,** 251–253. Æ *antoninianus*. ℞. LIBERTAS AVGG. Libertas stg. l.	£8	£24
567 **Volusian,** 251–253. Æ *antoninianus*. ℞. CONCORDIA AVGG. Concordia seated l.	£8	£24
568 **Aemilian,** 252–253. Æ *antoninianus*. ℞. PACI AVG. Pax stg. l.	£45	£120
569 **Valerian I,** 253–260. Billon *antoninianus*. ℞. VICTORIA AVGG. Victory stg. l.	£4	£12

570    576

	F	*VF*
570 **Gallienus,** 253–268. Æ *antoninianus*. ℞. DIANAE CONS . AVG. Antelope	£3	£10
571 **Salonina,** wife of Gallienus. Æ *antoninianus*. ℞. PIETAS AVG. Pietas stg. l.	£3	£10
572 **Valerian II Caesar,** 253–255. Billon *antoninianus*. ℞. PIETAS AVGG. Sacrificial implements	£8	£25
573 **Saloninus Caesar,** 259. Billon *antoninianus*. ℞. SPES PVBLICA. Spes advancing l.	£8	£25
574 **Macrianus,** usurper in the East, 260–261. Billon *antoninianus*. ℞. SOL. INVICTO. Sol stg. l.	£30	£100
575 **Quietus,** usurper in the East, 260–261. Billon *antoninianus*. ℞. ROMAE AETERNAE. Roma seated l.	£30	£100

	F	VF
576 **Postumus,** usurper in the West, 259–268. Æ *antoninianus*. ℞. MONETA AVG. Moneta stg. l.	£5	£15
577 **Laelianus,** usurper in the West, 268. Æ *antoninianus*. ℞. VICTORIA AVG. Victory advancing r.	£75	£225
578 **Marius,** usurper in the West, 268. Æ *antoninianus*. ℞. VICTORIA AVG. Victory advancing r.	£28	£80
579 **Victorinus,** usurper in the West, 268–270. N *aureus*. ℞. LEG . XX . VAL . VICTRIX. Boar l.	£3,500	£10,000
580 Æ *antoninianus*. ℞. SALVS AVG. Salus stg. l.	£4	£12
581 **Claudius II Gothicus,** 268–270. Æ *antoninianus*. ℞. MARTI PACIF. Mars advancing l.	£3	£10
582 **Tetricus I,** usurper in the West, 270–273. Æ *antoninianus*. LAETITIA AVG. Laetitia stg. l.	£3	£10
583 **Tetricus II Caesar,** usurper in the West, 270–273. Æ *antoninianus*. ℞. SPES AVGG. Spes advancing l.	£4	£12

584A   584B   584C

	F	VF
584 **Barbarous radiates.** British and Continental copies of Æ *antoniniani*, mostly of Claudius II (A), Tetricus I (B) and Tetricus II (C)	£1.50	£4
585 **Quintillus,** 270. Æ *antoninianus*. ℞. FIDES MILIT. Fides stg. l.	£10	£30
586 **Aurelian,** 270–275. Æ *antoninianus*. ℞. SECVRIT . AVG. Securitas stg. l.	£4	£12

587   596

	F	VF
587 **Severina,** wife of Aurelian. Æ *antoninianus*. ℞. PROVIDEN . DEOR. Fides and Sol stg.	£10	£30
588 **Tacitus,** 275–276. Æ *antoninianus*. ℞. CLEMENTIA TEMP. Clementia stg. l.	£7	£22
589 **Florianus,** 276. Æ *antoninianus*. ℞. SALVS AVG. Salus stg. l.	£20	£65
590 **Probus,** 276–282. Æ *antoninianus*. ℞. ABVNDANTIA AVG. Abundantia stg. r.	£4	£12
591 **Carus,** 282–283. Æ *antoninianus*. ℞. PAX EXERCITI. Pax stg. l.	£10	£30
592 **Numerian,** 283–284. Æ *antoninianus*. ℞. ORIENS AVG. Sol advancing l.	£8	£25
593 **Carinus,** 283–285. Æ *antoninianus*. ℞. AETERNIT . AVG. Aeternitas stg. l.	£7	£22
594 **Diocletian,** 284–305, London mint reopened *c.* 297. R *argenteus*. ℞. VIRTVS MILITVM. Tetrarchs sacrificing before camp-gate	£75	£200
595 Æ *antoninianus*. ℞. CLEMENTIA TEMP. Diocletian and Jupiter stg.	£4.50	£14
596 Æ *follis*. ℞. GENIO POPVLI ROMANI. Genius stg. l., LON (London) *mm.*	£10	£35

597   600

Diocletian *continued*	F	VF
597 *Æ follis*. ℞. Similar, no *mm*. (London)	£9	£30
598 — ℞. Similar, other *mms*.	£6	£20
599 **Maximianus,** 286–310. *R argenteus*. ℞. VIRTVS MILITVM. Tetrarchs sacrificing before camp gate	£70	£200
600 *Æ antoninianus*. ℞. SALVS AVGG. Salus stg. l.	£4.50	£14
601 *Æ follis*. ℞. GENIO POPVLI ROMANI. Genius stg. l., LON. *mm*.	£12	£40
602 — ℞. Similar, no *mm*.	£9	£30
603 **Carausius,** commander of the Roman Channel fleet, who took power in Britain and Northern Gaul, 287–293. *London mint N aureus*. ℞. PAX AVG. Pax stg. l., no *mm*.	£7500	£17,500

604   623

		F	VF
604	*R denarius*. ℞. CONSER AVG. Neptune seated l.	£550	£1500
605	*Æ antoninianus*. ℞. ADVENTVS AVG. Emperor riding l.	£70	£200
606	— ℞. COHR . PRAEF. Four standards	£85	£250
607	— ℞. COMES AVG. Victory stg. l.	£30	£85
608	— ℞. CONCORD . EXERCI. Four standards	£55	£150
609	— ℞. CONCORDIA MILITVM. Clasped hands	£55	£150
610	— ℞. CONSERVAT . AVG. Sol stg. l.	£70	£200
611	— ℞. FELICIT . TEMP. Felicitas stg. l.	30	£85
612	— ℞. FIDES MILITVM. Fides stg. l.	£70	£200
613	— ℞. FORTVNA AVG. Fortuna stg. l.	£25	£70
614	— ℞. GENIVS AVG. Genius stg. l.	£70	£200
615	— ℞. GERMANICVS MAX . V. Trophy between captives	£175	£450
616	— ℞. LAETITIA AVG. Laetitia stg. l.	£25	£70
617	— ℞. LEG . II . AVG. Capricorn l.	£70	£200
618	— ℞. LEG XX . V . V. Boar r.	£80	£220
619	— ℞. MARS VLTOR. Mars walking r.	£70	£200
620	— ℞. MONETA AVG. Moneta stg. l.	£25	£70
621	— ℞. ORIENS AVG. Sol walking r.	£30	£85

		F	VF
622	Æ *antoninianus*. ℞. PACATOR ORBIS. Bust of Sol r.	£120	£350
623	— ℞. PAX AVG. Pax stg. l.	£20	£60
624	— ℞. PIAETAS AVG. Pietas sacrificing at altar	£30	£85
625	— ℞. SALVS AVG. Salus feeding serpent	£25	£75
626	— ℞. SECVRIT . PERP. Securitas stg. l.	£30	£85
627	— ℞. VICTORIA AVG. Victory walking r.	£30	£85

628   643

628	Æ *antonianianus*. Struck in the name of Diocletian. ℞. PAX AVGGG. Pax stg. l.	£28	£75
629	Æ *antoninianus*. Struck in the name of Maximianus. ℞. PROVIDENTIA AVG. Providentia stg. l.	£28	£75
630	*Colchester or Clausentum mint. Æ denarius.* ℞. CONCORDIA MILITVM. Clasped hands	£175	£450
631	Æ *antoninianus*. ℞. ABVNDANTIA AVG. Abundantia stg. l.	£30	£85
632	— ℞. APOLINI CON . AV. Griffin walking r.	£110	£300
633	— ℞. CONCORDIA AVGGG. Two emperors stg.	£135	£400
634	— ℞. CONSTANT . AVG. Nude male stg. r.	£70	£200
635	— ℞. EXPECTATE VENI. Britannia stg. r.	£110	£300
636	— ℞. FELICITAS AVG. Galley	£50	£150
637	— ℞. GENIO BRITANNI. Genius stg. l.	£150	£420
638	— ℞. HILARITAS AVG. Hilaritas stg. l.	£28	£75
639	— ℞. IOVI CONSERV. Jupiter stg. l.	£30	£80
640	— ℞. LEG. I. MIN. Ram stg. r.	£70	£200
641	— ℞. LIBERALITAS AVG. Carausius seated with subordinates	£85	£250
642	— ℞. PAX AVG. Pax stg. l.	£25	£70
643	— ℞. PROVID . AVG. Providentia stg. l.	£28	£75
644	— ℞. RENOVAT . ROMA. She-wolf suckling Romulus and Remus	£80	£220
645	— ℞. RESTIT . SAECVL. Carausius and Victory stg.	£80	£220
646	— ℞. ROMAE AETER. Roma seated l.	£35	£90
647	— ℞. SAECVLARES AVG. Lion walking r.	£70	£200
648	— ℞. SOLI INVICTE. Sol in quadriga	£70	£200
649	— ℞. SPES PVBLICA. Spes walking r.	£28	£75
650	— ℞. TEMP . FELICIT. Felicitas stg. l.	£28	£75
651	— ℞. VIRTVS AVG. Mars stg. r.	£25	£70
651A	Æ *antoninianus*. Struck in the name of Diocletian. ℞. PAX AVGGG. Pax stg. l.	£28	£75
652	Æ *antoninianus*. Struck in the name of Maximianus. ℞. PAX AVGGG. Pax stg. l.	£28	£75

653   662

		F	VF
653	**Carausius, Diocletian and Maximianus.** Æ *antoninianus*. Struck by Carausius. CARAVSIVS ET FRATRES SVI. Jugate busts of three emperors l. ℞. PAX AVGGG. Pax stg. l.	£600	£1750
654	**Allectus,** chief minister and murderer of Carausius, 293–296. *London mint. N aureus*. ℞. PAX AVG. Pax stg. l.	£7500	£20,000
655	Æ *antoninianus*. ℞. AEQVITAS AVG. Aequitas stg. l.	£25	£70
656	— ℞. COMES AVG. Minerva stg. l.	£25	£70
657	— ℞. FORTVNA AVG. Fortuna seated l.	£65	£180
658	— ℞. HILARITAS AVG. Hilaritas stg. l.	£22	£60
659	— ℞. LAETITIA AVG. Laetitia stg. l.	£30	£80
660	— ℞. LEG . II. Lion walking l.	£175	£450
661	— ℞. ORIENS AVG. Sol stg. l.	£70	£200
662	— ℞. PAX AVG. Pax stg. l.	£30	£80
663	— ℞. PIETAS AVG. Pietas stg. l.	£25	£70
664	— ℞. PROVIDENTIA AVG. Providentia stg. l.	£35	£90
665	— ℞. SAECVLI FELICITAS. Emperor stg. r.	£55	£160
666	— ℞. SALVS AVG. Salus feeding serpent	£25	£70
667	— ℞. SPES PVPLICA. Spes holding flower	£22	£65
668	— ℞. TEMPORVM FELICI. Felicitas stg. l.	£22	£65
669	— ℞. VICTORIA AVG. Victory stg. r.	£22	£65
670	— ℞. VIRTVS AVG. Mars stg. r.	£25	£70
671	Æ *quinarius*. ℞. VIRTVS AVG. Galley	£20	£60
672	*Colchester or Clausentum mint*. Æ *antoninianus*. ℞. ABVND . AVG. Abundantia stg. l.	£30	£80
673	— ℞. ADVENTVS AVG. Emperor riding l.	£85	£240
674	— ℞. DIANAE REDVCI. Diana leading stag	£70	£200
675	— ℞. FELICITAS SAECVLI. Felicitas stg. l.	£70	£200
676	— ℞. FIDES EXERCITVS. Four standards	£55	£150
677	— ℞. IOVI CONSERVATORI. Jupiter stg. l.	£70	£200

678   681

678	— ℞. MONETA AVG. Moneta stg. l.	£35	£100
679	— ℞. PAX AVG. Pax stg. l.	£30	£80
680	— ℞. ROMAE AETERN. Roma in temple	£80	£230

		F	VF
681	Æ *quinarius.* ℞. LAETITIA AVG. Galley	£30	£80
682	— ℞. VIRTVS AVG. Galley	£22	£60

683   698

		F	VF
683	**Constantius I,** Caesar 293–305, Augustus 305–306, campaigned in Britain and died at York. Æ *follis.* ℞. GENIO POPVLI ROMANI. Genius stg. l., no *mm.*	£12	£35
684	Æ *follis.* ℞. MEMORIA FELIX. Eagles beside altar. PLN. *mm.*	£11	£30
685	Æ *radiate.* ℞. CONCORDIA MILITVM. Constantius and Jupiter stg.	£9	£25
686	**Galerius,** Caesar 293–305, Augustus 305–311. Æ *follis.* ℞. GENIO IMPERATORIS. Genius stg. l.	£6	£15
687	— ℞. GENIO POPVLI ROMANI. Genius stg. l., no *mm.*	£7	£20
688	**Galeria Valeria,** wife of Galerius. Æ *follis.* ℞. VENERI VICTRICI. Venus stg. l.	£32	£85
689	**Severus II,** 306–307. Æ *follis.* ℞. FIDES MILITVM. Fides seated l.	£28	£75
690	Æ *follis.* ℞. GENIO POPVLI ROMANI. Genius stg. l., no *mm.*	£32	£85
691	Æ *radiate.* ℞. CONCORDIA MILITVM. Severus and Jupiter stg.	£18	£50
692	**Maximinus II,** 309–313. Æ *follis.* ℞. GENIO AVGVSTI. Genius stg. l.	£6	£15
693	— ℞. GENIO POP . ROM. Genius stg. l. PLN. *mm.*	£9	£25
694	**Maxentius,** 306–312, Æ *follis.* ℞. CONSERV . VRB SVAE. Roma in temple	£9	£25
695	**Licinius I,** 308–324. Æ *follis.* ℞. GENIO POP . ROM. Genius stg. l. PLN. *mm.*	£6.50	£18
696	Æ 3. ℞. SOLI INVICTO COMITI. Sol stg. l.	£3.50	£9
697	**Licinius II Caesar,** 317–324. Æ 3. ℞. PROVIDENTIAE CAESS. Camp gate	£5	£14
698	**Constantine I, the Great,** 307–337. Came to power in Britain, following his father's death at York. London mint closed 325. Æ *follis.* ℞. SOLI INVICTO COMITI. Sol stg. l. PLN *mm.*	£11	£30
699	Æ 3. ℞. BEATA TRANQVILLITAS. Altar. PLON *mm.*	£5.50	£15
700	Æ 3. ℞. VOT . XX in wreath	£2	£5

701

		F	VF
701	**Commemorative issues.** Æ 3/4, commencing A.D. 330. Bust of Roma. ℞. She-wolf suckling Romulus and Remus	£3	£8
702	Æ 3/4. Bust of Constantinopolis. ℞. Victory stg. l.	£3	£8
703	**Fausta,** wife of Constantine. Æ 3. ℞. SPES REIPVBLICAE. Fausta stg.	£11	£30
704	— ℞. Similar. PLON *mm.*	£22	£60

		F	*VF*
705	**Helena,** mother of Constantine. Æ 3. ℞. SECVRITAS REIPVBLICE. Helena stg. l.	£8	£25
706	— ℞. Similar. PLON *mm.*	£22	£60

707   714

		F	*VF*
707	**Theodora,** second wife of Constantius I, struck after her death. Æ 4. ℞. PIETAS ROMANA. Pietas holding child	£5	£14
708	**Crispus Caesar,** 317–326. Æ 3. ℞. CAESARVM NOSTRORVM VOT . V. Wreath	£4	£12
709	— ℞. PROVIDENTIAE CAESS. Camp gate. PLON *mm.*	£6	£15
710	**Delmatius Caesar,** 335–337. Æ 3. ℞. GLORIA EXERCITVS. Two soldiers stg.	£11	£30
711	**Hannibalianus Rex,** 335–337. Æ 4. ℞. SECVRITAS PVBLICA. Euphrates reclining	£85	£250
712	**Constantine II Caesar,** 317–337. Æ 3. ℞. BEAT . TRANQLITAS. Altar. PLON *mm.*	£6	£15
713	Æ 3/4. ℞. GLORIA EXERCITVS. Two soldiers stg.	£9	£25
714	**Constans,** 337–350. Visited Britain in 343. Æ *centenionalis.* ℞. FEL . TEMP . REPARATIO. Constans stg. on galley	£6	£15

715   723   733   741

		F	*VF*
715	**Constantius II,** 337–361. Æ *centenionalis.* ℞. FEL . TEMP . REPARATIO. Soldier spearing fallen horseman	£4	£12
716	Æ 3. ℞. PROVIDENTIAE CAESS. Camp gate. PLON *mm.*	£12	£35
717	**Magnentius,** usurper in the West, 350–353. Æ *centenionalis.* ℞. VICTORIAE DD . NN . AVG . ET CAE. Two Victories	£7	£20
718	**Decentius Caesar,** usurper in the West, 351–353. Æ *centenionalis.* ℞. VICTORIAE DD . NN . AVG . ET . CAE. Two Victories	£12	£35
719	**Constantius Gallus Caesar,** 351–354. Æ *centenionalis.* ℞. FEL . TEMP REPARATIO. Soldier spearing fallen horseman	£9	£25

		F	*VF*
720	**Julian II,** 360–363. *R siliqua.* ℞. VOT . X . MVLT . XX within wreath . . .	£18	£50
721	Æ 3. ℞. Similar	£7	£20
722	**Jovian,** 363–364. Æ 3. ℞. VOT . V . within wreath	£18	£50
723	**Valentinian I,** 364–375. Æ 3. ℞. SECVRITAS REIPVBLICAE. Victory advancing l.	£4	£10
724	**Valens,** 364–378. *R siliqua.* ℞. VRBS ROMA. Roma seated l.	£14	£40
725	Æ 3. ℞. GLORIA ROMANORVM. Valens dragging captive	£4	£10
726	**Gratian,** 367–383. *R siliqua.* ℞. VRBS ROMA. Roma seated l.	£18	£50
727	Æ 3. ℞. CONCORDIA AVGGG. Constantinopolis seated l.	£7	£18
728	**Valentinian II,** 375–392. *R siliqua.* ℞. VICTORIA AVGGG. Victory advancing l.	£22	£60
729	Æ 2. ℞. GLORIA ROMANORVM. Valentinian stg. on galley	£9	£25
730	Æ 4. ℞. SALVS REIPVBLICAE. Victory advancing l.	£3	£8
731	**Theodosius I,** 379–395. Æ 2. ℞. GLORIA ROMANORVM. Theodosius stg. on galley	£9	£25
732	Æ 4. ℞. SALVS REIPVBLICAE. Victory advancing l.	£2.50	£6
733	**Magnus Maximus,** usurper in the West, 383–388, proclaimed emperor by the Roman army in Britain, *N solidus.* ℞. VICTORIA AVGG. Two emperors seated, Victory between them; AVGOB *mm.* (London)	£2750	£8000
734	*R siliqua.* ℞. VICTORIA AVGG. Victory advancing l. AVGPS *mm.* (London)	£225	£600
735	— ℞. VIRTVS ROMANORVM. Roma seated l.	£25	£65
736	**Flavius Victor,** usurper in the West, 387–388. Æ 4. ℞. SPES ROMANORVM. Camp gate	£18	£50
737	**Eugenius,** usurper in the West, 392–394. *R siliqua.* ℞. VIRTVS ROMANORVM. Roma seated l.	£90	£250
738	**Arcadius,** 383–408. Æ 2. ℞. GLORIA ROMANORVM. Arcadius stg. r. . .	£9	£25
739	**Honorius,** 393–423, during whose reign the so-called "Roman withdrawal" from Britain took place. *R siliqua.* ℞. VIRTVS ROMANORVM. Roma seated l.	£25	£65
740	Æ 3. ℞. VIRTVS EXERCITI. Honorius stg. r.	£7	£20
741	**Constantine III,** usurper in the West, proclaimed emperor in Britain, 407–411. *R siliqua.* ℞. VICTORIA AVGGGG. Roma seated l.	£100	£300
742	**Valentinian III,** 425–455, during whose reign the last vestiges of Roman rule in Britain disappeared. Æ 4. ℞. VOT . PVB. Camp gate	£18	£50

EARLY ANGLO-SAXON PERIOD, *c.* 600–*c.* 775

The withdrawal of Roman forces from Britain early in the 5th century A.D. and the gradual decline of central administration resulted in a rapid deterioration of the money supply. The arrival of Teutonic raiders and settlers hastened the decay of urban commercial life and it was probably not until late in the 6th century that renewed political, cultural and commercial links with the kingdom of the Merovingian Franks led to the appearance of small quantities of Merovingian gold *tremisses* (one-third solidus) in England. A purse containing such pieces was found in the Sutton Hoo ship-burial. Native Anglo-Saxon gold *thrymsas* were minted from about the 630s, initially in the style of their continental prototypes or copied from obsolete Roman coinage and later being made in pure Anglo-Saxon style. By the middle of the 7th century the gold coinage was being increasingly debased with silver, and gold had been superseded entirely by silver by about 675.

These silver coins, contemporary with the *deniers* or *denarii* of the Merovingian Franks, are the first English pennies, though they are commonly known today as *sceattas* (a term more correctly translated as "treasure" or "wealth"). They provide important material for the student of Anglo-Saxon art.

Though the earliest sceattas are a transition from the gold thrymsa coinage, coins of new style were soon developed which were also copied by the Frisians of the Low Counties. Early coins appear to have a standard weight of 20 grains (1.29 gms) and are of good silver content, though the quality deteriorates early in the 8th century. These coins exist in a large number of varied types, and as well as the official issues there are mules and other varieties which are probably contemporary imitations. Many of the sceattas were issued during the reign of Aethelbald of Mercia, but as few bear inscriptions it is only in recent years that research has permitted their correct dating and the attribution of certain types to specific areas. Some silver sceats of groups II and III and most types of groups IV to X were issued during the period (A.D. 716–757) when Aethelbald, King of Mercia, was overlord of the southern English. In Northumbria very debased sceattas or *stycas* continued to be issued until the middle of the ninth century. Though a definitive classification has not yet been developed, the arrangement given below follows the latest work on the series: this list is not exhaustive.

The reference "*B.M.C.*" is to the type given in *British Museum Catalogue: Anglo-Saxon Coins*, and *not* the item number.

North, J. J. *English Hammered Coinage*, Vol. 1, *c.* 650–1272 (1980).

Metcalf, D. M. "A stylistic analysis of the 'porcupine' sceattas". *Num. Chron.*, 7th ser., Vol. VI (1966).

Rigold, S. E. "The two primary series of sceattas", *B.N.J.*, xxx (1960).

Sutherland, C. H. V. *Anglo-Saxon Gold Coinage in the light of the Crondall Hoard* (1948).

ᚠᚪᚦ ᚻᚱᚳ·ᚷᛈ ᚻᚾᛁ ᛁ ᚩᚴ ᚳᚣᛘᛏᛒᛗᛖᛚᛝ ᛞ ᛟ ᚪ ᚨ ᛠ ᚣ

f u th o r k · z w h n i j ih p x s t b e m l ng d œ a æ ea y
Early Anglo-Saxon Runes

GOLD

A. Anglo-Merovingian types

751 **Thrymsa** (*c.* 1.32 gms). Name and portrait of Bishop Leudard (chaplain to Q. Bertha of Kent). ℞. Cross. *N. 1* . . . . *Unique*

752 *Canterbury.* Bust r., moneyer's name. ℞. Cross, mint name. *N. 2* . . . . . . *Extremely rare*

753   762   763

753 No mint name. Bust l. ℞. Cross. *N. 3–5, 7* . . . . *Extremely rare*

754 Bust r. ℞. Cross. *N. 6–9, 12* . . . . *Extremely rare*

755 Cross both sides. *N. 10* . . . . *Extremely rare*

756 Bust r. ℞. Cross, runic letters. *N. 11* . . . . *Extremely rare*

GOLD

33

B. Roman derivatives

		F	VF
757	**Solidus.** Bust r. copied from 4th cent. solidus. ℞. Various. *N. 13, 14*	*Extremely rare*	
758	— Runic inscription on reverse. *N. 15*	*Extremely rare*	
759	**Thrymsa.** Radiate bust r. ℞. Clasped hands. *N. 16*	*Extremely rare*	
760	Bust r., hands raised to cross. ℞. Camp gate. *N. 17*	*Extremely rare*	
761	Helmeted bust r. ℞. Cross, runic inscription. *N. 18*	*Extremely rare*	
762	Diad. bust r. ℞. "Standard", TOV / XX in centre. *N. 19. M.* —	*Extremely rare*	
763	— Similar. ℞. Victory protecting "two emperors". *N. 20*	£1250	£2500

C. "London" and derived issues

764 765 767

764	**Thrymsa.** Facing bust, no legend. ℞. Greek cross, LONDVNIV. *N. 21* . . .	*Extremely rare*	
765	Head r. or l. ℞. Plain cross, legend jumbled. *N. 22–24*	*Extremely rare*	

D. "Witmen" group

766	**Thrymsa.** Bust r. with trident centre. ℞. Cross with forked limbs, moneyer's name. *N. 25*	*Extremely rare*	
767	— Similar, but blundered legend on reverse. *N. 25 var.*	£1700	£3500
768	— ℞. Cross potent. *N. 26*	£1700	£3500

E. "York" group

769 771 772

769	**Thrymsa.** Three crosses with geometric squared design below. ℞. Small cross. *N. 27*	*Extremely rare*	

F. "Regal" coinages

770	**Solidus** (4.12 gms). Diad. bust r., moneyer's name around. ℞. Cross potent on steps. *N. 28*	*Extremely rare*	
771	**Thrymsa.** Diad. bust r., AVDVARLD REGES. ℞. Orb with cross, moneyer's name. *N. 29*	£2350	£5500
772	Diad. bust l., moneyer's name around. ℞. Cross and pellets, legend of X s. *N. 30*	*Extremely rare*	
773	Diad. bust r. ℞. Cross botonée, PADA in runes. *N. 31*	£1700	£3750

Miscellaneous issues

774	**Thrymsa.** Crude bust r. ℞. Standing figure with arms outstretched. *N. 33* .	*Extremely rare*	
775	Crude bust or head r. ℞. Various. *N. 35, 38*	*Extremely rare*	
776	Forked cross both sides, and other types. *N. 36, 37, 39*	*Extremely rare*	

EARLY ANGLO-SAXON PERIOD

SILVER

I. **Transitional types struck in silver,** by thrymsa moneyers, *c.* 675–690   *F*   *VF*

779   780   781

777	**Sceat.** *Kentish.* As 773, diad. bust r. R. *Pada* in runes across field. *N. 154* .	£700	£1500
778	— Obv. Similar. R. Cross on steps. *B.M.C. type 2*	*Extremely rare*	
778A	As 763. R. Victory over two emperors. *B.M.C. 1*	*Extremely rare*	
779	— Diad. bust r., TNC to r. R. Cross with annulet in each angle, *Pada* in runes in legend. *B.M.C. 3*	£650	£1450
780	— *"Varimundus".* As 761, helmeted bust r. with sceptre. R. Cross pattée, TmVNVmVC, etc. *Rigold VB, 4–9*	£650	£1450

II. **Primary Sceattas,** *c.* 690–725

783   785   786

781	Series A, *Kentish.* Radiate bust r., usually of good style, TIC to r. R. "Standard". *B.M.C. 2a*	£100	£225
782	Series B, *Kentish.* Diad. bust r. R. Bird above cross on steps. *B.M.C. 26* . .	£120	£275
783	— Diad. head r. within serpent-circle or bust r. R. Bird above cross and two annulets, serpent-circle around. *B.M.C. 27a*	£100	£225
784	— (Bz.) Diad. head r. of poorer style. R. Bird and cross larger and cruder. *B.M.C. 27b* (see also 791)	£125	£300
785	Series C, *East Anglian (?) Runic.* Radiate bust r. somewhat as 781. *Epa* (etc.) in runes to r. R. Neat "Standard" type. *B.M.C. 2b; Rigold R1* (see also 832, and for Frisian copies nos. 839 and 840)	£125	£300
786	*Early "porcupines".* Porcupine-like figure, body with annulet at one end, triangle at other. R. "Standard" with four pellets around central annulet. *Metcalf D*	£85	£200

787   789   790

787	— "Porcupine" has insect-like body with fore-leg. R. "Standard" with four lines and central annulet. *Metcalf G*	£75	£150
788	— "Porcupine" with parallel lines in curve of body. R. "Standard" with VOIC-like symbols	£75	£150
789	— Figure developed into plumed bird. R. "Standard" has groups of triple pellets. *B.M.C. type 6*	£125	£300
790	*Slightly later "porcupines" of reduced weight.* As 788 but various symbols in "standard" (some varieties are Frisian imitations—see 841–2 below) . .	£75	£150

III. **"Mercian" types,** *c.* 705–730. More than one mint, possibly including London; the fineness dropping from good silver to under .500.

791 792 793

		F	VF
791	Derivative of 784, but bird and cross larger and cruder, no serpent circles. *B.M.C. 27b*	£100	£300
792	Two heads face-to-face, cross with trident base between. ℞. Four birds clockwise around cross. *B.M.C. 37*	£110	£325
793	Man holding two crosses. ℞. Bird and branch. *B.M.C. 23b*	£150	£400
794	Diad. bust r. with bird or cross. ℞. Hound and tree. *B.M.C. 42*	£175	£450
795	Diad. bust r. with chalice. ℞. Man standing with cross and bird. *B.M.C. 20*	£150	£400
796	Diad. bust r. with cross. ℞. Wolf curled head to tail. *B.M.C. 32a*	£150	£400
797	— Similar, but wolf-headed serpent	£150	£400
798	— Similar, but wolf-serpent within torque. *B.M.C. 32b*	£150	£400
799	— Similar, but wolf's head r. or l. with long tongue. *B.M.C. 33*	£200	£500
800	— Obv. Similar. ℞. Celtic cross or shield. *B.M.C. 34*	£150	£400

IV. **Types of similar style or finess,** *of uncertain political attribution*

		F	VF
800A	Kneeling archer r., tree behind. ℞. Bird on branch r., head turned l. *B.M.C.* —	*Extremely rare*	
801	As 791, but cross before head. ℞. Large and small bird. *B.M.C. 36*	£150	£350
802	Bust r., lettering around or with cable border. ℞. Bird r. in torque. *B.M.C. 38*	£175	£400
803	Bust l. within cable border. ℞. Man with two crosses. *B.M.C. 21*	£200	£450
804	Facing bust. ℞. Interlaced cruciform pattern. *B.M.C. 52*	£350	£750

797 805 806

V. **South Wessex types,** *c.* 725–750. Found predominantly in excavations at Hamwic (Southampton)

		F	VF
805	Scutiform design (shield with bosses). ℞. Bird and branch as 794. *B.M.C. type 39*	£175	£400
806	Jewel-head, roundels around. ℞. Bird and branch. *B.M.C. 49*	£175	£400
807	Scutiform design. ℞. Wolf-head whorl. *B.M.C. 48*	£175	£400

VI.   **South Saxon types,** *c.* 720–750

		F	VF
808	Diad. bust r. cross before. ℞. "Standard". *B.M.C. 3a*	£125	£300
809	— Similar but crude style and of very base silver	£100	£225

808   815   816

VII.   **"Dragon" types,** *c.* 725–735?

		F	VF
810	Two standing figures, long cross between. ℞. Monster looking back to r. or l. *B.M.C. type 41b*	£175	£400
811	One standing figure, cross either side. ℞. As last. *B.M.C. 23a and 40*	£175	£400
812	Four interlaced shields. ℞. As last. *B.M.C. 43*	£175	£400
813	Bust r., cross before. ℞. As last. *N. 114*	*Extremely rare*	
814	Wolf's head facing. ℞. As last. *N. 122*	£350	£750
815	Wolf and twins. ℞. Bird in vine. *B.M.C. 7*	£200	£450
816	Diad. bust r. + LEV. ℞. "Porcupine" l. *B.M.C. 9*	£175	£400
817	Facing head. ℞. Fantastic animal r. or l. *N. 143–146*	£250	£575

VIII.   **"London issue"** *of around .400 silver content or less, c. 740–750*

		F	VF
818	Diad. bust r., LVNDONIA (sometimes blundered). ℞. Man holding two long crosses. *B.M.C. type 12*	£400	£850
819	— Obv. As last. ℞. "Porcupine" to l. *B.M.C. 12/15*	£350	£750
820	— Obv. As last. ℞. Seated figure r. holding sceptre. *B.M.C. 13*		*Unique*
821	— Obv. As last but bust l. ℞. Scutiform design. *B.M.C. 14*	£350	£750
822	Diad. bust r. with cross, no legend. ℞. As 818. *B.M.C. 15a*	£200	£450
823	— As last. ℞. Man standing with branch and cross, or two branches. *B.M.C. 15b*	£200	£450
824	Diad. bust r. with floral scroll. ℞. As last	£200	£450
825	— As last. ℞. Man with two crosses. *B.M.C. 16*	£150	£350
826	As 813 but bust l. *B.M.C. 17*	£175	£400
827	Diad. bust r. with cross. ℞. Man standing with cross and bird. *B.M.C. 18* .	£200	£450
828	Diad. bust l. with cross. ℞. As last. *B.M.C. 19*	£200	£450
829	Victory standing with wreath. ℞. Man with two crosses. *B.M.C. 22*	£300	£650

818   831

IX.   **"Wolf-head whorl"** *types, mostly of about .300 silver or less, c. 740–750*

		F	VF
830	Man standing holding two crosses. ℞. Wolf-head whorl. *B.M.C. 23e*	£150	£350
831	Sphinx or female centaur with outstretched wings. ℞. As above. *B.M.C. 47* See also No. 807.	£250	£575

832

	F	VF

X. East Anglian types, *of about .500 silver or less, c.* 735–750. Struck to a standard of 15 grs./0.97 gm. or less

832	Crude radiate bust l. or r., *Epa, Wigraed,* or *Spi,* etc., in runes. ℞. "Standard". *Rigold R2* (compare with 785)	£120	£275
833	— Similar. ℞. Cross with each limb ending in annulet. *Rigold R2Z, N. 160*	£200	£450
833A	Saltire in square. ℞. Cross ending in annulets. *B.M.C. 51*	£110	£250
834	Bird r. looking back. ℞. "Standard" with four annulets in saltire. *B.M.C. 46*	£200	£450
835	"Standard" both sides. *N. 55–57*	*Extremely rare*	
836	Fantastic bird r. or l. ℞. Fantastic quadruped l. or r. *B.M.C. 44*	£150	£350

836   837   839

XI. Late sceattas, *on a restored silver standard, c.* 750–775. These probably include some specimens of 830 and 831 and the following types:

837	"Porcupine". ℞. *Aethili/raed* in runes in two lines. *B.M.C. 4*	£750	£1750
838	"Porcupine". ℞. Small cross, S E D E in angles. *N. 47*	*Extremely rare*	

XII. Frisian sceattas, *c.* 700–750. A number of large sceatta hoards have been found in the Netherlands and Lower Rhine area. Some of the coins are now known to have been minted in Frisia but some also circulated in England

839	Crude radiate bust l. or r., as 832, sometimes crude runes. ℞. Plain cross with pellets or annulets in angles. *Rigold R3. B.M.C. 2c*	£65	£150
840	"Standard". ℞. Cross and pellets. *B.M.C. 50*	£70	£175
841	"Porcupine" with III, XII or XIII in curve. ℞. "Standard". *Metcalf A, B & C*	£70	£175
842	"Porcupine" has a triangle attached to curve or an outline of pellets. *Metcalf E & F*	£70	£175

843   844

843	Facing "Wodan" head. ℞. Monster. *B.M.C. 31*	£110	£225
844	— Similar. ℞. Two men with staves or long cross. *B.M.C. 30a & b*	£150	£325

XIII. **Uncertain issues**

847

		F	VF
846	**Ealdfrith** (? possibly sub-king of Lindsey, *c.* 790). Ӕ *sceat.* Pellet in annulet. ℞. Fantastic animal l. with trifid tail		*Extremely rare*
847	**Beonna,** King of East Anglia, *c.* 758. Ӕ *sceat.* Pellet in centre, Runic inscription. ℞. EFE in Roman characters around saltire cross	£500	*Extremely rare*
847A	— Similar. ℞. Name in Runic		*Extremely rare*
847B	— Similar. ℞. Interlace pattern		*Extremely rare*

KINGS OF NORTHUMBRIA

In the North a series of silver sceats was struck with the king's name on the obverse and a fantastic animal on the reverse.

Towards the end of the eighth century the coinage degenerated to one of base silver and finally to copper or brass; from the second reign of Aethelred I the design becomes standardised with the king's name retained on the obverse but with the moneyer's name on the reverse and in the centre of both sides a cross, pellet or rosette, etc.

A parallel series of ecclesiastical coins was struck by the Archbishops of York. The coinage continued until the conquest of Northumbria by the Danes and the defeat of Osbert in 867, almost a century after introduction of the broad silver penny in Southern England.

852	**Eadberht** (737–758). Ӕ *sceat.* . Small cross. ℞. Fantastic quadruped to l. or r.	£350	£800
	Aethelwald Moll (759–765). See Archbishop Ecgberht of York		

853   859   861

853	**Alcred** (765–774). Ӕ *sceat.* As 852	£350	£800
854	**Aethelred I,** first reign (774–779). Ӕ *sceat.* As last	£350	£800
855	**Aelfwald I** (779–788). Ӕ *sceat.* As last	£400	£950
856	— — Small cross. ℞. With name of moneyer CVDBEVRT	£375	£900
857	**Aethelred I,** second reign (789–796). Ӕ *sceat.* Similar. ℞. SCT CVD (St. Cuthbert), shrine		*Extremely rare*
858	— Small cross. ℞. With moneyer's name	£225	£550
	The last and the rest of the sceats, *except where otherwise stated, have on the obv. the king's name, and on the rev. the moneyer's name: in the centre on both sides is a cross, a pellet, a rosette, etc. During the following reign the silver sceat becomes debased and later issues are only brass or copper.*		
859	**Eanred** (810–*c.* 854). Base Ӕ *sceat*	£30	£65
859A	— Ӕ *penny.* Bust r. ℞. Cross, part moline part crosslet		*Unique*
860	— Æ *sceat*	£15	£35
861	**Aethelred II,** first reign (*c.* 854–*c.* 858). Æ *sceat*	£12	£25
862	— ℞. Quadruped	£400	£950

	F	VF

863 **Redwulf** (*c.* 858). Æ *sceat* £40   £90

864 **Aethelred II,** second reign (*c.* 858–*c.* 862). Æ *sceat*, mainly of the moneyer
EARDWVLF £20   £45

865 **Osbert** (*c.* 862–867). Æ *sceat* £55   £125
*Coins with blunaered legends are worth less than those with normal readings,
and to this series have been relegated those coins previously attributed to Eardwulf
and Aelfwald II.*

ARCHBISHOPS OF YORK

866   868

866 **Ecgberht** (732 *or* 734–766). Æ *sceat*, with king Eadberht. As illustration,
or holds cross and crozier £300   £375

866A —— with Aethelwald Moll. Cross each side . . . . *Extremely rare*

867 —— with Alchred. Cross each side . . . . *Extremely rare*

868 **Eanbald II** (796–*c.* 830). Æ *sceat*. Ṛ. With name of moneyer £50   £125

869 — Æ *sceat*, as last £40   £90

870   871

870 **Wigmund** (837–854). Gold *solidus*. Facing bust. Ṛ. Cross in wreath . . . .   *Unique*

871 — Æ *sceat*, various £20   £40

872 **Wulfhere** (854–900). Æ *sceat* £85   £175

MIDDLE ANGLO-SAXON PERIOD, *c.* 780–973

In the kingdom of the Franks a reformed coinage of good quality *deniers* struck on broad flans had been introduced by Pepin in 755 and continued by his son Charlemagne and his descendants. A new coinage of *pennies* of similar size and weighing about 20 grains (1.3 gms.) was introduced into England, probably by Offa, the powerful king of Mercia, about 775/780, though early pennies also exist of two little known kings of Kent, Heaberht and Ecgberht, of about the same period.

The silver penny (*Lat.* "denarius", hence the *d.* of our *£. s. d.*) remained virtually the sole denomination of English coinage for almost five centuries, with the rare exception of occasional gold coins and somewhat less rare silver halfpence. The penny reached a weight of 24 grains, i.e., a "pennyweight" during the reign of Aelfred the Great. Silver pennies of this period normally bear the ruler's name, though not always his portrait, and the name of the moneyer responsible for their manufacture.

Pennies were issued by various rulers of the Heptarchy for the kingdoms of Kent, Mercia, East Anglia and Wessex (and possibly Anglian Northumbria), by the Danish settlers in the Danelaw and the Hiberno-Norse kings of York, and also by the Archbishops of Canterbury and a Bishop of London. Under Eadgar, who became the sole ruler of England, a uniform coinage was instituted throughout the country, and it was he who set the pattern for the "reformed" coinage of the later Anglo-Saxon and Norman period.

Halfpence are known from the age of Aelfred to that of Eadgar, but they are rare and were probably never made in large quantities. To provide small change pennies were sometimes cut or broken in half.

Nos. 873–1387 are all silver **pennies** except where stated.

KINGS OF KENT

		F	VF
873	**Heaberht** (*c.* 765). Monogram for REX. ℞. Five annulets, each containing a pellet, joined to form a cross		*Unique*
874	**Ecgberht** (*c.* 780). Similar. ℞. Varied ......*from*	£1250	£3000
875	**Eadberht Praen** (796–798). As illustration. ℞. Varied	£1250	£3000

875   877

		F	VF
876	**Cuthred** (798–807). *Canterbury*. Various types without portrait ...*from*	£500	£1250
877	— As illustration	£550	£1300

878   879

		F	VF
878	**Anonymous** (*c.* 822–823). *Canterbury*. As illustration	£650	£1650
879	**Baldred** (*c.* 823–825). *Canterbury*. Head or bust r. ℞. Varied	£750	£1850
880	— Cross each side	£650	£1650
881	*Rochester*. Diademed bust r. ℞. Varied	*Extremely rare*	

ARCHBISHOPS OF CANTERBURY

882 885

		F	VF
882	**Jaenberht** (765–792). His name around central ornament or cross and wedges. ℞. OFFA REX in two lines	£1750	£4500
883	— His name in three lines. ℞. OFFA REX between the limbs of Celtic cross	£2250	£5500
884	**Aethelheard** (el. 792, cons. 793, d. 805). With Offa as overlord. First issue (792–793), with title *Pontifex*	£1600	£4000
885	— Second issue (793–796), with title *Archiepiscopus*	£1200	£3000
886	With Coenwulf as overlord. Third issue (796–805)	£1150	£2750
887	**Wulfred** (805–832). Group I (805–c. 810). As illustration. ℞. Crosslet *(unique)*, alpha-omega . . . .*from*	£800	£2000
888	— Group II (*c.* 810). As last. ℞. DOROVERNIA C monogram	£550	£1350
889	— Group III (pre 823). Bust extends to edge of coin. ℞. As last	£600	£1500
890	— Groups IV and V (*c.* 822–823). Anonymous under Ecgberht. Moneyer's name in place of the Archbishop's. ℞. DOROBERNIA CIVITAS in three or five lines	£525	£1300
891	— Group VI (*c.* 823–825). Baldred type. Crude portrait. ℞. DRVR CITS in two lines	£550	£2000
892	— Group VII (*c.* 832). Second monogram (Ecgberht) type. Crude portrait r., PLFRED. ℞. DORIB C. Monogram as 1035	£550	£2000

887 894

		F	VF
893	**Ceolnoth** (833–870). Group I with name CIALNOÐ. Tonsured bust facing. ℞. Varied . . . .*from*	£425	£1050
894	— Group II. Similar but CEOLNOÐ. ℞. Types of Aethelwulf of Wessex . .	£525	£1250
895	— Group III. Diad. bust r. ℞. Moneyer's name in and between lunettes . .	£500	£1150

896

		F	VF
896	**Aethered** (870–889). Bust r. ℞. As illustration or with long cross with lozenge panel	£1750	£4500
897	— Cross pattée. ℞. ELF / STAN		*Unique*

Archbishops of Canterbury *continued*

898

		F	VF
898	**Plegmund** (890–914). DORO in circle. ℞. As illustration above, various moneyers ....*from*	£350	£850
899	— Similar, but title EPISC, and XDF in centre	£600	£1500
900	— Small cross pattée. ℞. Somewhat as last	£325	£800
901	— Crosses moline and pommée on *obv.*	£600	£1500

KINGS OF MERCIA

Until 825 Canterbury was the principal mint of the Kings of Mercia and some moneyers also struck coins for the Kings of Kent and Archbishops.

GOLD

902   903

902	**Offa** (757–796). Gold *dinar*. Copy of Arabic dinar of Caliph Al Mansur, dated 157 A.H. (A.D. 774), with OFFA REX added on *rev.*	*Unique*
903	Gold *penny*. Bust r., moneyer's name. ℞. Standing figure, moneyer's name	*Unique*

SILVER

904   905

		F	VF
904	*Canterbury.* Group I (*c.* 784–*c.* 787). Early coins without portraits, small flans. Various types ....*from*	£700	£1950
905	— Group II (*c.* 787–*c.* 792). Various types with portrait, small flans .*from*	£1100	£2750
906	— — — Various types without portraits, small flans ....*from*	£700	£1750

Offa *continued*

907   909

		F	VF
907	*Canterbury*. Group III (*c*. 792–796). Various types without portrait, large flans . . . .*from*	£750	£1850
908	*East Anglia*. Copies of Group II and III, possibly struck *c*. 790. Ornate, crude, and sometimes with runic letters	£650	£1650
909	**Cynethryth** (wife of Offa). Coins as Group II of Offa. As illustration	£4000	£10,000
910	— *O*. As *rev*. of last. ℞. EOBA on leaves of quatrefoil	£2500	£6500
911	**Eadberht** (Bishop of London, died 787/789). EADBERHT EP in three lines. ℞. Name of Offa . . . . *The attribution to this particular cleric is uncertain.*	*Extremely rare*	
912	**Coenwulf** (796–821). Group I (796–805). *Canterbury* and *London*. Without portrait. His name in three lines. ℞. Varied	£450	£1100
913	— *Canterbury*. Name around m as illus. below. ℞. Moneyer's name in two lines	*Unique*	

914   915

914	— *Both mints*. Tribrach type as illustration	£375	£900
915	— Group II (*c*. 805–810). *Canterbury*. With portrait. Small flans. ℞. Varied but usually cross and wedges	£475	£1150
916	— Groups II and IV (*c*. 810–820). *Canterbury*. Similar but larger flans. ℞. Varied	£450	£1100
917	— *Rochester*. Large diad. bust of coarse style. ℞. Varied. (Moneyers: Dun, Ealhstan)	£500	£1200
918	— *London*. With portrait generally of Roman style. ℞. Crosslet	£525	£1250
919	— *E. Anglia*. Crude diad. bust r. ℞. Moneyer's name LVL on leaves in arms of cross	£475	£1150
920	— — *O*. as last. ℞. Various types . . . .*from*	£450	£1100

921   929

		F	VF
921	**Ceolwulf I** (821–823). *Canterbury*. Group I. Bust r. ℞. Varied. (Moneyers: Oba, Sigestef)	£650	£1600
922	— — Group II. Crosslet. ℞. Varied	£550	£1350
923	— — Group III. Tall cross with MERCIORŪ. ℞. Crosslet. SIGESTEF DOROBERNIA		*Unique*
924	— *Rochester*. Group I. Bust r. ℞. Varied	£550	£1350
925	— — Group IIA. As last but head r.	£600	£1500
926	— — Group IIB. Ecclesiastical issue by Bp. of Rochester. With mint name, DOROBREBIA, but no moneyer		*Extremely rare*
927	— *East Anglia*. Crude style and lettering with barbarous portrait. ℞. Varied	£550	£1375
928	**Beornwulf** (823–825). Bust r. ℞. Moneyer's name in three lines	£1500	£3750
929	— ℞. Cross crosslet in centre	£1250	£3000
930	Crude copy of 928 but moneyer's name in two lines with crosses between .		*Extremely rare*

931   933

931	**Ludica** (825–827). Bust r. ℞. Moneyer's name in three lines as 928		*Extremely rare*
932	— Similar. ℞. Moneyer's name around cross crosslet in centre, as 929		*Extremely rare*
933	**Wiglaf**, first reign (827–829). Crude head r. ℞. Crosslet	£1750	£4500

934

934	Second reign (830–840). Cross and pellets. ℞. Moneyer's name in and between lunettes of pellets	£1750	£4500

935

		F	VF
935	**Berhtwulf** (840–852). Various types with bust . . . .*from*	£700	£1750
936	— Cross potent over saltire. ℞. Cross potent	£750	£1850
937	Berhtwulf with Aethelwulf of Wessex. As before. ℞. IAETHELWLF REX, cross pommée over cross pattée		*Unique*
938	**Burgred** (852–874). *B.M.C. type A*. Bust r. ℞. Moneyer's name in and between lunettes	£100	£210
939	— — B. Similar but lunettes broken in centre of curve	£110	£230

938   939   940   941

		F	VF
940	— — C. Similar but lunettes broken in angles	£110	£230
941	— — D. Similar but legend divided by two lines with a crook at each end .	£100	£210
942	— — E. As last, but m above and below	£350	£900
943	**Ceolwulf II** (874–*c.* 880). Bust r. ℞. Two emperors seated, Victory above .		*Unique*

944

		F	VF
944	— ℞. Moneyer's name in angles of long cross with lozenge centre	£2000	£5000

KINGS OF EAST ANGLIA

946   948

		F	VF
	Beonna (*c.* 760). See no. 847		
946	**Aethelberht** (d. 794). As illustration	*Only 3 known*	
947	**Eadwald** (*c.* 798). King's name in three lines. ℞. Moneyer's name in quatrefoil or around cross	*Extremely rare*	
948	**Aethelstan I** (*c.* 825–840). Bust r. or l. ℞. Crosslet or star	£750	£2000
949	Bust r. ℞. Moneyer's name in three or four lines	£750	£2000
950	Alpha or A. ℞. Varied	£450	£1100
951	*O.* and *rev.* Cross with or without wedges or pellets in angles	£450	£1100
952	— Similar, with king's name both sides	£600	£1500
952A	Name around ship in centre. ℞. Moneyer Eadgar, pellets in centre. (Possibly the earliest of his coins.)	*Unique*	
953	**Aethelweard** (*c.* 840–*c.* 855), A, Omega or cross and crescents. ℞. Cross with pellets or wedges	£750	£1850

953   954

954	**Edmund** (855–870). Alpha or A. ℞. Cross with pellets or wedges	£450	£1100
955	— *O.* Varied. ℞. Similar	£450	£1100

For the St. Edmund coins and the Danish issues struck in East Anglia having on them the name of Aethelred I of Wessex and Alfred, see Danish East Anglia.

VIKING COINAGES

Danish East Anglia, c. 885–915

956 957

	F	VF

956 **Aethelstan II** (878–890), originally named Guthrum? Cross pattée. ℞. Moneyer's name in two lines £1000 £2500

957 **Oswald** (unknown except from his coins). Alpha or A. ℞. Cross pattée .. *Extremely rare*

958 — Copy of Carolingian "temple" type. ℞. Cross and pellets .... *Unique fragment*

959 **Aethelred I.** As last, with name of Aethelred I of Wessex. ℞. As last, or cross-crosslet .... *Extremely rare*

960 **St. Edmund,** memorial coinage, Æ *penny*, type as illus. below, various legends of good style £75 £175

961 — Similar, but barbarous or semi-barbarous legends £65 £150

962 *Halfpenny.* Similar £400 £1000

961 963

963 **St. Martin of Lincoln.** As illustration £1500 £3750

964 **Alfred.** (Viking imitations, usually of very barbarous workmanship.) Bust r. ℞. *Londonia* monogram £400 £1200

965 — Similar, but *Lincolla* monogram .... *Extremely rare*

966 970

966 — Small cross, as Alfred group II (*Br. 6*), various legends, some read REX DORO ....*from* £200 £500

967 — Similar. ℞. 'St. Edmund type' A in centre £500 £1500

968 — Two emperors seated. ℞. As 964. (Previously attributed to Halfdene) . *Unique*

969 *Halfpenny.* As 964 and 965 ....*from* £500 £1500

970 — As 966 .... £450 £1350

Danish Northumbria, *c.* **898–915**   *F*   *VF*

971 **Alfred** (Imitations). ELFRED between ORSNA and FORDA. ℞. Moneyer's
name in two lines £300   £750

972 — *Halfpenny.* Similar, of very crude appearance . . . .   *Extremely rare*

971   975

973 **Alfred/Plegmund.** *Obv.* ELFRED REX PLEGN . . . .   *Extremely rare*

974 **Plegmund.** Danish copy of 900 . . . .   £300   £750

975 **Earl Sihtric.** Type as 971. SCELDFOR between GVNDI BERTVS. ℞. SITRIC
COMES in two lines . . . .   *Extremely rare*

Viking Coinage of York?

References are to "The Classification of Northumbrian Viking Coins in the Cuerdale hoard", by
C. S. S. Lyon and B. H. I. H. Stewart, in Numismatic Chronicle, 1964, p. 281ff.

976 **Siefred.** C . SIEFRE DIIS REX in two lines. ℞. EBRAICE CIVITAS (or con-
tractions), small cross. *L. & S. Ia, Ie, Ii* £200   £550

977 — Cross on steps between. ℞. As last. *L. & S. If, Ij* £275   £750

978 — Long cross. ℞. As last. *L. & S. Ik* . . . .   *Extremely rare*

979 SIEFREDVS REX, cross crosslet within legend. ℞. As last. *L. & S. Ih* £130   £350

980 SIEVERT REX, cross crosslet to edge of coin. ℞. As last. *L. & S. Ic, Ig, Im*   £130   £350

981 — Cross on steps between. ℞. As last. *L. & S. Il* £240   £650

982 — Patriarchal cross. ℞. DNS DS REX, small cross. *L. & S. Va* £150   £400

983 — — ℞. MIRABILIA FECIT, small cross. *L. & S. VIb* £185   £500

984 REX, at ends of cross crosslet. ℞. SIEFREDVS, small cross. *L. & S. IIIa, b*   £140   £385

985 — Long cross. ℞. As last. *L. & S. IIIc* £120   £325

986 *Halfpenny.* Types as 977, *L. & S. Ib*; 980, *Ic*; and 983, *VIb* . . . .   *Extremely rare*

980   993

987 **Cnut.** CNVT REX, cross crosslet to edge of coin. ℞. EBRAICE CIVITAS,
small cross. *L. & S. Io, Iq* £90   £200

988 — — ℞. CVNNETTI, small cross. *L. & S. IIc* £100   £225

989 — Long cross. ℞. EBRAICE CIVITAS, small cross. *L. & S. Id, In, Ir* £75   £175

990 — — ℞. CVNNETTI, small cross. *L. & S. IIa, IId* £75   £175

991 — Patriarchal cross. ℞. EBRAICE CIVITAS, small cross. *L. & S. Ip, Is* . .   £75   £175

992 — — ℞.—*Karolus* monogram in centre. *L. & S. It* £400   £1000

993 — — ℞. CVNNETTI, small cross. *L. & S. IIb, IIe* £50   £125

		F	VF

994 *Halfpenny.* Types as 987, *L. & S. Iq*; 989, *Id*; 991, *Is*; 992, *Iu*; 993, *IIb* and *e* . . . . *from*   £450   £1100

995 As 992, but CVNNETTI around *Karolus* monogram. *L. & S. IIf* £450   £1100

995   998

996 **Cnut and/or Siefred.** CNVT REX, patriarchal cross. ℞. SIEFREDVS, small cross. *L. & S. IIId* £110   £235

997 — — ℞. DNS DS REX, small cross. *L. & S. Vc.* £150   £325

998 — — ℞. MIRABILIA FECIT. *L. & S. VId* £140   £300

999 EBRAICE C, patriarchal cross. ℞. DNS DS REX, small cross. *L. & S. Vb* . .   £120   £250

1000 — — ℞. MIRABILIA FECIT. *L. & S. VIc* £140   £300

1001 DNS DS REX in two lines. ℞. ALVALDVS, small cross. *L. & S. IVa* £1500

1002 DNS DS O REX, similar. ℞. MIRABILIA FECIT. *L. & S. VIa* £250   £550

1003 *Halfpenny.* As last. *L. & S. VIa* . . . .   *Extremely rare*

1004 **"Cnut".** Name blundered around cross pattée with extended limbs. ℞. QVENTOVICI around small cross. *L. & S. VII* £300   £650

1005 — *Halfpenny.* Similar. *L. & S. VII* £450   £1000
Possibly not Northumbrian; the reverse copied from the Carolingian coins of Quentovic, N. France.

1006 **St. Peter coinage.** Early issues. SCI PETRI MO in two lines. ℞. Cross pattée   £175   £400

1007 — Similar. ℞. "Karolus" monogram . . . .   *Extremely rare*

1008 *Halfpenny.* Similar. ℞. Cross pattée £1000   £2250

1006   1009

1009 **Regnald** (blundered types). RAIENALT, head to l. or r. ℞. EARICE CT, "Karolus" monogram £1250   £3000

1010 — Open hand. ℞. Similar £1000   £2500

1011 — Hammer. ℞. Bow and arrow £1250   £3000

1012 — Similar. ℞. Sword . . . .   *Extremely rare*

English Coins of the Hiberno-Norse Vikings

Early period, *c.* **919–925**

1013 **Sihtric** (921–927). SITRIC REX, sword. ℞. Cross or T £1500   £3750

1015   1016

		F	VF

1014 **St. Peter coinage.** Late issues. SCI PETRI MO, sword and hammer. ℞.
     EBORACEI, cross and pellets £350 £850
1015 — Similar. ℞. Voided hammer £450 £1100
1016 — Similar. ℞. Solid hammer £750 £1850
     St. Peter coins with blundered legends are rather cheaper.

Later period, 939–954 (after the battle of Brunanburh). All struck at York except the first two which
were struck at Derby.

1017 **Anlaf Guthfrithsson,** 939–941. Flower type. Small cross, ANLAF REX TO
     D. ℞. Flower above moneyer's name £2500 £6000
1018 — Circular type. Small cross each side, ANLAF CVNVNC MOT £2500 £6000
1019 — Raven type. As illustration, CVNVNC £2000 £5000

1019   1020

1020 **Anlaf Sihtricsson,** first reign, 941–944. Triquetra type. As illus., CVNVNC.
     ℞. Danish standard £2000 £5000
1021 — Circular type (a). Small cross each side, CVNVNC £2000 £5000
1022 — Cross moline type, CVNVNC. ℞. Small cross .... *Extremely rare*
1023 — Two line type. Small cross. ℞. ONLAF REX. ℞. Name in two lines ... £2000 £5000
1024 **Regnald Guthfrithsson,** 943–944. Triquetra type. As 1020. REGNALD
     CVNVNC £3000 £7500
1025 — Cross moline type. As 1022, but REGNALD CVNVNC £2500 £6000
1026 **Sihtric Sihtricsson,** *c.* 942. Triquetra type. As 1020, SITRIC CVNVNC ... *Unique*

1025   1030

1027 — Circular type. Small cross each side. SITRIC CVNVNC .... *Unique*
1028 **Eric,** first reign, 948. Two line type. Small cross, ERICVS REX A; ERIC
     REX AL; or ERIC REX EFOR. ℞. Name in two lines £2500 £6000
1029 **Anlaf Sihtricsson,** second reign, 948–952. Circular type (b). Small cross
     each side. ONLAF REX £2750 £6500
1030 **Eric,** second reign, 952–954. Sword type. ERIC REX in two lines, sword
     between. ℞. Small cross £2750 £6500

KINGS OF WESSEX

Later, KINGS OF ALL ENGLAND

All are silver pennies unless otherwise stated

BEORHTRIC, 786–802

Beorhtric was dependent on Offa of Mercia and married a daughter of Offa.

1031

		F	VF
1031	As illustration	*Extremely rare*	
1032	Alpha and omega in centre. ℞. Omega in centre	*Extremely rare*	

ECGBERHT, 802–839

King of Wessex only, 802–825; then also of Kent, Sussex, Surrey, Essex and East Anglia, 825–839, and of Mercia also, 829–830.

1033	*Canterbury.* Group I. Diad. hd. r. within inner circle. ℞. Various . . . *from*	£1450	£5000
1034	— II. Non-portrait types. ℞. Various . . . *from*	£750	£3000

1035

1035	— III. Bust r. breaking inner circle. ℞. DORIB C.	£1250	£3750
1036	*London.* Cross potent. ℞. LVN / DONIA / CIVIT		*Unique*
1037	— — ℞. REDMVND MONE around TA	£1500	£4500
1038	*Rochester*, royal mint. Non-portrait types with king's name ECGBEORHT . . . *from*	£1150	£3500
1039	— — Portrait types, ECGBEORHT . . . *from*	£1350	£4250
1040	*Rochester*, bishop's mint. Bust r. ℞. SCS ANDREAS (APOSTOLVS)	£1450	£5000
1041	*Winchester.* SAXON monogram or SAXONIORVM in three lines. ℞. Cross	£1150	£3500

AETHELWULF, 839–858

Son of Ecgberht; sub-King of Essex, Kent, Surrey and Sussex, 825–839; King of all southern England, 839–855; King of Essex, Kent and Sussex only, 855–858. No coins are known of his son Aethelbald who ruled over Wessex proper, 855–860.

1042

		F	VF
1042	*Canterbury.* Phase I (839–c. 843). Head within inner circle. ℞. Various. *Br. 3*	£300	£650
1043	— — Larger bust breaking inner circle. ℞. A. *Br. 1 and 2*	£300	£650
1044	— — Cross and wedges. ℞. SAXONIORVM in three lines in centre. *Br. 10*	£275	£60
1045	— — Similar, but OCCIDENTALIVM in place of moneyer. *Br. 11*	£250	£800
1046	— Phase II (c. 843–848?). Cross and wedges. ℞. Various, but chiefly a form of cross or a large A. *Br. 4*	£275	£600
1047	— — New portrait, somewhat as 1043. ℞. As last. *Br. 7*	£275	£600
1048	— — Smaller portrait. ℞. As last, with *Chi/Rho* monogram. *Br. 7*	£300	£650
1049	— Phase III (c. 848/851–c. 855). DORIB in centre. ℞. CANT mon. *Br. 5*	£275	£600
1050	— — CANT mon. ℞. CAN M in angles of cross. *Br. 6*	£300	£650

1044   1051

1051	— Phase IV (c. 855–859). Type as Aethelberht. New neat style bust. ℞. Large voided long cross. *Br. 8*	£225	£500
1052	*Winchester.* SAXON mon. ℞. Cross and wedges. *Br. 9*	£350	£800

AETHELBERHT, 858–865/866

Son of Aethelwulf; sub-King of Kent, Essex and Sussex, 858–860; King of all southern England, 860–865/6.

1053	As illustration below	£200	£500
1054	*O.* Similar. ℞. Cross fleury over quatrefoil	£700	£1500

1053

AETHELRED I, 865/866–871

Son of Aethelwulf, succeeded his brother Aethelberht.

		F	VF
1055	As illustration	£200	£500
1056	Similar, but moneyer's name in four lines	£600	£1500

For another coin with the name Aethelred see 959 under Viking coinages.

1055

ALFRED THE GREAT, 871–899

Brother and successor to Aethelred, Aelfred had to contend with invading Danish armies for much of his reign. In 878 he and Guthrum the Dane divided the country, with Aelfred holding all England south and west of Watling Street. Aelfred occupied London in 886.

Types with portraits

1057	Bust r. ℞. As Aethelred I. *Br. 1 (name often* AELBRED)	£400	£900
1058	— ℞. Long cross with lozenge centre, as 944. *Br. 5*	£1500	£3500
1059	— ℞. Two seated figures, as 943. *Br. 2*		Unique
1060	— ℞. As Archbp. Aethered; cross within large quatrefoil. *Br. 3*		Unique

1057   1062

1061	*London.* Bust r. ℞. LONDONIA monogram	£600	£1400
1062	— — ℞. Similar, but with moneyer's name added	£800	£2000
1063	— *Halfpenny.* Bust r. ℞. LONDONIA monogram as 1061	£1000	£2500
1064	*Gloucester.* ℞. ÆT GLEAPA in angles of three limbed cross		Unique

Types without portraits

1065	King's name on limbs of cross, trefoils in angles. ℞. Moneyer's name in quatrefoil. *Br. 4*		Unique

1066   1069

1066	Cross pattée. ℞. Moneyer's name in two lines. *Br. 6*	£200	£450
1067	— As last, but neater style, as Edw. the Elder	£225	£500
1068	— *Halfpenny.* As 1066	£650	£1650
1069	*Canterbury.* As last but DORO added on *obv. Br. 6a*	£350	£750

For other pieces bearing the name of Alfred see under the Viking coinages.

1070	*Exeter?* King's name in four lines. ℞. EXA vertically		Extremely rare
1071	*Winchester?* Similar to last, but PIN		Extremely rare
1072	"Offering penny". Very large and heavy. AELFRED REX SAXORVM in four lines. ℞. ELIMO in two lines i.e. (*Elimosina,* alms)		Extremely rare

EDWARD THE ELDER, 899–924

Eadward, the son of Aelfred, aided by his sister Aethelflaed 'Lady of the Mercians', annexed al England south of the Humber and built many new fortified boroughs to protect the kingdom.

1074

		F	*VF*
1073	**Rare types.** *Br. 1. Bath?* ℞. BA	*Extremely rare*	
1074	— 2. *Canterbury.* Cross moline in pommée. ℞. Moneyer's name	£700	£1750
1075	— 3. *Chester?* Small cross. ℞. Minster	£750	£1850
1076	— 4. — Small cross. ℞. Moneyer's name in single line	£625	£1500
1077	— 5. — ℞. Two stars	£850	£2000

1078 1082

1078	— 6. — ℞. Flower above central line, name below	£850	£2000
1079	— 7. — ℞. Floral design with name across field	£850	£2000
1080	— 8. — ℞. Bird holding twig	*Extremely rare*	
1081	— 9. — ℞. Hand of Providence	£1000	£2500
1082	— 10. — ℞. City gate of Roman style	*Extremely rare*	
1083	— 11. — ℞. Anglo-Saxon burg	£750	£1850

1084 1087

1084	**Ordinary types.** *Br. 12.* Bust l. ℞. Moneyer's name in two lines ....*from*	£400	£1000
1085	— — As last, but in *gold*		*Unique*
1086	— 12a. Similar, but bust r. of crude style	£350	£850
1087	— 13. Small cross. ℞. Similar	£125	£300
1088	*Halfpenny.* Similar to last	£650	£1500

AETHELSTAN, 924–939

Aethelstan, the eldest son of Eadward, decreed that money should only be coined in a borough, that every borough should have one moneyer and that some of the more important boroughs should have more than one moneyer.

1089   1094

		F	VF
1089	**Main issues.** Small cross. ℞. Moneyer's name in two lines	£225	£450
1090	Diad. bust r. ℞. As last	£650	£1500
1091	— ℞. Small cross	£550	£1350
1092	Small cross both sides	£200	£425
1093	— Similar, but mint name added	£300	£700
1094	Crowned bust r. As illustration. ℞. Small cross	£450	£1100
1095	— Similar, but mint name added	£450	£1100

1100   1104

1096	**Local Issues.** *N.W. mints.* Star between two pellets. ℞. As 1089	£550	£1250
1097	— Small cross. ℞. Floral ornaments above and below moneyer's name	£550	£1250
1098	— Rosette of pellets each side	£250	£550
1099	— Small cross one side, rosette on the other side	£275	£650
1100	*York.* Small cross. ℞. Tower over moneyer's name	£550	£1250
1101	— Similar, but mint name added	£750	£1750
1102	— Bust in high relief r. or l. ℞. Small cross	£500	£1150
1103	— Bust r. in high relief. ℞. Cross-crosslet	£500	£1150
1104	*Lincoln?* Helmeted bust r. ℞. As last	£600	£1500

EADMUND, 939–946

Eadmund, the brother of Aethelstan, extended his realm over the Norse kingdom of York.

1105   1107

		F	VF
1105	Small cross or rosette. ℞. Moneyer's name in two lines with crosses or rosettes between . . . .*from*	£125	£275
1106	Crowned bust r. ℞. Small cross	£300	£650
1107	Similar, but with mint name	£400	£850
1108	Small cross either side, or rosette on one side	£175	£375
1109	Cross of five pellets. ℞. Moneyer's name in two lines	£200	£425
1110	Small cross. ℞. Flower above name	£750	£1750
1111	Helmeted bust r. ℞. Cross-crosslet	£750	£1750

1112

1112	*Halfpenny.* As 1105 . . . .*from*	£950	£2000

EADRED, 946–955

Eadred was another of the sons of Eadward. He lost the kingdom of York to Eric Bloodaxe.

1113   1115

1113	As illustration. ℞. Moneyer's name in two lines	£125	£250
1114	— Similar, but mint name after REX	£300	£650
1115	Crowned bust r. As illustration	£350	£750
1116	— ℞. Similar, with mint-name added	£400	£850
1117	Rosette. ℞. As 1113	£125	£250
1118	Small cross. ℞. Rosette	£135	£285
1119	— ℞. Flower enclosing moneyer's name. *B.M.C. II*	*Extremely rare*	
1120	*Halfpenny.* Similar to 1113 . . . .*from*	£750	£1500

HOWEL DDA, d. 949–950

Grandson of Rhodri Mawr, Howel succeeded to the kingdom of Dyfed *c.* 904, to Seisyllog *c.* 920 and became King of Gwynedd and all Wales, 942.

1121

	F	VF
1121 HOPÆL REX, small cross or rosette. ℞. Moneyer's name in two lines . . .		*Unique*

EADWIG, 955–959

Elder son of Eadmund, Eadwig lost Mercia and Northumbria to his brother Eadgar in 957.

1122

	F	VF
1122 *Br. 1.* Type as illustration	£150	£375
1123 — — Similar, but mint name in place of crosses	£375	£850
1123A— Similar to 1122, but star in place of cross on *obv.*		*Unique*
1124 — 2. As 1122, but moneyer's name in one line	£600	£1350
1125 — 3. Similar. ℞. Floral design	£675	£1450
1126 — 4. Similar. ℞. Rosette or small cross	£250	£550
1127 — 5. Bust r. ℞. Small cross (*Possibly an altered coin of Eadgar*)	*Extremely rare*	

1128

1128 *Halfpenny.* Small cross. ℞. Flower above moneyer's name		*Unique*

EADGAR, 959–975

King in Mercia and Northumbria from 957; King of all England 959–975.

It is now possible on the basis of the lettering to divide up the majority of Eadgar's coins into issues from the following regions: N.E. England, N.W. England, York, East Anglia, Midlands, S.E. England, Southern England, and S.W. England. (*Vide* "Anglo-Saxon Coins", ed. R. H. M. Dolley.)

1129   1135

		F	VF
1129	*Br. 1.* Small cross. ℞. Moneyer's name in two lines, crosses between, trefoils top and bottom	£80	£200
1130	— — ℞. Similar, but rosettes top and bottom (a N.W. variety)	£80	£200
1131	— — ℞. Similar, but annulets between	£80	£200
1132	— — ℞. Similar, but mint name between (a late N.W. type)	£125	£275
1133	— 2. — ℞. Floral design	£750	£1600
1134	— 4. Small cross either side	£80	£200
1135	— — Similar, with mint name	£250	£550
1136	— — Rosette either side	£125	£275
1137	— — Similar, with mint name	£200	£450
1138	— 5. Large bust to r. ℞. Small cross	£350	£750
1139	— — Similar, with mint name	£500	£1000
1140	*Halfpenny.* (8½ grains.) *Br. 3.* Small cross. ℞. Flower above name. *See also 1141 below.*	*Extremely rare*	
1140A	— — ℞. Mint name around cross (Chichester)	*Unique*	
1140B	— Bust r. ℞. 'Londonia' monogram	*Extremely rare*	

LATE ANGLO-SAXON PERIOD

In 973 Eadgar introduced a new coinage. A royal portrait now became a regular feature and the reverses normally have a cruciform pattern with the name of the mint in addition to that of the moneyer. Most fortified towns of burghal status were allowed a mint, the number of moneyers varying according to their size and importance; some royal manors also had a mint and some moneyers were allowed to certain ecclesiastical authorities. In all some seventy mints were active about the middle of the 11th century (see list of mints pp. 65–67).

The control of the currency was retained firmly in the hands of the central government, unlike the situation in France and the Empire where feudal barons and bishops controlled their own coinage. Coinage types were changed at intervals to enable the Exchequer to raise revenue from new dies and periodic demonetization of old coin types helped to maintain the currency in a good state. No halfpence were minted during this period, but pennies were often sheared into two halves.

1141

		F	VF
EADGAR, 959–975 *continued*			
1141 **Penny.** Type 6. Small bust l. ℞. Small cross, name of moneyer and mint ..		£450	£950

EDWARD THE MARTYR, 975–978

Son of Eadgar and Aethelflaed, Eadward was murdered at Corfe, reputedly on the orders of his stepmother Aelfthryth.

1142

1142 Type as illustration above		£650	£1500

AETHELRED II, 978–1016

He was the son of Eadgar and Aelfthryth. His reign was greatly disturbed by incursions of Danish fleets and armies which massive payments of money failed to curb. His later by-name 'the Unready' comes from *Unrede*, 'no counsel', a play on his given name.

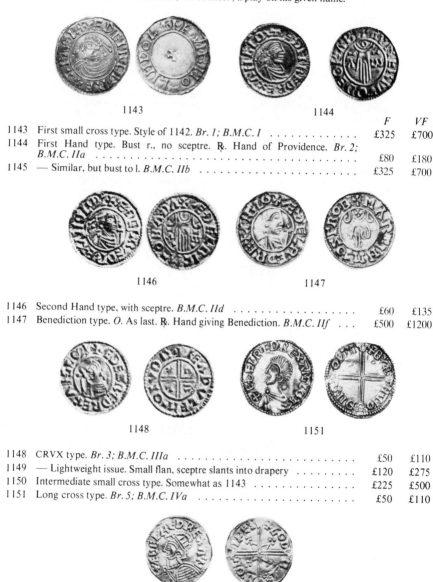

1143   1144

		F	VF
1143	First small cross type. Style of 1142. *Br. 1; B.M.C. I*	£325	£700
1144	First Hand type. Bust r., no sceptre. ℞. Hand of Providence. *Br. 2; B.M.C. IIa*	£80	£180
1145	— Similar, but bust to l. *B.M.C. IIb*	£325	£700

1146   1147

1146	Second Hand type, with sceptre. *B.M.C. IId*	£60	£135
1147	Benediction type. *O*. As last. ℞. Hand giving Benediction. *B.M.C. IIf* . . .	£500	£1200

1148   1151

1148	CRVX type. *Br. 3; B.M.C. IIIa*	£50	£110
1149	— Lightweight issue. Small flan, sceptre slants into drapery	£120	£275
1150	Intermediate small cross type. Somewhat as 1143	£225	£500
1151	Long cross type. *Br. 5; B.M.C. IVa*	£50	£110

1152

1152	Helmet type. *Br. 4; B.M.C. VIII*	£55	£110
1153	— — Similar, but struck in **gold**		*Unique*

		F	VF
1154	Last small cross type. As 1143, but different style	£45	£100
1155	— Similar, but bust to edge of coin. *B.M.C. Id*	£250	£550

1154   1156

1156 Agnus Dei type. *Br. 6; B.M.C. X* . . . .   *Extremely rare*

CNUT, 1016–1035

Son of Swegn Forkbeard, King of Denmark, Cnut was acclaimed King by the Danish fleet in England in 1014 but was forced to leave. He returned in 1015 and in 1016 agreed on a division of the country with Eadmund Ironsides, the son of Aethelred. No coins of Eadmund are known and on his death in November 1016 Cnut secured all England, marrying Emma, widow of Aethelred.

Main types

1157   1158   1159   1160

		F	VF
1157	Quatrefoil type. *Br. 2; B.M.C. VIII*	£70	£140
1158	Helmet type. *Br. 3; B.M.C. XIV*	£55	£120
1159	Short cross type. *Br. 4; B.M.C. XVI*	£50	£110
1160	Jewel cross type. *Br. 6; B.M.C. XX.* Type as 1163	£500	£1200
	[Note. *This type is now considered to be a posthumus issue struck under the auspices of his widow, Aelfgifu Emma.*]		

Scandinavian Imitations

		F	VF
1161	Small cross type, as Aethelred II. *Br. 1; B.M.C. 1*	£250	£550
1162	Long cross type, as Aethelred II. *Br. 5; B.M.C. IVa*	£250	£550

HAROLD I, 1035–1040

Harold, the son of Cnut and Aelgifu of Northampton, initially acted as regent for his half-brother Harthacnut on Cnut's death, was then recognised as King in Mercia and the north, and King throughout England in 1037.

1163   1165

		F	VF
1163	Jewel cross type, as illustration. *Br. 1; B.M.C. 1*	£200	£400
1164	Long cross and trefoils type. *Br. 2; B.M.C. V*	£150	£350
1165	— Similar, but fleur de lis in place of trefoils. *B.M.C. Vc*	£150	£350

HARTHACNUT, 1035–1042

He was heir to Cnut but lost the throne to his half-brother Harold owing to his absence in Denmark. On Harold's death he recovered his English realm.

1167   1168

		F	VF
1166	**Early period, 1036.** Jewel cross type, as 1163; bust l. *Br. 1; B.M.C. I*	£700	£1500
1167	— Similar, but bust r. *B.M.C. Ia*	£650	£1400
1168	**Restoration, 1040–1042.** Arm and sceptre type, with name Harthacnut. *Br. 2; B.M.C. II*	£800	£1750
1169	— Similar, but with name "Cnut"	£500	£1100

1169   1170

		F	VF
1170	**Danish types,** of various designs, some of English type mostly struck at Lund, Denmark (now Sweden) ....*from*	£150	£300

EDWARD THE CONFESSOR, 1042–1066

Edward was the son of Aethelred II and Emma of Normandy. A number of new mints were opened during his reign.

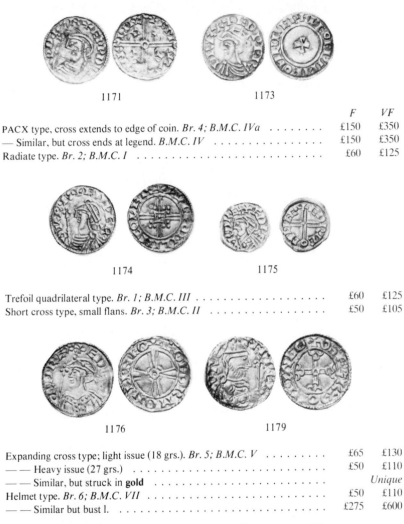

1171   1173

		F	VF
1171	PACX type, cross extends to edge of coin. *Br. 4; B.M.C. IVa*	£150	£350
1172	— Similar, but cross ends at legend. *B.M.C. IV*	£150	£350
1173	Radiate type. *Br. 2; B.M.C. I*	£60	£125

1174   1175

1174	Trefoil quadrilateral type. *Br. 1; B.M.C. III*	£60	£125
1175	Short cross type, small flans. *Br. 3; B.M.C. II*	£50	£105

1176   1179

1176	Expanding cross type; light issue (18 grs.). *Br. 5; B.M.C. V*	£65	£130
1177	— — Heavy issue (27 grs.)	£50	£110
1178	— — Similar, but struck in **gold**		*Unique*
1179	Helmet type. *Br. 6; B.M.C. VII*	£50	£110
1180	— — Similar but bust l.	£275	£600

1181   1182

1181	Sovereign type. *Br. 7; B.M.C. IX*	£70	£125
1182	Hammer cross type. *Br. 8; B.M.C. XI*	£50	£105

1183　　　　　　　　　　　　1184

		F	VF
1183	Facing bust type. *Br. 9; B.M.C. XIII*	£45	£105
1184	Pyramids type. *Br. 10; B.M.C. XV*	£70	£150

1185

1185	Large facing bust with sceptre. ℞. Similar	£950	£2000
	Most York coins of this reign have an annulet in one quarter of the reverse.		

HAROLD II, 1066

Harold was the son of Godwin Earl of Wessex. He was the brother-in-law of Edward the Confessor and was recognised as King on Edward's death. He defeated and killed Harald of Norway who invaded the north, but was himself defeated and killed at the Battle of Hastings by William of Normandy.

1186　　　　　　　　　　　　1187

1186	Bust l. with sceptre. ℞. PAX across centre of *rev. B.M.C. I*	£300	£650
1187	Similar, but without sceptre. *B.M.C. Ia*	£350	£850
1188	Bust r. with sceptre	£600	£1250

ANGLO-SAXON, NORMAN AND EARLY PLANTAGENET MINTS

In Anglo-Saxon times coins were struck at a large number of towns. The place of mintage is normally given on all coins from the last quarter of the 10th century onwards, and generally the name of the person responsible (e.g. BRVNIC ON LVND). Below we give a list of the mints, showing the reigns (Baronial of Stephen's reign omitted), of which coins have been found. After the town names we give one or two of the spellings as found on the coins, although often they appear in an abbreviated or extended form. On the coins the Anglo-Saxon and Norman *w* is like a P or Γ and the *th* is Ð. We have abbreviated the king's names, etc.:

Alf	—	Alfred the Great	Wi	—	William I
EE	—	Edward the Elder	Wii	—	William II
A'stan	—	Aethelstan	He	—	Henry I
EM	—	Edward the Martyr	St	—	Stephen (regular issues)
Ae	—	Aethelred II	M	—	Matilda
Cn	—	Cnut	HA	—	Henry of Anjou
Hi	—	Harold I	WG	—	William of Gloucester
Ht	—	Harthacnut	T	—	"Tealby" coinage
ECfr	—	Edward the Confessor	SC	—	Short cross coinage
Hii	—	Harold II	LC	—	Long cross coinage

Axbridge (ACXEPO, AGEPOR) Ae, Cn, Ht.
Aylesbury (AEGEL) Ae, Cn, ECfr.
Barnstaple (BEARDA, BARDI), Edwig, Ae-Hi, ECfr, Wi, He.
Bath (BADAN) EE-Edmund, Edwig-ECfr, Wi, He, St.
Bedford (BEDANF, BEDEF) Edwig-T.
Bedwyn (BEDEΓIN) ECfr, Wi.
Berkeley (BEORC) ECfr.
Bramber ? (BRAN) St.
Bridport (BRIPVT, BRIDI) A'stan, Ae, Cn, Ht, ECfr, Wi.
Bristol (BRICSTO) Ae-T, M, HA, LC.
Bruton (BRIVT) Ae-Cn, ECfr.
Buckingham (BVCIN) EM-Hi, ECfr.
Bury St. Edmunds (EDMVN, SEDM, SANTEA) A'stan?, ECfr, Wi, He-LC.
Cadbury (CADANB) Ae, Cn.
Caistor (CASTR) EM, Ae, Cn.
Cambridge (GRANTE) Edgar-Wii.
Canterbury (DORO, CAENT, CANTOR, CANTΓAR) Alf, A'stan, Edgar-LC.
Cardiff (CAIRDI, CARDI, CARITI) Wi, He, St, M.
Carlisle (CAR, CARDI, EDEN) He-LC.
Castle Gotha ? (GEOÐA, IOÐA) Ae-Ht.
Castle Rising (RISINGE) St.
Chester (LEIGECES, LEGECE, CESTRE) A'stan, Edgar-T.
Chichester (CISSAN CIV, CICES, CICST) A'stan, Edgar-St, SC.
Chippenham ? (CIPEN) St.
Christchurch, see Twynham.
Cissbury (SIÐEST) Ae, Cn.
Colchester (COLEAC, COLECES) Ae-Hi, ECfr-T.
Crewkerne (CRVCERN) Ae, Cn.
Cricklade (CROCGL, CRIC, CREC) Ae-Wii.
Derby (DEOR, DIORBI, DERBI) A'stan, Edgar-ECfr, Wi-St.
Dorchester (DORCE, DORECES) Ae-ECfr, Wi-He, WG.
Dover (DOFER) A'stan, Edgar-St.
Droitwich (PICC, PICNEH) ECfr, Hii.
Dunwich (DVNE) St.
Durham (DVRE DVRHAN) Wi, St-LC.
Exeter (EAXANC, EXEC, XECST) Alf, A'stan, Edwig-LC.
Eye (EI, EIE) St.
Frome ? (FRO) Cn-ECfr.
Gloucester (GLEAΓEC, GLEΓ, GΓ) Alf, A'stan, Edgar-St, HA, T, LC.
Guildford (GILDEF) EM-Cn, Ht-Wii.

Hastings (HAESTIN) Ae-St.
Hedon, near Hull (HEDVN) St.
Hereford (HEREFOR) A'stan, Ae-St, HA, T, LC.
Hertford (HEORTF) A'stan, Edwig-Hi, ECfr, Wi, Wii.
Horncastle ? (HORN) EM, Ae.
Horndon ? (HORNIDVNE) ECfr.
Huntingdon (HVNTEN) Edwig-St.
Hythe (HIÐEN) ECfr, Wi, Wii.
Ilchester (IVELCE, GIFELCST, GIVELC) Edgar, EM-He, T, LC.
Ipswich (GIPESΓIC) Edgar-SC.
Kings Lynn (LENN, LENE) SC.
Langport (LANCPOR) A'stan, Cn, Hi, ECfr.
Launceston (LANSTF, SANCTI STEFANI) Ae, Wi, Wii, St, T.
Leicester (LIGER, LIHER, LEHRE) A'stan, Edgar-T.
Lewes (LAEPES) A'stan, Edgar-T.
Lichfield (LIHFL) SC.
Lincoln (LINCOLNE, NICOLE) Edgar-LC.
London (LVNDENE) Alf-LC.
Louth ? (LVD) Ae.
Lydford (LYDAN) EM-Hi, ECfr.
Lympne (LIMEN) A'stan, Edgar-Cn.
Maldon (MAELDVN, MAELI) A'stan, Ae-Hi, ECfr, Wii.
Malmesbury (MALD, MEALDMES) Ae-Wii, HA.
Marlborough (MAERLEB) Wi, Wii.
Milbourne Port (MYLE) Ae, Cn.
Newark (NEPIR, NIPOR) Edwig, Eadgar, Ae, Cn.
Newcastle (NEWEC, NIVCA) St, T, LC.
Newport (NIPAN, NIPEP) Edgar, ECfr.
Northampton (HAMTVN, NORHANT) Edwig, Edgar-Wi, He-LC.
Norwich (NORPIC) A'stan-LC.
Nottingham (SNOTINC) A'stan, Ae-St.
Oxford (OXNAFOR, OXENEF) A'stan, Edmund, Edred, Edgar-St, M, T-LC.
Pembroke (PAN, PAIN) He-T.
Pershore (PERESC) ECfr.
Peterborough (MEDE, BVR) Ae, Cn, Wi.
Petherton (PEÐR) ECfr.
Pevensey (PEFNESE, PEVEN) Wi, Wii, St.
Reading (READIN) ECfr.
Rhuddlan (RVDILI, RVLA) Wi, SC.
Rochester (ROFEC) A'stan, Edgar-He, SC.
Romney (RVME, RVMNE) Ae-Hi, ECfr-He.
Rye (RIE) St.
Salisbury (SAEREB, SALEB) Ae-ECfr, Wi-He, T.
Sandwich (SANPIC) ECfr, Wi-St.
Shaftesbury (SCEFTESB, SCEFITI) A'stan, Ae-St.
Shrewsbury (SCROBES, SALOP) A'stan, Edgar-LC.
Southampton (HAMWIC, HAMTVN) A'stan, Edwig-Cn.
Southwark (SVDGE, SVDΓEEORC) Ae-St.
Stafford (STAFF, STAEF) A'stan, Ae-Hi, ECfr, Wi, Wii, St, T.
Stamford (STANFOR) Edgar-St.
Steyning (STAENIG) Cn-Wii.
Sudbury (SVDBI, SVB) Ae, Cn, ECfr, Wi-St.
Swansea (SWENSEI) HA?
Tamworth (TOMPEARÐGE, TAMPRÐ) A'stan, Edwig-Hi, ECfr, Wi-St.
Taunton (TANTVNE) Ae, Cn, Ht-St.
Thetford (ÐEOTFOR, TETFOR) Edgar-T.
Torksey (TORC, TVRC) EM-Cn.
Totnes (DARENT VRB, TOTANES, TOTNESE) A'stan, Edwig-Cn, Wii.
Twynham, now Christchurch (TPIN, TVEHAM) Wi, He.
Wallingford (PELING, PALLIG) A'stan, Edgar-He, T, LC.
Wareham (PERHAM) A'stan, Ae, Cn, Ht-St, M, WG.
Warminster (PORIME) Ae-Hi, ECfr.
Warwick (PAERING, PERPIC) A'stan, Edgar-St.
Watchet (PECEDPORT, PICEDI) Ae-ECfr, Wi-St.

Wilton (PILTVNE) Edgar-LC.
Winchcombe (PINCELE, PINCL) Edgar-Cn, Ht-Wi.
*Winchester (*PINTONIA, PINCEST) Alf-A'stan, Edwig-LC.
Worcester (PIHRAC, PIHREC) Ae-Hi, ECfr-SC.
York (EBORACI, EOFERPIC) A'stan, Edmund, Edgar-LC.

The location of the following is uncertain.
AESTHE *(? Hastings)* Ae.
BRYGIN *(? Bridgnorth,* but die-links with NIPAN and with *Shaftesbury)* Ae.
DERNE, DYR (E. Anglian mint) ECfr
DEVITVN *(? Welsh Marches* or *St. Davids)* Wi
EANBYRIG, Cn.
MAINT, Wi.
ORSNAFORDA *(? Horsforth or Orford)* Alf.
WEARDBYRIG *(? Warborough)* A'stan, Edgar.

EDWARDIAN AND LATER MINTS

London, Tower: Edw. I–Geo. III.
    ,,   *Tower Hill:* Geo. III–Eliz. II.
    ,,   *Durham House:* Hen. VIII (posth.)–Edw. VI.
Aberystwyth: Chas. I.
    ,,   *-Furnace:* Chas. I.
Barnstaple?: Chas. I.
Berwick-on-Tweed: Edw. I–Edw. III.
Birmingham, Heaton: Vic., Geo. V.
    ,,   *King's Norton:* Geo. V.
    ,,   *Soho:* Geo. III.
Bombay, India (branch mint): Geo. V.
Bristol: Edw. I, Edw. IV, Hen. VI rest., Hen. VIII–Edw. VI, Chas. I, Wm. III.
Bury St. Edmunds: Edw. I–Edw. III.
Calais: Edw. III–Hen. IV, Hen. VI.
Canterbury: Edw. I–Edw. III, Edw. IV, Hen. VII–Edw. VI.
Carlisle: Chas. I.
Chester: Edw. I, Chas. I, Wm. III.
Colchester: Chas. I.
Coventry: Edw. IV, Chas. I(?).
Durham: Edw. I–Edw. IV, Rich. III–Hen. VIII.
Exeter: Edw. I, Chas. I, Wm. III.
Hartlebury Castle, Worcs.: Chas. I.
Kingston-upon-Hull: Edw. I.
Lincoln: Edw. I.
Llantrisant: Eliz. II (decimal coinage).
Melbourne, Australia (branch mint): Vic.–Geo. V.
Newark: Chas. I.
Newcastle-upon-Tyne: Edw. I.
Norwich: Edw. IV, Wm. III.
Ottawa, Canada (branch mint): Edw. VII–Geo. V.
Oxford: Chas. I.
Perth, Australia (branch mint): Vic.–Geo. V.
Pontefract: Chas. I.
Pretoria, South Africa (branch mint): Geo. V.
Reading: Edw. III.
Scarborough: Chas. I.
Shrewsbury: Chas. I.
Southwark: Hen. VIII–Edw. VI.
Sydney, Australia (branch mint): Vic.–Geo. V.
Tournai, Belgium: Hen. VIII.
Truro: Chas. I.
Worcester: Chas. I.
York: Edw. I, Edw. III–Edw. IV, Rich. III–Edw. VI, Chas. I, Wm. III.

NORMAN KINGS AND THEIR SUCCESSORS

There were no major changes in the coinages following the Norman conquest. The controls and periodic changes of type made in the previous reigns were continued. Nearly seventy mints were operating during the reign of William I; these had been reduced to about fifty-five by the middle of the 12th century and, under Henry II, first to thirty and later to eleven. By the second half of the 13th century the issue of coinage had been centralized at London and Canterbury, with the exception of two ecclesiastical mints. Of the thirteen types with the name PILLEMVS, PILLELM, etc. (William), the first eight have been attributed to the Conqueror and the remaining five to his son William Rufus.

From William I to Edward II inclusive all are silver pennies unless otherwise stated.

WILLIAM I, 1066–1087

William Duke of Normandy was the cousin of Edward the Confessor. After securing the throne of England he had to suppress several rebellions.

1250   1251

		F	VF
1250	**Penny.** Profile left type. *Br. I*	£150	£400
1251	Bonnet type. *Br. II*	£115	£250

1252   1253

		F	VF
1252	Canopy type. *Br. III*	£175	£500
1253	Two sceptres type. *Br. IV*	£125	£325

1254   1255

		F	VF
1254	Two stars type. *Br. V*	£95	£225
1255	Sword type. *Br. VI*	£200	£500

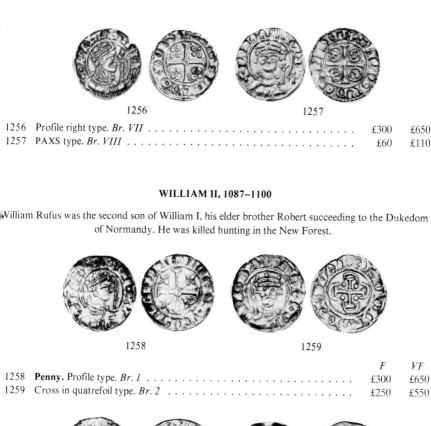

1256

1257

1256 Profile right type. *Br. VII* £300   £650
1257 PAXS type. *Br. VIII* £60   £110

WILLIAM II, 1087–1100

William Rufus was the second son of William I, his elder brother Robert succeeding to the Dukedom
of Normandy. He was killed hunting in the New Forest.

1258

1259

		F	VF
1258	**Penny.** Profile type. *Br. 1*	£300	£650
1259	Cross in quatrefoil type. *Br. 2*	£250	£550

1260

1261

		F	VF
1260	Cross voided type. *Br. 3*	£250	£550
1261	Cross pattée and fleury type. *Br. 4*	£300	£700

1262

1262 Cross fleury and piles type. *Br. 5* £600   £1250

HENRY I, 1100–1135

Fifteen types were minted during this reign. In 1108 provision was made for minting round half-pence again, none having been struck since the time of Eadgar, but few can have been made as only one specimen has survived. The standard of coinage manufacture was now beginning to deteriorate badly. Many genuine coins were being cut to see if they were plated counterfeits and there was a reluctance by the public to accept such damaged pieces. About 1112 an extraordinary decision was taken ordering the official mutilation of all new coins by snicking the edges, thus ensuring that cut coins had to be accepted. Pennies of types VII to XII (Nos. 1268–1273) usually have a cut in the flan that sometimes penetrated over a third of the way across the coin.

At Christmas 1124 the famous 'Assize of the Moneyers' was held at Winchester when all the moneyers in England were called to account for their activities and a number are said to have been mutilated for issuing coins of inferior quality.

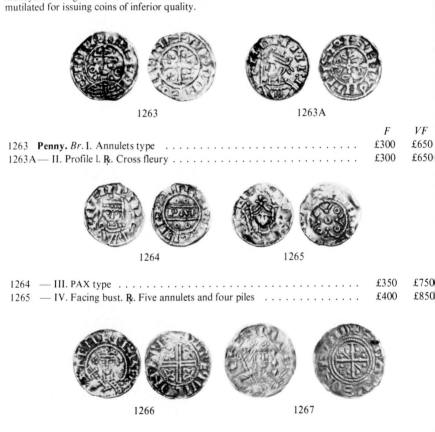

1263   1263A

		F	VF
1263 **Penny.** *Br.* I. Annulets type		£300	£650
1263A— II. Profile l. ℞. Cross fleury		£300	£650

1264   1265

		F	VF
1264 — III. PAX type		£350	£750
1265 — IV. Facing bust. ℞. Five annulets and four piles		£400	£850

1266   1267

		F	VF
1266 — V. — ℞. Voided cross with fleur in each angle		£500	£1100
1267 — VI. Pointing bust and stars type		£900	£1850

1268

		F	VF
1268 — VII. Facing bust. ℞. Quatrefoil with piles		£325	£70

1269   1270

		F	VF
1269	*Br.* VIII. Large bust l. R̸. Cross with annulet in each angle	£600	£1250
1270	— IX. Facing bust. R̸. Cross in quatrefoil	£475	£950

1271   1272

| 1271 | — X. Small facing bust in circle. R̸. Cross fleury . . . . | £275 | £600 |
| 1272 | — XI. Very large bust l. R̸. "Double inscription" around small cross pattée | £725 | £1500 |

1273   1274

| 1273 | — XII. Small bust l. R̸. Cross with annulet in each angle . . . . | £350 | £750 |
| 1274 | — XIII. Star in lozenge fleury type . . . . | £275 | £600 |

1275   1276

| 1275 | — XIV. Pellets in quatrefoil type . . . . | £125 | £300 |
| 1276 | — XV. Quadrilateral on cross fleury type . . . . | £120 | £275 |

1277

| 1277 | *Halfpenny.* Facing head. R̸. Cross potent with pellets in angles . . . . | *Unique* |

STEPHEN, 1135–1154
and the Civil War and Anarchy, 1138–1153

Stephen of Blois, Count of Boulogne and a nephew of Henry I, hastily crossed the Channel on his uncle's death and secured the throne for himself, despite Henry's wishes that his daughter Matilda should succeed him. She was the widow of the German emperor Henry V, and was then married to Geoffrey, Count of Anjou. Two years later Matilda arrived in England to claim the throne, supported by her half-brother Robert of Gloucester. During the protracted civil war that ensued Matilda and later her son, Henry of Anjou, set up an alternative court at Bristol and held much of the west of England, striking coins at mints under their control. Many irregular coins were struck during this troublous period, some by barons in their own name. Particularly curious are the coins from the Midlands and E. Anglia which have Stephen's head defaced, now believed to have been issued during the Interdict of 1148. In 1153, following the death of Stephen's son, Eustace, a treaty between the two factions allowed for the succession of Duke Henry and a uniform coinage was once more established throughout the kingdom.

B.M.C.—British Museum Catalogue: *Norman Kings*, 2 vols. (1916). *M.*—Mack, R. P., "Stephen and the Anarchy 1135–54", *BNJ*, XXXV (1966), pp. 38–112.

STEPHEN
Regular regal issues

	1278		1280	

		F	VF
1278	**Penny.** Cross moline (Watford) type. Bust r., with sceptre. ℞. Cross moline with lis in angles. *B.M.C. I; M. 3–42*	£100	£250
1279	— Similar, but obv. reads PERERIC or PERERICM. *M. 43–50*	£550	£1250
1280	Voided cross type. Facing bust with sceptre. ℞. Voided cross pattée with mullets in angles. *East and South-east mints only. B.M.C. II; M. 53–66*	£200	£450

	1281		1282	

1281	Cross fleury type. Bust l. with sceptre. ℞. Cross fleury with trefoils in angles. *East and South-east mints only. B.M.C. VI; M. 77–99*	£800	£2500
1282	Cross pommée (Awbridge) type. Bust half-left with sceptre. ℞. Voided cross pommée with lis in angles. *B.M.C. VII; M. 99z–135b*	£300	£650

For B.M.C. types III, IV & V, see 1300–1302.

Local and irregular issues of the Civil War

A. Coins struck from erased or defaced dies

1283   1288

		F	VF
1283	As 1278, with king's bust defaced with long cross. *East Anglian mints. M. 137–147*	£400	£1000
1284	— Similar, but king's bust defaced with small cross. *Nottingham. M. 149*	£500	£1250
1285	— Similar, but sceptre defaced with bar or cross. *Nottingham, Lincoln and Stamford. M. 148 and 150–154*	£400	£1000
1286	— Similar, but king's name erased. *Nottingham. M. 157*	£500	£1250
1286A	— Other defacements	*Extremely rare*	

B. South-Eastern variant

1287	As 1278, but king holds mace instead of sceptre. *Canterbury. M. 158*	*Extremely rare*	

C. Eastern variants

1288	As 1278, but roundels in centre or on limbs of cross or in angles. *Suffolk mints. M. 159–168*	£600	£1200
1288A	As 1278, but star before sceptre and annulets at tips of fleurs on reverse. *Suffolk mints. M. 188*	£1000	£2500
1289	As 1278, but thick plain cross with pellet at end of limbs, lis in angles. *Lincoln. M. 169–173*	£600	£1200
1290	— Similar, but thick plain cross superimposed on cross moline. *M. 174*	*Extremely rare*	
1290A	As 1278. ℞. Quadrilateral over voided cross. *M. 176*	*Extremely rare*	
1290B	As 1278. ℞. Long cross to edge of coin, fleurs outwards in angles. *Lincoln. M. 186–187*	*Extremely rare*	

D. Southern variants

1291	As 1278, but with large rosette of pellets at end of obverse legend. *M. 184–185*	*Extremely rare*	
1292	— Similar, but star at end of obverse legend. *M. 187y*	*Extremely rare*	
1293	Crowned bust r. or l. with rosette of pellets before face in place of sceptre. ℞. As 1280, but plain instead of voided cross. *M. 181–183*	*Extremely rare*	

1295

1295	As 1278, but usually collar of annulets. ℞. Voided cross moline with annulet at centre. *Southampton. M. 207–212*	£800	£2000

E. Midland variants

1296

		F	VF
1296	As 1278, but cross moline on reverse has fleured extensions into legend. *Leicester.M. 177–178*	£1000	£2500
1297	As 1278 but crude work. ℞. Voided cross with lis outwards in angles. *Tutbury.M. 179*	*Extremely rare*	
1298	Somewhat similar. ℞. Voided cross with martlets in angles. *Derby.M. 175* ..	£1200	£3000

1298   1300

1299	As 1278. ℞. Plain cross with T-cross in each angle. *M. 180*	*Extremely rare*	
1300	Facing bust with three annulets on crown. ℞. Cross pattée, fleurs inwards in angles. *Northampton or Huntingdon*(?). *B.M.C. III; M. 67–71*	£1200	£3000

1301   1302

1301	Facing bust with three fleurs on crown. ℞. Lozenge fleury, annulets in angles. *Lincoln or Nottingham. B.M.C. IV; M. 72–75*	£1250	£3250
1302	Bust half-right with sceptre. ℞. Lozenge with pellet centre, fleurs inwards in angles. *Leicester. B.M.C. V; M. 76*	£1250	£3250
1303	**Robert,** Earl of Leicester(?). As 1280, but reading ROBERTVS. *M. 269* ..	*Extremely rare*	

F. North-east and Scottish border variants

1304	As 1278, but star before sceptre and annulets at tips of fleurs on reverse. *M. 188*	£1000	£2500
1305	As 1278, but a voided cross extending to outer circle of reverse. *M. 189–192*	*Extremely rare*	
1306	As 1278, but crude style, with Stephen's name. *M. 276–279 and 281–282*	£700	£1750
1307	— Similar. ℞. Cross crosslet with cross-pattée and crescent in angles. *M. 288*	*Extremely rare*	

		F	VF
1308	**David I** (K. of Scotland). As 1305, but with name DAVID REX. *M. 280* . .		*Extremely rare*
1309	**Henry** (Earl of Northumberland, son of K. David). hENRIC ERL. As 1278.		
	M. 283–285	£1200	£3000
1310	— Similar. ℞. Cross fleury. *M. 286–287*	£1000	£2500
1311	— As 1307, but with name NENCI : COM on obverse. *M. 289*	£1200	£2750

G. "Ornamented" series. *So-called 'York Group' but probably minted in Northern France*

1312	As 1278, with obverse inscription NSEPEFETI, STEFINEI or RODBDS. ℞. WIS Đ . GNETA, etc., with ornament(s) in legend (sometimes retrograde). *M. 215–216 and 227*	*Extremely rare*

1313   1315

1313	Flag type. As 1278, but king holds lance with pennant, star to r. ℞. As 1278, mostly with four ornaments in legend. *M. 217*	£1250	£3000
1313A	— Similar, but with eight ornaments in reverse inscription. *M. 217*	£1250	£3000
1314	As 1278, but STIEN and ornaments, sceptre is topped by pellet in lozenge. ℞. Cross fleury over plain cross, ornaments in place of inscription. *M. 218*		*Extremely rare*
1314A	King stg. facing, holding sceptre and long standard with triple-tailed pennon. ℞. Cross pattée, crescents and quatrefoils in angles, pellets around, ornaments in legend		*Unique*
1315	**Stephen and Queen Matilda.** Two standing figures holding sceptre, as illustration. ℞. Ornaments in place of inscription. *M. 220*	£2500	£5000

1316   1320

1316	**Eustace.** EVSTACIVS, knight stg. r. holding sword. ℞. Cross in quatrefoil, EBORACI EDTS (or EBORACI TDEFL). *M. 221–222*		*Extremely rare*
1317	— Similar, but ThOMHS FILIuS VIF. *M. 223*		*Extremely rare*
1318	— Similar, but mixed letters and ornaments in rev. legend. *M. 224*		*Extremely rare*
1319	[EVSTA] CII . FII . IOANIS, lion passant r., collonade (or key?) below. ℞. Cross moline with cross-headed sceptres in angles, mixed letters and ornaments in legend		*Unique*
1320	Lion rampant r., looped object below, EISTAOhIVS. ℞. Cross fleury with lis in angles, mostly, ornaments in legend. *M. 226*	£1400	£3500

F   VF

1321   **Rodbert.** Knight on horse r., RODBERTVS IESTV (?). ℞. As 1314. *M. 228*   *Extremely rare*

1321   1322

1322   **Bishop Henry.** Crowned bust r., crozier and star to r., HENRICVS EPC. ℞.
       Somewhat as last, STEPhANVS REX. *M. 229* . . . .   *Extremely rare*

H.   Uncertain issues

1323   Crowned bust r. with sceptre, ‑NEPΓ:. ℞. Cross pattée with annulets in
       angles (as Hen. I type XIII). *M. 272* . . . .   *Extremely rare*

1324   Crowned facing bust with sceptre, star to r. (as Hen. I type XIV). ℞. As
       last. *M. 274* . . . .   *Extremely rare*

1325   Other types . . . .   *Extremely rare*

ANGEVINS

1326   1331

1326   **Matilda,** Dowager Empress, Countess of Anjou (in England 1139–1148).
       As 1278, but cruder style, MATILDI IMP. etc. *M. 230–240* £750   £1500

1326A Obv. similar. ℞. Cross pattée over cross fleury (Cardiff hoard) . . . .   *Extremely rare*

1326B Similar, but triple pellets or plumes at end of cross (Cardiff hoard) . . . .   *Extremely rare*

1327   **Duke Henry,** son of Matilda and Geoffrey of Anjou, Duke of Normandy
       from 1150 (in England 1147–1149–1150 and 1153–1154). As 1278 but
       hENRICVS, etc. *M. 241–245* £2250   £5000

1327A As 1295 but hENRIC. *M. 246* . . . .   *Extremely rare*

1327B As 1326B, but hENNENNVS R, etc. . . . .   *Extremely rare*

1328   Obverse as 1278. ℞. Cross crosslet in quatrefoil. *M. 254* . . . .   *Extremely rare*

1329   Crowned bust r. with sceptre. ℞. Cross fleury over quadrilateral fleury.
       M. 248–253 . . . .   £2250   £5000

1330   Crowned facing bust, star each side. ℞. Cross botonnée over a
       quadrilateral pommée. *M. 255–258* £2250   £5000

1331   Obverse as 1330. ℞. Voided cross botonnée over a quadrilateral pommée.
       M. 259–261 . . . .   £2250   £5000

1332   **William,** Earl of Gloucester (succeeded his father, Earl Robert, in 1147).
       Type as Henry of Anjou, no. 1329. *M. 262* . . . .   *Unique*

1333   Type as Henry of Anjou, no. 1330. *M. 263* . . . .   *Unique*

1334   Type as Henry of Anjou, no. 1331. *M. 264–268* £2500   £5500

1335   **Brian Fitzcount,** Lord of Wallingford (?). Type as Henry of Anjou, no.
       1330. *M. 270* . . . .   *Unique*

1336   **Patrick,** Earl of Salisbury (?). Helmeted bust r. holding sword, star behind.
       ℞. As Henry of Anjou, no. 1329. *M. 271* . . . .   *Extremely rare*

HENRY II, 1154–1189

Cross-and-crosslets ("Tealby") Coinage, 1158–1180

Coins of Stephen's last type continued to be minted until 1158. Then a new coinage bearing Henry's name replaced the currency of the previous reign which contained a high proportion of irregular and sub-standard pennies. The new Cross and Crosslets issue is more commonly referred to as the "Tealby" coinage, over 5000 of these pennies having been discovered at Tealby, Lincolnshire in 1807. Thirty mints were employed in this recoinage, but once the re-minting had been completed not more than a dozen mints were kept open. The issue remained virtually unchanged for twenty-two years apart from minor variations in the king's portrait. The coins tend to be poorly struck.

A   B   C

Penny

		fair	F
1337	Class A. No hair	£12	£35
1338	— B. Similar but mantle varies	£15	£40
1339	— C. Decorated collar, curl of hair	£12	£35

D   E   F

1340	— D. Decoration continues along shoulder	£15	£40
1341	— E. Similar bust, but shoulder not decorated	£18	£45
1342	— F. Hair in long ringlet to r. of bust	£18	£45

Mints and classes of the Cross-and-Crosslets coinage

Approximate dates for the various classes are as follows:

A 1158–1161, B and C 1161–1165, D 1165–1168, E 1168–1170 and F 1170–1180.

Bedford	A – – – – –	Ilchester	A B C D– F	Pembroke	A – – – – –
Bristol	A B C D E F	Ipswich	– B C D E F	Salisbury	A – – – – –
Bury St. Edmunds	A B C D E F	Launceston	A – – – – –	Shrewsbury	A – – – – –
Canterbury	A B C D E F	Leicester	A – – – – –	Stafford	A – C – – –
Carlisle	A – C D E F	Lewes	– – – – ? F	Thetford	A – C D– F
Chester	A – – D – –	Lincoln	A B C D E F	Wallingford	A – – – – –
Colchester	A – C – E –	London	A B C D E F	Wilton	A – – – – –
Durham	A B C – – –	Newcastle	A – C D E F	Winchester	A – C D? –
Exeter	A B C D– –	Northampton	A – C ? – –	York	A – C D– –
Gloucester	A – – – – –	Norwich	A B C D– F		
Hereford	A – C – – –	Oxford	A – – D E –		

"Short Cross" coinage of Henry II (1180–1189)

In 1180 a coinage of new type, known as the Short Cross coinage, replaced the Tealby issue. The new coinage is remarkable in that it covers not only the latter part of the reign of Henry II, but also the reigns of his sons Richard and John and his grandson Henry III, and the entire issue bears the name "hENRICVS". There are no English coins with names of Richard or John. The Short Cross coins can be divided chronologically into various classes: eleven mints were operating under Henry II and tables of mints, moneyers and classes are given for each reign.

1a　　　　　　　1b　　　　　　　1c

		F	VF
1343	Class 1a. Narrow face, square E, sometimes square C, round M	£150	£400
1344	— 1b. Curls usually 2 to l., 5 to r., round Є and C, square M, stop before REX	£30	£80
1345	— 1c. First evidence of degradation, more curls to r. than to l., no stop in obv. legend	£25	£70

Mints, moneyers, and classes for Henry II

London: Aimer (1b, c), Alain (1b, c), Alain V (1b), Alward (1b), Davi (1b, c), Filip Aimer (1a, b), Gilebert (1c), Godard (1b), Henri (1a, b), Henri Pi (1a, b), Iefrei or Gefrei (1a, b, c), Johan (1a, b), Osber (1b), Pieres (1a, b, c), Pieres M (1a, b), Randul (1a, b), Raul (1b, c), Reinald (1b), Ricard (1c), Stivene (1c), Willelm (1a, b, c) . . . . *from*　£25

Carlisle: Alain (1a, b, c) . . . . *from*　£80

Exeter: Asketil (1a, b), Iordan (1a, b), Osber (1a, b), Raul (1b), Ricard (1b, c), Roger (1b) . . . . *from*　£60

Lincoln: Edmund (1b, c), Girard (1b), Hugo (1b), Lefwine (1b, c), Rodbert (1b), Walter (1b), Will . D.F. (1b), Willelm (1b, c) . . . . *from*　£50

Northampton: Filipe (1a, b), Gefrei (1b), Hugo (1a, b), Raul (1a, b, c), Reinald (1a), Simund (1b), Walter (1a, b, c), Willelm (1a, b) . . . . *from*　£65

Norwich: Reinald (1b, c), Willelm (1b) . . . . *from*　£65
　　　　(Current research may indicate that these coins are of the Northampton mint).

Oxford: Asketil (1b), Iefri (1b), Owein (1b), Ricard (1b, c), Rodbert (1b), Robert F. B. (1b), Sagar (1b) . . . . *from*　£65

Wilton: Osber (1a, b), Rodbert (1a, b) . . . . *from*　£60

Winchester: Adam (1b, c), Clement (1a, b), Gocelm (1a, b, c), Henri (1a), Osber (1a, b), Reinir (1b), Ricard (1b), Rodbert (1a, b) . . . . *from*　£30

Worcester: Edric (1b), Godwine (1b), Osber (1b, c), Oslac (1b) . . . . *from*　£60

York: Alain (1b), Everard (1a, b, c), Gerard (1b), Hugo (1b, c), Hunfrei (1b), Isac (1a, b), Turkil (1a, b, c), Willelm (1b) . . . . *from*　£30

RICHARD I, 1189–1199

Pennies of Short Cross type continued to be issued throughout the reign, all bearing the name hENRICVS. The coins of class 4, which have very crude portraits, continued to be issued in the early years of the next reign. The only coins bearing Richard's name are from his territories of Aquitaine and Poitou in western France.

| 2 | 3a | 3b | 4a | 4b |

'Short Cross" coinage (reading HENRICVS)

			F	VF
346	Class 2a. Round face; 5 pearls in crown; mass of small curls at both sides of head		£65	£165
347	— 3a. Long thin face; 7 or more pearls in crown; 3 or 4 curls at either side of head; beard of small curls, large pellet eyes		£60	£150
347A	— 3b. Similar, but annulet eyes		£45	£115
348	— 4a. Similar, but beard of pellets		£28	£80
348A	— 4b. Very crude bust, hair represented by only one or two crescents each side		£28	£70
348B	— 4a*. As 4a, but colon stops on reverse		£35	£90

Mints, moneyers, and classes for Richard I

		F
London: Aimer (2–4b), Alain (4a), Davi (2), Fulke (3–4b), Goldwine (4a), Henri (4a–4b), Pieres (2), Raul (2), Ricard (2–4b), Stivene (2–4b), Willelm (2–4b)	*from*	£28
Canterbury: Goldwine (2–4b), Hernaud (4b), Io(h)an (4b), Meinir (2–4b), Reinald (2–4a), Reinaud (4b), Roberd (2–4b), Samuel (4b), Ulard (3–4b)	*from*	£28
Carlisle: Alain (3–4b)	*from*	£110
Durham: Adam (4a), Alain (4a–b)	*from*	£125
Exeter: Ricard (3)	*from*	£90
Lichfield: Ioan (2)	*Extremely rare*	
Lincoln: Edmund (2), Lefwine (2), Willelm (2, 4a)	*from*	£45
Northampton: Geferi (4a), Roberd (3), Waltir (3)	*from*	£90
Norwich: Randal (4a–b), Willelm (4a–b)	*from*	£90
Shrewsbury: Ive (4b), Reinald (4a, 4b), Willelm (4a)	*from*	£150
Winchester: Gocelm (2–3), Osber (3–4), Pires (3–4), Willelm (2–4)	*from*	£50
Worcester: Osber (2)	*Extremely rare*	
York: Davi (4b?), Everard (2–4b), Hue (3–4b), Nicole (4b), Turkil (2–4b)	*from*	£28

JOHN, 1199–1216

"Short Cross" coinage *continued.* All with name hENRICVS

The Short Cross coins of class 4 will have continued during the early years of John's reign, but in 1205 a re-coinage was initiated and new Short Cross coins of better style replaced the older issues. Coins of classes 5a and 5b were issued in the re-coinage in which sixteen mints were employed. Only ten of these mints were still working by the end of class 5. The only coins to bear John's name are the pennies, halfpence and farthings issued for Ireland.

| 4c | 5a | 5b | 5c | 6a1 | 6a2 |

		F	*VF*
1349	Class 4c. Somewhat as 4b, but letter S is reversed	£35	£8(
1350	— 5a. New coinage of neat style and execution; realistic face; 5 pearls to crown; letter S is reversed; *mm* cross pommée	£35	£8(
1350A	— — with ornamented letters	£35	£10(
1350B	— 5a/5b or 5b/5a mules	£35	£9(
1351	— 5b. Similar, but S normal and *mm* reverts to cross pattée	£20	£4(
1352	— 5c. Similar, but letter X composed of 4 strokes in the form of a St. Andrew's cross	£20	£4(
1353	— 6a1. Coarser style; letter X composed of 2 strokes in the form of a St. Andrew's cross	£17	£4(
1353A	— 6a2. Similar, but letter X has arms at right angles and with rounded ends	£17	£4(

Mints, moneyers and classes for John

		F
London: Abel (5c–6a), Adam (5b–c), Alexander (5a?), Andreu (5b), Arnaud (5b), Beneit (5b–c), Fulke (4c–5b), Henri (4c–5b), Ilger (5b–6a), Iohan (5a–b), Rauf (5c–6a), Rener (5b–c), Ricard (4c–5b), Ricard B (5b–c), Ricard T (5b), Walter (5c–6a), Willelm (4c–5b), Willelm B (5b–c), Willelm L (5b–c), Willelm T (5b–c) .	*from*	£1?
Bury St. Edmunds: Fulke (5b–c)	*from*	£30
Canterbury: Andreu (5b), Arnaud (5a–c), Coldwine (4c–5c), (H)erraud (5a), Hue (4c–5c), Io(h)an (4c–5c), Iohan B (5b–c), Iohan M (5b–c), Rauf (Vc?), Roberd (4c–5c), Samuel (4c–5c), Simon (5a–c), Simun (4c–5b), Walter (5b)	*from*	£17
Carlisle: Tomas (5b)	*from*	£110
Chichester: Pieres (5b), Rauf (5a–b), Simon (5a–b), Willelm (5b)	*from*	£50
Durham: Pieres (4c–6a)	*from*	£100
Exeter: Gilebert (5a–b), Iohan (5a–b), Ricard (5a–b)	*from*	£45
Ipswich: Alisandre (5a–c), Iohan (5b–c)	*from*	£50
Kings Lynn: Iohan (5b), Nicole (5b), Willelm (5b)	*from*	£175
Lincoln: Alain (5a), Andreu (5a–c), Hue (5b–c), Iohan (5a), Rauf (5a–b), Ricard (5a), Tomas (5b)	*from*	£40
Northampton: Adam (5b–c), Randul (4c), Roberd (5b), Roberd T (5b)	*from*	£45

		F
Norwich: Gifrei (5b–c), Iohan (5a–c), Reinald (5a), Reinaud (5a–b)	*from*	£45
Oxford: Ailwine (5b), Henri (5b), Miles (5b)	*from*	£50
Rhuddlan: An irregular issue probably struck during this reign. Halli, Henricus, Tomas, Simond	*from*	£90
Rochester: Alisandre (5b), Hunfrei (5b)	*from*	£150
Winchester: Adam (5a–c), Andreu (5b–c), Bartelme (5b–c), Henri (5a), Iohan (5a–c), Lukas (5b), Miles (5a–c), Rauf (5b–c), Ricard (5b)	*from*	£25
York: Davi (4c–5b), Iohan (5a–b), Nicole (4c–5c), Renaud (5b), Tomas (5b) . . .	*from*	£30

HENRY III, 1216–72

"Short Cross" coinage *continued* (1216–47)

The Short Cross coinage continued for a further thirty years during which time the style of portraiture and workmanship deteriorated. By the 1220s minting had been concentrated at London and Canterbury, one exception being the mint of the Abbot of Bury St. Edmunds.

| 6b | 6c | 7 early | 7 middle | 7 late |

"Short Cross" coinage, 1216–47	F	VF
1354 Class 6b. Very tall lettering; early coins have a head similar to 6a, but later issues have a long thin face	£15	£35
1355 — 6c. Pointed face	£15	£35
1355A — — Ornamental lettering	£50	£135
1356 — 7. No stops between words in rev. legend; no neck	£12	£30

| 8a | 8b1 | 8b2 | 8b3 |

	F	VF
1357 — 8a. New style; *mm* cross pattée; letter X curule shaped	*Extremely rare*	
1357A — 8b1. Similar; *mm* cross pommée	£30	£100
1357B — 8b2. Cruder version; wedge shaped letter X	£30	£100
1357C — 8b3. Very crude version; letter X is cross pommée	£30	£100

Mints, moneyers, and classes for Henry III "Short Cross" coinage

		F
London: Abel (6b–7), Adam (7), (H)elis (7), Giffrei (7), Ilger (6b–7), Ledulf (7), Nicole (7–8), Rau(l)f (6b–7), Ricard (7), Terri (7), Walter (6b–6c)	*from*	£12
Bury St. Edmunds: Io(h)an (7–8), Norman (7), Rauf (6b–7), Simund (7), Willelm (7)	*from*	£27.50
Canterbury: Henri (6b–7), Hiun (6b–c), Iun (7), Io(h)an (6b–8), Ioan Chic (7), Ioan F. R. (7), Nicole (7–8), Norman (7), Osmund (7), Roberd (6b–7), Robert Vi (7), Roger (6b–7), Roger of R (7), Salemun (7), Samuel (6b–7), Simon (7), Simun (6b–7), Tomas (7), Walter (6b–7), Willem (7–8), Willem Ta (7)	*from*	£12
Durham: Pieres (7)	*from*	£125
Winchester: Henri (6c), Iohan (6c)	*from*	£22.50
York: Iohan (6c), Peres (6c), Tomas (6c), Willelm (6c)	*from*	£150

"Long Cross" coinage (1247–72)

By the middle of Henry's reign the coinage in circulation was in a poor state, being worn and clipped. In 1247 a fresh coinage was ordered, the new pennies having the reverse cross extended to the edge of the coin to help safeguard the coins against clipping. The earliest of these coins have no mint or moneyers' names. A number of provincial mints were opened for producing sufficient of the Long Cross coins, but these were closed again in 1250, only the royal mints of London and Canterbury and the ecclesiastical mints of Durham and Bury St. Edmunds remaining open.

In 1257, following the introduction of new gold coinages by the Italian cities of Brindisi (1232), Florence (1252) and Genoa (1253), Henry III issued a gold coinage in England. This was a gold "Penny" valued at 20 silver pence and twice the weight of the silver penny. The coinage was not a success, being undervalued, and coinage ceased after a few years—few have survived.

Without sceptre

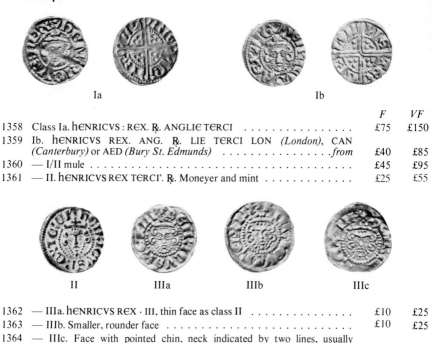

Ia   Ib

		F	VF
1358	Class Ia. hENRICVS : REX. ℞. ANGLIE TERCI	£75	£150
1359	Ib. hENRICVS REX. ANG. ℞. LIE TERCI LON *(London)*, CAN *(Canterbury)* or AED *(Bury St. Edmunds)* . . . .*from*	£40	£85
1360	— I/II mule	£45	£95
1361	— II. hENRICVS REX TERCI'. ℞. Moneyer and mint	£25	£55

II   IIIa   IIIb   IIIc

		F	VF
1362	— IIIa. hENRICVS REX · III, thin face as class II	£10	£25
1363	— IIIb. Smaller, rounder face	£10	£25
1364	— IIIc. Face with pointed chin, neck indicated by two lines, usually REX : III	£10	£25

With sceptre

IVa   IVb   Va   Vb   Vc

		F	VF
1365	Class IVa. Similar to last, but with sceptre	£50	£110
1366	— IVb. Similar, but new crown with half-fleurs and large central fleur . . .	£60	£130
1367	— Va. With class IV bust, round eyes, from now on legend begins at 10 o'clock	£12.50	£30
1368	— Vb. Narrower face, wedge-tailed R, round eyes	£10	£25
1369	— Vc. As last, but almond-shaped eyes	£10	£25

Vd	Ve	Vf	Vg	Vh

		F	VF
1370	— Vd. Portrait of quite different style; new crown with true-shaped fleur .	£35	£85
1371	— Ve. Similar, with jewelled or beaded crown	£90	£225
1372	— Vf. New style larger face, double-banded crown	£17.50	£40
1373	— Vg. Single band to crown, low central fleur, curule chair shaped X . . .	£15	£35
1374	— Vh. Crude copy of Vg, with pellets in lieu of fleur	£22.50	£50
1375	— Vi. Similar to last, but triple line of pellets for beard	*Extremely rare*	

Vi	1376

1376	**Gold penny** of 20d. As illustration	*Extremely rare*

Note. *A very fine specimen sold at auction in June 1985 for £65,000.*

Mints, Moneyers, and classes for Henry III "Long Cross" coinage

		F
London: Davi or David (IIIc–Vf), Henri (IIIa–Vd, f, g), Ion, Ioh, Iohs, or Iohan (Vc–g), Nicole (Ib/II mule, II–Vc), Renaud (Vg–i), Ricard (IIIc–Vg), Robert (Vg), Thomas (Vg), Walter (Vc–g), Willem (Vc–g and gold penny)	*from*	£10
Bristol: Elis (IIIa, b, c), Henri (IIIb), Iacob (IIIa, b, c), Roger (IIIa, b, c), Walter (IIIb, c)	*from*	£22.50
Bury St. Edmunds: Ion or Iohs (II–Va, Vg, h, i), Randulf (Va–f), Renaud (Vg), Stephane (Vg)	*from*	£17.50
Canterbury: Alein (Vg, h), Ambroci (Vg), Gilbert (II–Vd/c mule, Vf, g), Ion, Ioh, Iohs, or Iohanes (IIIe–Vd, f, g), Nicole or Nichole (Ib/II mule, II–Vh), Ricard (Vg, h), Robert (Vc–h), Walter (Vc–h), Willem or Willeme (Ib/II mule, II–Vd, f, g) . .	*from*	£10
Carlisle: Adam (IIIa, b), Ion (IIIa, b), Robert (IIIa, b), Willem (IIIa, b)	*from*	£85
Durham: Philip (IIIb), Ricard (V, b, c), Roger (Vg), Willem (Vg)	*from*	£90
Exeter: Ion (II–IIIc), Philip (II–IIIc), Robert (II–IIIc), Walter (II–IIIb)	*from*	£40

		F
Gloucester: Ion (II–IIIc), Lucas (II–IIIc), Ricard (II–IIIc), Roger (II–IIIc)	*from*	£25
Hereford: Henri (IIIa, b), Ricard (IIIa, b, c), Roger (IIIa, b, c), Walter (IIIa, b, c) .	*from*	£40
Ilchester: Huge (IIIa, b, c), Ierveis (IIIa, b, c), Randulf (IIIa, b, c), Stephe (IIIa, b, c)	*from*	£60
Lincoln: Ion (II–IIIc), Ricard (II–IIIc), Walter (II–IIIc), Willem (II–IIIc)	*from*	£25
Newcastle: Adam (IIIa, b), Henri (IIIa, b, c), Ion (IIIa, b, c), Roger (IIIa, b, c) . .	*from*	£22
Northampton: Lucas (II–IIIb), Philip (II–IIIc), Tomas (II–IIIc), Willem (II–IIIc)	*from*	£25
Norwich: Huge (II–IIIc), Iacob (II–IIIc), Ion (II–IIIc), Willem (II–IIIc)	*from*	£35
Oxford: Adam (II–IIIc), Gefrei (II–IIIc), Henri (II–IIIc), Willem (II–IIIc)	*from*	£40
Shrewsbury: Lorens (IIIa, b, c), Nicole (IIIa, b, c), Peris (IIIa, b, c), Ricard (IIIa, b, c)	*from*	£70
Wallingford: Alisandre (IIIa, b), Clement (IIIa, b), Ricard (IIIa, b), Robert (IIIa, b)	*from*	£42
Wilton: Huge (IIIb, c), Ion (IIIa, b, c), Willem (IIIa, b, c)	*from*	£45
Winchester: Huge (II–IIIc), Iordan (II–IIIc), Nicole (II–IIIc), Willem (II–IIIc) . .	*from*	£22.50
York: Alain (II–IIIb), Ieremie (II–IIIb), Ion (II–IIIc), Rener (II–IIIc), Tomas (IIIb, c)	*from*	£25

EDWARD I, 1272–1307

"Long Cross" coinage *continued* (1272–79). With name hENRICVS

The earliest group of Edward's Long Cross coins are of very crude style and only known of Durham and Bury St. Edmunds. Then, for the last class of the type, pennies of much improved style were issued at London, Durham and Bury, but in 1279 the Long Cross coinage was abandoned and a completely new coinage substituted.

VI   VII

	F	VF
1377 Class VI. Crude face with new realistic curls, Є and N ligate	£15	£45
1378 — VII. Similar, but of improved style, usually with Lombardic U.	£100	£250

Mints, moneyers, and classes for Edward I "Long Cross" coinage

		F
London: Phelip (VII), Renaud (VI, VII)	*from*	£85
Bury St. Edmunds: Ioce (VII), Ion or Ioh (VI, VII)	*from*	£16
Durham: Roberd (VI), Robert (VII)	*from*	£100

New Coinage (from 1279).

A major recoinage was embarked upon in 1279 which introduced new denominations. In addition to the penny, halfpence and farthings were also minted and, for the first time, a four penny piece called a "Groat" (from the French *Gros*).

As mint administration was now very much centralized, the practice of including the moneyer's name in the coinage was abandoned (except for a few years at Bury St. Edmunds). Several provincial mints assisted with the recoinage during 1279–81, then minting was again restricted to London, Canterbury, Durham and Bury.

The provincial mints were again employed for a subsidiary re-coinage in 1299–1302 in order to remint light-weight coins and the many illegal *esterlings* (foreign copies of the English pennies or *Sterlings*, mainly from the Low Countries, are usually poorer quality than the English coins).

1379

		F	VF
1379	**Groat.** (= 4d.; wt. 89 grs.). Type as illustration but several minor varieties	£1200	£2750

Most extant specimens show traces of having been mounted on the obverse and gilded on the reverse; unmounted coins are worth more.

	1a	1b	1c		

		F	VF
1380	**Penny.** *London.* Class 1a. Crown with plain band, ЄDW RЄX; Lombardic N on obv.	£200	£550
1381	— 1b. — ЄD RЄX; no drapery on bust, Roman N	£175	£425
1382	— 1c. — ЄDW RЄX; Roman N, normal or reversed; small lettering	£14	£35
1383	— 1d. — ЄDW R;—; large lettering and face	£12	£30
1384	— — — Annulet below bust (for the Abbot of Reading)	£135	£325

	1d (1384)	2a	2b		

		F	VF
1385	— 2a. Crown with band shaped to ornaments; large face and short neck similar to 1d; usually broken left petal to central fleur of crown	£16	£40
1386	— 2b. — tall bust; long neck; N reversed	£12	£30

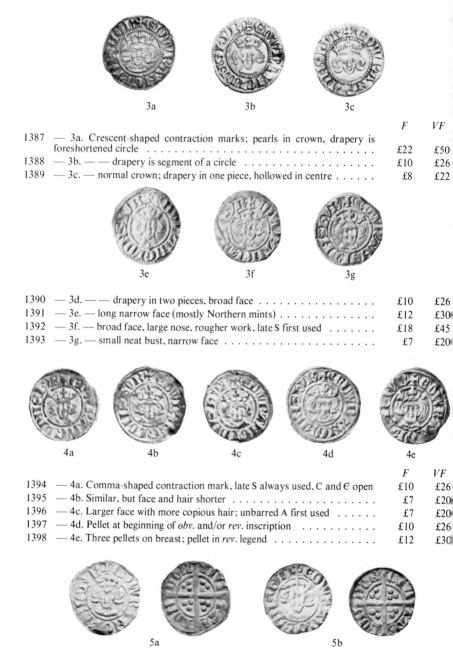

3a   3b   3c

		F	VF
1387	— 3a. Crescent-shaped contraction marks; pearls in crown, drapery is foreshortened circle	£22	£50
1388	— 3b. —— drapery is segment of a circle	£10	£26
1389	— 3c. — normal crown; drapery in one piece, hollowed in centre	£8	£22

3e   3f   3g

		F	VF
1390	— 3d. —— drapery in two pieces, broad face	£10	£26
1391	— 3e. — long narrow face (mostly Northern mints)	£12	£30
1392	— 3f. — broad face, large nose, rougher work, late S first used	£18	£45
1393	— 3g. — small neat bust, narrow face	£7	£20

4a   4b   4c   4d   4e

		F	VF
1394	— 4a. Comma-shaped contraction mark, late S always used, C and Є open	£10	£26
1395	— 4b. Similar, but face and hair shorter	£7	£20
1396	— 4c. Larger face with more copious hair; unbarred A first used	£7	£20
1397	— 4d. Pellet at beginning of obv. and/or rev. inscription	£10	£26
1398	— 4e. Three pellets on breast; pellet in rev. legend	£12	£30

5a   5b

		F	VF
1399	— 5a. Well spread coins, pellet on breast, A normally unbarred	£30	£65
1400	— 5b. Coins more spread, tall lettering, long narrow face, pellet on breast	£30	£65

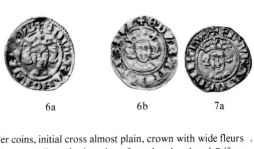

6a   6b   7a

		F	VF
1401	— 6a. Smaller coins, initial cross almost plain, crown with wide fleurs . . .	£100	£250
1402	— 6b. Initial cross well pattée; lettering of good style; closed Є (from now on)	£35	£85
1403	— 7a. Rose on breast; almond-shaped eyes, double barred N	£32	£80

7b   8a   8b   9a   9b

1404	— 7b. — — longer hair, new crown	£40	£100
1405	— 8a. Smaller crown; top-tilted S; longer neck	£25	£60
1406	— 8b. Not unlike 9a, but top-tilted S	£25	£60
1407	— 9a. Narrow face, flatter crown, star on breast	£14	£35
1408	— 9b. Small coins; Roman N, normal, un-barred, or usually of pot-hook form; often star or pellet on breast	£6	£17

10b   10c   10d   10f

1409	— 10a. Bi-foliate (from now on), long narrow face, narrow-waisted lettering, ЄDWARD R	£15	£35
1410	— 10b. — — — ЄDWAR R	£15	£35
1411	— 10c. — — — ЄDWA R	£8	£20
1412	— 10d. Broader face and larger crown, more ornate lettering	£5	£15
1413	— 10e. Square face with short neck; thin initial cross	£5	£15
1414	— 10f. Thicker and more dumpy initial cross	£9	£22

* Prices are for full flan, well struck coins.*
*   The prices for the above types are for London. We can sometimes supply coins of the following mints (see over page); types struck in brackets.*

Berwick type I	Type II	Type III	Type IV

		F	VF
1415	*Berwick-on-Tweed.* (Blunt types I–IV) . . . . *from*	£20	£50
1416	*Bristol.* (2; 3b; c, d; 3f, g; 9b) . . . . *from*	£16	£34
1417	*Bury St. Edmunds.* Robert de Hadelie (3c, d, g; 4a, b, c) . . . . . . *from*	£50	£120
1418	— Villa Sci Edmundi (4e; 5b; 6b; 7a; 8a–10f) . . . . *from*	£18	£40
1419	*Canterbury.* (2; 3b–g; 4; 5; 7a; 9; 10) . . . . *from*	£8	£20
1420	*Chester.* (3g; 9b) . . . . *from*	£35	£75
1421	*Durham.* King's Receiver (9b; 10a, b, e, f) . . . . *from*	£16	£35
1422	— Bishop de Insula (2; 3b, c, e, g; 4a) . . . . *from*	£18	£40
1423	— Bishop Bec (4b, c, d; 5b; 6b; 7a; 8b; 9; 10b–f) mostly with *mm.* cross moline . . . . *from*	£18	£40
1424	— — (4b) cross moline in one angle of *rev.*	£120	£250
1425	*Exeter.* (9b)	£35	£75
1426	*Kingston-upon-Hull.* (9b)	£40	£110
1427	*Lincoln.* (3c, d, f, g) . . . . *from*	£16	£34
1428	*Newcastle-upon-Tyne.* (3e; 9b; 10) . . . . *from*	£18	£40
1429	*York.* Royal mint (2; 3b, c, d, f; 9b) . . . . *from*	£12	£26
1430	— Archbishop's mint (3e, g; 9b). ℞. Quatrefoil in centre . . . . *from*	£18	£40

1431	1436

1431	**Halfpenny,** *London.* Class IIIb. Drapery as segment of circle	£30	£75
1432	— IIIc. Normal drapery as two wedges	£35	£85
1433	— IIIg. Similar, larger letters, wider crown	£30	£75
1433A	— — IV c. Comma abbreviation mark, thick waisted s.	£35	£85
1433B	— — Pellet before LON	£40	£95
1434	— IVe. Usually three pellets on breast, one on *rev.*	£35	£85
1434A	— VI. Double barred N, small lettering	£35	£85
1435	—VII. Double barred N, large lettering	£32	£80
1436	IX. Pot-hook N, usually no star on breast, crown band curved at fleurs . .	£25	£65
1437	— X.ЄDWAR R ANGL DNS hYB, thick waisted letters	£25	£65

The above prices are for London; halfpence of the mints given below were also struck.

1438	*Berwick-on-Tweed.* (Blunt types II and III) . . . . *from*	£65	£175
1439	*Bristol.* (IIIc; IIIg)	£50	£175
1440	*Lincoln.* (IIIc)	£55	£135
1441	*Newcastle.* (IIIe). With single pellet in each angle of *rev.*	£100	£325
1442	*York.* (IIIb)	£85	£200

1443   1445

	F	VF
1443 **Farthing,** *London.* Class I. Heavy weight (6.85 grains), ЄDWARDVS REX. ℞. LONDONIЄNSIS, bifoliate crown	£45	£160
1443A — — — trifoliate crown	£55	£150
1444 — II. Similar, but reversed N's	£40	£120
1445 — IIIc. As class I, but different bust	£35	£115
1446 — IIIg. Lighter weight (5.5 grs.), Є R ANGLIЄ, no inner circle on obv.	£40	£120
1446A — — Reads CIVITAS LONDON, narrow crown.	£55	£150
1446B — — — Wider crown	£55	£150
1447 — VII. Similar, double barred N, pellet eyes	£60	£160
1448 — VIII. Є R ANGL DN, closed Є	£40	£120
1449 — IX. Pot-hook N	£40	£120
1450 — X or XI. ЄDWARDVS REX A or AN inner circle both sides	£30	£90

The above prices are for London; farthings of the mints given below were also struck.

1452

	F	VF
1451 *Berwick-on-Tweed.* (Blunt type III)	£150	£350
1452 *Bristol.* (II; III as illustration) . . . . *from*	£100	£250
1453 *Lincoln.* (III) . . . . *from*	£135	£325
1453A *Newcastle* (IIIe) single pellet in *rev.* quarters	*Extremely rare*	
1454 *York.* (II; III) . . . . *from*	£125	£300

For further information on the pennies of Edward I and II see the articles by K. A. Jacob in "Notes on English Silver Coins, 1066–1648", and for the mint of Berwick-on-Tweed, see the article by C. E. Blunt, in the Num. Chron., 1931.

EDWARD II, 1307–27

The coinage of this reign differs only in minor details from that of Edward I. No groats were issued in the years c. 1282–1351.

11a   12   13   14

15a   15b   15c

		F	VF
1455	**Penny,** *London.* Class 11a. Broken spear-head or pearl on l. side of crown; long narrow face, straight-sided N	£10	£26
1456	— 11b. — Є with angular back (till 15b), N with well-marked serifs	£10	£26
1457	— 11c. — — A of special form	£30	£65
1458	— 12. Central fleur of crown formed of three wedges	£20	£45
1459	— 13. Central fleur of crown as Greek double axe	£16	£40
1460	— 14. Crown with tall central fleur; large smiling face with leering eyes	£12	£30
1461	— 15a. Small flat crown with both spear-heads usually bent to l.; face of 14	£16	£40
1462	— 15b. — very similar, but smaller face	£16	£40
1463	— 15c. — large face, large Є	£18	£45

The prices of the above types are for London. We can sometimes supply coins of the following mints; types struck in brackets.

Type 5   Type 6   Type 7

		F	VF
1464	*Berwick-on-Tweed.* (Blunt types V, VI and VII) ....from	£40	£85
1465	*Bury St. Edmunds.* (11; 12; 13; 15) ....from	£16	£40
1466	*Canterbury.* (11; 12; 13; 14; 15) ....from	£16	£40
1467	*Durham.* King's Receiver (11a; 14); mm. plain cross ....from	£25	£55
1468	— Bishop Bec. (11a), mm. cross moline	£25	£55
1469	— Bishop Kellawe (11; 12; 13), crozier on *rev.* ....from	£24	£50
1470	— Bishop Beaumont (13; 14; 15), mm. lion with lis ....from	£24	£50
1471	Sede Vacante (15c); mm. plain cross	£55	£135
1472	**Halfpenny** of *London.* ЄDWARDVS REX A(NG)	£55	£135
1473	— — *Berwick-on-Tweed.* (Blunt type V)	£80	£200
1474	**Farthing** of *London.* ЄDWARDVS REX (AN)G	£65	£160
1475	— *Berwick-on-Tweed.* (Blunt type V)	*Extremely rare*	

* *Prices are for full flan, well struck coins.*

EDWARD III, 1327–77

During Edward's early years small quantities of silver coin were minted following the standard of the previous two reigns, but in 1335 halfpence and farthings were produced which were well below the .925 Sterling silver standard. In 1344 an impressive gold coinage was introduced comprising the Florin or Double Leopard valued at six shillings, and its half and quarter, the Leopard and the Helm. The design of the Florin was based on the contemporary gold of Philip de Valois of France. The first gold coinage was not successful and it was replaced later the same year by a heavier coinage, the Noble valued at 6s. 8d, i.e., 80 pence, half a mark or one third of a pound, together with its fractions. The Noble was lowered in weight in two stages over the next few years, being stabilized at 120 grains in 1351. With the signing of the Treaty of Bretigni in 1360 Edward's title to the Kingdom of France was omitted from the coinage, but it was resumed again in 1369.

In 1344 the silver coinage had been re-established at the old sterling standard, but the penny was reduced in weight to just over 20 grains and in 1351 to 18 grains. Groats were minted again in 1351 and were issued regularly henceforth until the reign of Elizabeth.

Subsequent to the treaty with France which gave England a cross-channel trading base at Calais, a mint was opened there in 1363 for minting gold and silver coins of English type. In addition to coins of the regular English mints the Abbot of Reading also minted silver pence and a halfpence with a scallop shell badge while coins from Berwick display one or two boars' heads.

Mintmarks

6	1	2	3	74	4	5	7a

1334–51	Cross pattée (6)	1356	Crown (74)
1351–2	Cross 1 (1)	1356–61	Cross 3 (4)
1351–7	Crozier on cross end (76a, *Durham*)	1361–9	Cross potent (5)
1352–3	Cross 1 broken (2)	1369–77	Cross pattée (6)
1354–5	Cross 2 (3)		Plain cross (7a)
			Cross potent and four pellets

The figures in brackets refer to the plate of mintmarks on page 313.

GOLD

Third coinage, 1344–51
First period, 1344

1476	1477	1478

1476	**Florin** or **Double Leopard.** (= 6s.; wt. 108 grs.). King enthroned beneath canopy; crowned leopard's head each side. ℞. Cross in quatrefoil		*Extremely rare*
1477	**Half-florin** or **Leopard.** Leopard sejant with banner l. ℞. Somewhat as last		*Extremely rare*
1478	**Quarter-florin** or **Helm.** Helmet on fleured field. ℞. Floriate cross		*Extremely rare*

Second period, 1344–46

		F	VF
1479	**Noble** (= 6s. 8d., wt. 138$\frac{6}{13}$ grs.). King stg. facing in ship with sword and shield. ℞. L in centre of royal cross in tressure	*Extremely rare*	
1480	**Quarter-noble.** Shield in tressure. ℞. As last	£550	£1100

Third period, 1346–51

1481	**Noble** (wt. 128$\frac{4}{7}$ grs.). As 1479, but Є in centre; large letters	£500	£1200
1482	**Half-noble.** Similar	*Extremely rare*	
1483	**Quarter-noble.** As 1480, but Є in centre	£200	£400

Fourth coinage, 1351–77

Reference: L. A. Lawrence, *The Coinage of Edward III from 1351.*
Pre-treaty period, 1351–61. With French title.

1488   1498

1484	**Noble** (wt. 120 grs.), series B (1351). Open Є and C, Roman M ; *mm.* cross 1 (1)	£325	£600
1485	— — *rev.* of series A (1351). Round lettering, Lombardic M and N ; closed inverted Є in centre	£350	£675
1486	C (1351–1352). Closed Є and C, Lombardic M ; *mm.* cross 1 (1)	£275	£550
1487	D (1352–1353). *O.* of series C. ℞. *Mm.* cross 1 broken (2)	£400	£700
1488	E (1354–1355). Broken letters, V often has a nick in r. limb; *mm.* cross 2 (3)	£250	£525
1489	F (1356). *Mm.* crown (74)	£325	£600
1490	G (1356–1361). *Mm.* cross 3 (4). Many varieties		£450
1491	**Half-noble,** B. As noble with *rev.* of series A, but closed Є in centre not inverted	£175	£425
1492	C. *O.* as noble. *Rev.* as last	£200	£450
1493	E. As noble	£450	£800
1494	G. As noble. Many varieties	£175	£375
1495	**Quarter-noble,** B. Pellet below shield. ℞. Closed Є in centre	£125	£225
1496	C. *O.* of series B. *Rev.* details as noble	£130	£275
1497	E. *O.* as last. *Rev.* details as noble, pellet in centre	£150	£300
1498	G. *Mm.* cross 3 (4). Many varieties	£100	£200

Transitional treaty period, 1361. Aquitaine title added and FRANC omitted on the noble and, rarely, the half-noble; irregular sized letters; *mm.* cross potent (5).

		F	VF
1499	**Noble.** ℞. Pellets or annulets at corners of central panel	£325	£650
1500	**Half-noble.** Similar	£175	£425
1501	**Quarter-noble.** Similar. Many varieties	£110	£225

1499   1503

Treaty period, 1361–69. Omits FRANC, new letters, usually curule-shaped X ; *mm.* cross potent (5).

1502	**Noble.** *London.* Saltire before EDWARD	£235	£500
1503	— Annulet before EDWARD	£235	£500
1504	*Calais.* C in centre of *rev.*, flag at stern of ship	£275	£620
1505	— — without flag	£265	£575

1506   1508

1506	**Half-noble.** *London.* Saltire before EDWARD	£175	£400
1507	— Annulet before EDWARD	£175	£400
1508	*Calais.* C in centre of *rev.*, flag at stern of ship	£275	£625
1509	— — without flag	£275	£625
1510	**Quarter-noble.** *London.* As 1498. ℞. Lis in centre	£100	£225
1511	— — annulet before EDWARD	£100	£225
1512	*Calais.* ℞. Annulet in centre	£125	£250
1513	— — cross in circle over shield	£135	£275
1514	— ℞. Quatrefoil in centre; cross over shield	£135	£275
1515	— — crescent over shield	£225	£475

Post-treaty period, 1369–1377. French title resumed.

		F	VF
1516	**Noble.** *London.* Annulet before ЄD. ℞. Treaty period die	£275	£550
1517	— — — crescent on forecastle	£300	£585
1518	— — post-treaty letters. ℞. Є and pellet in centre	£250	£525
1519	— — — ℞. Є and saltire in centre	£325	£600
1520	*Calais.* Flag at stern. ℞. Є in centre	£275	£550

1521

1521	— — *Rev.* as 1518, with Є and pellet in centre	£235	£500
1522	— As 1520, but without flag. ℞. C in centre	£250	£575
1523	**Half-noble.** *London. O.* Treaty die. *Rev.* as 1518	*Extremely rare*	
1524	*Calais.* Without AQT, flag at stern. ℞. Є in centre	£325	£700
1525	— — ℞. Treaty die with C in centre	£350	£725

SILVER

First coinage, 1327–35 (.925 fineness)

1526   1530   1535

1526	**Penny.** *London.* As Edw. II; class XVd with Lombardic n's	£160	£350
1527	*Bury St. Edmunds.* Similar	*Extremely rare*	
1528	*Canterbury; mm.* cross pattée with pellet centre	£140	£300
1529	— — three extra pellets in one quarter	£140	£300
1530	*Durham.* ℞. Small crown in centre	£350	£750
1531	*York.* As 1526, but quatrefoil in centre of *rev.*	£90	£200
1532	— — — pellet in each quarter of *mm.*	£90	£200
1533	— — — three extra pellets in one quarter	£90	£200
1534	— — — Roman N on *obv.*	£90	£200
1535	*Berwick* (1333–1342, Blunt type VIII). Bear's head in one quarter of *rev.*	£225	£500
1536	**Halfpenny.** *London.* ЄDWARDVS RЄX AII(G)*, neat work, flat crown	£100	£225
1537	*Berwick* (Bl. VIII). Bear's head in one or two quarters	£90	£200
1538	**Farthing.** *London.* ЄDWARDVS RЄX A*, flat crown	£100	£300
1539	*Berwick* (Bl. VIII). As 1537	£160	£350

1537 1540

Second coinage, 1335–43 (.833 fineness)

		F	VF
1540	**Halfpenny.** *London.* ЄDWARDVS RЄX A(NG)*, rough work, tall crown ..	£20	£55
1541	*Reading.* Escallop in one quarter	£175	£375
1542	**Farthing.** *London.* As halfpenny	£115	£250

Third or florin coinage, 1344–51. Bust with bushy hair. (.925 fine, 18 grs.)

1543 1555

		F	VF
1543	**Penny.** *London.* Class 1. ЄDW, Lombardic n's	£13	£35
1544	— 2, ЄDWA, n's, but sometimes N's on *rev.*	£10	£27
1545	— 3, ЄDW, N's, sometimes reversed or n's on *rev.*	£8	£23
1546	— 4, ЄDW, no stops, reversed N's, but on *rev.* sometimes n's, N's or double-barred N's	£9	£25
	There are also five unusual varieties of obv.		
1547	*Canterbury.* ЄDWA, n's	£45	£95
1548	— ЄDW, reversed N's	£40	£85
1549	*Durham*, Sede Vacante (1345). A, ЄDW R. ℞. No marks	£100	£250
1550	— — B, similar, ЄDWAR R	£150	£350
1551	— Bp. Hatfield. C, similar, but pellet in centre of *rev.*	£100	£250
1552	— — — Crozier on *rev.*	£100	£250
1553	— — — — with pellet in centre of *rev.*	£100	£250
1554	— — D, ЄDWARDVS RЄX AIn, crozier on *rev.*	£200	£450
1555	*Reading.* O. as 1546. ℞. Escallop in one quarter	£225	£450
1556	*York.* O. as 1546. ℞. Quatrefoil in centre	£45	£115
1557	**Halfpenny.** *London.* ЄDWARDVS RЄX(An)	£10	£30
1558	— — pellet either side of crown	£17	£40
1559	— — saltire either side of crown and in one quarter of *rev.*	£15	£35
1560	*Reading.* O. similar. ℞. Escallop in one quarter	£185	£450
1561	*Continental imitation.* Mostly reading ЄDWARDIENSIS	£18	£45
1562	**Farthing.** *London.* ЄDWARDVS RЄX	£90	£200
1562A	*Reading.* As last. ℞. As halfpenny		*Unique*

Fourth coinage, 1351–77

Reference: L. A. Lawrence, *The Coinage of Edward III from 1351.*
Pre-treaty period, 1351–61. With French title.

1567 1570

		F	VF
1563	**Groat** (= 4d., 72 grs.). *London*, series B (1351). Roman M, open C and Є; *mm.* cross 1	£100	£300
1564	— — — crown in each quarter		*Unique*
1565	— C (1351–2). Lombardic m, closed C and Є, R with wedge-shaped tail; *mm.* cross 1	£20	£85
1566	— D (1352–3). R with normal tail; *mm.* cross 1 or cross 1 broken (2)	£25	£105
1567	— E (1354–5). Broken letters, V often with nick in r. limb; *mm.* cross 2 (3)	£17	£75
1568	— — — lis on breast	£20	£85
1569	— F (1356). *Mm.* crown (74)	£25	£105
1570	— G (1356–61). Usually with annulet in one quarter and sometimes under bust, *mm.* cross 3 (4). Many varieties	£20	£85
1571	*York*, series D. As London	£35	£130
1572	— E. As London	£30	£110

1573 1574

1573	**Halfgroat.** *London*, series B. As groat	£50	£140
1574	— C. As groat	£15	£45
1575	— D. As groat	£17	£50
1576	— E. As groat	£15	£45
1577	— F. As groat	£20	£55
1578	— G. As groat	£17	£50
1579	— — — annulet below bust	£20	£55

		F	VF
1580	*York*, series D. As groat	£25	£60
1581	— E. As groat	£20	£50
1582	— — lis on breast	£35	£85

1584	1587	1591

1583	**Penny.** *London*. Series A (1351). Round letters, Lombardic m and n, annulet in each quarter; *mm.* cross pattée	£30	£60
1584	— C. Details as groat, but annulet in each quarter	£12	£30
1585	— D. Details as groat, but annulet in each quarter	£12	£30
1586	— E. Sometimes annulet in each quarter	£12	£30
1587	— F. Details as groat	£15	£35
1588	— G. Details as groat	£12	£30
1589	— — annulet below bust	£15	£35
1590	— — saltire in one quarter	£25	£50
1591	*Durham*, Bp. Hatfield. Series A. As 1583, but extra pellet in each quarter, VIL LA crozier DVRREM	£150	£350
1592	— C. Details as groat. ℞. Crozier, CIVITAS DVNЄLMIЄ	£30	£70
1593	— D — — —	£30	£77
1594	— E — — —	£25	£60
1595	— F — Є. Crozier, CIVITAS DVRЄMЄ	£30	£70
1596	— G — — —	£18	£45
1597	— — — — — annulet below bust	£20	£50
1598	— — — — — saltire in one quarter	£20	£50
1599	— — — — — annulet on each shoulder	£20	£50
1600	— — — — — trefoil of pellets on breast	£25	£60
1601	— — — ℞. Crozier, CIVITAS DVRЄLMIЄ	£30	£70
1602	*York*, Royal Mint. Series D	£18	£40
1603	— — E	£12	£25
1604	— Archb. Thorsby. Series D. ℞. Quatrefoil in centre	£16	£35
1605	— — G —	£12	£25
1606	— — — — annulet or saltire on breast	£13	£30
1607	**Halfpenny.** *London*. Series E. ЄDWARDVS RЄX An	£75	£175
1608	— G, but with *obv.* of F (*mm.* crown). Annulet in one quarter	*Extremely rare*	
1609	**Farthing.** *London*. Series E. ЄDWARDVS RЄX	*Extremely rare*	

Transitional treaty period, 1361. French title omitted, irregular sized letters; *mm.* cross potent (5).

		F	VF
1610	**Groat.** *London.* Annulet each side of crown	£90	£300
1611	**Halfgroat.** Similar, but only seven arches to tressure	£80	£225

1611   1612

1612	**Penny,** *London.* Omits REX, annulet in two upper qtrs. of *mm.*	£40	£110
1613	*York,* Archb. Thoresby. Similar, but quatrefoil enclosing pellet in centre of *rev.*	£40	£110
1614	*Durham,* Bp. Hatfield. Similar. ℞. Crozier, CIVITAS DORELME	£40	£110
1615	**Halfpenny.** Two pellets over *mm.,* EDWARDVS REX An	£75	£150

Treaty period, 1361–69. French title omitted, new letters, usually "Treaty" X ; *mm.* cross potent (5).

1616	**Groat,** *London.* Many varieties	£25	£90
1617	— Annulet before EDWARD	£30	£100
1618	— Annulet on breast	£60	£175
1619	*Calais.* As last	£100	£350

1621   1635

1620	**Halfgroat,** *London.* As groat	£20	£50
1621	— — Annulet before EDWARDVS	£15	£40
1622	— — Annulet on breast	£45	£120
1623	*Calais.* As last	£100	£300
1624	**Penny,** *London.* EDWARD AnGL R, etc.	£15	£35
1625	— — — pellet before EDWARD	£20	£45
1626	*Calais.* ℞. VILLA CALESIE	£55	£135
1627	*Durham.* ℞. DIVITAS DVNELMIS	£40	£100
1628	— ℞. Crozier, CIVITAS DVREME	£25	£65
1629	*York,* Archb. Thoresby. Quatrefoil in centre of *rev.*, EDWARDVS DEI G REX An	£30	£65
1630	— — — EDWARDVS REX ANGLI	£15	£35
1631	— — — — quatrefoil before ED and on breast	£13	£33
1632	— — — — annulet before ED	£20	£45
1633	— — — EDWARD AnGL R DnS HYB	£27	£60

		F	VF
1634	**Halfpenny.** ЄDWARDVS RЄX An, pellet stops	£20	£45
1635	— Pellet before ЄD, annulet stops	£22	£50
1636	**Farthing.** ЄDWARDVS RЄX, pellet stops	£80	£180

Post-treaty period, 1369–77. French title resumed, X like St. Andrew's cross; *mm.* 5, 6, 7a.

1637   1638

1637	**Groat.** Various readings, *mm.* cross pattée	£85	£250
1638	— — row of pellets across breast (chain mail)	£190	£600
1639	— row of annulets below bust (chain mail); *mm.* cross potent with four pellets	£165	£500
1640	**Halfgroat.** Various readings	£65	£165
1641	— row of pellets one side of breast (chain mail)	£165	£525
1642	**Penny,** *London.* No marks on breast	£33	£85
1643	— Pellet or annulet on breast	£45	£110
1644	— Cross or quatrefoil on breast	£38	£100
1645	*Durham,* Bp. Hatfield. *Mm.* 7a, CIVITAS DVnOLM, crozier	£38	£100
1646	— — — annulet on breast	£45	£110
1647	— — — — lis on breast	£33	£85
1648	*York,* Archb. Thoresby or Neville. ℞. Quatrefoil in centre	£22.50	£60
1649	— — — lis on breast	£45	£95
1650	— — — annulet on breast	£27.50	£60
1651	— — — cross on breast	£27.50	£60

1652

1652	**Farthing.** ЄDWARD RЄX ANGL, large head without neck	£150	£300

RICHARD II, 1377–99

There was no significant change in the coinage during this reign. Noteworthy is the first appearance of symbols on the ship's rudder on some of the gold coins. The earlier silver coins have a portrait like that on the coins of Edward III, but the king's head and the style of lettering were altered on the later issues.

Reference: *Silver coinages of Richard II, Henry IV and V.* (B.N.J. 1959–60 and 1963).

Mintmark: cross pattée (6)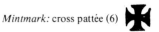

GOLD

	1655		1657

			F	VF
1653	**Noble,** *London.* With altered *obv.* and/or *rev.* die of Edw. III . . . . . *from*		£550	£1250
1654	— Lettering as Edw. III, lis over sail		£450	£1100
1655	— Straight-sided letters, annulet over sail		£400	£1000
1656	— Late issue, fish-tail lettering; no marks, or trefoil by shield		£450	£1050
1657	— — — lion or lis on rudder		£575	£1250
1658	— — small dumpy lettering; escallop or crescent on rudder and/or trefoil over sail or by shield . . . .*from*		£525	£1150

	1658		1662

1659	*Calais.* Flag at stern, otherwise as 1653 . . . . *from*	£500	£1025
1660	— — as 1655, but quatrefoil over sail	£475	£1000
1661	— — as 1656; no marks	£500	£1025
1662	— — — lion on rudder	£540	£1100
1663	— — as 1658	£475	£1000

1664   1672/3

		F	VF
1664	**Half-noble,** *London*. As 1653	£525	£1200
1665	— as 1655	£450	£1000
1666	— as 1656; lion on rudder	£475	£1100
1667	— as 1658; crescent on rudder	£525	£1200
1668	*Calais*. Flag at stern, otherwise as 1653	£475	£1100
1669	— — as 1655; quatrefoil over sail	£475	£1100
1670	— — as 1656; lion on rudder	£450	£1000
1671	— — as 1658, but one var. has saltire behind rudder	£525	£1200
1672	**Quarter-noble,** *London*. R in centre of *rev*.	£200	£425
1673	— Lis or pellet in centre of *rev*.	£175	£375
1674	— — *obv*. die of Edw. III altered	£225	£475
1675	— — escallop over shield	£250	£525
1676	— — trefoil of annulets over shield	£200	£450
1677	— — quatrefoil, cross or slipped trefoil over shield .... *from*	£175	£400

SILVER

		F	VF
1678	**Groat.** I. Style of Edw. III, F (*i.e. et*) before FRANC, etc.	£250	£650
1679	II. New lettering, retrograde Z before FRANC, etc.	£200	£550
1680	III. Bust with bushy hair, "fishtail" serifs to letters	£250	£650
1681	IV. New style bust and crown, crescent on breast	£850	£2000

1682

		F	VF
1682	**Halfgroat.** II. New lettering	£200	£450
1683	III. As 1680	£210	£475
1684	— — with *obv*. or *rev*. die of Edw. III	£375	£850
1684A	— opposite mule, with *obv*. of Edw. III, *rev*. R. III	£375	£850
1685	IV. As 1681, but no crescent	£550	£1200

		F	VF
1686	**Penny,** *London.* I. Lettering as 1678, RICARDVS REX AnGLIE	£175	£450
1688	— II. As 1679, Z FRAnC lis on breast	£175	£450
1689	— III. As 1680, RICARD REX AnGLIE, fish-tail letters	£200	£500

1689   1692

1690	*York.* I. Early style, usually with cross or lis on breast, quatrefoil in centre of *rev.* . . . . *Fair* £20		£60
1691	— II. New bust and letters, no marks on breast . . . . *Fair* £17		£55
1692	— Local dies. Pellet above each shoulder, cross on breast, REX AnGLIE . . . . *Fair* £15		£40
1693	— — — REX DNS EB . . . . *Fair* £17		£50
1694	— — — REX AnG FRAnC . . . . *Fair* £17		£50
1695	— III. As 1680, REX AnGL Z FRANC . . . . *Fair* £15		£45
1695A	— Similar, but with scallop mark after TAS . . . . *Fair* £25		£90
1696	— IV. Very bushy hair, new letters, no crescent. ℞. R in centre of quatrefoil	£225	£475
1697	*Durham.* Cross or lis on breast, DVnOLM	£250	£625

1699   1701   1704

1698	**Halfpenny.** Early style. LONDON, saltire or annulet on breast	£45	£100
1699	Intermediate style. LOnDOn, no marks on breast	£30	£60
1700	Late style. Similar, but fishtail letters	£50	£115
1701	**Farthing.** Small bust and letters	£125	£275
1702	— — rose after REX	£150	£325
1703	Large head, no bust	£175	£375
1704	Rose in each angle of *rev.* instead of pellets	£325	£600

HENRY IV, 1399–1413

In 1412 the standard weights of the coinage were reduced, the noble by 12 grains and the penny by 3 grains, partly because there was a scarcity of bullion and partly to provide revenue for the king, as Parliament had not renewed the royal subsidies. As in France, the royal arms were altered, three fleur-de-lis taking the place of the four or more lis previously displayed.

Mintmark: cross pattée (6)

Heavy coinage, 1399–1412   GOLD

1707   1708

		F	VF
1705	**Noble** (120 grs.), *London.* Old arms with four lis in French quarters; crescent or annulet on rudder	—	£6000
1706	— New arms with three lis; crescent, pellet or no marks on rudder	—	£6000
1707	*Calais.* Flag at stern, old arms; crown on or to l. of rudder	*Extremely rare*	
1708	— — new arms; crown or star on rudder	*Extremely rare*	
1709	**Half-noble,** *London.* Old arms	*Extremely rare*	
1710	— new arms	*Extremely rare*	
1711	*Calais.* New arms	*Extremely rare*	
1712	**Quarter-noble,** *London.* Crescent over old arms	£750	£1500
1713	— — — new arms	£650	£1300
1714	*Calais.* New arms. ℞. *Mm.* crown	£850	£1750

1710   1715

Light coinage, 1412–13

1715	**Noble** (108 grs.). Trefoil, or trefoil and annulet, on side of ship. ℞. Trefoil in one quarter	£1000	£2000
1716	**Half-noble.** Similar, but always with annulet	£6000	—
1717	**Quarter-noble.** Trefoils, or trefoils and annulets beside shield, lis above. ℞. Lis in centre	£400	£800

SILVER

Heavy coinage, 1399–1412

1718	1722	1723

		F	VF
1718	**Halfgroat** (36 grs.). Star on breast	£800	£2000
1719	**Penny**, *London*. Similar, early bust with long neck	£500	£1250
1720	— later bust with shorter neck, no star	£500	£1250
1721	*York*. Early bust with long neck	£450	**£1000**
1722	— later bust with broad face, round chin	£450	£1000
1723	**Halfpenny**. Early small bust	£225	£500
1724	Later large bust, with rounded shoulders annulets by neck	£225	£500
1725	**Farthing**. Face without neck	£400	£800

Light coinage, 1412–13

1728	1731	1737

		F	VF
1726	**Groat** (60 grs.). I. Pellet to l., annulet to r. of crown; altered die of Richard II	£1500	£3500
1727	New dies; II. Annulet to l., pellet to r. of crown, 8 or 10 arches to tressure	£1250	£3000
1728	— III. Similar but 9 arches to tressure	£1250	£3000
1729	**Halfgroat**. Pellet to l., annulet to r. of crown	£800	£2000
1730	Annulet to l., pellet to r. of crown	£800	£2000
1731	**Penny**, *London*. Annulet and pellet by crown; trefoil on breast and before CIVI	£500	£1050
1732	— — annulet or slipped trefoil before LON	£500	£1050
1733	— Pellet and annulet by crown		*Unique*
1734	*York*. Annulet on breast. ℞. Quatrefoil in centre	£450	£1000
1735	*Durham*. Trefoil on breast, DVnOLM	£650	£1400
1736	**Halfpenny**. Struck from heavy dies	£225	£525
1737	New dies; annulet either side of crown or none	£225	£525
1738	**Farthing**. Face, no bust; slipped trefoil after REX	£475	£950

HENRY V, 1413–22

There was no change of importance in the coinage of this reign. There was, however, a considerable development in the use of privy marks which distinguished various issues, except for the last issue of the reign when most marks were removed. The Calais mint, which had closed in 1411, did not re-open until early in the next reign.

Mintmarks

Cross pattée (4, but with pellet centre).   Pierced cross (18).

GOLD

1744   1755

		F	VF
1739	**Noble.** A. Quatrefoil over sail and in second quarter of *rev.* Short broad letters, no other marks	*Extremely rare*	
1740	— B. Ordinary letters; similar, or with annulet on rudder	£500	£900
1741	— C. Mullet by sword arm, annulet on rudder	£450	£750
1742	— — broken annulet on side of ship	£300	£525
1743	— D. Mullet and annulet by sword arm, trefoil by shield, broken annulet on ship	£325	£575
1744	— E. Mullet, or mullet and annulet by sword arm, trefoil by shield, pellet by sword point and in one quarter, annulet on side of ship	£350	£650
1745	— — Similar, but trefoil on ship instead of by shield	£400	£700
1746	— F. Similar, but no pellet at sword point, trefoil in one quarter	£350	£700
1747	— G. No marks; annulet stops, except for mullet after first word	£575	£1050
1748	**Half-noble.** B. As noble; Hen. IV *rev.* die	*Extremely rare*	
1749	— C. Broken annulet on ship, quatrefoil below sail	£375	£800
1750	— — Mullet over shield, broken annulet on *rev.*	£350	£700
1751	— F. Similar, but no annulet on ship, usually trefoil by shield	£400	£850
1752	— F/E. As last, but pellet in 1st and annulet in 2nd quarter	£450	£1000
1753	— G. As noble, but quatrefoil over sail, mullet sometimes omitted after first word of *rev.*	£500	£1150
1754	**Quarter-noble.** A. Lis over shield and in centre of *rev.* Short broad letters; quatrefoil and annulet beside shield, stars at corners of centre on *rev.*	£225	£425
1755	— C. Ordinary letters; quatrefoil to l., quat. and mullet to r. of shield	£140	£275
1756	— — — annulet to l., mullet to r. of shield	£125	£250

	F	VF
1757 **Quarter-noble.** F. Ordinary letters; trefoil to l., mullet to r. of shield	£175	£350
1758 — G — no marks, except mullet after first word	£175	£350

SILVER

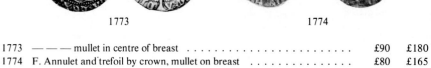

1759   1762

	F	VF
1759 **Groat.** A. Short broad letters; "emaciated" bust	£450	£950
1760 — — muled with Hen. IV *obv.* or *rev.*	£500	£1000
1761 — — muled with later *rev.* of Hen. V	£400	£850
1762 B. Ordinary letters; 'scowling' bust	£250	£500
1762A — — mullet in centre of breast	£250	£500
1763 — — muled with Hen. IV or later Hen. V	£275	£600
1764 C. Normal bust	£55	£1100
1765 — — mullet on r. shoulder	£40	£900
1767 G. Normal bust; no marks	£100	£200
1768 **Halfgroat.** A. As groat, but sometimes with annulet and pellet by crown . .	£250	£500
1769 B. Ordinary letters; no marks	£120	£250
1770 — — muled with Hen. IV or class C	£160	£325
1771 C. Tall neck, broken annulet to l. of crown	£60	£120
1772 — — — mullet on r. shoulder	£55	£110

1773   1774

	F	VF
1773 — — — mullet in centre of breast	£90	£180
1774 F. Annulet and trefoil by crown, mullet on breast	£80	£165
1775 G. New neat bust: no marks	£70	£150

1778   1791

		F	VF
1776	**Penny.** *London.* A. Letters, bust and marks as 1768	£50	£130
1777	— B. Altered A *obv.*, with mullet and broken annulet added by crown. ℞. Ordinary letters	£65	£175
1778	— C. Tall neck, mullet and broken annulet by crown	£20	£55
1779	— D. Similar, but whole annulet	£25	£75
1780	— F. Mullet and trefoil by crown	£27	£80
1781	— G. New neat bust, no marks, DI GRA	£25	£75
1782	*Durham.* C. As 1778 but quatrefoil at end of legend	£45	£135
1783	— D. As 1779	£40	£125
1784	— G. Similar, but new bust. ℞. Annulet in one qtr.	£50	£160
1785	*York.* C. As 1778, but quatrefoil in centre of *rev.*	£20	£55
1786	— D. Similar, but whole annulet by crown	£20	£55
1787	— E. As last, but pellet above mullet	£40	£110
1788	— F. Mullet and trefoil by crown	£27	£75
1789	— — Trefoil over mullet to l., annulet to r. of crown	£22	£60
1790	— G. Mullet and trefoil by crown (London dies)	£22	£60
1791	— — Mullet and lis by crown, annulet in one qtr. (usually local dies and muled with Henry VI)	£22	£70

1796   1798

		F	VF
1792	**Halfpenny.** A. Emaciated bust, annulets by crown	£28	£70
1793	— altered dies of Hen. IV	£38	£100
1794	C. Ordinary bust, broken annulets by crown	£18	£40
1795	D. Annulets, sometimes broken, by hair	£18	£40
1796	F. Annulet and trefoil by crown	£20	£45
1797	G. New bust; no marks, usually muled with Henry VI	£75	£175
1798	**Farthing.** G. Small face with neck	£85	£250

HENRY VI, First Reign, 1422–61

The supply of gold began to dwindle early in the reign, which accounts for the rarity of gold after 1426. The Calais mint was re-opened in 1424 and for some years a large amount of coin was struck there. It soon stopped minting gold; the mint was finally closed in 1440. A royal mint at York was opened for a short time in 1423/4.

Marks used to denote various issues become more prominent in this reign and can be used to date coins to within a year or so.

Reference: *Heavy Coinage of Henry VI*, by C. A. Whitton (B.N.J. 1938–41).

Mintmarks

| 7a | 105 | 18 | — | 8 | 9 | 15 |

1422–60 Plain cross (7a, intermittently)	1427–34 Cross patonce (8)
Lis (105, on gold)	Cross fleurée (9)
1422–27 Pierced cross (18)	1434–35 Voided cross (15)
1422–34 Cross pommée	1435–60 Cross fleury (9)
	1460 Lis (105, on *rev.* of some groats)

For Restoration marks see p. 121.

GOLD

Annulet issue, 1422–7

![coin 1799]

1799

		F	VF
1799	**Noble.** *London.* Annulet by sword arm, and in one spandrel on *rev.*; trefoil stops on *obv.* with lis after hENRIC, annulets on *rev.*, with mullet after IhC	£300	£575
1800	— Similar, but *obv.* from Henry V die	£600	£1200
1801	— As 1799, but Flemish imitative coinage	£200	£425
1802	*Calais.* As 1799, but flag at stern and C in centre of *rev.*	£450	£900
1803	— — with h in centre of *rev.*	£425	£800
1804	*York.* As London, but with lis over stern	£425	£800
1805	**Half-noble.** *London.* As 1799	£250	£500
1806	— Similar, but *obv.* from Henry V die	£350	£675
1807	*Calais.* As noble, with C in centre of *rev.*	£625	£1100
1808	— — with h in centre of *rev.*	£325	£675
1809	*York.* As noble	£350	£725

	F	VF
1810 **Quarter-noble.** *London.* Lis over shield; *mm.* large lis	£125	£250
1811 — — — trefoil below shield	£175	£400
1812 — — — pellet below shield	*Extremely rare*	
1813 *Calais.* Three lis over shield; *mm.* large lis	£200	£400
1814 — Similar but three lis around shield	£225	£450
1815 — As 1810, but much smaller *mm.*	£175	£375
1816 *York.* Two lis over shield	£225	£450

1814   1819

Rosette-mascle issue, 1427–30

1817 **Noble.** *London.* Lis by sword arm and in *rev.* field; stops, rosettes, or rosettes and mascles	£475	£1000
1818 *Calais.* Similar, with flag at stern	£450	£1200
1819 **Half-noble.** *London.* Lis in *rev.* field; stops, rosettes and mascles	£450	£950
1820 *Calais.* Similar, flag at stern; stops, rosettes	£575	£1250
1821 **Quarter-noble.** *London.* As 1810; stops, as noble	£225	£475
1822 — without lis over shield	£200	£450
1823 *Calais.* Lis over shield, rosettes r. and l., and rosette stops	£325	£500

Pinecone-mascle issue, 1430–4

1824 **Noble.** *London.* Stops, pinecones and mascles	£525	£1100
1825 **Half-noble.** *London.* O. Rosette-mascle die. ℞. As last	*Extremely rare*	
1826 **Quarter-noble.** As 1810, but pinecone and mascle stops	*Unique*	

Leaf-mascle issue, 1434–5

1827 **Noble.** Leaf in waves; stops, saltires with two mascles and one leaf	£1000	£2500
1828 **Half-noble.** (Fishpool Hoard)	*Unique*	
1829 **Quarter-noble.** As 1810; stops, saltire and mascle; leaf on inner circle of *rev.*	£1350	£2750

Leaf-trefoil issue, 1435–8

1830 **Noble.** Stops, leaves and trefoils	*Extremely rare*	
1830A **Half noble.** Mule with Annulet Issue reverse die	*Unique*	
1831 **Quarter-noble.** Similar	*Unique*	

Trefoil issue, 1438–43

1832 **Noble.** Trefoil below shield and in *rev.* legend	£1000	£2500

Leaf-pellet issue, 1445–54

1833 **Noble.** Annulet, lis and leaf below shield	£1000	£2500

Cross-pellet issue, 1454–60

1834 **Noble.** Mascle at end of *obv.* legend	*Unique*	

SILVER

Annulet issue, 1422–7

1835   1840

		F	VF
1835	**Groat.** *London.* Annulet in two quarters of *rev.*	£20	£55
1836	*Calais.* Annulets at neck. ℞. Similar	£15	£35
1837	— — no annulets on *rev.*	£20	£50
1838	*York.* Lis either side of neck. ℞. As 1835	£500	£950
1839	**Halfgroat.** *London.* As groat	£17	£43
1840	*Calais.* As 1836	£14	£30
1841	— — no annulets on *rev.*	£17	£43
1842	— — only one annulet on *rev.*	£22	£55
1843	*York.* As groat	£500	£1000
1844	**Penny.** *London.* Annulets in two qtrs.	£15	£35
1845	*Calais.* Annulets at neck. ℞. As above	£13	£26
1846	— — only one annulet on *rev.*	£17	£40
1847	*York.* As London, but lis at neck	£500	£950
1848	**Halfpenny.** *London.* As penny	£20	£42
1849	*Calais.* Similar, but annulets at neck	£18	£40
1850	*York.* Similar, but lis at neck	£350	£700
1851	**Farthing.** *London.* As penny, but *mm.* cross pommée	£175	£350
1852	*Calais.* Similar, but annulets at neck	£275	£550

1843   1849   1852

Annulet-trefoil sub-issue

		F	VF
1853	**Groat.** *London.* As 1835, but trefoil of pellets to l. of crown (*North*)	£50	£125
1854	*Calais.* Similar, but annulets by neck also	£40	£105
1855	**Halfgroat.** *Calais.* Similar	£50	£125
1856	**Penny.** *Calais.* Similar	£60	£150
1857	— — only one annulet on *rev.*	£75	£185

Rosette-mascle issue, 1427–30. All with rosettes (early) or rosettes and mascles somewhere in the legends.

		F	VF
		F	VF
1858	**Groat.** *London*	£32	£75
1859	*Calais*	£18	£40
1860	— mascle in two spandrels (as illus. 1863)	£35	£90

1861   1863   1872

1861	**Halfgroat.** *London*	£25	£60
1862	*Calais*	£18	£38
1863	— mascle in two spandrels, as illustrated	£35	£90
1864	**Penny,** *London*	£24	£50
1865	*Calais*	£18	£40
1866	*York.* Archb. Kemp. Crosses by hair, no rosette	£18	£40
1867	— — Saltires by hair, no rosette	£18	£40
1868	— — Mullets by crown	£18	£40
1869	*Durham*, Bp. Langley. Large star to l. of crown, no rosette, DVnOLMI	£60	£160
1870	**Halfpenny,** *London*	£22	£45
1871	*Calais*	£18	£40
1872	**Farthing,** *London*	£110	£225
1873	*Calais. Mm.* cross pommée	£120	£250

1879   1884

Pinecone-mascle issue, 1430–4. All with pinecones and mascles in legends

1874	**Groat,** *London*	£27	£65
1875	*Calais*	£22	£55
1876	**Halfgroat,** *London*	£22	£50
1877	*Calais*	£20	£45
1878	**Penny,** *London*	£35	£80
1879	*Calais*	£24	£55
1880	*York*, Archb. Kemp. Mullet by crown, quatrefoil in centre of *rev.*	£20	£42
1881	— — rosette on breast, no quatrefoil	£18	£40
1882	— — mullet on breast, no quatrefoil	£40	£85
1883	*Durham*, Bp. Langley. DVnOLMI	£75	£200
1884	**Halfpenny,** *London*	£20	£45
1885	*Calais*	£20	£45

Pinecone-mascle issue, *continued.*

		F	*VF*
1886	**Farthing,** *London*	£100	£225
1887	*Calais. Mm.* cross pommée	£150	£325

Leaf-mascle issue, 1434–5. Usually with a mascle in the legend and a leaf somewhere in the design.

1888	**Groat,** *London.* Leaf below bust	£40	£100
1889	— — *rev.* of last or next coinage	£35	£90
1890	*Calais.* Leaf below bust, and usually below MЄVM	£28	£75
1891	**Halfgroat,** *London.* No leaf, pellet under TAS and DON	£30	£70
1892	*Calais.* Leaf below bust, and sometimes on *rev.*	£32	£75
1893	**Penny,** *London.* Leaf on breast, no stops on *rev.*	£24	£55
1894	*Calais.* Leaf on breast and below SIЄ	£20	£45
1895	**Halfpenny,** *London.* Leaf on breast and on *rev.*	£20	£45
1896	*Calais.* Leaf on breast and below SIЄ	£45	£100

1892   1897   1912

Leaf-trefoil issue, 1435–8. Mostly with leaves and trefoil of pellets in the legends.

1897	**Groat,** *London.* Leaf on breast	£37	£90
1898	— without leaf on breast	£30	£75
1899	*Calais.* Leaf on breast	*Extremely rare*	
1900	**Halfgroat,** *London.* Leaf on breast; *mm.* plain cross	£22	£48
1901	— *O. mm.* cross fleury; leaf on breast	£22	£48
1902	— — without leaf on breast	£22	£48
1903	**Penny,** *London.* Leaf on breast	£18	£40
1903A	*Calais.* Similar	*Unique*	
1904	*Durham,* Bp. Neville. Leaf on breast. ℞. Rings in centre, no stops, DVnOLM	£80	£200
1905	**Halfpenny,** *London.* Leaf on breast	£22	£50
1906	— without leaf on breast	£24	£55
1907	**Farthing,** *London.* Leaf on breast; stops, trefoil and saltire on *obv.*	£100	£250

Trefoil issue, 1438–43. Trefoil of pellets either side of neck and in legend, leaf on breast.

1908	**Groat,** *London.* Sometimes a leaf before LON	£35	£85
1909	— Fleurs in spandrels, sometimes extra pellet in two qtrs.	£40	£90
1910	— Trefoils in place of fleurs at shoulders, none by neck, sometimes extra pellets	£35	£80
1911	*Calais*	£100	£250
1912	**Halfpenny,** *London*	£45	£100

EDWARD IV, First Reign, 1461–70

In order to increase the supply of bullion to the mint the weight of the penny was reduced to 12 grains in 1464, and the current value of the noble was raised to 8s. 4d. Later, in 1465, a new gold coin was issued, the Ryal or "Rose Noble", weighing 120 grains and having a value of 10s. However, as 6s. 8d. had become the standard professional fee the old noble was missed, and a new coin was issued to take its place, the Angel of 80 grains.

Royal mints were opened at Canterbury and York to help with the re-coinage, and other mints were set up at Bristol, Coventry and Norwich, though they were not open for long.

Reference: C. E. Blunt and C. A. Whitton, *The Coinage of Edward IV and Henry VI (Restored),* B.N.J. 1945–7.

Mintmarks

105	9	7a	33	99	28	74	11

1461–4	Lis (105)	1467–70	Lis (105, *York*)	
	Cross fleury (9)	1467–8	Crown (74)	often
	Plain cross (7a)		Sun (28)	combined
1464–5	Rose (33 and 34)	1468–9	Crown (74)	sometimes
1464–7	Pall (99, *Canterbury*)		Rose (33)	combined
1465–6	Sun (28)	1469–70	Long cross	often
1466–7	Crown (74)		fitchée (11)	combined
			Sun (28)	

GOLD

Heavy coinage, 1461–4

		F	VF
1946	**Noble** (= 6s. 8d., wt. 108 grs.). Normal type, but *obv.* legend commences at top left, lis below shield; *mm.* -/lis	£4000	£8000
1947	— Quatrefoil below sword arm; *mm.* rose/lis	*Extremely rare*	
1948	— ℞. Roses in two spandrels; *mm.* rose	*Extremely rare*	
1949	**Quarter noble**	*Unique*	

1946   1950

Light coinage, 1464–70

1950	**Ryal** or rose-noble (= 10s., wt. 120 grs.), *London.* Type as next illus. Large fleurs in spandrels; *mm.* 33–74	£325	£550
1951	— — Small trefoils in spandrels; *mm.* 74–11	£300	£525
1952	— Flemish imitative coinage (mostly 16th cent.)	£200	£400

Light coinage, *continued.*

		F	VF
1953	*Bristol.* B in waves, large fleurs; *mm.* 28, 74	£350	£750
1954	—— small fleurs in spandrels; *mm.* 74, 28	£350	£750
1955	*Coventry.* C in waves; *mm.* sun	£650	£1400
1956	*Norwich.* N in waves; *mm.* sun, rose?	£800	£1750
1957	*York.* Є in waves, large fleurs in spandrels, *mm.* 28, 105	£375	£800
1958	—— small fleurs, *mm.* 105, 28	£375	£800
1959	**Half-ryal,** *London.* As 1950	£250	£500
1960	*Bristol.* B in waves; *mm.* 28–28/74	£500	£1100
1961	*Coventry.* C in waves; *mm.* sun	£850	£1800
1962	*Norwich.* N in waves; *mm.* rose	£750	£1600

1963

1963	*York.* Є in waves; *mm.* 28, 105, 33/105	£275	£600
1964	**Quarter-ryal.** Shield in tressure of eight arcs, rose above. ℞. Somewhat as half ryal; *mm.* 28/33		*Unique?*
1965	Shield in quatrefoil, ℞ above, rose on l., sun on r.; *mm.* 33/28–74/33	£200	£425
1966	—— sun on l., rose on r.; *mm.* 74–11	£225	£475

1967

1967	**Angel** (= 6s. 8d., wt. 80 grs.). St. Michael spearing dragon. ℞. Ship, rays of sun at masthead, large rose and sun beside mast; *mm.* -/33		*Extremely rare*
1968	—— small rose and sun at mast; *mm.* -/74		*Extremely rare*

First reign

SILVER

1972   1985

Heavy coinage, 1461–4

		F	VF
1969	**Groat** (60 grs.). Group I, lis on neck, pellets by crown; *mm.* 9, 7a, 105, 9/105	£75	£175
1970	— Lis on breast, no pellets; *mm.* plain cross, 7a/105	£75	£165
1971	— — with pellets at crown; *mm.* plain cross	£75	£165
1972	II, quatrefoils by neck, crescent on breast; *mm.* rose	£75	£165
1973	III, similar, but trefoil on breast; *mm.* rose	£75	£165
1974	— — — eye in *rev.* inner legend, *mm.* rose	£75	£165
1975	— Similar, but no quatrefoils by bust	£85	£175
1976	— — Similar, but no trefoil on breast	£85	£175
1977	IV, annulets by neck, eye after TAS; *mm.* rose	£70	£150
1978	**Halfgroat.** I, lis on breast, pellets by crown and extra pellets in two qtrs.; *mm.* 9, 7a	£140	£300
1979	II, quatrefoils at neck, crescent on breast; *mm.* rose	£160	£350
1980	III, similar, but trefoil on breast, eye on *rev.*; *mm.* rose	£160	£350
1981	— Similar, but no mark on breast	£150	£325
1982	IV, annulets by neck, sometimes eye on *rev.*; *mm.* rose	£140	£300
1983	**Penny** (15 grs.), *London.* I, marks as 1978, but mascle after REX; *mm.* plain cross	£135	£275
1984	— II, quatrefoils by neck; *mm.* rose	£125	£250
1985	— III, similar, but eye after TAS; *mm.* rose	£120	£225
1986	— IV, annulets by neck; *mm.* rose	£150	£350
1987	*York*, Archb. Booth. Quatrefoils by bust, voided quatrefoil in centre of *rev.*; *mm.* rose	£120	£250
1988	*Durham.* O. of Hen. VI. ℞. DVnOLIn	£160	£350
	Some of the Durham pennies from local dies may belong to the heavy coinage period, but if so they are indistinguishable from the light coins.		
1989	**Halfpenny.** I, as 1983, but no mascle	£100	£200
1990	II, quatrefoils by bust; *mm.* rose	£65	£160
1991	— saltires by bust; *mm.* rose	£110	£220
1992	III, no marks by bust; *mm.* rose	£70	£175
1993	IV, annulets by bust; *mm.* rose	£70	£175
1994	**Farthing.** I, as 1989	*2 known*	

Light coinage, 1464–70. There is a great variety of groats and we give only a selection. Some have pellets in one quarter of the reverse, or trefoils over the crown; early coins have fleurs on the cusps of the tressure, then trefoils or no marks on the cusps, while the late coins have only trefoils.

		F	VF
1995	**Groat** (48 grs.), *London.* Annulets at neck, eye after TAS; *mm.* 33 (struck from heavy dies, IV)	£50	£125
1996	— — — Similar, but new dies, eye after TAS or DOn	£45	£115
1997	— Quatrefoils at neck, eye; *mm.* 33 (heavy dies, III)	£50	£125
1998	— — — Similar, but new dies, eye in *rev.* legend	£40	£110
1999	— No marks at neck, eye; *mm.* 33	£65	£150

2000   2002

2000	— Quatrefoils at neck, no eye; *mm.* 33, 74, 28, 74/28, 74/33, 11/28	£20	£45
2001	— — — rose or quatrefoil on breast; *mm.* 33, 74/28	£22	£60
2002	— No marks at neck; *mm.* 28, 74, 11/28, 11	£22	£60
2003	— Trefoils or crosses at neck; *mm.* 11/33, 11/28, 11	£22	£60
2004	*Bristol.* B on breast, quatrefoils at neck; *mm.* 28/33, 28, 28/74, 74, 74/28	£25	£65
2005	— — trefoils at neck; *mm.* 28	£30	£80
2006	— — no marks at neck; *mm.* 28	£35	£90
2007	— Without B, quatrefoils at neck; *mm.* 28	£28	£75
	Bristol is variously rendered as BRESTOLL, BRISTOLL, BRESTOW, BRISTOW.		
2008	*Coventry.* C on breast, quatrefoils at neck, COVETRE; *mm.* 28/33, 28	£75	£160
2009	— — Local dies, similar; *mm.* rose	£75	£160
2010	— — — as last, but no C or quatrefoils	£80	£200
2011	*Norwich.* n on breast, quatrefoils at neck, nORWIC or nORVIC, *mm.* 28/33, 28	£60	£150
2012	*York.* Є on breast, quatrefoils at neck, ЄBORACI; *mm.* 28, 105/74, 105, 105/28	£30	£75
2013	— Similar, but without Є on breast, *mm.* 105	£38	£85
2014	— Є on breast, trefoils at neck; *mm.* 105/28, 105	£25	£60
2015	**Halfgroat,** *London.* Annulets by neck (heavy dies); *mm.* 33	£85	£200
2016	— Quatrefoils by neck; *mm.* 33/-, 28/-, 74, 74/28	£30	£75
2017	— Saltires by neck; *mm.* 74, 74/28	£30	£75
2018	— Trefoils by neck; *mm.* 74, 74/28, 11/28	£25	£65
2019	— No marks by neck; *mm.* 11/28	£65	£160

Light coinage, silver, *continued.*

		F	VF
2020	**Halfgroat,** *Bristol.* Saltires or crosses by neck; *mm.* 33/28, 28, 74, 74/- ..	£65	£150
2021	— Quatrefoils by neck; *mm.* 28/-, 74, 74/-	£65	£140
2022	— Trefoils by neck; *mm.* 74	£75	£175
2023	— No marks by neck; *mm.* 74/28	£75	£175
2024	*Canterbury,* Archb. Bourchier (1464–7). Knot below bust; quatrefoils by neck; *mm.* 99/-, 99, 99/33, 99/28	£18	£40
2025	— — — quatrefoils omitted *mm.* 99	£18	£40
2026	— — — saltires by neck; *mm.* 99/-, 99/28	£20	£45
2026A	— — — trefoils by neck; *mm.* 99	£20	£45

2027   2030

		F	VF
2027	— — — wedges by hair and/or neck; *mm.* 99, 99/33, 99/28	£20	£50
2028	— — As 2024 or 2025, but no knot	£25	£60
2029	— Royal mint (1467–9). Quatrefoils by neck; *mm.* 74, 74/-	£17	£40
2030	— — Saltires by neck; *mm.* 74/-, 74	£20	£45
2031	— — Trefoils by neck; *mm.* 74, 74/-, 74/28, 33	£20	£45
2032	— No marks by neck; *mm.* 28	£50	£125
2033	*Coventry.* Crosses by neck; *mm.* sun		*Unique*
2034	*Norwich.* Saltires by neck; *mm.* sun		*Extremely rare*
2035	*York.* Quatrefoils by neck; *mm.* sun, lis, lis/-	£35	£110
2036	— Saltires by neck; *mm.* lis	£30	£80
2037	— Trefoils by neck; *mm.* lis, lis/-	£30	£80
2038	— Є on breast, quatrefoils by neck; *mm.* lis/-	£35	£85
2039	**Penny** (12 grs.), *London.* Annulets by neck (heavy dies); *mm.* 33	£70	£160
2040	— Quatrefoils by neck; *mm.* 28, 74	£20	£50
2041	— Trefoil and quatrefoil by neck; *mm.* 74	£28	£65
2042	— Saltires by neck; *mm.* 74	£28	£65
2043	— Trefoils by neck; *mm.* 74, 11	£20	£50
2044	— No marks by neck; *mm.* 11		*Extremely rare*
2045	*Bristol.* Crosses, quatrefoils or saltires by neck, BRISTOW; *mm.* crown ..	£60	£150
2046	— Quatrefoils by neck; BRI(trefoil)STOLL	£75	£185
2047	— Trefoil to r. of neck BRISTOLL	£100	£250
2048	*Canterbury,* Archb. Bourchier. Quatrefoils or saltires by neck, knot on breast; *mm.* pall	£35	£80
2049	— — Similar, but no marks by neck	£55	£125
2050	— — As 2048, but no knot	£40	£90
2051	— — Crosses by neck, no knot	£40	£90
2052	— Royal mint. Quatrefoils by neck; *mm.* crown	£90	£200

Light coinage silver, *continued.*

		F	VF
2053	**Penny,** *Durham,* King's Receiver (1462–4). Local dies, mostly with rose in centre of *rev.; mm.* 7a, 33	£20	£60
2054	— Bp. Lawrence Booth (1465–70). B and D by neck, B on *rev.; mm.* 33 . .	£22	£65
2055	— — Quatrefoil and B by neck; *mm.* 28	£24	£70
2056	— — B and quatrefoil by neck; *mm.* 74	*Extremely rare*	
2057	— — D and quatrefoil by neck; *mm.* 74	£26	£75
2058	— — Quatrefoils by neck; *mm.* crown	£30	£90
2059	— — Trefoils by neck; *mm.* crown	£30	£90
2060	— — Lis by neck; *mm.* crown	£30	£90
2061	*York,* Sede Vacante (1464–5). Quatrefoils at neck, no quatrefoil in centre of *rev.; mm.* 28, 33	£50	£125
2062	— Archb. Neville (1465–70). Local dies, G and key by neck, quatrefoil on *rev.; mm.* 33, 7a	£50	£125

2063   2068

		F	VF
2063	— — London-made dies, similar; *mm.* 28, 105, 11	£22	£70
2064	— — Similar, but no marks by neck; *mm.* large lis	*Extremely rare*	
2065	— — — Quatrefoils by neck; *mm.* large lis	£20	£45
2066	— — — Trefoils by neck; *mm.* large lis	£30	£65
2067	**Halfpenny,** *London.* Saltires by neck; *mm.* 34, 28, 74	£25	£55
2068	— Trefoils by neck; *mm.* 28, 74, 11	£22	£45
2069	— No marks by neck; *mm.* 11	*Unique?*	
2070	*Bristol.* Crosses by neck; *mm.* 74	£110	£250
2071	— Trefoils by neck; *mm.* 74	£90	£200
2072	*Canterbury,* Archb. Bourchier. No marks; *mm.* pall	£100	£225
2072A	— — — Trefoils by neck, *mm.* pall	£100	£225
2073	— Royal mint. Saltires by neck; *mm.* crown	£65	£140
2074	— — Trefoils by neck; *mm.* crown	£60	£125
2075	*York,* Royal mint. Saltires by neck; *mm.* lis/-, sun/-	£65	£140
2076	— Trefoils by neck; *mm.* lis/-	£60	£125
2077	**Farthing,** *London.* ЄDWARD DI GRA RЄX, no marks at neck, *mm.* 33 . . .	*Extremely rare*	
2077A	— Trefoils by neck, *mm.* 74	*Extremely rare*	

HENRY VI RESTORED, Oct. 1470–Apr. 1471

The coinage of this short restoration follows closely that of the previous reign. Only angel gold was issued, the ryal being discontinued. Many of the coins have the king's name reading hЄnRICV—a distinguishing feature.

Mintmarks

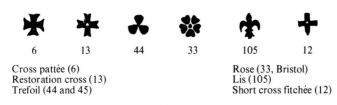

| 6 | 13 | 44 | 33 | 105 | 12 |

Cross pattée (6)
Restoration cross (13)
Trefoil (44 and 45)

Rose (33, Bristol)
Lis (105)
Short cross fitchée (12)

GOLD

2079

		F	VF
2078	**Angel,** *London.* As illus. but no B ; *mm.* -/6, 13, -/105, none	£650	£1300
2079	*Bristol.* B in waves; *mm.* -/13, none	£800	£1500
2080	**Half-angel,** *London.* As 2078; *mm.* -/6, -/13, -/105	£1250	£2750
2081	*Bristol.* B in waves; *mm.* -/13		*Unique*

SILVER

| 2082 | | | 2084 |

2082	**Groat,** *London.* Usual type; *mm.* 6, 6/13, 6/105, 13, 13/6, 13/105, 13/12 .	£120	£250
2083	*Bristol.* B on breast; *mm.* 13, 13/33, 13/44, 44, 44/13, 44/33, 44/12	£150	£350
2084	*York.* Є on breast; *mm.* lis, lis/sun	£125	£300
2085	**Halfgroat,** *London.* As 2082; *mm.* 13, 13/-	£200	£450
2086	*York.* Є on breast; *mm.* lis	*Extremely rare*	
2087	**Penny,** *London.* Usual type; *mm.* 6, 13, 12	£200	£450
2087A	*Bristol.* Similar; *mm.* 12		*Unique?*
2088	*York.* G and key by neck; *mm.* lis	£175	£350
2089	**Halfpenny,** *London.* As 2087; *mm.* 12	£200	£450
2090	*Bristol.* Similar; *mm.* cross		*Unique?*

EDWARD IV, Second Reign, 1471–83

The Angel and its half were the only gold denominations issued during this reign. The main types and weight standards remained the same as those of Edward's first reign light coinage. The use of the "initial mark" as a mintmark to denote the date of issue was now firmly established.

Mintmarks

33	12	55	44	55	28	56	17

37	6	18	19	20	31	11	38

1471–83	Rose (33, *York & Durham*)	1473–7	Cross pattée (6)
			Pierced cross 1 (18)
1471	Short cross fitchée (12)	1477–80	Pierced cross and pellet (19)
1471–2	Annulet (large, 55)		Pierced cross 2 (18)
	Trefoil (44)		Pierced cross, central pellet (20)
	Rose (33, *Bristol*)		Rose (33, *Canterbury*)
1471–3	Pansy (30, *Durham*)	1480–3	Heraldic cinquefoil (31)
1472–3	Annulet (small, 55)		Long cross fitchée (11, *Canterbury*)
	Sun (28, *Bristol*)		Halved sun and rose (38)?
1473–7	Pellet in annulet (56)		
	Cross and four pellets (17)		
	Cross in circle (37)		

GOLD

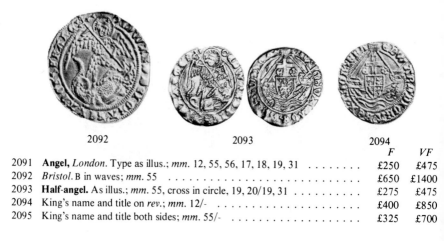

2092   2093   2094

		F	VF
2091	**Angel,** *London.* Type as illus.; *mm.* 12, 55, 56, 17, 18, 19, 31	£250	£475
2092	*Bristol.* B in waves; *mm.* 55	£650	£1400
2093	**Half-angel.** As illus.; *mm.* 55, cross in circle, 19, 20/19, 31	£275	£475
2094	King's name and title on *rev.*; *mm.* 12/-	£400	£850
2095	King's name and title both sides; *mm.* 55/-	£325	£700

SILVER

2101   2106

		F	VF
2096	**Groat,** *London.* Trefoils on cusps, no marks by bust; *mm.* 12–37	£25	£60
2097	— — roses by bust; *mm.* 56	£40	£100
2098	— Fleurs on cusps; no marks by bust; *mm.* 18–20	£25	£55
2099	— — pellets by bust; *mm.* 18 (2)	£60	£175
2100	— — rose on breast; *mm.* 31	£25	£60
2101	*Bristol.* B on breast; *mm.* 33, 33/55, 28/55, 55, 55/-, 28	£50	£150
2102	*York.* Є on breast; *mm.* lis	£60	£175
2103	**Halfgroat,** *London.* As 2096; *mm.* 12–31	£25	£60
2104	*Bristol.* B on breast; *mm.* 33/12	*Extremely rare*	
2105	*Canterbury* (Royal mint). As 2103; *mm.* 33, 11, 11/31, 31	£18	£45
2106	— C on breast; *mm.* rose	£18	£45
2107	— — Ŗ. C in centre; *mm.* rose	£18	£45
2108	— — Ŗ. Rose in centre; *mm.* rose	£20	£50
2109	*York.* Є on breast; *mm.* lis	£75	£200
2110	**Penny,** *London.* No marks by bust; *mm.* 12–31	£24	£60
2111	*Bristol.* Similar; *mm.* rose	*Unique?*	
2112	*Canterbury* (Royal). Similar; *mm.* 33, 11	£65	£140
2113	— C on breast; *mm.* 33	£80	£175

2115   2116   2123

2114	*Durham,* Bp. Booth (1471–6). No marks by neck; *mm.* 12, 44	£22	£60
2115	— — D in centre of *rev.*; B and trefoil by neck; *mm.* 44, 33, 56	£23	£65
2116	— — — two lis at neck; *mm.* 33	£23	£60
2117	— — — crosses over crown, and on breast; *mm.* 33	£20	£55
2118	— — — crosses over crown, V under CIVI; *mm.* 33, 30 . . . . , . .	£20	£55
2119	— — — B to l. of crown, V on breast and under CIVI	£20	£55
2120	— — — As last but crosses at shoulders	£20	£55
2121	— Sede Vacante (1476). Ŗ. D in centre; *mm.* 33	£50	£150
2122	— Bp. Dudley (1476–83). V to r. of neck; as last	£22	£60
2123	— — D and V by neck; as last, but *mm.* 31	£20	£55

Nos. 2117–2123 are from locally-made dies.

Second reign, silver, *continued.*

2125   2134

		F	VF
2124	*York*, Archb. Neville (1471–2). Quatrefoils by neck. ℞. Quatrefoil; *mm.* 12 (over lis)		*Extremely rare*
2125	—— Similar, but G and key by neck; *mm.* 12 (over lis)	£15	£35
2126	—— Neville suspended (1472–5). As last, but no quatrefoil in centre of *rev.*	£18	£37
2126A	—— no marks by bust, similar	£90	£225
2127	—— No marks by neck, quatrefoil on *rev.*; *mm.* 55, cross in circle, 33	£18	£40
2128	—— Similar but Є and rose by neck; *mm.* 33	£18	£40
2129	— Archb. Neville restored (1475–6). As last, but G and rose	£20	£45
2130	—— Similar, but G and key by bust	£18	£40
2131	— Sede Vacante (1476). As 2127, but rose on breast; *mm.* 33	£20	£45
2132	— Archb. Lawrence Booth (1476–80). B and key by bust, quatrefoil on *rev.*; *mm.* 33, 31	£15	£35
2133	— Sede Vacante (1480). Similar, but no quatrefoil on *rev.*; *mm.* 33	£18	£37
2134	— Archb. Rotherham (1480–3). T and slanting key by neck, quatrefoil on *rev.*; *mm.* 33	£15	£35
2135	——— Similar, but star on breast		£350
2136	——— Star on breast and to r. of crown	£70	**£150**
2137	**Halfpenny,** *London.* No marks by neck; *mm.* 12–31	£18	£50
2138	— Pellets at neck; *mm.* 18	£20	£55
2139	*Canterbury* (Royal). C on breast and in centre of *rev.*; *mm.* rose	£70	£150
2140	— C on breast only; *mm.* rose	£60	£130
2141	— Without C either side; *mm.* 11	£70	£160
2142	*Durham*, Bp. Booth. No marks by neck. ℞. DERAM, D in centre; *mm.* rose	£90	£200
2143	——— Similar, but V to l. of neck	£90	£200

EDWARD IV or V

Mintmark: Halved sun and rose.

The consensus of opinion now favours the last year of Edward IV for the introduction of the halved-sun-&-rose mintmark, but it is suggested that the earliest coins of Edward V's reign were struck from these Edw. IV dies. The coins are very rare.

GOLD

		F	VF
2144	**Angel.** As 2091	£700	£1750
2145	**Half-angel.** As 2093	*Extremely rare*	

2145 2146

SILVER

		F	VF
2146	**Groat.** As 2098	£325	£750
2147	**Penny.** As 2110	£400	£900
2148	**Halfpenny.** As 2137	£300	£700

EDWARD V, 1483

On the death of Edward IV, 9th April, 1483, the 12-year-old Prince Edward was placed under the guardianship of his uncle, Richard, Duke of Gloucester, but within eleven weeks Richard usurped the throne and Edward and his younger brother were confined to the Tower and were later murdered there. Very few coins of this reign have survived. The boar's head was a personal badge of Richard, Edward's 'Protector'.

Mintmarks: Boar's head on *obv.*, halved sun and rose on *rev.*

GOLD

		F	VF
2149	**Angel.** As 2091	*Extremely rare*	
	Note. *A fine specimen sold at auction in June 1985 for £11,200.*		
2150	**Half-angel.** Similar	*Unique*	

EDWARD V

SILVER

2151

		F	VF
2151	**Groat.** As 2098	£3000	£7500
2152	**Halfgroat.** As 2103	*Unknown?*	
2153	**Penny.** As 2110	*Unknown?*	

RICHARD III, 1483–5

Richard's brief and violent reign was brought to an end on the field of Bosworth. His coinage follows the pattern of the previous reigns. The smaller denominations of the London mint are all rare.

Mintmarks

38	62	63	105	33

Halved sun and rose, 3 styles (38, 39 and another with the sun more solid, see *North*).
Boar's head, narrow (62) wide (63).
Lis (105, *Durham*)
Rose only (33).

GOLD

2154	**Angel.** Reading ЄDWARD but with R (over Є) and rose by mast; *mm.* sun and rose	*Unique*	
2155	— Similar, but boar's head *mm.* on *obv.*	*Extremely rare*	

2156   2158

2156	Reading RICARD or RICAD. Ɍ. R and rose by mast; *mm.* various combinations	£700	£1500
2157	— Similar, but R by mast over Є (?)	£750	£1600
2158	**Half-angel.** Ɍ. R and rose by mast; *mm.* boar's head	*Extremely rare*	

SILVER

2159   2160

		F	VF
2159	**Groat,** *London. Mm.* various combinations	£225	£450
2160	— Pellet below bust	£225	£450
2161	*York. Mm.* sun and rose (*obv.*)	£400	£900
2162	**Halfgroat.** *Mm.* sun and rose or on *obv.* only	£750	£1500
2163	Pellet below bust; *mm.* sun and rose	£800	£1600
2164	— *mm.* boar's head (*obv.*)	£850	£1750
2165	**Penny,** *London. Mm.* boar's head (*obv.*)		*Unique*

This was the R. Carlyon-Britton specimen. It was stolen from our premises Feb. 1962.

2168   2169

2166	*York,* Archb. Rotherham. ℞. Quatrefoil in centre; *mm.* sun and rose	£300	£550
2167	— — T and upright key at neck; *mm.* rose	£200	£375
2168	— — — *mm.* boar's head	£200	£375
2169	*Durham,* Bp. Sherwood. S on breast. ℞. D in centre; *mm.* lis	£165	£325
2170	**Halfpenny,** *London. Mm.* sun and rose	£325	£600
2171	— *Mm.* boar's head		*Extremely rare*

HENRY VII, 1485–1509

For the first four years of his reign Henry's coins differ only in name and mintmark from those of his predecessors, but in 1489 radical changes were made in the coinage. Though the pound sterling had been a denomination of account for centuries a pound coin had never been minted. Now a magnificent gold pound was issued which, from the design of the king enthroned in majesty, was called a 'Sovereign'. The reverse had the royal arms set in the centre of a Tudor rose. A few years later the angel was restyled and St. Michael, who is depicted about to thrust Satan into the Pit with a cross-topped lance, is no longer a feathered figure but is clad in armour of Renaissance style. A gold ryal of ten shillings was also minted again for a brief period.

The other major innovation was the introduction of the Shilling in the opening years of the 16th century. It is remarkable for the very fine profile portrait of the King which replaces the representational image of a monarch that had served on the coinage for the past couple of centuries. This new portrait was also used on groats and halfgroats but not on the smaller denominations.

Mintmarks

| 39 | 41 | 40 | 42 | 33 | 11 | 7a | 123 |

| 105 | 76b | 31 | 78 | 30 | 91 | 43 | 57 |

| 85 | 94 | 118 | 21 | 33 | 53 |

1485–7	Halved sun and rose (39)	1495–8	Pansy (30)
	Lis upon sun and rose (41)		Tun (123, *Canterbury*)
	Lis upon half rose (40)		Lis (105, *York*)
	Lis-rose dimidiated (42)	1498–9	Crowned leopard's head (91)
	Rose (33, *York*)		Lis issuant from rose (43)
1487	Lis (105)		Tun (123, *Canterbury*)
	Cross fitchy (11)	1499–1502	Anchor (57)
1487–8	Rose (33)	1502–4	Greyhound's head (85)
	Plain cross (7a, *Durham*)		Lis (105, profile issue only)
1488–9	No marks		Martlet (94, *York*)
1489–93	Cinquefoil (31)	1504–5	Cross-crosslet (21)
	Crozier (76b, *Durham*)	1504–9	Martlet (94, *York* and
1492	Cross fitchy (11, gold only)		*Canterbury*)
1493–5	Escallop (78)		Rose (33, *York* and
	Dragon (118, gold only)		*Canterbury*)
	Lis (105, *Canterbury* and	1505–9	Pheon (53)
	York)		
	Tun (123, *Canterbury*)		

The coins are placed in groups, as in Brooke, *English Coins*, to correspond to the classification of the groats.

GOLD

		F	VF
2172	**Sovereign** (20s; wt. 240 grs.). Group I. Large figure of king sitting on throne with low back. ℞. Large Tudor rose bearing small shield; *mm.* 11		*Extremely rare*
2173	II. *O.* Somewhat similar but no lis as background. ℞. Large shield crowned on large Tudor rose; *mm.* 31		*Unique*

2174

<table>
<tr><td></td><td></td><td>F</td><td>VF</td></tr>
</table>

2174 III. King on high-backed very ornamental throne, with greyhound and
dragon on side pillars. ℞. Shield on Tudor rose; *mm.* 118 . . . .   £5500 £12,500

2175 IV. Similar but throne with high canopy breaking legend and broad seat,
mm. 105/118 . . . .   £5000 £11,500

2176 — Similar but narrow throne with a portcullis below the king's feet (like
Henry VIII); *mm.* 105/21, 105/53 . . . .   £5250 £11500

2177 **Double-sovereign** and **Treble-sovereign** from sovereign dies. These
piedforts were probably intended as presentation pieces . . . .   *Unique*

2178

2178 **Ryal** (10s.). As illustration: *mm.* 11 . . . .   £6500 £15000

2181   2183

Gold

		F	VF
2179	**Angel** (6s. 8d). I. Angel of old type with one foot on dragon. ℞. PЄR CRVCЄM, etc., *mm.* 39, 41, 40, 33	£235	£500
2180	—— Name altered from RICARD and h on *rev.* from Є	£400	£850
2181	II. As 2179, but *mm.* none, 31/-, 31/78	£210	£425
2182	—— ℞. IhC AVTЄ TRANSIЄNS etc.; *mm.* none	£275	£575
2183	III. New dies, angel with both feet on dragon; *mm.* 78, 30, 43, 57, 85 (large straight lettering)	£210	£425
2184	—— ℞. IhC AVG TRANSIЄNS, etc.; *mm.* 78	£250	£525
2185	IV. Small square lettering; *mm.* 85	£210	£475
2186	— Tall thin lettering; *mm.* 21	£210	£425
2187	V. Large crook-shaped abbreviation after hЄnRIC; *mm.* 21, 21 and 53, 53	£210	£425
2188	**Half-angel or angelet.** I. Mm. 39 (old dies altered), 41	£250	£500
2189	III. Angel with both feet on dragon: *mm.* 30, 57/30, 57/85	£165	£350
2190	IV. Small square lettering; *mm.* 33	£175	£370
2191	— Tall thin lettering; *mm.* 33/21	£175	£370
2192	V. As angel; *mm.* pheon	£165	£350

SILVER

Facing bust issues. Including "Sovereign" type pennies.

2194    2195

		F	VF
2193	**Groat.** I. Open crown; *mm.* 39, 40, 40/41, 41, 42	£50	£120
2194	—— crosses or saltires by neck, 33, 11, 105 . . . . . . *from*	£70	£135
2195	II. Crown with two unjewelled arches; *mm.* none, 31	£27	£60
2196	—— similar but crosses by neck; *mm.* none, -/105	£35	£90
2197	—— ℞. Portcullis over long cross; *mm.* -/lis	*Extremely rare*	

2198    2199    2201

		F	VF
2198	IIIa. Crown with two jewelled arches, bust as types I & II; *mm.* 31	£32	£75
2198A	IIIb. Similar, but new bust with realistic hair; *mm.* 78, 30	£27	£60
2199	IIIc. Crown with one plain and one jewelled arch; *mm.* 30, 91, 43, 43/57, 57, 57/85, 85	£27	£60
2200	IVa. Wide single arch crown; arch is single bar with 4 crockets; *mm.* 85, 85/33, 21	£26	£65

		F	*VF*
2201	IVb. — Similar, but arch is double bar with 6 uprights as jewels; *mm.* 85, 21/85,21	£25	£65
2202	**Halfgroat,** *London.* I. Open crown, tressure unbroken; *mm.* 41, 40/-	£225	£500
2203	—IIIa. Double arched crown, rosettes on tressure; *mm.* 78	£25	£55
2204	—IIIb. Similar, nothing on tressure. ℞. Lozenge panel in centre; *mm.* lis	£25	£55
2205	——Similar, but also with lis on breast	£25	£55
2206	— IIIc. Unarched crown with tressure broken. ℞. Lozenge panel in centre; *mm.* lis	£20	£45
2206A	———Similar but smaller dies and much smaller lettering	£20	£45

2211   2214

		F	*VF*
2207	*Canterbury,* Archb. Morton. I. Open crown, crosses by neck. ℞. m in centre; *mm.* tun	£30	£75
2208	—— II. Similar, but double-arched crown; *no mm.*	£17	£40
2209	— King and Archb. jointly. As last but without m; (a) early lettering, trefoil stops; *mm.* lis, tun and lis/lis	£12	£30
2210	—— (b) ornate lettering, rosette stops; *mm.* tun and lis/-, tun/lis, tun ...	£12	£30
2211	—— (c) — saltire or no stops; *mm.* 123, 123 & 30/123	£11	£30
2212	*York,* Royal Mint. (a) Double-arched crown, lis on breast (rarely omitted). ℞. Lozenge panel in centre; *mm.* lis	£20	£45
2213	—— (b) Similar, but unarched crown, tressure broken	£12	£30
2214	— Archb. Savage. (a) Double-arched crown, keys at neck, no tressure; ornate lettering; *mm.* martlet	£12	£30
2215	—— (b) Similar, but fleured tressure, small square lettering	£12	£30
2216	—— (c) As last, but tall thin lettering	£12	£30
2217	— Sede Vacante (1507/8). As last but no keys	£17	£45

2221   2226

		F	*VF*
2218	**Penny.** Old type. *London*; *mm.* 41	£100	£250
2219	———crosses by bust, *mm.* small cross	*Extremely rare*	
2220	— *Canterbury,* Archb. Morton. Open crown, *mm.* tun. ℞. m in centre ..	£100	£250
2221	—— King and Archb. jointly, arched crown; *mm.* tun	£40	£100
2222	— *Durham,* Bp. Sherwood. S on breast. ℞. D in centre; *mm.* 7a	£75	£175
2223	— *York,* Archb. Rotherham. With or without cross on breast, *mm.* 41, T and cross at neck. ℞. h in centre	£35	£90
2224	———T and trefoil at neck. ℞. Quatrefoil in centre and two extra pellets	£40	£100

Facing bust issues.

		F	VF
2225	**Penny.** "Sovereign" type. *London.* Early lettering, trefoil stops, no pillars to throne; no *mm.*	£45	£110
2226	———— single pillar on king's right side; no *mm.* or 31	£20	£50
2227	—— Ornate letters, rosette stops, single pillar; *mm.* lis	£25	£60
2228	———— saltire stops, two pillars; *mm.* none, 30	£20	£50
2229	—— Similar, but small square lettering; no *mm.*	£20	£50
2230	——— Similar, but lettering as profile groats two double pillars; *mm.* 21, 53	£25	£60
2231	— *Durham*, Bp. Sherwood. Crozier to r. of king, throne with one pillar. ℞. D and S beside shield	£28	£70
2232	—— Throne with two pillars, no crozier. ℞. As last	£28	£70
2233	—— Bp. Fox. Throne with one pillar. ℞. Mitre above shield, RD or DR at sides	£25	£60
2234	—— Similar, but two pillars	£28	£70

2231   2233   2235

		F	VF
2235	*York*, Archb. Rotherham. Keys below shield; early lettering, trefoil stops, no pillars to throne	£18	£45
2236	———— single pillar	£18	£45
2237	———— ornate lettering, rosette or no stops, single pillar	£18	£45
2238	—————— two pillars sometimes with crosses between legs of throne	£18	£45

2245   2248   2249

		F	VF
2239	**Halfpenny,** *London.* I. Open crown; *mm.* 41, 42	£40	£100
2240	——— trefoils at neck; no *mm.*, rose	£40	£100
2241	——— crosses at neck; *mm.* 33, 11?	£25	£70
2242	— II. Arched crown; *mm.* cinquefoil, none?	£18	£45
2243	——— saltires at neck; no *mm.*	£15	£40
2244	— III. Crown with lower arch, ornate lettering; no *mm.*	£18	£45
2245	— V. Much smaller portrait; *mm.* pheon	£25	£60
2246	*Canterbury*, Archb. Morton. I. Open crown. ℞. 𝔪 in centre	£75	£175
2247	—— II. Similar, but arched crown, saltires by bust; *mm.* profile eye (82)	£100	£225
2248	— King and Archb. III. Arched crown; *mm.* none, 105	£45	£110
2249	*York*, Archb. Savage. Arched crown, key below bust	£45	£110
2250	**Farthing,** hᴇnRIC DI GRA RᴇX (A)	£150	£300

Profile issue

2253

		F	VF
2251	**Testoon** (1s.). Type as groat. hҽnRIC (VS); *mm.* lis	£4000	£8500
2252	— hҽnRIC VII; *mm.* lis	£4500	£10000
2253	— hҽnRIC SҽPTIM; *mm.* lis	£6000	£12500

2254   2258

2254	**Groat,** *Tentative issue* (contemporary with full-face groats). Double band to crown, hҽnRIC VII; *mm.* none, 105/-, -/105: 105/85, 105, 85, 21	£125	£275
2255	— — tressure on *obv.; mm.* 21	£2000	£4500
2256	— — hҽnRIC (VS); *mm.* 105, -/105, 105/85, none	£350	£750
2257	— — hҽnRIC SҽPTIM; *mm.* -/105	£2250	£5500
2258	*Regular issue.* Triple band to crown; *mm.* 21, 21 and 53/21, 21/21 and 53, 53	£40	£100

2261   2263

2259	**Halfgroat,** *London.* As last; *mm.* 105, 53/105, 53	£35	£80
2260	— — no numeral after King's name, no *mm.,* -/lis	£150	£350
2261	*Canterbury,* King and Archb. As London, but *mm.* 94, 33	£30	£65
2262	*York,* Archb. Bainbridge. As London, but two keys below shield; *mm.* 94, 33	£25	£65
2263	— — XB beside shield; *mm.* 33/94	£150	£350

HENRY VIII, 1509–47

Henry VIII is held in ill-regard by numismatists as being the author of the debasement of England's gold and silver coinage; but there were also other important numismatic innovations during his reign. For the first sixteen years of the reign the coinage closely followed the pattern of the previous issues, even to the extent of retaining the portrait of Henry VII on the larger silver coins.

In 1526, in an effort to prevent the drain of gold to continental Europe, the value of English gold was cried up by 10%, the sovereign to 22s. 0d. and the angel to 7s. 4d., and a new coin valued at 4s. 6d.—the Crown of the Rose—was introduced as a competitor to the French *écu au soleil*. The new crown was not a success and within a few months it was replaced by the Crown of the Double Rose valued at 5 shillings but made of gold of only 22 carat fineness, the first time gold had been minted below the standard $23\frac{1}{4}$ carat. At the same time the sovereign was again revalued to 22s. 6d. and the angel to 7s. 6d., with a new coin, the George Noble, valued at 6s. 8d. (one-third pound).

The royal cyphers on some of the gold crowns and half-crowns combine the initial of Henry with those of his queens: Katherine of Aragon, Anne Boleyn and Jane Seymour. The architect of this coinage reform was the Chancellor, Cardinal Thomas Wolsey, but besides his other changes he had minted at York a groat bearing his initials and cardinal's hat in addition to the other denominations normally authorized for the ecclesiastical mints.

In view of Henry's final break with Rome in 1534, followed by the Act of Supremacy of 1535, it was hardly surprising that the Church's coining privileges in England were finally terminated and the mints of Durham and York (ecclesiastical) were closed.

In 1544, to help finance the king's inordinate extravagances, it was decided to extend the process of debasement. Initially all the "fine" gold coins were reduced in quality to 23 carat then the following year gold was issued of 22 carat and later of 20 carat fineness. Concurrently the silver coins were reduced from the sterling standard fineness of 11 oz. 2 dwt. (i.e. .925 silver) to 9 oz. (.750), and later to 6 oz. (.500) and eventually 4 oz. (.333) fineness. Henry's nickname of "Old Coppernose" was earned, not through his own personal characteristics, but by his last poor 'silver' coins which soon displayed their two-thirds copper content once they became slightly worn.

Mintmarks

| 53 | 69 | 70 | 108 | 33 | 94 | 73 | 11 |

| 105 | 22 | 23 | 30 | 78 | 15 | 24 | 110 |

1509–26	Pheon (53)		Lis (105, *Canterbury, Durham*)
	Castle (69)		
	Castle with H (70, gold)	1509–14	Martlet (94, *York*)
	Portcullis crowned (108)	1509–23	Radiant star (22, *Durham*)
	Rose (33, *Canterbury*)	1514–26	Star (23, *York*)
	Martlet (94, *Canterbury*)		Pansy (30, *York*)
	Pomegranate (73, but broader, *Cant.*)		Escallop (78, *York*)
			Voided cross (15, *York*)
	Cross fitchée (11, *Cant.*)	1523–26	Spur rowel (24, *Durham*)

52	72a	44	8	65a	114	121	90

36	106	56	S	Є	116

1526–44	Rose (33)		1526–32	Cross patonce (8, *Cant.*)
	Lis (105)			T (114, *Canterbury*)
	Sunburst (110)			Uncertain mark (121,
	Arrow (52)			*Canterbury*)
	Pheon (53)		1529–44	Radiant star (22, *Durham*)
	Lis (106)		1530–44	Key (90, *York*)
	Star (23, *Durham*)		1533–44	Catherine wheel (36
1526–9	Crescent (72a, *Durham*)			*Canterbury*)
	Trefoil (44 variety,		1544–7	Lis (105 and 106)
	Durham)			Pellet in annulet (56)
	Flower of eight petals and			S
	circle centre (*Durham*)			Є or E
1526–30	Cross (7a, sometimes		1546–7	WS monogram (116, *Bristol*)
	slightly voided, *York*)			
	Acorn (65a, *York*)			

GOLD

First coinage, 1509–26

2264

		F	VF
2264	**Sovereign** (20s.). As last sov. of Hen. VII; *mm.* 108	£3000	£7000
2265	**Angel** (6s. 8d.). As Hen. VII, but henRIC? VIII DI GRA REX, etc.; *mm.* 53, 69, 70, 108	£200	£450
2266	**Half-angel.** Similar; *mm.* 69, 70, 108 (sometimes without VIII)	£200	£450

Second coinage, 1526–44

		F	VF
2267	**Sovereign** (22s. 6d.). As 2264, but *mm.* 110, 105, 105/52	£3000	£7000
2268	**Angel** (7s. 6d.). As 2265, but henRIC VIII D G R etc.; *mm.* 110, 105	£250	£550
2269	**Half-angel.** Similar; *mm.* 105	£400	£900

Second coinage gold

2270   2272

		F	*VF*
2270	**George-noble** (6s. 8d.). As illustration; *mm.* rose	£2500	£6000
2270A	— Similar, but more modern ship with three masts, without initials hR. ℞. St. George brandishing sword behind head		*Unique*
2271	**Half-George-noble.** Similar		*Unique*
2272	**Crown of the rose** (4s. 6d.). As illustration; *mm.* rose		*Extremely rare*

2279   2285

2273	**Crown of the double-rose** (5s.). Double-rose crowned, hK (Henry and Katherine of Aragon) both crowned in field. ℞. Shield crowned; *mm.* rose .	£175	£350
2274	— hK both sides; *mm.* rose/lis, lis, arrow	£200	£375
2275	— hK / hA or hA / hK ; *mm.* arrow	£225	£550
2276	— hR / hK or hI / hR ; *mm.* arrow	*Both unique*	
2277	— hA (Anne Boleyn); *mm.* arrow	£250	£575
2278	— hA / hR ; *mm.* arrow	*Extremely rare*	
2279	— hI (Jane Seymour); *mm.* arrow	£225	£500
2280	— hK / hI ; *mm.* arrow	£250	£650
2281	— hR / hI ; *mm.* arrow	£250	£675
2282	— hR (Rex); *mm.* arrow	£200	£375
2283	— — but with hIBERIE REX ; *mm.* pheon	£400	£1000
2284	**Halfcrown.** Similar but king's name on *rev.*, no initials; *mm.* rose	£165	£375
2285	— hK uncrowned on *obv.*; *mm.* rose	£150	£350
2286	— hK uncrowned both sides; *mm.* rose/lis, lis, arrow	£160	£360
2287	— hI uncrowned both sides; *mm.* arrow	£200	£400
2288	— hR uncrowned both sides; hIB REX ; *mm.* pheon	£275	£750

Third coinage, 1544–7

2291

		F	VF
2289	**Sovereign, I** (20s., wt. 200 grs., 23 ct.). As illustration but king with larger face and larger design; *mm*. lis	£4000	£9500
2290	II (20s., wt. 200 or 192 grs., 23, 22 or 20 ct.). *London*. As illustration; *mm*. lis, pellet in annulet/lis	£1600	£3500
2291	— *Southwark*. Similar; *mm*. S, Є/S	£1550	£3350
2292	— — Similar but Є below shield; *mm*. S/Є	£1625	£3500
2293	— *Bristol*. As London but *mm*. WS/-	£1700	£4250
2294	**Half-sovereign** (wt. 96 grs.), *London*. As illus.; *mm*. lis, pellet in annulet	£200	£575
2295	— Similar, but with annulet on inner circle (*rev*.)	£225	£600
2296	*Southwark*. *Mm*. S	£225	£600
2297	— Є below shield; *mm*. S, Є	£200	£550
2298	*Bristol*. Lombardic lettering; *mm*. WS/ WS/-	£350	£900

2303   2304

2299	**Angel.** Annulet by angel's head and on ship, hЄnRIC' 8; *mm*. lis	£175	£400
2300	— Similar, but annulet one side only or none	£190	£420
2301	**Half-angel.** Annulet on ship; *mm*. lis	£165	£375
2302	— No annulet in ship	£190	£425
2303	— Three annulets on ship; *mm*. lis	£225	£450
2304	**Quarter-angel.** *Mm*. lis	£185	£425

		F	VF
2305	**Crown,** *London.* As 2283, but hᗺnRIC' 8; Lombardic lettering; *mm.* 56 . .	£140	£300
2306	— without RVTILAnS; *mm.* 56	£150	£325
2307	— — with annulet on inner circle	£175	£375
2308	*Southwark.* As 2305; *mm.* S, ᗺ, E/S, S/ᗺ	£175	£375
2309	*Bristol.* hᗺnRIC VIII. ℞. DEI GRA, etc.; *mm.* WS, -/WS	£140	£300
2310	— Similar but hᗺnRIC(VS) 8	£140	£300
2311	**Halfcrown,** *London.* As 2288 but hᗺnRIC' 8; *mm.* 56	£125	£275
2312	— — with annulet on inner circle	£135	£285
2313	*Southwark.* As 2311; *mm.* S	£160	£375
2314	— *O.* hᗺnRIC 8 ROSA SINᗺ SPIn. ℞. DEI GRA, etc.; *mm.* ᗺ	£175	£400
2315	*Bristol. O.* RVTILAnS, etc. ℞. hᗺnRIC 8; *mm.* WS/-	£170	£375

For other gold coins in Henry's name, see page 142.

SILVER

First coinage, 1509–26

2316   2327

		F	VF
2316	**Groat.** Portrait of Hen. VII. *London;* *mm.* 53, 69, 108	£75	£200
2317	— *Tournai;* *mm.* crowned T. ℞. CIVITAS TORnACᗺn *	£175	£550
2318	**Halfgroat.** Portrait of Hen. VII. *London;* *mm.* 108	£60	£150
2319	— *Canterbury,* Archb. Warham. POSVI *rev.;* *mm.* rose	£70	£180
2320	— — — WA above shield; *mm.* martlet	£30	£100
2321	— — — WA beside shield; *mm.* cross fitchée	£40	£120
2322	— — CIVITAS CAnTOR *rev.,* similar; *mm.* 73, 105, 11/105	£30	£90
2323	— *York,* POSVI *rev.,* Archb. Bainbridge (1508–14). Keys below shield; *mm.* martlet	£30	£90
2324	— — — XB beside shield; *mm.* martlet	£45	£125
2325	— — — Archb. Wolsey (1514–30). Keys and cardinal's hat below shield; *mm.* 94, 22	£70	£170
2326	— — CIVITAS ᗺBORACI *rev.* Similar; *mm.* 22, 23, 30, 78, voided cross .	£25	£60
2327	— — As last with TW beside shield; *mm.* voided cross	£27	£70
2327A	— *Tournai.* As 2317		*Unique*

* Other non-portrait groats and half-groats exist of this mint, captured during an invasion o France in 1513.

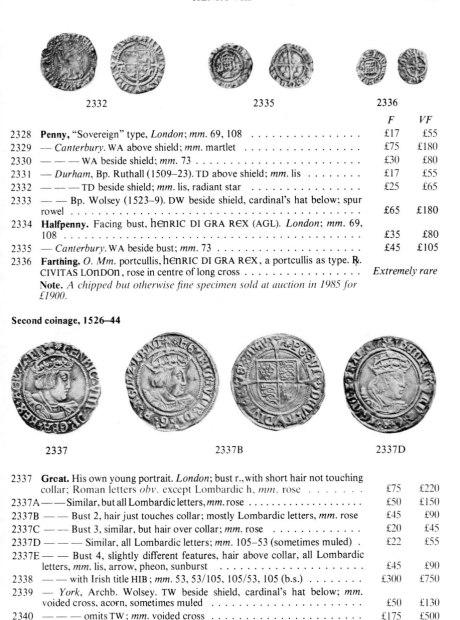

	2332	2335	2336		
				F	VF

2328 **Penny,** "Sovereign" type, *London; mm.* 69, 108 . . . . £17 £55

2329 — *Canterbury*. WA above shield; *mm.* martlet £75 £180

2330 — — WA beside shield; *mm.* 73 . . . . £30 £80

2331 — *Durham*, Bp. Ruthall (1509–23). TD above shield; *mm.* lis £17 £55

2332 — — — TD beside shield; *mm.* lis, radiant star £25 £65

2333 — — Bp. Wolsey (1523–9). DW beside shield, cardinal's hat below; spur rowel £65 £180

2334 **Halfpenny.** Facing bust, hꞒnRIC DI GRA RꞒX (AGL). *London; mm.* 69, 108 . . . . £35 £80

2335 — *Canterbury*. WA beside bust; *mm.* 73 . . . . £45 £105

2336 **Farthing.** *O. Mm.* portcullis, hꞒnRIC DI GRA RꞒX, a portcullis as type. ℞. CIVITAS LOnDOn, rose in centre of long cross . . . . *Extremely rare*

Note. *A chipped but otherwise fine specimen sold at auction in 1985 for £1900.*

Second coinage, 1526–44

2337	2337B	2337D

2337 **Groat.** His own young portrait. *London*; bust r., with short hair not touching collar; Roman letters *obv.* except Lombardic h, *mm.* rose £75 £220

2337A — — Similar, but all Lombardic letters, *mm.* rose £50 £150

2337B — — Bust 2, hair just touches collar; mostly Lombardic letters, *mm.* rose £45 £90

2337C — — Bust 3, similar, but hair over collar; *mm.* rose £20 £45

2337D — — — Similar, all Lombardic letters; *mm.* 105–53 (sometimes muled) . £22 £55

2337E — — Bust 4, slightly different features, hair above collar, all Lombardic letters, *mm.* lis, arrow, pheon, sunburst £45 £90

2338 — — with Irish title HIB; *mm.* 53, 53/105, 105/53, 105 (b.s.) £300 £750

2339 — *York*, Archb. Wolsey. TW beside shield, cardinal's hat below; *mm.* voided cross, acorn, sometimes muled £50 £130

2340 — — — omits TW; *mm.* voided cross £175 £500

Second Coinage Silver

	2342			2343			2348

		F	*VF*
2341	**Halfgroat.** Similar. *London*; *mm.* rose to arrow	£35	£80
2342	— — with Irish title HIB; *mm.* pheon	£400	£1000
2343	— *Canterbury*, Archb. Warham (—1532). ℞. CIVITAS CAnTOR, WA beside shield; *mm.* 121, 121/33, 8, 8/T, T	£17	£45
2344	— — — nothing by shield; *mm.* 121, 121/-	£30	£70
2345	— — Archb. Cranmer (1533—). TC beside shield; *mm.* 36, 36/-	£23	£60
2346	— *York*, Archb. Wolsey (—1530). ℞. CIVITAS EBORACI, TW beside shield, hat below; *mm.* voided cross	£23	£60
2347	— — Sede Vacante (1530/1). No marks; *mm.* key	£30	£65
2348	— — Archb. Lee (1531–44). EL or LE beside shield; *mm.* key	£23	£50

	2350		2354		2359

		F	*VF*
2349	**Penny,** "Sovereign" type, h . D . G . ROSA SInE SPInA , *London*; *mm.* rose to arrow	£20	£50
2350	— *Canterbury*. WA beside shield; *mm.* 121, 8, T	£60	£150
2351	— — TC beside shield; *mm.* 36	£50	£135
2352	— *Durham*, Bp. Wolsey (—1529). TW beside shield, hat below; *mm.* 23, 72a, 44	£30	£80
2353	— — Sede Vacante (1529–30). No marks; *mm. obv.* only, 23/-, 22/- . . .	£30	£85
2354	— — Bp. Tunstall (1530—). CD beside shield; *mm.* 23, 23/-, 22/-	£25	£70
2355	— *York*. EL beside shield; *mm.* key	£65	£150
2356	**Halfpenny.** Facing bust, h D G ROSA SIE SPIA. *London*; *mm.* rose to pheon?	£23	£50
2357	— *Canterbury*. WA beside bust; *mm.* 8?, T	£20	£45
2358	— — TC beside bust; *mm.* 36	£45	£100
2359	— *York*. TW beside bust; *mm.* cross voided	£55	£125
2360	— — Sede Vacante. Key below bust; *mm.* cross voided	£50	£110
2361	— — EL or LE beside bust; *mm.* key	£45	£90
2362	**Farthing.** *O.* RVTILANS ROSA, portcullis; *mm.* lis? ℞. HD . . . . . , long cross with pellet in each angle	*Extremely rare*	
2363	— — *mm.* arrow. ℞. hE. . D G . . AC, rose on long cross	*Extremely rare*	

Third coinage, 1544–7

Fair   Fine

2365

2384

		Fair	Fine
2364	**Testoon.** *Tower.* hꞓnRIC'. VIII, etc. ℞. Crowned rose between h and R.POSVI, etc.; *mm.* lis, two lis, and pellet in annulet	£100	£275
2365	— hꞓnRIC' 8 ; *mm.* lis, pellet in annulet	£90	£250
2366	— — annulet on inner circle of one or both sides; *mm.* pellet in annulet	£105	£300
2367	*Southwark.* As 2365. ℞. CIVITAS LOnDOn; *mm.* S, Є	£100	£275
2368	*Bristol. Mm.* -/WS monogram	£110	£350

Bust 1   Bust 2   Bust 3

		F	VF
		F	*VF*
2369	**Groat.** *Tower.* As 2365, busts 1, 2, 3; *mm.* lis	£30	£135
2370	— — annulet on inner circle	£40	£165
2371	*Southwark.* As 2367, busts 1, 2, 3, 4; no *mm.* or lis; S or S and Є in forks .	£35	£150
2372	*Bristol. Mm.* -/WS monogram	£37	£160
2373	*Canterbury.* Busts 1 var., 2; no *mm.*, 105/-	£37	£160
2374	*York.* Busts 1 var., 2, 3, no *mm.*	£37	£160
2375	**Halfgroat.** *Tower.* As 2365, bust 1; *mm.* lis, none	£50	£140
2376	*Southwark.* As 2367, bust 1; no *mm.*; S or Є in forks	£40	£135
2377	*Bristol. Mm.* -/WS monogram	£30	£125
2378	*Canterbury.* Bust 1; no *mm.*	£20	£100
2379	*York.* Bust 1; no *mm.*	£30	£125
2380	**Penny.** *Tower.* Facing bust; no *mm.* or lis	£25	£100
2381	*Southwark.* Facing bust; *mm.* S, Є	£35	£115
2382	*Bristol.* Facing bust; no *mm.*	£30	£110
2383	*Canterbury.* Facing bust; no *mm.*	£30	£115
2384	*York.* Facing bust; no *mm.*	£30	£110
2385	**Halfpenny.** *Tower.* Facing bust; no *mm.* or lis	£35	£115
2386	*Bristol.* Facing bust; no *mm.*	£65	£175
2387	*Canterbury.* Facing bust; no *mm.*	£37	£125
2388	*York.* Facing bust; no *mm.*	£37	£125

HENRY VIII POSTHUMOUS COINAGE, 1547–51

These coins were struck during the reign of Edward VI but bear the name and portrait of Henry VIII, except in the case of the half-sovereigns which bear the youthful head of Edward.

Mintmarks

| 56 | 105 | 52 | K | E | 116 |

| 66 | 115 | 33 | 122 | t | 94 |

1547	Annulet and pellet (56)	1549	TC monogram (115, *Bristol*)
1547–8	Lis (105)		Lis (105, *Canterbury*)
1547–9	Arrow (52)		Rose (33, *Canterbury*)
	K		Grapple (122)
	Roman E (*Southwark*)	1549/50	t (*Canterbury*)
	WS monogram (116, *Bristol*)	1550/1	Martlet (94)
1548–9	Bow (66, *Durham House*)		

GOLD

		F	VF
2389	**Sovereign,** *London.* As no. 2290, but Roman lettering; *mm.* lis	£1550	£3750
2390	— *Bristol.* Similar but *mm.* WS	£1700	£4250

| 2391 | | 2395 |

		F	VF
2391	**Half-sovereign.** As no. 2294, but with youthful portrait. *London*; *mm.* 52, 56, 105, 122, 94	£200	£550
2392	— — — K below shield; *mm.* -/K, none	£225	£575
2393	— — — grapple below shield; *mm.* grapple, none	£235	£600
2394	— *Southwark. Mm.* E, and usually E below shield, or none	£200	£550
2395	**Crown.** As no. 2305. *London*; *mm.* 52, -/K, 122, 94	£175	£525
2396	— Similar but transposed legends without numeral; *mm.* arrow/-	£250	£625
2397	— *Southwark.* Similar; *mm.* E	*Extremely rare*	
2398	— — King's name on *obv.*; *mm.* E/-	*Extremely rare*	
2399	**Halfcrown.** As no. 2311. *London*; *mm.* 52, K /-, 122/-, 94	£200	£500
2400	— *Southwark. Mm.* E, E/-, -/E	£200	£500

SILVER

		Fair	Fine
2401	**Testoon.** *Tower.* As 2365 with sleeve stops one side; no *mm.* or 56	£80	£275
2402	*Southwark.* As 2367; *mm.* S/E	£125	£375

Some of the Bristol testoons, groats and halfgroats with WS
*monogram were struck after the death of Henry VIII but cannot
be distinguished from those struck during his reign.*

Bust 4   Bust 5   Bust 6

		F	VF
2403	**Groat.** *Tower.* Busts 4, 5, 6 (and, rarely, 2). ℞. POSVI , etc.; *mm.* 105, 52, -/52, K /-, -/K , K , -/122, -/94, 94, 94/105, -/105, 105/94, none	£32	£140
2404	*Southwark.* Busts 4, 5, 6. ℞. CIVITAS LONDON ; no *mm.* lis, -/Æ ; S and Є or roses in forks	£34	£150
2405	*Durham House.* Bust 6. ℞. REDDE CVIQUE QVOD SVVM EST ; *mm.* bow .	£110	£375
2406	*Bristol. Mm.* WS on *rev.* (busts may vary from normal)	£45	£175
2407	— — *Mm.* TC on *rev.* Similar	£70	£275
2408	*Canterbury.* Busts 5, 6; no *mm.* or rose	£30	£125
2409	*York.* Busts 4, 5, 6; no *mm.* or lis	£32	£140
2410	**Halfgroat.** Bust l. *Tower.* POSVI, etc.; *mm.* 52, -/52, 52/K , -/K , 52/122, -/122, 105/94	£22	£90
2411	— *Southwark.* CIVITAS LONDON ; *mm.* 25, E , -/E, none	£20	£80
2412	— *Durham House.* ℞. REDD, etc.; *mm.* bow	£135	£300
2413	— *Bristol. Mm.* WS on *rev.*	£25	£100
2414	— — *mm.* TC on *rev.*	£38	£125
2415	— *Canterbury.* No *mm.* or t	£20	£80
2416	— *York.* No *mm.* (also bust 6)	£22	£90

2422   2418   2427

		F	VF
2417	**Penny.** *Tower.* CIVITAS LONDON. Facing bust; *mm.* 52/-, -/52, -/K , 122/-, -/122, none	£18	£100
2418	— — three-quarter bust; no *mm.*	£18	£100
2419	*Southwark.* As 2417; *mm.* E	£55	£175
2420	*Durham House.* As groat but shorter legend	£135	£400
2421	*Bristol.* Facing bust; no *mm.*	£22	£120
2422	*Canterbury.* Similar	£18	£100
2423	— three-quarters facing bust; no *mm.*	£18	£100
2424	*York.* Facing bust; no *mm.*	£18	£100
2425	— three-quarters facing bust; no *mm.*	£22	£120
2426	**Halfpenny.** *Tower.* 52?, none	£42	£150
2427	*Canterbury.* No *mm.*	£24	£110
2428	*York.* No *mm.*	£42	£150

EDWARD VI, 1547–53

Coinage in his own name

While base coins continued to be issued bearing the name of Henry VIII, plans were made early in Edward's reign to reform the coinage. As a first step, in 1549, the standard of the gold was raised to 22 carat and "silver" was increased to 50% silver content. Baser shillings were issued in 1550, but finally, in 1551, it was decided to resume the coinage of some "fine" gold and a new silver coinage was ordered of 11 oz. 1 dwt. fineness, i.e. almost up to the ancient standard. At the same time four new denominations were added to the coinage—the silver crown, halfcrown, sixpence and threepence. Pennies continued to be struck in base silver.

The first dates on English coinage appear in Roman numerals during this reign; MDXLVIII = 1548; MDXLIX = 1549; MDL = 1550; MDLI = 1551.

Mintmarks

66	52	35	115	E	53	122
44	t	T	111	Y	126	94	91A
92	105	y	97	123	78	26

1548–9	Bow (66, *Durham House*)	1549–50	6 (126 gold only)
1549	Arrow (52)	1550	Martlet (94)
	Rose (35)	1550–1	Leopard's head (91A)
	TC monogram (115, *Bristol*)		Lion (92)
	Roman E (*Southwark*)		Lis (105)
	Pheon (53)		Rose (33)
	Grapple (122)	1551	Yor y (117)
	Trefoil (44 variety)		Ostrich's head (97, gold only)
	t or T (*Canterbury*)	1551–3	Tun (123)
1549–50	Swan (111)		Escallop (78)
	Roman Y	1552–3	Pierced mullet (26, *York*)

GOLD

First period, Apr. 1547–Jan. 1549

2429   2431

		F	VF
2429	**Half-sovereign.** As 2391, but reading EDWARD 6. *Tower; mm.* arrow ...	£400	£850
2430	— *Southwark* (Usually with E or Є below shield); *mm.* E	£350	£750

F   VF

2431   **Crown.** RVTILANS, etc., crowned rose between E R both crowned. ℞.
       EDWARD 6, etc., crowned shield between ER both crowned; *mm.* arrow . .   *Unique*
2432   **Halfcrown.** Similar, but initials not crowned . . . .   *Extremely rare*

Second period, Jan. 1549–Apr. 1550

2433

2433   **Sovereign.** As illustration; *mm.* arrow, Y £1750   £4000

2435   2438

2434   **Half-sovereign.** Uncrowned bust. *London.* TIMOR etc., MDXLIX on *obv.*;
       mm. arrow . . . .   *Extremely rare*
2435   — — SCVTVM, etc., as illustration; *mm.* arrow, **6**, Y £450   £1250
2436   — *Durham House.* Similar with MDXLVIII at end of *obv.* legend; *mm.* bow   *Extremely rare*
2437   — — LVCERNA, etc., on *obv.*; *mm.* bow . . . .   *Extremely rare*
2438   Crowned bust. *London.* EDWARD VI, etc. ℞. SCVTVM, etc.; *mm.* 52, 122,
       111, Y, 94 . . . .   £400   £1100
2439   — *Durham House.* Half-length bust; *mm.* bow . . . .   *Unique*
2440   — — King's name on *obv.* and *rev.*; *mm.* bow £4000   £7500

2441   2444

2441   **Crown.** Uncrowned bust, as 2435; *mm.* arrow, **6**, Y, 52 . . . .   £625   £1500
2442   Crowned bust, as 2438; *mm.* 52, 122, 111, Y £600   £1400

Second period gold

		F	VF
2443	**Halfcrown.** Uncrowned bust; *mm.* arrow, Y	£600	£1500
2444	Crowned bust, as illus. above; *mm.* 52, 52/111, 122, Y	£550	£1400
2445	Similar, but king's name on *rev.*; *mm.* 52, 122	£600	£1500

Third period, 1550–3

2446	**"Fine" sovereign** (= 30s.). King on throne; *mm.* 97, 123	£8000	£20000
2447	**Double sovereign.** From the same dies	*Extremely rare*	

2448   2451

2448	**Angel** (= 10s.). As illustration; *mm.* 97, 123	£4000	£8000
2449	**Half-angel.** Similar, *mm.* 97		*Unique*
2450	**Sovereign.** (= 20s.). Half-length figure of king r., crowned and holding sword and orb. ℞. Crowned shield with supporters; *mm.* y, tun	£750	£1750
2451	**Half-sovereign.** As illustration above; *mm.* y, tun	£550	£1200
2452	**Crown.** Similar, but for *rev.* legend; *mm.* y, tun	£800	£1750
2453	**Halfcrown.** Similar	£800	£2000

SILVER

First period, Apr. 1547–Jan. 1549

2459   2460

2454	**Shilling.** Tower Mint. Crowned bust r. ℞.TIMOR, etc.MDXLVII, crowned garnished shield, ER at sides; *mm.* rose (? A pattern)	*Extremely rare*	
2455	**Groat.** Similar. *Tower.* ℞. Shield over cross, POSVI, etc.; *mm.* arrow	£325	£850
2456	— *Southwark.* ℞. CIVITAS LONDON ; *mm.* E or none	£350	£900
2457	**Halfgroat.** *Tower.* As groat	£300	£700
2458	*Southwark.* As groat; *mm.* arrow, E	£250	£600
2459	*Canterbury.* Similar. No *mm.*	£250	£600
2460	**Penny.** *Tower.* As halfgroat, but E.D.G. etc. ℞. CIVITAS LONDON ; *mm.* arrow	£225	£700
2461	— *Southwark.* As last, but *mm.* E	£225	£700
2462	*Bristol.* Similar, but no *mm.*	£225	£600

		F	VF
2463	**Halfpenny.** *Tower. O.* As 2460, *mm*. E (?). ℞. Cross and pellets	*Extremely rare*	
2464	— *Bristol.* Similar, but no *mm.*	£275	£600

Second period, Jan. 1549–Apr. 1550

2471

		Fair	Fine
2465	**Shilling.** As illus. *London.* MDXLIX or MDL; *mm*. 52–91A . . .	£15	£50
2466	— — Similar, but legends transposed, MDXLIX; *mm*. 52, 35, Y or none	£25	£80
	Note. *(2465 and 2466) Normally 80 grains, there are lighter (60 gns) slightly thinner coins of better appearance, although the silver content remains the same.*		
2467	— *Bristol.* MDXLIX; *mm.* TC	£200	£750
2468	— *Canterbury.* MDXLIX; *mm*. T or t	£40	£125
2469	— *Durham House.* ℞. TIMOR etc. MDXLIX; *mm*. bow	£175	£500
2470	— — Similar, but legends transposed	£185	£600
2471	— — No date. ℞. INIMICOS etc.	£100	£350
2472	— — Similar, but legends transposed	£125	£400
	For coins of Edward VI countermarked see p. 154.		

Third period, 1550–3
Base issue

2473	2475		2477

2473	**Shilling.** As 2465, MDL, MDLI; *mm*. lis, lion, rose	£25	£110
	For coins of Edward VI countermarked, see p. 154.		
2474	**Penny.** *London. O.* Rose. ℞. Shield; *mm*. escallop	£25	£75
2475	— — *York. Mm*. mullet, as illustration	£20	£50
2476	**Halfpenny.** As penny, but single rose	£75	£250
2477	**Farthing.** *O.* Portcullis. ℞. Cross and pellets	*Extremely rare*	

Fine silver issue

2478

			F	VF
2478	**Crown.** King on horseback with date below horse. ℞. Shield on cross; *mm.* y, 1551; tun, 1551–3		£200	£500

2479

2479	**Halfcrown.** Walking horse with plume; *mm.* y, 1551	£150	£425
2480	Galloping horse without plume; *mm.* tun, 1551–3	£200	£500
2481	Large walking horse without plume; *mm.* tun, 1553	£375	£1000
2482	**Shilling.** Facing bust, rose l., value VII r. *mm.* y, tun	£35	£110

2482   2483   2486

2483	**Sixpence.** *London.* As illustration	£50	£175
2484	*York.* As last, but CIVITAS EBORACI; *mm.* mullet	£175	£450
2485	**Threepence.** *London.* As sixpence, but III; *mm.* tun	£125	£400
2486	*York.* As 2484, but III by bust	£200	£500
2487	**Penny.** "Sovereign" type; *mm.* tun	*Extremely rare*	

MARY, 1553–4

All Mary's gold coin was struck in 23 carat $3\frac{1}{2}$ grain gold, the "crown" gold denominations being temporarily discontinued. The mintmarks appear at the end of the first word of the legends.

Mintmarks

Pomegranate   Half-rose (or half-rose and castle)

GOLD

2488

		F	VF
2488	**"Fine" Sovereign** (= 30s.). Queen enthroned. ℞. Shield on rose, MDLIII, MDLIIII and undated	£1600	£3500
2489	**Ryal** (= 15s.). Queen in ship, MDLIII	*Extremely rare*	
	Note. *A very fine specimen sold at auction in November 1985 for £13,000.*		
2490	**Angel** (= 10s.). Usual type; *mm.* pomegranate, half-rose	£450	£1000
2491	**Half-angel.** Similar; *mm.* pomegranate	£2000	£5000

2489   2492

SILVER

2492	**Groat.** Crowned bust l. ℞. VERITAS, etc.	£50	£150
2493	**Halfgroat.** Similar	£300	£750
2494	**Penny.** Similar, but M . D. G. ROSA, etc.	£300	£750
2495	— As last. ℞. CIVITAS LONDON	£250	£650
2495A	— Base penny. Similar to 2474 but M.D.G. etc.	£40	£125

PHILIP AND MARY, 1554–8

The groats and smaller silver coins of this period have Mary's portrait only, but the shillings and sixpences show the bust of the queen's husband, Philip of Spain.

Mintmarks

Lis (105)   ⚜   Half-rose and castle   ⌗

GOLD

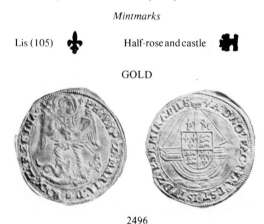

2496

		F	VF
2496	**Angel.** As illustration; *mm.* lis	£1350	£2650
2497	**Half-angel.** Similar	*Extremely rare*	

SILVER

2505   2510

2498	**Shilling.** Busts face-to-face, full titles, undated	£90	£275
2499	— — — also without mark of value	£180	£475
2500	— — 1554	£65	£250
2501	— English titles only 1554, 1555	£70	£275
2502	— — without mark of value, 1554, 1555	£200	£600
		Fair	
2503	— — date below bust, 1554, 1555 . . . . *Fair* £125		
2504	— — As last, but without ANG., 1555 . . . . *Fair* £150		
2505	**Sixpence.** Similar. Full titles, 1554	£125	£450
2506	— English titles only, 1555, 1557	£110	£400
2506A	— As last but heavy beaded i.C. on obv. 1555. (? Irish 4d. obv. mule) .	*Extremely rare*	
2507	— — date below bust, 1554, 1557 . . . . *Fair* £125		
2508	**Groat.** Crowned bust of Mary l. ℞. POSIMVS etc.; *mm.* lis	£50	£150
2509	**Halfgroat.** Similar, but POSVIM	£450	£950
2510	**Penny.** Similar to 2495, but P . Z . M . etc.; *mm.* lis	£300	£750
2511	**Base penny.** Similar to 2495A, but P . Z . M . etc.; *mm.* halved rose and H (or castle)	£40	£125

Note. *Similar pence of the York mint were made for currency in Ireland (see* Coins and Tokens of Ireland, *no.6502).*

ELIZABETH I, 1558–1603

Elizabeth's coinage is particularly interesting on account of the large number of different denominations issued. 'Crown' gold coins were again issued as well as the 'fine' gold denominations. In 1559 the base shillings of Edward VI second and third coinages were called in and countermarked for recirculation at reduced values. The normal silver coinage was initially struck at .916 fineness as in the previous reign but between 1560 and 1577 and after 1582 the old sterling standard of .925 was restored. Between 1578 and 1582 the standard was slightly reduced and the weights were reduced by 1/32nd in 1601. Gold was similarly reduced slightly in quality 1578–82, and there was a slight weight reduction in 1601.

To help alleviate the shortage of small change, and to avoid the expense of minting an impossibly small silver farthing, a threefarthing piece was introduced which would provide change if a penny was tendered for a farthing purchase. The sixpence, threepence, threehalfpence and threefarthings were marked with a rose behind the queen's head to distinguish them from the shilling, groat, halfgroat and penny.

Coins of exceedingly fine workmanship were produced in a screw press introduced by Eloye Mestrelle, a French moneyer, in 1561. With parts of the machinery powered by a horse-drawn mill, the coins produced came to be known as "mill money". Despite the superior quality of the coins produced the machinery was slow and inefficient compared to striking by hand. Mestrelle's dismissal was engineered in 1572 and six years later he was hanged for counterfeiting.

Mintmarks

| 106 | 21 | 94 | 23 | 53 | 33 | 107 | 92 |

| 74 | 71 | 26 | 77 | 65b | 27 | 7 | 14 |

| 113 | 60 | 54 | 79 | 72b | 86 | 123 | 124 |

| 90 | 57 | 0 | 1 | 2 |

1558–60	Lis (106)		1578–9	Greek cross (7)
1560–1	Cross crosslet (21)		1580–1	Latin cross (14)
	Martlet (94)		1582	Sword (113)
1560–6	Star (23, milled)		1582–3	Bell (60)
1561–5	Pheon (53)		1582–4	A (54)
1565	Rose (33)		1584–6	Escallop (79)
1566	Portcullis (107)		1587–9	Crescent (72b)
1566–7	Lion (92)		1590–2	Hand (86)
1567–70	Coronet (74)		1592–5	Tun (123)
	Lis (105, milled)		1594–6	Woolpack (124)
1569–71	Castle (71)		1595–8	Key (90)
1570	Pierced mullet (26, milled)		1597–1600	Anchor (57)
1572–3	Ermine (77)		1600	**0**
1573–4	Acorn (65b)		1601	**1**
1573–7	Eglantine (27)		1602	**2**

GOLD

Hammered Coinage

First to Third issues, 1559–78. ('Fine' gold of .979, 'Crown' gold of .916 fineness. Sovereigns of 240 grs. wt.). Mintmarks: lis to eglantine.

2512

		F	VF
2512	**'Fine' Sovereign** of 30 sh. Queen enthroned, tressure broken by throne. ℞. Arms on rose; *mm.* lis, cross-crosslet	£1400	£3000
2513	**Angel.** St. Michael. ℞. Ship. Wire line inner circles; *mm.* lis, 21	£300	£650
2514	— — Similar, but beaded inner circles; ship to r.; *mm.* 106, 21, 74, 77–27	£250	£500
2515	— — — Similar, but ship to l.; *mm.* 77–27	£275	£550
2516	**Half Angel.** As 2513, wire line inner circles; *mm.* lis	*Extremely rare*	
2517	— As 2514, beaded inner circles; *mm.* 106, 21, 74, 77–27	£180	£425
2518	**Quarter Angel.** Similar; *mm.* 106, 74, 77–27	£175	£400

2513   2520

2519	**Half Pound** of 10 sh. Young crowned bust l. ℞. Arms. Wire line inner circles; *mm.* lis	£400	£900
2520	— Similar, but beaded inner circles; *mm.* 21, 33–71	£325	£700
2521	**Crown.** As 2519; *mm.* lis	*Extremely rare*	
2522	— 2520; *mm.* 21, 33–71	£250	£625
2523	**Half Crown.** As 2519; *mm.* lis	*Extremely rare*	
2524	— As 2520; *mm.* 21, 33–71	£275	£650

Fourth Issue, 1578–82 ('Fine' gold only of .976). Mintmarks: Greek cross, Latin cross and sword.

		F	VF
2525	**Angel.** As 2514; *mm.* 7, 14, 113	£275	£600
2526	**Half Angel.** As 2517; *mm.* 7, 113	£180	£425
2527	— Similar, but without E and rose above ship; *mm.* 14	£375	£800
2528	**Quarter Angel.** As last; *mm.* 7, 14, 113	£175	£400

Fifth Issue, 1583–1600 ('Fine' gold of .979, 'crown' gold of .916; pound of 174.5 grs. wt.). Mintmarks: bell to **O**.

2529

		F	VF
2529	**Sovereign** (30 sh.). As 2512, but tressure not broken by back of throne; *mm.* 54–124	£1250	£2500
2530	**Ryal** (15 sh.). Queen in ship; *mm.* 54–86	£2250	£6000
2531	**Angel.** As 2514; *mm.* 60–123, 90–**O**	£250	£500
2532	**Half Angel.** As 2517; *mm.* 60–57	£180	£425
2533	**Quarter Angel.** As 2518; *mm.* 60–57	£175	£400
2534	**Pound** (20 sh.). Old bust l., with elaborate dress and profusion of hair; *mm.* 123–**O**	£650	£1400
2535	**Half Pound.** Similar; *mm.* 123–**O**	£450	£800
2536	**Crown.** Similar; *mm.* 123–90, **O**	£275	£650
2573	**Half Crown.** Similar; *mm.* 123–**O**	£250	£600

2534   2541

Sixth Issue, 1601–3 ('Fine' gold of .979, 'crown' gold of .916; Pound of 172 grs. wt.). Mintmarks: **1** and **2**

		F	VF
2538	**Angel.** As 2514; *mm.* **1, 2**	£300	£650
2539	**Pound.** As 2534; *mm.* **1, 2**	£800	£1800
2540	**Half Pound.** As 2535; *mm.* **1, 2**	£600	£1150
2541	**Crown.** As 2536; *mm.* **1, 2**	£400	£850
2542	**Half Crown.** As 2537; *mm.* **1, 2**	£275	£650

Milled Coinage, 1561–70

2543	**Half Pound.** Crowned bust l.; *mm.* star, lis	£750	£1750
2544	**Crown.** Similar; *mm.* star, lis	£900	£2250
2545	**Half Crown.** Similar; *mm.* star, lis	£1400	£3150

SILVER

Hammered Coinage

Countermarked Edward VI base shillings (1559)

2546   2547

2546	**Fourpence-halfpenny.** Edward VI 2nd period shillings countermarked on obverse with a portcullis; *mm.* 66, 52, t, 111 and Y	*Extremely rare*
2547	**Twopence-farthing.** Edward VI 3rd period shillings countermarked on obverse with a seated greyhound; *mm.* 92, 105 and 33	*Extremely rare*

First Issue, 1559–60 (.916 fine, shillings of 96 grs.)

2548

2548	**Shilling.** Without rose or date, ELIZABET(H), wire-line inner circles; *mm.* lis	£175	£500
2549	— Wire-line and beaded circles; *mm.* lis	£85	£250

2551

		F	VF
2550	**Groat.** Without rose or date, wire-line inner circles; *mm.* lis	£110	£250
2551	— Wire-line and beaded circles; *mm.* lis	£40	£100
2551A	Similar, with small bust, ? from half groat punch; *mm.* lis	*Extremely rare*	
2552	**Halfgroat.** Without rose or date, wire-line inner circles; *mm.* lis	£150	£350
2553	**Penny.** Without rose or date, wire-line inner circles; *mm.* lis	£115	£275
2554	Similar, but dated 1558	*Extremely rare*	

Second Issue, 1560–1 (.925 fineness, shilling of 96 grs.)

2555	**Shilling.** Without rose or date, beaded circles, ET instead of Z ; *mm.* cross crosslet, martlet	£50	£150
2556	**Groat.** As last, *mm.* cross crosslet, martlet	£50	£150
2557	**Halfgroat.** As last, *mm.* cross crosslet, martlet	£25	£80
2558	**Penny.** As last, *mm.* cross crosslet, martlet	£13	£35

Third Issue, 1561–77 (Same fineness and weight as last)

2561   2567   2571

		F	VF
2559	**Sixpence.** With rose and date 1561, large flan (27 mm. or more), large bust with hair swept back; *mm.* pheon	£150	£325
2560	— large flan, regular bust; *mm.* pheon	£25	£75
2561*	— 1561–77, regular flan and bust (up to 26.5 mm.); *mm.* pheon to eglantine	£17	£65
2562	Without rose, 1561; *mm.* pheon	*Extremely rare*	
2563	Without date; *mm.* lion, crown, ermine	*Extremely rare*	
2564	**Threepence.** With rose and date 1561, large flan (21 mm.); *mm.* pheon . . .	£22	£75
2565	— 1561–77, regular (19 mm.); *mm.* pheon to eglantine	£10	£38
2566	Without rose, 1568; *mm.* coronet		*Unique*
2567	**Halfgroat.** Without rose or date; *mm.* portcullis to castle	£25	£75
2568	**Threehalfpence.** With rose and date 1561, large flan (17 mm.); *mm.* pheon	£40	£100
2569	— 1561–2, 1564–70, 1572–7, regular flan (16 mm.); *mm.* pheon to eglantine	£25	£65
2570	**Penny.** Without rose or date; *mm.* 33–71, 27	£12	£35
2571	**Threefarthings.** With rose and date 1561–2, 1568, 1572–7; *mm.* 53, 74, 77–27 . . . . *fair* £15	£60	£175

* There are many different bust varieties within this issue.

Fourth Issue, 1578–82 (.921 fineness, shilling of 95.6 grs.)

			F	VF
2572	**Sixpence.** As 2561, 1578–82; *mm.* 7–113		£20	£60
2573	**Threepence.** As 2565, 1578–82; *mm.* 7–113		£18	£65
2574	**Threehalfpence.** As 2569, 1578–9, 1581–2; *mm.* 7–113		£20	£70
2575	**Penny.** As 2570; *mm.* 7–113		£15	£40
2576	**Threefarthings.** As 2571, 1578–9, 1581–2; *mm.* 7–113 . . . . *Fair* £25		£75	£175

2573   2577   2581

Fifth Issue, 1582–1600 (.925 fineness, shilling of 96 grs.)

		F	VF
2577	**Shilling.** Without rose and date, ELIZAB; *mm.* bell to **O**	£25	£90
2578	**Sixpence.** With rose and date 1582–1600; *mm.* bell to **O**	£20	£65
2579	**Halfgroat.** Without rose and date, E, D, G, ROSA etc., two pellets behind bust. ℞. CIVITAS LONDON; *mm.* bell to **O**	£10	£35
2580	**Penny.** As last, but no marks behind bust; *mm.* bell to **O**	£10	£35
2581	**Halfpenny.** Portcullis. ℞. Cross and pellets; *mm.* none, A to **O**	£30	£90

Sixth Issue, 1601–2 (.925 fineness, shilling of 93 grs.)

		F	VF
2582	**Crown.** Similar to illustration below; *mm.* **1, 2**	£275	£850

2583

		F	VF
2583	**Halfcrown.** Similar, *mm.* **1, 2**	£175	£500
2584	**Shilling.** As 2577, *mm.* **1, 2**	£30	£100
2585	**Sixpence.** With rose and date 1601–2; *mm.* **1, 2**	£25	£75
2586	**Halfgroat.** As 2579, *mm.* **1, 2**	£12	£35
2587	**Penny.** As 2580, *mm.* **1, 2**	£12	£35
2588	**Halfpenny.** As 2581, *mm.* **1, 2**	£25	£85

Milled coinage

2592

		F	VF
2589	**Shilling.** Without rose or date; *mm.* star. Plain dress, large size	£250	£700
2590	— decorated dress, large size (over 31 mm.)	£110	£375
2591	— — intermediate size (30–31 mm.)	£75	£225
2592	— — small size (under 30 mm.)	£80	£230
2593	**Sixpence.** Small bust, large rose, 1561; *mm.* star	£22	£65

2594   2601

		F	VF
2594	Tall narrow bust with plain dress, large rose, 1561–2; *mm.* star . . . *from*	£22	£80
2595	— similar, but decorated dress, 1562	£20	£65
2596	Large broad bust, elaborately decorated dress, small rose, 1562; *mm.* star	£20	£65
2597	— — cross pattée on *rev.*, 1562–4; *mm.* star	£30	£115
2598	— similar, but with low ruff, pellet border, 1563–4, 1566	£40	£150
2599	Small bust, 1567–8; *mm.* lis	£27	£100
2600	Large crude bust breaking legend; 1570, *mm.* lis; 1571, *mm.* castle	£80	£200
2601	**Groat.** As illustration	£100	£300
2602	**Threepence.** With rose, small bust with plain dress, 1561	£50	£150
2603	Tall narrow bust with large rose, 1562	£40	£125
2604	Short bust with small rose, 1562	£65	£165
2605	Cross pattée on *rev.*, 1563–4	£120	£325
2606	**Halfgroat.** As groat	£110	£375
2607	**Threefarthings.** E . D . G . ROSA, etc., with rose. ℞. CIVITAS LONDON, shield with 1563 above	*Extremely rare*	

Portcullis money

Trade coins of 8, 4, 2, and 1 Testerns were coined at the Tower Mint in 1600/1 for the first voyage of the incorporated "Company of Merchants of London Trading into the East Indies". The coins bear the royal arms on the obverse and a portcullis on the reverse and have the *mm.* **O**. They were struck to the weights of the equivalent Spanish silver 8, 4, 2 and 1 reales.

		F	VF
2607A	Eight testerns	£750	£1800
2607B	Four testerns	£400	£1000
2607C	Two testerns	£500	£1300
2607D	One testern	£300	£750

JAMES I, 1603–25

With the accession of James VI of Scotland to the English throne, the royal titles and coat of arms are altered on the coinage; on the latter the Scottish rampant lion and the Irish harp now appear in the second and third quarters. In 1604 the weight of the gold pound was reduced and the new coin became known as the 'Unite'. Fine gold coins of $23\frac{1}{2}$ carat and crown gold of 22 carat were both issued, and a gold four-shilling piece was struck 1604–19. In 1612 all the gold coins had their values raised by 10%; but in 1619 the Unite was replaced by a new, lighter 20s. piece, the 'Laurel', and a lighter rose-ryal, spur-ryal and angel were minted.

In 1613 the King granted Lord Harrington a licence to coin farthings of copper as a result of repeated public demands for a low value coinage; this was later taken over by the Duke of Lennox. Towards the end of the reign coins made from silver sent to the mint from the Welsh mines had the Prince of Wales's plumes inserted over the royal arms.

Mintmarks

125	105	33	79	84	74	90

60	25	71	45	32	123	132

72b	7a	16	24	125	105	46

First coinage
1603–4   Thistle (125)
1604–5   Lis (105)
Second coinage
1604–5   Lis (105)
1605–6   Rose (33)
1606–7   Escallop (79)
1607   Grapes (84)
1607–9   Coronet (74)
1609–10   Key (90)
1610–1   Bell (60)
1611–12   Mullet (25)
1612–13   Tower (71)
1613   Trefoil (45)

           Cinquefoil (32)
1613–15   Tun (123)
1615–16   Closed book (132)
1616–17   Crescent (72b, gold)
1617–18   Plain cross (7a)
1618–19   Saltire cross (16)
1619
Third coinage
1619–20   Spur rowel (24)
1620–1   Rose (33)
1621–3   Thistle (125)
1623–4   Lis (105)
1624   Trefoil (46)

GOLD

First coinage, 1603–4 (Obverse legend reads D'. G'. ANG : SCO : etc.)

2608   2612

		F	VF
2608	**Sovereign** (= 20s.). King crowned r., half-length, first bust with plain armour. ℞. EXVRGAT, etc.; *mm.* thistle	£700	£1600
2609	— second bust with decorated armour; *mm.* 125, 105	£750	£1750
2610	**Half-sovereign.** Crowned bust r. ℞. EXVRGAT, etc.; *mm.* thistle	£2000	£4500
2611	**Crown.** Similar. ℞. TVEATVR, etc.; *mm.* 125, 105/125	£1000	£2500
2612	**Halfcrown.** Similar; *mm.* thistle, lis	£500	£1000

N.B. *The Quarter-Angel of this coinage is considered to be a pattern, having the reverse of the half-crown although coin weights are known.*

Second coinage, 1604–19 (Obverse legend reads D' G' MAG : BRIT : etc.)

2613   2614

2613	**Rose-ryal** (= 30s., 33s. from 1612). King enthroned. ℞. Shield on rose; *mm.* 33–90, 25–132	£800	£1900
2614	**Spur ryal** (= 15s., 16s. 6d. from 1612). King in ship; *mm.* 33, 79, 74, 25–32, 132	£2000	£4750
2615	**Angel** (= 10s., 11s. from 1612). Old type; *mm.* 33–74, 60–16	£350	£850
2616	— pierced for use as touch-piece	£150	£350
2617	**Half-angel** (= 5s., 5s. 6d. from 1612). Similar; *mm.* 71–132, 7a, 16	£1300	£3000

Second coinage gold

2620   2627

		F	VF
2618	**Unite** (= 20s., 22s. from 1612). Half-length second bust r. ℞. FACIAM etc.; *mm.* lis or rose	£275	£525
2619	— fourth bust; *mm.* rose to cinquefoil	£235	£425
2620	— fifth bust; *mm.* cinquefoil to saltire	£215	£400
2621	**Double-crown.** Third bust r. ℞. HENRICVS, etc.; *mm.* lis or rose	£160	£375
2622	Fourth bust; *mm.* rose to bell	£160	£375
2623	Fifth bust; *mm.* mullet to saltire	£175	£400
2624	**Britain crown.** First bust r.; *mm.* lis to coronet	£135	£275
2625	Third bust; *mm.* key to cinquefoil	£135	£275
2626	Fifth bust; *mm.* cinquefoil to saltire	£125	£250
2627	**Thistle crown** (= 4s.). As illus.; *mm.* lis to cross	£125	£275
2628	— IR only on one side	£140	£300
2629	**Halfcrown.** I' D' G' ROSA SINE SPINA. First bust; *mm.* lis to coronet	£115	£250
2630	Third bust; *mm.* key to trefoil	£120	£275
2631	Fifth bust; *mm.* cinquefoil to cross	£110	£225

Third coinage, 1619–25

		F	VF
2632	**Rose-ryal** (= 30s.; 196½ grs.). King enthroned. ℞. XXX above shield; lis, lion and rose emblems around; *mm.* 24–105	£1250	£3000
2633	Similar but plain back to throne; *mm.* 46	£1350	£3250

2634   2635

		F	VF
2634	**Spur-ryal.** (= 15s.). As illus.; *mm.* 24–125, 46	£1600	£3250
2635	**Angel.** (= 10s.) of new type; *mm.* 24–46	£500	£1150
2636	— pierced for use as touch-piece	£200	£450

		F	VF
2637	**Laurel** (= 20s.; 140½ grs.). First (large) laur. bust l.; *mm.* 24	£250	£550
2638	Second to fourth busts; *mm.* 24–46	£225	£425
2639	Fifth, small rather crude bust; *mm.* trefoil	£1500	£3500

2641   2642

		F	VF
2640	**Half-laurel.** First bust; *mm.* spur rowel	£225	£425
2641	Fourth bust; *mm.* 24–46	£175	£375
2642	**Quarter-laurel.** Second or fourth bust; *mm.* 24–46	£125	£200
	For busts on the laurels, see North.		

SILVER

First coinage, 1603–4

		F	VF
2643	**Crown.** King on horseback. ℞. EXVRGAT, etc., shield; *mm.* thistle, lis . . .	£325	£1000
2644	**Halfcrown.** Similar	£225	£650
2645	**Shilling.** First bust, square-cut beard. ℞. EXVRGAT, etc.; *mm.* thistle . . .	£50	£175
2646	—Second bust, beard merges with collar; *mm.* thistle, lis	£30	£85

2647   2648

		F	VF
2647	**Sixpence.** First bust; 1603, *mm.* thistle	£35	£105
2648	Second bust; 1603–4; *mm.* thistle, lis	£30	£100
2649	**Halfgroat.** As illustration but II; *mm.* thistle, lis	£25	£60
2650	**Penny.** Similar, but I behind head; *mm.* thistle, lis	£25	£50

2650   2651

		F	VF
2651	**Halfpenny.** As illustration; *mm.* thistle, lis	£25	£55

Second coinage, 1604–19

		F	VF
2652	**Crown.** King on horseback. ℞. QVAE DEVS, etc.; *mm.* 105–84	£225	£600
2653	**Halfcrown.** Similar; *mm.* 105, 79, 123	£175	£525
2654	**Shilling.** Third bust, beard cut square and stands out (*cf.* illus. 2657); *mm.* lis, rose	£30	£100
2655	— Fourth bust, armour plainer (*cf.* 2658); *mm.* 33–74	£25	£90
2656	— Fifth bust, similar, but hair longer; *mm.* 74–7a	£25	£95

2657   2658

2657	**Sixpence.** Third bust; 1604–5; *mm.* lis, rose	£30	£90
2658	— Fourth bust; 1605–15; *mm.* rose to tun	£25	£85
2658A	— Fifth bust, 1618; *mm.* plain cross		*Unique*

2660   2663

2659	**Halfgroat.** As illus. but larger crown on *obv.*; *mm.* lis to coronet	£10	£30
2660	— Similar, but smaller crown on *obv.*; *mm.* coronet to cross	£15	£40
2661	**Penny.** As halfgroat but no crowns; *mm.* lis to cross and none	£10	£30
2661A	— Similar, but without I.C. on one or both sides	£10	£30
2662	— As before but TVEATVR legend both sides; *mm.* mullet	*Extremely rare*	
2663	**Halfpenny.** As illus.; *mm.* lis to mullet, cinquefoil	£20	£40

Third coinage, 1619–25

2664	**Crown.** As 2652, but mostly with bird-headed harp, colon stops on *obv.*, no stops on *rev.*; *mm.* 33–46	£175	£475
2665	— — plume over shield; *mm.* 125–46	£200	£525

2666   2667

2666	**Halfcrown.** As 2664; all have bird-headed harp	£100	£300
2666A	— — Similar but no ground line; *mm.* rose	£125	£350
2667	— — plume over shield; *mm.* 125–46	£110	£350

		F	VF
2668	**Shilling.** Sixth (large) bust, hair longer and very curly; *mm.* 24–46	£30	£90
2669	— — plume over shield; *mm.* 125–46	£40	£125

2670   2672

		F	VF
2670	**Sixpence.** Sixth bust; 1621–4; *mm.* 33–46	£30	£90
2671	**Halfgroat.** As 2660 but no stops on *rev.*; *mm.* 24–46 and none	£10	£25
2672	**Penny.** As illus.; *mm.* 24, 105, 46 and none	£10	£25
2672A	— Similar but without I.C. on one or both sides	£10	£25
2673	**Halfpenny.** As 2663, but no *mm.*	£20	£35

COPPER

For mintmarks see *English Copper, Tin and Bronze Coins in the British Museum, 1558–1958.*

2675   2676   2679

		F	VF
2674	**Farthing.** "Harington", small size. 1a, letter or other mark below crown (originally tinned surface) . . . . *from*	£15	£40
2675	— — 1b, central jewel on circlet of crown with *mm.* below or crown unmodified	£20	£45
2676	— 2, normal size of coin; *mm.* on *rev.*	£10	£20
2677	"Lennox". 3a; *mm. rev.* only	£5	£16
2678	— 3b; *mm.* both sides	£4	£14
2679	— — 3c; *mm. obv.* only	£4	£14
2680	— — 3d; larger crown	£4	£14
2681	— 4; oval type, legend starts at bottom l.	£15	£40

CHARLES I, 1625–49

Numismatically, this reign is one of the most interesting of all the English monarchs. Some outstanding machine-made coins were produced by Nicholas Briot, a French die-sinker, but they could not be struck at sufficient speed to supplant hand-hammering methods. In 1637 a branch mint was set up at Aberystwyth to coin silver extracted from the Welsh mines. After the king's final breach with Parliament the parliamentary government continued to issue coins at London with Charles's name and portrait until the king's trial and execution. The coinage of copper farthings continued to be manufactured privately under licences held first by the Duchess of Richmond, then by Lord Maltravers and later by various other persons. The licence was finally revoked by Parliament in 1644.

During the Civil War coins were struck at a number of towns to supply coinage for those areas of the country under Royalist control. Many of these coins have an abbreviated form of the "Declaration" made at Wellington, Shropshire, Sept., 1642, in which Charles promised to uphold the Protestant Religion, the Laws of England and the Liberty of Parliament. Amongst the more spectacular pieces are the gold triple unites and the silver pounds and half-pounds struck at Shrewsbury and Oxford, and the emergency coins made from odd-shaped pieces of silver plate during the sieges of Newark, Scarborough, Carlisle and Pontefract.

Mintmarks

105	10	96	71	57	88	101	35

87	107	60	75	123	57	119a	23

119b	98	112	81	120	109

Tower Mint under Charles I

1625	Lis (105)
1625–6	Cross Cavalry (10)
1626–7	Negro's head (96)
1627–8	Castle (71)
1628–9	Anchor (57)
1629–30	Heart (88)
1630–1	Plume (101)
1631–2	Rose (35)
1632–3	Harp (87)
1633–4	Portcullis (107)
1634–5	Bell (60)

1635–6	Crown (75)
1636–8	Tun (123)
1638–9	Anchor (57)
1639–40	Triangle (119a)
1640–1	Star (23)
1641–3	Triangle in circle (119b)

Tower Mint under Parliament

1643–4	P in brackets (98)
1644–5	R in brackets (112)
1645	Eye (81)
1645–6	Sun (120)
1646–8	Sceptre (109)

59	B	58 *var*	58

Briot's Mint

1631–2	Flower and B (59)		1638–9	Anchor and B (58)
1632	B			Anchor and mullet

Footnote. On mint mark no. 58 the 'B' below the anchor is sometimes shown as ๒

61 104 35 92 103 6 65b 71

89 91 *var.* 131 84 94 *var.* 64 93 34

102 67 127 128 129 25 83 100

134 71 130 A B 75

Provincial Mints

1638–42	Book (61, *Aberystwyth*)	
1642	Plume (104, *Shrewsbury*)	
	Pellets or pellet (*Shrewsbury*)	
1642–3	Rose (35, *Truro*)	
	Bugle (134, *Truro?*)	
1642–4	Lion (92, *York*)	
1642–6	Plume (103, *Oxford*)	
	Pellet or pellets (*Oxford*)	
	Lis (105, *Oxford*)	
1643	Cross pattée (6, *Bristol*)	
	Acorn (65b, *Bristol*)	
	Castle (71, *Worcester* or *Shrewsbury*)	
	Helmet (89, *Worcester* and *Shrewsbury*)	
1643–4	Leopard's head (91 *var. Worcester*)	
	Two lions (131, *Worcester*)	
	Lis (105, *Worcs.* or *Shrews.*)	
	Bunch of grapes (84, *Worcs.* or *Shrews.*)	
	Bird (94 var., *Worcs.* or *Shrews.*)	

1643–4	Boar's head (*Worcs.* or *Shrews.*)	
	Lion rampant (93, *Worcs.* or *Shrews.*)	
	Rosette (34, *Worcs.* or *Shrews.*)	
1643–5	Plume (102, *Bristol*)	
	Br. (67, *Bristol*)	
	Pellets (*Bristol*)	
	Rose (35, *Exeter*)	
	Rosette (34, *Oxford*)	
1643–6	Floriated cross (127, *Oxford*)	
1644	Cross pattée (6, *Oxford*)	
	Lozenge (128, *Oxford*)	
	Billet (129, *Oxford*)	
	Mullet (25, *Oxford*)	
1644–6	Gerb (83, *Chester*)	
	Pear (100, *Worcester*)	
	Lis (105, *Hereford?*)	
	Castle (71, *Exeter*)	
	Plume (130, see p. 182)	
	A (Ditto)	
1646	B (Ditto)	
1648–9	Crown (75, *Aberystwyth-Furnace*)	

GOLD

Tower mint, under the King, 1625–42

2687

		F	VF
2682	**Angel.** As for James I last issue, without mark of value; *mm.* lis and cross calvary	£550	£1400
2683	—— pierced for use as touch-piece	£200	£400

Tower Gold

		F	VF
2684	— X in field to r.; *mm.* 96–88	£450	£1200
2685	— — — pierced for use as touch-piece	£200	£400
2686	— X in field to l.; *mm.* 96, 88, 35–119a, 119b	£425	£1100
2687	— — — pierced for use as touch-piece	£200	£400

2688   2697

2688	**Unite** (= 20s.). First bust with ruff and collar of order, high double-crown. ℞. Square-topped shield; *mm.* 105, 10	£210	£425
2688A	— Similar, but extra garnishing to shield; *mm.* lis	£275	£525
2689	— Similar, but flat single-arched crown	£210	£475
2690	Second bust with ruff and armour nearly concealed with scarf; *mm.* 10–101	£185	£425
2690A	— Similar, but bust breaks inner circle; *mm.* as above?	£185	£425
2691	— As 2629; *mm.* anchor below bust	*Extremely rare*	
2692	Third bust, more armour visible. ℞. Oval shield with CR at sides; *mm.* 101, 35	£210	£475
2693	Fourth bust, small lace collar, Garter ribbon on breast. ℞. Oval shield with crowned CR at sides; *mm.* 87–23	£225	£485
2694	Sixth (Briot's) bust, large lace collar. ℞. Similar; *mm.* 57–119b	£250	£550
2695	— — with Briot's *rev.*; *mm.* 57	*Extremely rare*	
	Note. *An extremely fine example of this coin sold at auction for £4500 in 1986.*		
2696	**Double-crown.** First bust. ℞. Square-topped shield; *mm.* 105, 10	£175	£375
2697	Second bust. ℞. Similar; *mm.* 10–101	£150	£325
2698	Third bust. ℞. Oval shield with CR at sides; *mm.* 101, 35	£225	£475
2699	Fourth bust. ℞. Oval shield with crowned CR at sides; *mm.* 87–57	£185	£400
2700	Fifth bust as Aberystwyth silver. ℞. Similar; *mm.* 57, 119a	£250	£500
2701	Sixth bust. ℞. Normal; *mm.* 57–119b	£235	£475
2702	— ℞. Briot's square-topped shield; *mm.* 57	*Extremely rare*	
2703	**Crown.** First bust. ℞. Square-topped shield; *mm.* 105, 10	£125	£250
2704	Second bust. ℞. Similar; *mm.* 10–101	£115	£225
2705	— — ℞. As next; 101, 35	£135	£275
2706	Third bust. ℞. Oval shield with CR at sides; *mm.* 101	*Extremely rare*	
2707	Fourth bust. ℞. Oval shield with crowned CR at sides; *mm.* 87–119b	£125	£250
2708	Fifth (Aberystwyth) bust. ℞. Similar; *mm.* 57	£165	£350
2709	Sixth (Briot's) bust. ℞. Similar; *mm.* 57	*Unique*	

Gold

2703   2714

Tower mint, under Parliament, 1643–8. All Charles I types

		F	VF
2710	**Unite.** Fourth bust, as 2693; *mm.*(P)	£275	£700
2711	Sixth bust, as 2964; *mm.*(P),(R)	£350	£800
2712	Seventh bust, cruder style; *mm.* 81–109	£375	£875
2713	**Double-crown.** Fourth bust, as 2699; *mm.* eye	*Extremely rare*	
2714	Fifth bust, as 2700; *mm.* sun, sceptre	£325	£750
2715	Sixth bust, as 2701; *mm.*(P)	£400	£925
2716	Seventh bust, as 2712; *mm.* sun		*Unique*
2717	**Crown.** Fourth bust, as 2707; *mm.* (P) to sceptre	£200	£525

Nicholas Briot's coinage, 1631–2

2718 **Angel.** Type as Tower but smaller and neater; *mm.* -/B . . . .   *Extremely rare*

2719

2719	**Unite.** As illustration. ℞. FLORENT etc.	£750	£1900
2720	**Double-crown.** Similar but X. ℞. CVLTORES, etc.	£650	£1600
2721	**Crown.** Similar; *mm.* B	*Extremely rare*	

Provincial issues, 1638–49

Chester mint

2722 **Unite.** As Tower. Sixth bust but CR not crowned; *mm.* plume . . . .   *Extremely rare*

Shrewsbury mint, 1642 (See also 2749)

2723 **Triple unit,** 1642. Half-length figure l. holding sword and olive-branch; *mm.* : ℞. EXVRGAT, etc., around RELIG PROT, etc., in two wavy lines, III and three plumes above, date below . . . .   *Unique?*

Oxford mint, 1642–6

2724

		F	VF
2724	**Triple unite.** As last, but *mm.* plume, tall narrow bust, 1642	£1850	£3750
2725	Similar, but "Declaration" on continuous scroll, 1642–3	£1950	£4250
2726	As last, but larger bust, with scarf behind shoulder, 1643	£2150	£4500
2727	Similar, but without scarf, 1643	£1850	£3750
2728	Similar, but OXON below 1643, rosette stops	*Extremely rare*	
2729	Smaller size, 1644 / OXON	£1950	£4250
2730	— 1644 / OX	£2150	£4500
2731	**Unite.** Tall thin bust. ℞. "Declaration" in two wavy lines, 1642	£475	£1050
2732	— ℞. "Declaration" in three lines on continuous scroll, 1642–3	£475	£1050
2733	Larger bust. ℞. Similar, 1643	£575	£1250
2734	Shorter bust. ℞. Similar, 1643, 1645; *mm.* plume	£425	£950

2731

2735	— — 1644 / OX; *mm.* plume	£475	£1100
2736	Tall bust to edge of coin. ℞. Similar, 1643	£600	£1250
2737	As 2734. ℞. "Declaration" in three straight lines, 1644 / OX	*Extremely rare*	
2738	Longer, narrower bust. ℞. Similar	£550	£1200
2739	— ℞. Single plume above "Declaration", 1645–6 / OX	£600	£1250
2740	**Half-unite.** "Declaration" in three straight lines, 1642	*Extremely rare*	
2741	"Declaration" on scroll; *mm.* plume; 1642–3	£650	£1400
2742	Bust to bottom of coin, 1643	£575	£1150
2743	— 1644 / OX	*Extremely rare*	

Bristol mint, 1645

2744 **Unite.** Somewhat as 2734; *mm.* Br.; 1645 . . . . *Extremely rare*
2745 **Half-unite.** Similar . . . . *Unique?*

Truro mint, 1642–3

2746 **Unite.** *Mm.* rose. ℞. FLORENT, etc., crowned oval shield between C R . . . *Unique*
2747 — ℞. CVLTORES, etc., similar but no C R . . . . *Extremely rare*

Worcester mint, 1643–4

2748 **Unite.** No. *mm.* ℞. FLORENT, etc., double annulet stops, crowned oval
shield, lion's paws on either side of garniture . . . . *Extremely rare*
Note. *A fine example of this coin sold at auction in 1986 for £15,000.*

Salopia (Shrewsbury) mint, 1644

2749 **Unite.** As last, but *mm.* lis . . . . *Unique?*

Colchester besieged, 1648

2750 **Ten shillings.** Gateway of castle between CR ; below OBS COL 16 $\frac{S}{X}$ 48 . . . *Extremely rare*

Pontefract besieged, 1648–9. After the death of Charles I, in the name of Charles II

2751 **Unite.** DVM : SPIRO : SPERO around CR crowned. ℞. CAROLVS :
SECVNDVS : 1648, castle, OBS on l., PC above. *Octagonal* . . . . *Extremely rare*
2752 CAROL : II, etc., around HANC : DEVS, etc. ℞. POST : MORTEM, etc.,
around castle. *Octagonal* . . . . *Extremely rare*

SILVER

Tower mint, under the King, 1625–42

2759

	F	VF
2753 **Crown.** King on horseback with raised sword. 1a. Horse caparisoned with plume on head and crupper. ℞. Square-topped shield over long cross fourchée; *mm.* 105, 10	£175	£500
2754 — 1b. Similar, but plume over shield, no cross; *mm.* 105, 10, 71	£500	£1100
2755 — 2a. Smaller horse, plume on hd. only, cross on housings, king holds sword on shoulder. ℞. Oval garnished shield over cross fourchée, CR above; *mm.* harp	£150	£450
2756 — 2b[1]. — — plume divides CR, no cross; *mm.* 101, 35	£200	£525
2757 — 2b[2]. — — — with cross; *mm.* harp, plume	£250	£650

Tower Silver

		F	VF
2758	—3a. Horse without caparisons. ℞. Oval shield without CR ; *mm*. 60–23 ...	£175	£500
2759	— 3b. —— plume over shield; *mm*. 107, 75, 123	£200	£525
2760	"Briot" horse with ground-line; *mm*. 119b	£500	£1500

2762

		F	VF
2761	**Halfcrown.** As 2753. 1a¹. Rose on housings, ground-line; *mm*. lis	£90	£225
2761A	— Similar, but no rose on housings; *mm*. lis	£90	£235
2762	— 1a². Similar, but no rose or ground-line; *mm*. lis	£100	£250
2763	— 1a³. As last but clumsier horse and shield not over cross; *mm*. 10–71 .	£65	£165
2764	— 1a⁴. —— with ground-line; *mm*. lis	£450	£1000
2765	— 1b. —— plume over shield; *mm*. lis to anchor	£300	£600
2766	— 2/1b. As 2755 but rose on housings. ℞. As last; *mm*. heart, plume ...	£375	£850
2767	— 2a. As 2755. ℞. Flattened oval garnished shield without cross; *mm*. plume, rose, CR above, divided by rose (rare), lis over rose, lis	£50	£120
2768	— 2b. Similar, but large plume between the CR	£115	£275
2769	— 2c. As 2a, but differently garnished oval shield with CR at sides; *mm*. harp, portcullis	£50	£125
2770	— 2d. Similar, but with plume over shield; *mm*. harp	£225	£550

2771 2775

		F	VF
2771	— 3a¹. No caparisons on horse, upright sword, scarf flies out from waist. ℞. Round garnished shield, no CR; *mm*. 57, 60–57	£25	£90
2772	— 3b. —— plume over shield; *mm*. 107–123	£110	£250
2773	— 3a². — cloak flies from king's shoulder; *mm*. 123–23	£25	£90
2774	——— rough ground beneath horse; *mm*. 119a, 23	£25	£90
	Note. *(2771–4) See Brooker Coins of Charles I 340–52.*		
2775	— 4. Foreshortened horse, mane before chest, tail between legs; *mm*. 23, 119b	£22	£80

Tower Silver

2776

		F	VF
2776	**Shilling.** 1. Bust in ruff. ℞. Square-topped shield over cross fourchée; *mm.* lis, cross Calvary (normal weight 92¼ grs.)	£25	£120
2777	— — — light weight (81¾ grs.); *mm.* 10	£75	£200
2778	— 1b¹. As 2776, but plume over shield, no cross; *mm.* 105, 10	£80	£230
2779	— 1a. Bust in ruff and armour concealed by scarf. ℞. As 2776; 10–71	£25	£90
2780	— — — — light weight; *mm.* cross Calvary	£75	£210
2781	— 1b². As 2779, but plume over shield, no cross; *mm.* 10–101	£55	£175
2782	— 1b³. — — — cross; *mm.* negro's head	£350	£750
2783	— 2a. More armour visible. ℞. Oval shield, CR above; *mm.* plume, rose	£20	£75
2784	— 2b. — — plume over shield; *mm.* 101, 35	£100	£300
2785	— 3¹. Bust with lace collar. ℞. Flattish oval shield, CR at sides; *mm.* harp, portcullis	£20	£70
2786	— 3². — — plume over shield; *mm.* harp	£190	£400
2787	— 3a. — no inner circles, rounder shield without CR; *mm.* 60–123	£16	£60
2788	— 3b. — — plume over shield; *mm.* 60–123	£55	£125

2787   2791   2793

		F	VF
2789	— 4¹. Large Aberystwyth bust, small XII. ℞. Square-topped shield over cross fleury; *mm.* tun	£20	£70
2790	— 4¹. var. Similar, but rounder shoulders, large XII; *mm.* 57, 119a	£15	£55
2791	— 4². Smaller Aberystwyth bust with small double-arched crown, small XII; *mm.* tun	£15	£55
2792	— 4³. — single-arches, large XII; *mm.* 123, 57, 119a	£15	£55
2793	— 4⁴. Older (Briot's style) bust, very pointed beard; *mm.* 57–119b	£14	£50

Tower Silver

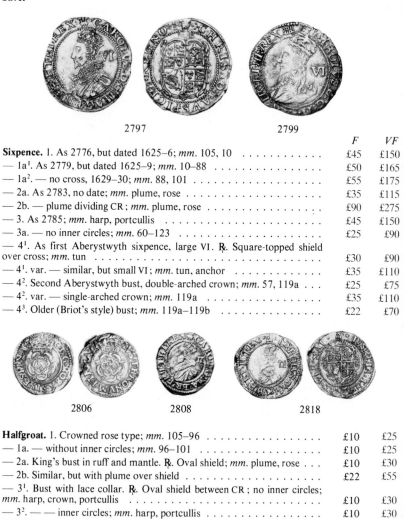

                    2797   2799

		F	VF
2794	**Sixpence.** 1. As 2776, but dated 1625–6; *mm*. 105, 10	£45	£150
2795	— 1a¹. As 2779, but dated 1625–9; *mm*. 10–88	£50	£165
2796	— 1a². — no cross, 1629–30; *mm*. 88, 101	£55	£175
2797	— 2a. As 2783, no date; *mm*. plume, rose	£35	£115
2798	— 2b. — plume dividing CR ; *mm*. plume, rose	£90	£275
2799	— 3. As 2785; *mm*. harp, portcullis	£45	£150
2800	— 3a. — no inner circles; *mm*. 60–123	£25	£90
2801	— 4¹. As first Aberystwyth sixpence, large VI. ℞. Square-topped shield over cross; *mm*. tun	£30	£90
2802	— 4¹. var. — similar, but small VI; *mm*. tun, anchor	£35	£110
2803	— 4². Second Aberystwyth bust, double-arched crown; *mm*. 57, 119a . . .	£25	£75
2804	— 4². var. — single-arched crown; *mm*. 119a	£35	£110
2805	— 4³. Older (Briot's style) bust; *mm*. 119a–119b	£22	£70

              2806   2808   2818

		F	VF
2806	**Halfgroat.** 1. Crowned rose type; *mm*. 105–96	£10	£25
2807	— 1a. — without inner circles; *mm*. 96–101	£10	£25
2808	— 2a. King's bust in ruff and mantle. ℞. Oval shield; *mm*. plume, rose . . .	£10	£30
2809	— 2b. Similar, but with plume over shield	£22	£55
2810	— 3¹. Bust with lace collar. ℞. Oval shield between CR ; no inner circles; *mm*. harp, crown, portcullis . .	£10	£30
2811	— 3². — — inner circles; *mm*. harp, portcullis	£10	£30
2812	— 3³. — — inner circle on *rev*.; *mm*. similar	£11	£35
2813	— 3⁴. — — inner circle on *obv*.; *mm*. similar	£10	£30
2814	— 3⁵. — — no CR , i.cs.; *mm*. portcullis	£10	£30
2815	— 3⁶. — — — i.c. on *obv*.; *mm*. portcullis	£10	£30
2816	— 3a¹. — ℞. Rounder shield, different garniture, no i.cs.; *mm*. 60–119b .	£10	£30
2817	— 3a². — — i.c. on *obv*.; *mm*. triangle	£10	£30
2818	— 3a³. — — i.cs. both sides; *mm*. 119a–119b	£10	£30
2819	— 3a⁴. Aberystwyth bust, no i.cs.; *mm*. anchor	£10	£30
2820	— 3a⁵. — i.c. on *rev*.; *mm*. anchor	£10	£30
2821	— 3a⁶. Very small bust, no i.cs.; *mm*. anchor	£10	£30

Tower Silver

2822   2829   2837

		F	
2822	**Penny.** 1. Rose each side; i.cs.; *mm.* negro's head, lis/ :, one or two pellets .	£8	£30
2823	— 1a. — no i.cs.; *mm.* lis, one or two pellets, anchor	£8	£30
2824	— 1b. — i.c. on *rev.*; *mm.* negro's head/two pellets	£10	£35
2825	— 2. Bust in ruff and mantle. ℞. Oval shield; i.cs.; *mm.* plume	£10	£35
2826	— 2¹. — — no i.cs.; *mm.* plume	£12	£40
2827	— 2a¹. More armour visible; no i.cs.; *mm.* plume, rose	£9	£30
2828	— 2a². — i.c. on *obv.*; *mm.* plume, rose	£12	£40
2829	— 2a³. — i.cs. both sides; *mm.* plume, rose	£10	£35
2830	— 2a⁴. — i.c. on *rev.*; *mm.* rose/plume	£20	£55
2831	— 3¹. Bust in lace collar. ℞. CR at sides of shield; no i.cs.; *mm.* harp, one or two pellets	£9	£30
2832	— 3². — similar but no CR ; *mm.* as last and 107	£10	£35
2833	— 3³. — — i.c. on *obv.*; *mm.* harp	£10	£35
2834	— 3⁴. — — i.c. on *rev.*; *mm.* harp	£10	£35
2835	— 3a¹. — similar, but shield almost round and with scroll garniture; no i.cs.; *mm.* bell, triangle, one or two pellets	£8	£25
2835A	— 3a¹ variety — i.c. on *obv.* only; *mm.* triangle/two pellets	£12	£35
2836	— 3a³. Aberystwyth bust; *mm.* one or two pellets or none	£8	£25
2837	**Halfpenny.** Rose each side; no legend or *mm.*	£15	£45

Tower mint, under Parliament, 1642–8. All Charles I type

2838	**Crown.** 4. Foreshortened horse; *mm.* (P) to sun	£175	£475
2839	— 5. Tall spirited horse; *mm.* sun	£225	£550
2840	**Halfcrown.** 3a³. As 2773, but coarse work; *mm.* (P) to sun	£25	£90
2841	— 4. Foreshortened horse; *mm.* (P)	*Extremely rare*	
2842	— 5. Tall horse; *mm.* sun, sceptre	£35	£110
2843	**Shilling.** 4⁴. Briot style bust but coarse work; *mm.* (P) to sun	£20	£75

2844   2845

2844	— 4⁵. Long narrow coarse bust; *mm.* sun, sceptre	£25	£80
2845	— 4⁶. Short broad older bust; *mm.* sceptre	£28	£95

Tower mint, under Parliament, Silver

		F	VF
2846	**Sixpence.** 4³. Briot style bust; *mm.*(P) to sun	£35	£100
2847	— 4⁴. Late Aberystwyth bust; *mm.*(R) to sceptre	£30	£85
2848	— 4⁵. Squat bust of crude style; *mm.* eye and sun	£65	£185
2849	**Halfgroat.** 3a³. As 2818; *mm.*(P) to sceptre	£20	£55
2850	— 3a⁷. Older, shorter bust, pointed beard; *mm.* eye to sceptre	£20	£55
2851	**Penny.** 3a². Older bust; *mm.* pellets	£18	£50

Nicholas Briot's coinage, 1631–9

First milled issue, 1631–2

2852	**Crown.** King on horseback. ℞. Crowned shield between C R crowned; *mm.* flower and B / B	£300	£700
2853	**Halfcrown.** Similar	£175	£500
2854	**Shilling.** Briot's early bust with falling lace collar. ℞. Square-topped shield over long cross fourchée; *mm.* as before	£110	£325
2855	**Sixpence.** Similar, but VI behind bust (sometimes no *mm.* on *rev.*) . . .	£65	£210

2855   2856

2856	**Halfgroat.** Briot's bust, B below, II behind. ℞. IVSTITIA, etc., square-topped shield over long cross fourchée	£40	£100
2857	**Penny.** Similar, but I behind bust	£30	£75

Second milled issue, 1638–9

2858

2858	**Halfcrown.** As 2853, but *mm.* anchor and B	£175	£450
2859	**Shilling.** Briot's late bust, the falling lace collar is plain with broad lace border, no scarf. ℞. As 2854 but cross only to inner circle; *mm.* anchor and B, anchor	£50	£160
2860	**Sixpence.** Similar, but VI; *mm.* 57, anchor and mullet	£35	£110

Briot's hammered issue, 1638–9

		F	VF
2861	**Halfcrown.** King on Briot's style horse with ground line. ℞. Square-topped shield; *mm.* anchor, triangle over anchor	£450	£1000
2862	**Shilling.** As 2859; *mm.* anchor, triangle over anchor. ℞. Square-topped shield over short cross fleury	£350	£800

Provincial and Civil War issues, 1638–49

York mint, 1643–4. *Mm.* lion

		F	VF
2863	**Halfcrown.** 1. Ground-line below horse. ℞. Square-topped shield between CR	£140	£375
2864	— 2. — ℞. Oval shield as Tower 3a	£150	£475
2865	— 3. No ground-line. ℞. Shield somewhat flattened	£125	£350
2866	— 4. As last, but EBOR below horse with head held low. Base metal, often very base	£110	£300
2867	— 5. Tall horse, mane in front of chest, EBOR below. ℞. Crowned square-topped shield between CR, flowers in legend	£100	£275
2868	— 6. As last, but shield is oval, garnished	£90	£265

2868   2872

		F	VF
2869	— 7. Similar, but horse's tail shows between legs. ℞. Shield as last, but with lion's skin garniture, no CR or flowers	£80	£250
2870	**Shilling.** 1. Bust as Tower 3¹. ℞. EBOR above square-topped shield over cross fleury	£50	£140
2871	— 2. Similar, but bust in plain armour, mantle; coarse work	£65	£185
2872	— 3. — ℞. EBOR below oval shield	£65	£185
2873	— 4. — Similar, but crowned oval shield	£50	£140
2874	— 5. — As last, but lion's skin garniture	£50	£140

2876   2877

		F	VF
2875	**Sixpence.** Crowned oval shield	£110	£275
2876	— — C R at sides	£85	£200
2877	**Threepence.** As type 1 shilling, but III behind bust	£30	£80

Aberystwyth mint, 1638/9–42. *Mm.* book.
Plume 1 = with coronet and band. Plume 2 = with coronet only

		F	VF
2878	**Halfcrown.** King on horseback, small plume 2 behind. ℞. Oval garnished shield with large plume above	£300	£750
2879	— plume 1 behind King, ground below horse	£350	£850
2880	As 2878, but more spirited horse, no ground, FRAN ET HIB	£400	£950
2881	**Shilling.** Bust with large square lace collar, plume 2 before, small XII. ℞. As before. No inner circles	£110	£270
2882	— inner circle on *rev.*	£125	£320
2883	As 2881, but large plume 1, large XII, inner circles	£110	£270
2884	As last, but small head, rounded lace collar	£125	£320
2885	Briot's bust as Tower 4[4], small square lace collar, plume 2, inner circles . .	£150	£350

2886

		F	VF
2886	**Sixpence.** As 2881, but small VI; no inner circles	£120	£300
2887	As 2884, but plume 2, inner circle *obv.*	£155	£360
2888	Similar, but with inner circles both sides	£120	£300
2889	— — later *rev.* with smaller square-shaped plume	£115	£275
2890	Bust as the first Oxford sixpence; with crown cutting inner circle	£155	£365
2891	**Groat.** Large bust, lace collar, no armour on shoulder. Crown breaks inner circle. ℞. Shield, plume 1 or 2	£25	£55
2892	— Similar, armour on shoulder, shorter collar. ℞. Similar	£30	£65
2893	— Smaller, neater bust not breaking circle. ℞. Similar	£25	£55

2891   2894   2895–9

		F	VF
2894	**Threepence.** Small bust, reads M . B . FR . ET . H . ℞. Shield, plume 1 or 2 above	£20	£45
2895	— Similar, but HI. ℞. Shield, plume 2 above	£23	£50
2896	— M : B : FR : ET . HI : ℞. Similar	£23	£50
2897	— M . B . F . ET . HIB. ℞. Similar	£28	£60
2898	— M : B : F : ET : HIB : ℞. Similar	£28	£60
2899	— MAG : B : F : ET . H : ℞. Similar	£25	£55

Aberystwyth, *continued.*

		F	VF
2900	**Halfgroat.** Bust as Tower type 3a. ℞. Large plume. No i.cs	£80	£250
2900A	Bust as 2881. ℞. As last	£80	£250
2901	Bust with round lace collar; inner circles	£80	£250
2902	Briot's bust, square lace collar; inner circles	£80	£250

2905   2907

2903	**Penny.** As 2900; CARO; no inner circles	£45	£135
2904	As 2901; CARO; inner circles	£45	£135
2905	As 2903; CAROLVS; inner circles	£43	£120
2906	Similar, but Briot's bust; inner circles	£55	£150
2907	**Halfpenny.** No legend. *O.* Rose. ℞. Plume	£100	£250

Aberystwyth-Furnace mint, 1648/9. *Mm.* crown

2908	**Halfcrown.** King on horseback. ℞. As 2878	£600	£1500
2909	**Shilling.** Aberystwyth type, but *mm.* crown	*Extremely rare*	
2910	**Sixpence.** Similar	*Extremely rare*	

2911   2913

2911	**Groat.** Similar	£135	£275
2912	**Threepence.** Similar	£175	£350
2913	**Halfgroat.** Similar. ℞. Large plume	£185	£375
2914	**Penny.** Similar	£600	£1250

Uncertain mint (? Hereford)

2915

		Fair	Fine
2915	**Halfcrown.** As illustration, dated 1645 or undated	£600	£1500

Shrewsbury mint, 1642. *Mm.* plume without band   *F*   *VF*

2917 **Pound.** King on horseback, plume behind, Aberystwyth style. ℞. Declaration between two straight lines, XX and three Shrewsbury plumes above, 1642 below £850 £2250

2918 Similar, but Shrewsbury horse walking over pile of arms £750 £1750

2919 As last, but cannon amongst arms and only single plume and XX above Declaration £1000 £2750

2920 **Half-pound.** As 2917, but X £375 £1150

2921 Similar, but only two plumes on *rev.* £450 £1350

2922 Shrewsbury horseman with ground-line £400 £1150

2923 — with cannon and arms below horse £350 £1100

2924 — no cannon in arms, no plume on *obv.* £350 £1100

2926

2925 **Crown.** Aberystwyth horseman . . . . *Unique*

2926 Shrewsbury horseman with ground-line £275 £850

2927 **Halfcrown.** *O.* From Aberystwyth die; *mm.* book. ℞. Single plume above Declaration, 1642 . . . . £250 £625

2928 Aberystwyth horseman, fat plume behind. ℞. Three plumes above Declaration £165 £400

2929 Shrewsbury horseman. ℞. As 2927, single plume £185 £475

2930 — ℞. 2: plume: 6, above Declaration £300 £750

2931 — with ground-line. ℞. Similar £275 £650

2932 — — ℞. As 2927, single plume £175 £450

2933 — — ℞. Three thin plumes above Declaration £110 £300

2934 — — — no plume behind king £125 £325

2935 **Shilling.** *O.* From Aberystwyth die; *mm.* book. ℞. Declaration type £135 £300

2936 *O.* From Shrewsbury die. ℞. Similar £150 £350

Oxford mint, 1642/3–6. *Mm.* usually plume with band, except on the smaller denominations when it is lis or pellets. There were so many dies used at this mint that we can only give a selection of the more easily identifiable varieties.

2937 **Pound.** Large horseman over arms, no exergual line, fine workmanship. ℞. Three Shrewsbury plumes and XX above Declaration, 1642 below £1050 £3450

2937

		F	VF
2938	— Similar, but three Oxford plumes, 1643	£1050	£3450
2939	Shrewsbury horseman trampling on arms, exergual line. ℞. As last, 1642 .	£650	£2100
2940	— — cannon amongst arms, 1642–3	£600	£1950
2941	— as last but exergue is chequered, 1642	£750	£2450
2942	Briot's horseman, 1643	£1150	£3700
2943	*O.* As 2937. ℞. Declaration in cartouche, single large plume above, 1644 OX below	£1500	£4500
2944	**Half-pound.** As next. ℞. Shrewsbury die, 1642	£275	£750
2945	Oxford dies both sides, 1642–3	£250	£700
2946	**Crown.** *O.* Shrewsbury die with ground-line. ℞. As last but V	£275	£750
2947	Oxford horseman with grass below, 1643	£400	£1100
2948	By Rawlins. King riding over a view of the city. ℞. Floral scrolls above and below Declaration, 1644 / OXON below (Beware forgeries!)	*Extremely rare*	
	Note. *An extremely fine specimen sold at auction in June 1974 for £20,000.*		
2949	**Halfcrown.** *O.* From Shrewsbury die, 1642	£135	£400
2950	℞. From Shrewsbury die, 1642	£105	£300
2951	Both Oxford dies, but Shrewsbury type horse, ground-line, 1642	£70	£190
2952	— — without ground-line, 1642	£90	£270
2953	Oxford type horse, ground-line, 1643	£75	£240

2954

2954	— without ground-line, 1643	£70	£200

Oxford Silver, *continued.*

		F	VF
2955	**Halfcrown.** Briot's horse, grass below, 1643	£80	£250
2956	—— large central plume, 1643, 1644 / OX	£90	£290
2957	— lumpy ground, 1643, 1643 / OX	£80	£225
2958	—— large central plume, 1643–4 / OX	£80	£250
2959	— plain ground, 1644–5 / OX	£80	£250
2960	—— large central plume, 1644 / OX	£80	£250
2961	——— Similar, but large date in script	£105	£350
2962	——— two small plumes at date, 1644 / OX	£225	£550
2963	Large horse (as Briot's, but clumsier), plain ground, 1644–5 / OX	£90	£300
2964	— lumpy ground, 1644–5 / OX	£90	£300
2965	—— large central plume, 1644 / OX	£90	£300
2966	— pebbly ground, 1645–6 / OX	£90	£300
2967	—— pellets or annulets by plumes and at date, 1645–6 / OX	£90	£300
2968	— grass below, 1645–6 / OX	£90	£350
2969	—— rosettes by plumes and at date, 1645 / OX	£110	£400
2970	**Shilling.** *O.* From Shrewsbury die. ℞. Declaration type, 1642	£75	£200
2971	Both Oxford dies. Small bust, 1642–3	£58	£160
2972	Similar, but coarser work, 1643	£58	£160
2973	Large bust of fine work, 1643	£58	£160
2974	— 1644–6 / OX	£65	£175
2975	Bust with bent crown, 1643	£65	£175
2976	— 1644 / OX	£65	£175
2977	Rawlins' dies. Fine bust with R on truncation, 1644	£80	£240
2978	—— 1644 / OX	£90	£270
2979	Small size, 1646, annulets or pellets at date	£100	£300

2980

		F	VF
2980	**Sixpence.** *O.* Aberystwyth die. ℞. With three Oxford plumes, 1642–3	£120	£275
2981	— ℞. With three Shrewsbury plumes, 1643	£120	£275
2982	— ℞. With Shrewsbury plume and two lis, 1644 / OX	£135	£325

2985   2991

		F	VF
2983	**Groat.** *O.* Aberystwyth die. ℞. As 2985	£35	£120
2984	As last but three plumes above Declaration	£75	£225

Oxford Silver, *continued.*

		F	VF
2985	**Groat.** As illustration, with lion's head on shoulder	£50	£135
2986	Large bust reaching to top of coin. ℞. As last	£50	£135
2987	Large bust to bottom of coin, lion's head on shoulder, legend starts at bottom l. ℞. As last	£60	£160
2988	Rawlins' die; similar, but no i.c., and with R on shoulder. ℞. As last	£60	£160
2989	O. As 2985. ℞. Large single plume and scroll above Declaration, 1645	£60	£160
2990	O. As 2987. ℞. As last	£60	£160
2991	O. As 2988. ℞. Large single plume above Declaration, which is in cartouche, 1645–6	£80	£200
2992	**Threepence.** O. Aberystwyth die. ℞. Declaration type, 1644 / OX	£50	£140
2993	Rawlins' die, R below shoulder. ℞. Aberystwyth die with oval shield; *mm.* book	£45	£140
2994	— ℞. Declaration type, three lis above, 1644 below	£50	£140
2995	— Similar, without the R , 1646 (over 1644)	£50	£140
2996	**Halfgroat.** ℞. Aberystwyth type with large plume	£55	£150
2997	— ℞. Declaration type, 1644 / OX	£80	£180

2995   2999

		F	VF
2998	**Penny.** O. Aberystwyth die; *mm.* book. ℞. Type, small plume	£75	£175
2999	— — ℞. Type, large plume	£75	£175
3000	— Rawlins' die with R . ℞. Type, small plume	£75	£175
3001	— Wider bust similar to the halfgroat. ℞. Similar	£90	£250
3002	— — ℞. Declaration type, 1644	£200	£550

Bristol mint, 1643–5. *Mm.* usually plume or Br., except on small denominations

		F	VF
3003	**Halfcrown.** O. Oxford die with or without groundline. ℞. Declaration, three Bristol plumes above, 1643 below	£90	£285
3004	— — Br. *mm.* on *rev.*, 1643	£85	£275
3005	King wears unusual flat crown, *obv. mm.* acorn? between four pellets. ℞. As 3003, 1643	£100	£295
3006	— Br. *mm.* on *rev.*, 1643–4	£100	£295
3007	Shrewsbury plume behind king. ℞. As last	£75	£210
3008	— Br. below date, 1644	£80	£250

Bristol Silver, *continued.*

3009   3024

		F	VF
3009	**Halfcrown.** Br. below horse and below date, 1644–5	£110	£320
3010	Br. also *mm.* on *rev.*, 1644–5	£85	£250
3011	**Shilling.** *O.* Oxford die. ℞. Declaration, 1643	£80	£215
3012	— — Similar, but Br. as *rev. mm.*, 1643–4	£80	£215
3013	Crude bust. ℞. As 3011, 1643	£80	£215
3014	— — Similar, but Br. as *rev. mm.*, 1644	£80	£215
3015	Bust of good style, plumelet before. ℞. As last, 1644–5	£80	£215
3016	— — Similar, but Br. below date instead of as *mm.*, 1644	£85	£235
3017	Bust with round collar, *mm.* Br. on its side. ℞. As last, 1644–5	£85	£235
3018	Bust with square collar. ℞. Br. as *mm.*, 1645	£80	£215
3019	**Sixpence.** Coarse bust, nothing before. ℞. Declaration, 1643	£140	£500
3020	— Plumelet before face, 1644	£125	£400
3021	**Groat.** Bust l. ℞. Declaration, 1644	£80	£250
3022	— Plumelet before face, 1644	£110	£350
3023	— Br. below date, 1644	£100	£300
3024	**Threepence.** *O.* Aberystwyth die; *mm.* book. ℞. Declaration, 1644	£100	£350
3025	Bristol die, plume before face, no *mm.*, 1644	£90	£300
3026	**Halfgroat.** Br. in place of date below Declaration	£100	£350
3027	**Penny.** Similar bust, I behind. ℞. Large plume with bands	£200	£550

Late 'Declaration' issues, 1645–6

(Previously given as Lundy Island and/or Appledore and Barnstaple/Bideford, it seems likely that coins marked A, 1645 may be Ashby de la Zouch and the coins marked B or with plumes may be Bridgnorth on Severn. A West Country provenance, or any association with Thomas Bushell now seems unlikely.)

3028	**Halfcrown.** A below horse and date and as *rev. mm.*, 1645	£700	£2000
3029	Similar but *rev.* from altered Bristol die (i.e. the A is over Br.)	£525	£1500
3030	As 3028 but without A below date 1645	£475	£1450
3031	A below horse and as *rev. mm.* Scroll above Declaration, B below 1646 . .	*Extremely rare*	
3032	Plumelet below horse. ℞. *Mm.* Shrewsbury plume; scroll above Declaration, 1646	£400	£1100
3033	— Similar, but plumelet below date	£450	£1250
3034	**Shilling.** Crowned bust l., *mm.* plume. ℞. Declaration type; *mm.* A and A below 1645	£350	£750
3035	— Similar, but plumelet before face	£350	£750
3036	— — ℞. Scroll above Declaration, 1646, *mm.* plumelet	£150	£350
3037	Large Shrewsbury plume before face. ℞. As last but *mm.* pellet	£175	£400

Late 'Declaration' Silver, *continued.*

3039   3044

		F	VF
3038	**Sixpence.** *O.* Plumelet before face; *mm.* ➤; 1645	£200	£500
3039	*O.* Large Shrewsbury plume before face; *mm.* B. ℞. Scroll above Declaration, 1646	£90	£225
3040	**Groat.** As 3038	*Extremely rare*	
3041	Somewhat similar, but *obv. mm.* plumelet; 1646	£100	£250
3042	**Threepence.** Somewhat as last but only single plumelet above Declaration, no line below, 1645	£80	£210
3043	— Scroll in place of line above, 1646 below	£70	£165
3044	**Halfgroat.** Bust l., II behind. ℞. Large plume with bands dividing 1646	£200	£450
	The penny listed under Bristol may belong to this series.		

Truro mint, 1642–3. *Mm.* rose

		F	VF
3045	**Half-pound.** King on horseback, face turned frontwards. ℞. CHRISTO, etc., round garnished shield. Struck from crown dies on thick flan	*Extremely rare*	
3046	**Crown.** Similar type	£135	£350
3047	— Shield garnished with twelve even scrolls	£160	£450
3048	King's face in profile, well-shaped flan, finer workmanship	£185	£475

3049

		F	VF
3049	**Halfcrown.** King on spirited horse galloping over arms. ℞. Oval garnished shield, 1642 in cartouche below	£900	£3000
3050	Similar, but no arms. ℞. Oblong shield, CR at sides	£700	£2500
3051	Galloping horse, king holds sword. ℞. Similar	£650	£2300
3052	— ℞. Similar, but CR above	£600	£1900
3053	Trotting horse. ℞. Similar, but CR at sides	£300	£750

Truro Silver, *continued.*

		F	VF
3054	**Halfcrown.** Walking horse, king's head in profile. R. Similar	£275	£725
3055	— R. Similar, but CR above	£325	£850
3056	**Shilling.** Small bust of good style. R. Oblong shield	£425	£1200
3057	— R. Round shield with eight even scrolls	£550	£1400
3058	— R. Oval shield with CR at sides	£250	£700
3059	Normal bust with lank hair. R. As last	£150	£450
3060	— R. As 3057	£450	£1300
3061	— R. Round shield with six scrolls	£150	£450

Truro or Exeter mint. *Mm.* rose

3064   3067–9

3062	**Halfcrown.** King on horseback, sash tied in bow. R. Oblong shield with CR at sides	£110	£300
3063	— R. Round shield with eight even scrolls	£70	£190
3064	— R. Round shield with six scrolls	£75	£200
3065	King's sash flies out behind. R. As 3063	£105	£275
3066	— R. Oblong shield, curved sides, little garniture	*Extremely rare*	
3067	Briot's horse with groundline. R. As 3063	£105	£275
3068	— R. As 3066		*Unique*
3069	— R. As 3064	£105	£275

Exeter mint, 1643–6. *Mm.* rose except where stated

3070	**Crown.** As 3046, but 1644 divided by *rev. mm.*	£125	£300
3071	Similar, but 1644 to l. of *mm.*	£110	£260
3072	Similar, but 1645 and *rev. mm.* EX	£125	£300
3073	King's sash in two loose ends; *mm.* castle/rose, 1645	£110	£260
3074	— *mm.* castle/EX, 1645	£150	£350
3075	— *mm.* castle, 1645	£110	£260
3076	**Halfcrown.** As 3049, but 1644 in legend	*Extremely rare*	
3077	Similar, but *mm.* castle, 1645		*Unique*
3078	Short portly figure, leaning backwards on ill-proportioned horse, 1644, 16 rose 44	£175	£450
3079	Briot's horse and groundline; 1644	£125	£350

Exeter Silver, *continued.*

3080

		F	*VF*
3080	**Halfcrown.** Horse with twisted tail; 1644–5	£120	£350
3081	— ℞. *Mm.* castle, 1645	£160	£450
3082	— ℞. *Mm.* EX, 1645	£160	£450
3083	— ℞. Declaration type; *mm.* EX, 1644–5	£750	£2100
3084	— — — EX also below 1644	£550	£1650
3085	**Shilling.** As 3061. 1644, 16 rose 44, 1645	£100	£265
3086	— ℞. Declaration type, 1645	£350	£1250
3087	**Sixpence.** As 3085. 1644, 16 rose 44	£90	£275
3088	**Groat.** Somewhat similar but 1644 at beginning of *obv.* legend	£75	£225

3089   3091

		F	*VF*
3089	**Threepence.** As illustration, 1644	£50	£150
3090	**Halfgroat.** Similar, but II. ℞. Oval shield, 1644	£80	£240
3091	— ℞. Large rose, 1644	£100	£300
3092	**Penny.** As last but I behind head	£135	£400

Worcester mint, 1643–4

3096

Worcester Silver, *continued.*

		F	VF
3093	**Halfcrown.** King on horseback l., W below; *mm.* two lions. ℞. Declaration type 1644	£350	£1050
3094	— ℞. Square-topped shield; *mm.* helmet, castle	£275	£850
3095	— ℞. Oval shield; *mm.* helmet	£275	£850
3096	Similar but grass indicated; *mm.* castle. ℞. Square-topped shield; *mm.* helmet or none. (Illustrated at foot of previous page)	£275	£850
3097	— ℞. Oval draped shield, lis or lions in legend	£300	£925
3098	— ℞. Oval shield CR at sides, roses in legend	£325	£1000
3099	— ℞. FLORENT etc., oval garnished shield with lion's paws each side ...	£400	£1150
3100	Tall king, no W or *mm.* ℞. Oval shield, lis, roses, lions or stars in legend ..	£275	£850
3101	— ℞. Square-topped shield; *mm.* helmet	£325	£1100
3102	— ℞. FLORENT, etc., oval shield	£400	£1150
3103	Briot type horse, sword slopes forward, ground-line. ℞. Oval shield, roses in legend	£275	£850
3104	— Similar, but CR at sides	£325	£1000
3105	Dumpy, portly king, crude horse. ℞. As 3100	£275	£850

3106

3106	Thin king and horse. ℞. Oval shield, stars in legend	£275	£800

Worcester or Salopia (Shrewsbury)

3111   3117

3107	**Shilling.** Bust of king l., faithfully rendered. ℞. Square-topped shield; *mm.* castle	£350	£1000
3108	— ℞. CR above shield; *mm.* helmet and lion	£350	£1000
3109	— ℞. Oval shield; *mm.* lion, pear	£325	£900

	F	VF

3110 **Shilling.** Bust a somewhat crude copy of last; *mm.* bird, lis. ℞. Square-topped shield with lion's paws above and at sides; *mm.* boar's head, helmet — £350 £1000

3111 — — CR above £350 £1000

3112 — ℞. Oval shield, lis in legend; *mm.* lis £300 £850

3113 — ℞. Round shield; *mm.* various £325 £900

3114 Bust r.; *mm.* pear. ℞. Oval shield, rose and lis in legend . . . . *Extremely rare*

3115 **Sixpence.** As 3110; *mm.* castle, castle/boar's hd. £500 £1250

3116 **Groat.** As 3112; *mm.* lis/helmet, rose/helmet £375 £850

3117 **Threepence.** Similar; *mm.* lis *obv.* £250 £650

3118 **Halfgroat.** Similar; *mm.* lis (*O.*) various (℞.) £275 £675

Salopia (Shrewsbury) mint, 1644

3119 **Halfcrown.** King on horseback l. SA below; *mm.* lis. ℞. Oval shield; *mm.* helmet . . . . *Extremely rare*

3120 — ℞. FLORENT, etc., oval shield, no *mm.* . . . . *Extremely rare*

3121 — SA erased or replaced by large pellet or cannon ball; *mm.* lis in legend, helmet £1200 £2750

3122 Tall horse and king, nothing below; *mm.* lis. ℞. Large round shield with crude garniture; *mm.* helmet £525 £1250

3123 — ℞. Small uncrowned square-topped shield with lion's paw above and at sides; *mm.* helmet £575 £1400

3124 — ℞. Small oval shield; *mm.* various £525 £1250

3125 — ℞. As 3120 . . . . £600 £1500

3126 Cruder work with little or no mane before horse. ℞. Round shield £525 £1250

3127 Grass beneath horse. ℞. Similar; *mm.* lis or rose £525 £1250

3128 Ground below horse. ℞. As 3120 . . . . £575 £1400

Hartlebury Castle (Worcs.) mint, 1646

3129

3129 **Halfcrown.** *O. Mm.* pear. ℞. HC (Hartlebury Castle) in garniture below shield; *mm.* three pears £1250 £3000

Chester mint, 1644

3130

	F	VF
3130 **Halfcrown.** As illus. ℞. Oval shield; *mm.* three gerbs and sword	£425	£1000
3131 As last. ℞. Crowned oval shield; *mm.* prostrate gerb, -/cinquefoil, and -/∴	£450	£1100
3131A — Similar, but without plume or CHST; *mm.* ∴, cinquefoil, prostrate gerb	£500	£1100
3132 — ℞. Crowned square-topped shield with CR at sides both crowned; *mm.* cinquefoil, rose in *rev.* legend	£525	£1350
3133 As 3130, but without plume or CHST. ℞. Declaration type, 1644; *mm.* plume, ∴ . . .	£475	£1200
3133A **Shilling.** Bust l. ℞. Oval garnished shield; *mm.* ∴ (obv. only)	*Extremely rare*	
3133B — — ℞. Square-topped shield; *mm.* as last	*Extremely rare*	
3134 **Threepence.** ℞. Square-topped shield; *mm.* prostrate gerb	£300	£650

Coventry (or Corfe Castle) mint? *Mm.* two interlocked C's

| 3135 **Halfcrown.** King on horseback l. ℞. Oval shield . . . . | *Extremely rare* | |

Carlisle besieged, 1644–5

| 3136 **Three shillings.** Large crown above C . R / . III . S. ℞. OBS . CARL / · 1645 . | *Extremely rare* | |
| 3137 Similar but : OBS : / · : CARL : · / · 1645 · . . . . | £1500 | £3500 |

3138

| 3138 **Shilling.** As illustration . . . . | £850 | £2250 |
| 3139 ℞. Legend and date in two lines . . . . | £900 | £2500 |

Note. *(3136–39) Round or Octagonal pieces exist.*

Newark besieged, several times 1645–6, surrendered May 1646

3140

		F	VF
3140	**Halfcrown.** Large crown between CR; below, XXX. ℞. OBS / NEWARK / 1645 or 1646	£135	£300
3141	**Shilling.** Similar but curious flat shaped crown, NEWARKE, 1645	£130	£275
3142	Similar but high arched crown, 1645	£100	£175
3143	—NEWARK, 1645 or 1646	£90	£200
3144	**Ninepence.** As halfcrown but IX, 1645 or 1646	£100	£225
3145	—NEWARKE, 1645	£95	£200
3146	**Sixpence.** As halfcrown but VI, 1646	£125	£300

Pontefract besieged, June 1648–March 1648–9

3147	**Two shillings** (lozenge shaped). DVM : SPIRO : SPERO around CR crowned. ℞. Castle surrounded by OBS, PC, sword and 1648	*Extremely rare*	
3148	**Shilling** (lozenge shaped, octagonal or round). Similar	£275	£600
3149	— Similar but XII to r. dividing PC	£250	£575

After the death of Charles I (30 Jan. 1648/9), in the name of Charles II

3149   3150

3150	**Shilling** (octagonal). *O.* As last. ℞. CAROLVS : SECVNDVS : 1648, castle gateway with flag dividing PC, OBS on l., cannon protrudes on r.	£225	£550
3151	CAROL : II : etc., around HANC : DE / VS : DEDIT / 1648. ℞. POST : MORTEM : PATRIS : PRO : FILIO around gateway etc. as last	£225	£550

Scarborough besieged, July 1644–July 1645

3165   3168

Type I. Castle with gateway to left, value punched below

3152	**Five shillings and eightpence**	*Extremely rare*
3153	**Crown.** Similar but SC also punched	*Extremely rare*
3154	**Three shillings and fourpence.** As 3152	*Extremely rare*
3155	**Three shillings.** Similar	*Extremely rare*
3156	**Two shillings and tenpence.** Similar	£4500
3157	**Halfcrown.** Similar	£3750
3158	**Two shillings and fourpence.** Similar	*Extremely rare*
3159	**Two shillings and twopence.** Similar	*Extremely rare*
3160	**Two shillings.** Similar	*Extremely rare*
3161	**One shilling and ninepence.** Similar	*Extremely rare*
3162	**One shilling and sixpence.** Similar	*Extremely rare*
3163	**One shilling and fourpence.** Similar	*Extremely rare*
3164	**One shilling and threepence.** Similar	*Extremely rare*
3165	**Shilling.** As illustration	*Extremely rare*
3166	**Sixpence.** Similar	*Extremely rare*
3167	**Groat.** Similar	*Extremely rare*

Type II. Castle with two turrets, value punched below

3168	**Two shillings.** Two castles	*Extremely rare*
3170	**One shilling and sixpence.** Single castle	*Extremely rare*
3171	**One shilling and fourpence.** Similar	£3000
3172	**One shilling and threepence.** Similar	*Extremely rare*
3173	**One shilling and twopence.** Similar	*Extremely rare*
3174	**One shilling and one penny.** Similar	*Extremely rare*
3175	**Shilling.** Similar	£3500
3176	**Elevenpence.** Similar	*Extremely rare*
3177	**Tenpence.** Similar	*Extremely rare*
3178	**Ninepence.** Similar	*Extremely rare*
3179	**Sevenpence.** Similar	*Extremely rare*
3180	**Sixpence.** Similar	*Extremely rare*

COPPER

For mintmarks see *English Copper, Tin and Bronze Coins in the British Museum, 1558–1958*, by C. Wilson Peck.

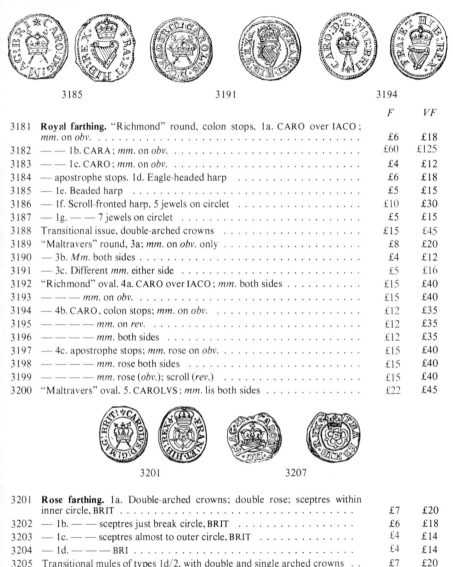

3185   3191   3194

		F	VF
3181	**Royal farthing.** "Richmond" round, colon stops, 1a. CARO over IACO; mm. on *obv.*	£6	£18
3182	— — 1b. CARA; *mm.* on *obv.*	£60	£125
3183	— — 1c. CARO; *mm.* on *obv.*	£4	£12
3184	— apostrophe stops. 1d. Eagle-headed harp	£6	£18
3185	— 1e. Beaded harp	£5	£15
3186	— 1f. Scroll-fronted harp, 5 jewels on circlet	£10	£30
3187	— 1g. — — 7 jewels on circlet	£5	£15
3188	Transitional issue, double-arched crowns	£15	£45
3189	"Maltravers" round, 3a; *mm.* on *obv.* only	£8	£20
3190	— 3b. *Mm.* both sides	£4	£12
3191	— 3c. Different *mm.* either side	£5	£16
3192	"Richmond" oval. 4a. CARO over IACO; *mm.* both sides	£15	£40
3193	— — — *mm.* on *obv.*	£15	£40
3194	— 4b. CARO, colon stops; *mm.* on *obv.*	£12	£35
3195	— — — — *mm.* on *rev.*	£12	£35
3196	— — — — *mm.* both sides	£12	£35
3197	— 4c. apostrophe stops; *mm.* rose on *obv.*	£15	£40
3198	— — — — *mm.* rose both sides	£15	£40
3199	— — — — *mm.* rose (*obv.*); scroll (*rev.*)	£15	£40
3200	"Maltravers" oval. 5. CAROLVS; *mm.* lis both sides	£22	£45

3201   3207

3201	**Rose farthing.** 1a. Double-arched crowns; double rose; sceptres within inner circle, BRIT	£7	£20
3202	— 1b. — — sceptres just break circle, BRIT	£6	£18
3203	— 1c. — — sceptres almost to outer circle, BRIT	£4	£14
3204	— 1d. — — — BRI	£4	£14
3205	Transitional mules of types 1d/2, with double and single arched crowns	£7	£20
3206	— 2. Single-arched crowns; single rose	£3	£9
3207	— 3. Sceptres below crown	£10	£30

COMMONWEALTH, 1649–60

The coins struck during the Commonwealth have inscriptions in English instead of Latin which was considered to savour too much of papacy. St. George's cross and the Irish harp take the place of the royal arms. The silver halfpenny was issued for the last time.

Coins with *mm.* anchor were struck during the protectorship of Richard Cromwell.

Mintmarks

1649–57 Sun 1658–60 Anchor

GOLD

3208   3213

		F	VF
3208	**Unite.** As illustration; *mm.* sun, 1649–57	£525	£1100
3209	— *mm.* anchor, 1658, 1660	£1000	£2750
3210	**Double-crown.** As illus., but X ; *mm.* sun, 1649–55, 57	£400	£850
3211	— *mm.* anchor, 1660	£1100	£2500
3212	**Crown.** As illus., but V ; *mm.* sun, 1649–55, 57	£275	£600
3213	— *mm.* anchor, 1658–60	£900	£2000

SILVER

		F	VF
3214	**Crown.** Same type; *mm.* sun, 1649, 51–4, 56	£200	£475
3215	**Halfcrown.** Similar; *mm.* sun, 1649, 1651–6	£65	£135
3216	— *mm.* anchor, 1658–1660 .... *Fair* £135	£325	
3217	**Shilling.** Similar; *mm.* sun, 1649, 1651–7	£40	£115
3218	— *mm.* anchor, 1658–60 .... *Fair* £110	£275	
3219	**Sixpence.** Similar; *mm.* sun, 1649, 1651–7	£40	£115
3220	— *mm.* anchor, 1658–60 .... *Fair* £80	£200	

3221   3223

		F	VF
3221	**Halfgroat.** As illustration	£15	£35
3222	**Penny.** Similar, but I above shields	£15	£35
3223	**Halfpenny.** As illustration	£15	£35

Oliver Cromwell. All said to be only patterns, but some circulated, especially the 1656 halfcrown and the shillings. Half broads exist, but are not contemporary.

GOLD

3224 **Fifty shillings.** Head l. ℞. Shield, 1656. Inscribed edge . . . .   *Extremely rare*

3225

		VF	*EF*
3225	**Broad** (= 20s.). Similar, but grained edge	£2500	£6000

SILVER

3227

		F	*VF*
3226	**Crown.** Bust l. ℞. Shield, 1658. Inscribed edge	£550	£1100
3227	**Halfcrown.** Similar, 1656, 1658	£250	£500
3228	**Shilling.** Similar, but grained edge, 1658	£200	£400
3229	**Sixpence.** Similar	*Extremely rare*	

COPPER

3230

3230 **Farthing.** Dr. bust l. ℞. CHARITIE AND CHANGE, shield £1200   £2250
      There are also other reverses.

SEVENTEENTH CENTURY TOKENS

As there was no authorized copper coinage under the Commonwealth, towns and traders took it into their own hands to issue small change. Between 1648 and 1672 there was an enormous and very varied issue of these tokens. They were mostly farthings and halfpennies, but there were also some pennies. No collection is truly representative unless it contains at least a few. Many collectors specialize in those of their own town or county.

	F
Price of commoner pennies	£28
— — — round halfpennies	£8
— — — octagonal halfpennies	£18
— — — heart-shaped halfpennies	£100
— — — square or lozenge-shaped halfpennies	£75
— — — round farthings	£5

For further details of seventeenth century tokens see *Trade Tokens issued in the Seventeenth Century* by G. C. Williamson, also Seaby's *British Tokens and their Values*, and *Seventeenth Century Tokens of the British Isles and their Values* by Michael Dickinson, to be published October 1986.

CHARLES II, 1660–85

For the first two years after the Restoration the same denominations, apart from the silver crown, were struck as were issued during the Commonwealth. In 1662 the hand hammering of coins was abandoned in favour of manufacture by the Roettiers improved mill and screw presses. As a prevention against clipping the larger coins were made with the edge inscribed DECVS ET TVTAMEN and the regnal year and the medium sized coins were given a grained edge.

The new gold coins were current for 100s., 20s. and 10s., and they came to be called "guineas" as the gold from which some of them were made was imported from Guinea by the Africa Company (whose badge was the Elephant and Castle). It was not until some years later that the guinea increased in value to 21s. and more. The Africa Co. badge is also found on some silver, and so is the plume symbol indicating silver from the Welsh mines. The four smallest silver denominations, though known today as "Maundy Money", were actually issued for general circulation: at this period the silver penny was probably the only coin distributed at the royal Maundy ceremonies. The smaller "machine" made coins were perhaps minted later than 1662.

A good regal copper coinage was issued for the first time in 1672, but later in the reign farthings were struck in tin (with a copper plug) in order to help the Cornish tin industry.

For the emergency issues struck in the name of Charles II in 1648/9, see the siege pieces of Pontefract listed under Charles I, nos. 3150–1.

Mintmark: Crown.

GOLD

Hammered coinage, 1660–2
First issue. Without mark of value

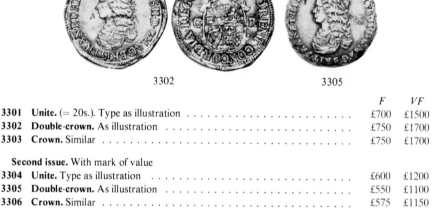

3302   3305

		F	VF
3301	**Unite.** (= 20s.). Type as illustration	£700	£1500
3302	**Double-crown.** As illustration	£750	£1700
3303	**Crown.** Similar	£750	£1700
	Second issue. With mark of value		
3304	**Unite.** Type as illustration	£600	£1200
3305	**Double-crown.** As illustration	£550	£1100
3306	**Crown.** Similar	£575	£1150

SILVER
First issue. Without inner circles or mark of value

3307	**Halfcrown.** Crowned bust, as 3309	£450	£1250
3308	**Shilling.** Similar	£150	£425
3309	**Sixpence.** Similar	£150	£400

		F	VF
3310	**Twopence.** Similar	£16	£40
3311	**Penny.** Similar	£18	£45
3312	As last, but without mintmark	£18	£45

3308   3313   3322

Second issue. Without inner circles, but with mark of value.

		F	VF
3313	**Halfcrown.** Crowned bust	£600	£1750
3314	**Shilling.** Similar	£300	£750
3315	**Sixpence.** Similar	£450	£1150
3316	**Twopence.** Similar, but *mm.* on *obv.* only	£12	£30
3317	Similar, but *mm.* both sides (machine made)	£10	£25
3318	Bust to edge of coin, legend starts at bottom l. (machine made, single arch crown)	£10	£25
3319	**Penny.** As 3317	£12	£30
3320	As 3318 (single arch crown)	£10	£25

3310   3317   3326

Third issue. With inner circles and mark of value

		F	VF
3321	**Halfcrown.** Crowned bust	£65	£240
3322	**Shilling.** Similar	£40	£140
3323	**Sixpence.** Similar	£50	£150
3324	**Fourpence.** Similar	£10	£30
3325	**Threepence.** Similar	£10	£30
3326	**Twopence.** Similar	£7	£20
3327	**Penny.** Similar	£15	£35

GOLD

Milled coinage

3328   3335

3328   Five guineas. First bust, pointed truncation

	F	VF		F	VF		F	VF
	£	£		£	£		£	£
1668	650.00	1250.00	1672	650.00	1250.00	1676	750.00	1500.00
1669	700.00	1300.00	1673	650.00	1250.00	1677	700.00	1300.00
1670	650.00	1150.00	1674	750.00	1400.00	1678	650.00	1200.00
1671	750.00	1450.00	1675	700.00	1300.00			

3329   — with elephant below bust

	F	VF		F	VF
1668	600.00	1100.00	1675	950.00	1800.00
1669	950.00	1800.00	1677/5	Extremely rare	

3330   — with elephant and castle below

	F	VF		F	VF
1675	Extremely rare		1677	750.00	1500.00
1676	700.00	1300.00	1678	850.00	1600.00

3331   Second bust, rounded truncation

	F	VF		F	VF		F	VF
1678	850.00	1600.00	1681	650.00	1200.00	1684	600.00	1100.00
1679	650.00	1200.00	1682	650.00	1200.00			
1680	700.00	1300.00	1683	650.00	1250.00			

3332   — with elephant and castle below

	F	VF		F	VF		F	VF
1680	Extremely rare		1682	700.00	1300.00	1684	650.00	1150.00
1681	850.00	1600.00	1683	850.00	1600.00			

3333   Two guineas. First bust, pointed truncation

	F	VF		F	VF
1664	350.00	850.00	1669	Extremely rare	
1665	Extremely rare		1671	450.00	1000.00

3334   — with elephant below, 1664 .... 275.00   600.00

3335   Second bust, rounded truncation

	F	VF		F	VF		F	VF
1675	375.00	800.00	1679	300.00	650.00	1683	250.00	550.00
1676	300.00	650.00	1680	400.00	1025.00	1684	375.00	750.00
1677	250.00	575.00	1681	250.00	575.00			
1678	250.00	550.00	1682	250.00	575.00			

3336   — with elephant and castle below

	F	VF		F	VF		F	VF
1676	275.00	600.00	1678	300.00	650.00	1683	500.00	1150.00
1677	Extremely rare		1682	250.00	475.00	1684	400.00	1050.00

3337   — with elephant only below, 1678 .... Extremely rare

N.B. *Overstruck dates are listed only if commoner than the normal date or if no normal date is known.*

Note. *Values for coins in EF (extremely fine) condition can be three or more times the value of VF (very fine) specimens.*

Milled gold

3343   3345

		F	VF
3338	**Guinea.** First bust, 1663	600.00	1450.00
3339	— with elephant below, 1663	500.00	1150.00
3340	Second bust, 1664	450.00	950.00
3341	— with elephant below, 1664		*Extremely rare*

3342   Third bust, normal portrait

	F £	VF £		F £	VF £		F £	VF £
1664 ...	225.00	700.00	1668 ...	225.00	700.00	1672 ...	275.00	850.00
1665 ...	225.00	700.00	1669 ...	275.00	850.00	1673 ...	450.00	1250.00
1666 ...	225.00	700.00	1670 ...	225.00	700.00			
1667 ...	225.00	700.00	1671 ...	225.00	700.00			

3343   — with elephant below

1664 ...	275.00	850.00	1665 ...	275.00	850.00	1668	*Extremely rare*

3344   Fourth bust, rounded truncation

1672 ...	175.00	600.00	1677 ...	150.00	450.00	1682 ...	175.00	650.00
1673 ...	175.00	650.00	1678 ...	150.00	500.00	1683 ...	150.00	450.00
1674 ...	275.00	900.00	1679 ...	150.00	450.00	1684 ...	175.00	650.00
1675 ...	225.00	700.00	1680 ...	150.00	475.00			
1676 ...	150.00	500.00	1681 ...	175.00	650.00			

3345   — with elephant and castle below

1674 ...	*Extremely rare*		1678 ...	425.00	1100.00	1682 ...	300.00	925.00
1675 ...	275.00	900.00	1679 ...	275.00	900.00	1683 ...	475.00	1400.00
1676 ...	175.00	575.00	1680 ...	475.00	1400.00	1684 ...	300.00	925.00
1677 ...	175.00	575.00	1681 ...	275.00	850.00			

3346   — with elephant below

1677 ...	*Extremely rare*	1678	*Extremely rare*

3347   **Half-guinea.** First bust, pointed truncation

1669 ...	200.00	600.00	1671 ...	250.00	750.00
1670 ...	150.00	425.00	1672 ...	250.00	750.00

3348   Second bust, rounded truncation

1672 ...	175.00	500.00	1677 ...	175.00	500.00	1682 ...	225.00	700.00
1673 ...	350.00	850.00	1678 ...	175.00	525.00	1683 ...	175.00	500.00
1674 ...	350.00	850.00	1679 ...	135.00	400.00	1684 ...	135.00	375.00
1675 ...	*Extremely rare*		1680 ...	350.00	850.00			
1676 ...	175.00	450.00	1681 ...	350.00	850.00			

3349   with elephant and castle below

1676 ...	*Extremely rare*		1680	*Extremely rare*		1684 ...	175.00	500.00
1677 ...	350.00	900.00	1682 ...	350.00	950.00			
1678/7 .	250.00	750.00	1683	*Extremely rare*				

SILVER

Milled coinage

3350

		F	VF
3350	**Crown.** First bust, rose below, edge undated, 1662	£35	£175
3351	— — edge dated, 1662	£45	£225
3352	— no rose, edge dated, 1662	£50	£275
3353	— — edge not dated, 1662	£45	£225
3354	— — new reverse, shields altered, 1663, regnal year on edge in Roman figures ANNO REGNI XV	£40	£200

3355

3355 Second bust, regnal year on edge in Roman figures

	F	VF		F	VF		F	VF
	£	£		£	£		£	£
1664 ...	45.00	200.00	1665 ...	200.00	900.00	1666 ..	50.00	250.00

3356 — — elephant below bust, 1666 .... | | | | | | | 175.00 | 700.00

3357 — regnal year on edge in words (e.g. 1667 = DECIMO NONO)

	F	VF		F	VF		F	VF
1667 ...	35.00	175.00	1669 ...	100.00	400.00	1671 ...	35.00	165.00
1668 ...	35.00	165.00	1670 ...	45.00	200.00			

3358 Third bust

	F	VF		F	VF		F	VF
1671 ...	35.00	165.00	1675/3 .	165.00	700.00	1679 ...	35.00	175.00
1672 ...	35.00	165.00	1676 ...	35.00	165.00	1680/79.	50.00	200.00
1673 ...	35.00	165.00	1677 ...	35.00	175.00			
1674 ...	*Extremely rare*		1678/7 .	110.00	450.00			

3359 Fourth bust

	F	VF		F	VF		F	VF
1679 ...	35.00	175.00	1681 ...	40.00	200.00	1683 ..	110.00	450.00
1680 ...	35.00	175.00	1682/1 .	45.00	225.00	1684 ...	115.00	475.00

3360 — elephant and castle below bust, 1681 .... | | | | | | | 950.00 | 2250.00

Milled Silver

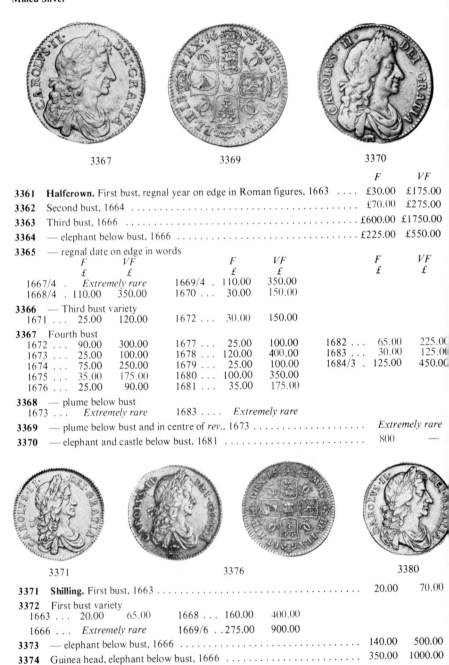

3367   3369   3370

		F	VF
3361	**Halfcrown.** First bust, regnal year on edge in Roman figures, 1663	£30.00	£175.00
3362	Second bust, 1664	£70.00	£275.00
3363	Third bust, 1666	£600.00	£1750.00
3364	— elephant below bust, 1666	£225.00	£550.00

3365 — regnal date on edge in words

	F	VF		F	VF		F	VF
	£	£		£	£		£	£
1667/4 .	*Extremely rare*		1669/4 .	110.00	350.00			
1668/4 .	110.00	350.00	1670 ...	30.00	150.00			

3366 — Third bust variety

	F	VF		F	VF
1671 ...	25.00	120.00	1672 ...	30.00	150.00

3367 Fourth bust

	F	VF		F	VF		F	VF
1672 ...	90.00	300.00	1677 ...	25.00	100.00	1682 ...	65.00	225.00
1673 ...	25.00	100.00	1678 ...	120.00	400.00	1683 ...	30.00	125.00
1674 ...	75.00	250.00	1679 ...	25.00	100.00	1684/3 .	125.00	450.00
1675 ...	35.00	175.00	1680 ...	100.00	350.00			
1676 ...	25.00	90.00	1681 ...	35.00	175.00			

3368 — plume below bust

1673 ...	*Extremely rare*	1683 .... *Extremely rare*

3369	— plume below bust and in centre of *rev.*, 1673	*Extremely rare*
3370	— elephant and castle below bust, 1681	800 —

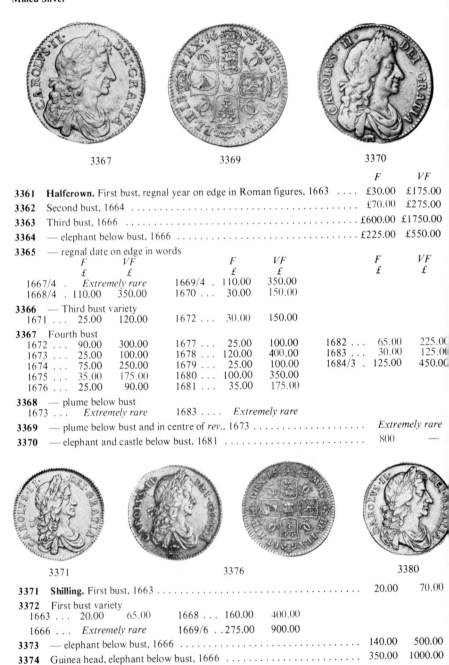

3371   3376   3380

		F	VF
3371	**Shilling.** First bust, 1663	20.00	70.00

3372 First bust variety

	F	VF		F	VF
1663 ...	20.00	65.00	1668 ...	160.00	400.00
1666 ...	*Extremely rare*		1669/6 ..	275.00	900.00

		F	VF
3373	— elephant below bust, 1666	140.00	500.00
3374	Guinea head, elephant below bust, 1666	350.00	1000.00

3375 Shilling. Second bust

	F £	VF £		F £	VF £		F £	VF £
1666 ...	Extremely rare		1673 ...	45.00	175.00	1679 ...	30.00	100.00
1668 ...	25.00	80.00	1674 ...	45.00	175.00	1680	Extremely rare	
1669 ...	Extremely rare		1675 ...	90.00	300.00	1681 ...	50.00	225.00
1670 ...	45.00	175.00	1676 ...	30.00	90.00	1682/1 ..	225.00	500.00
1671 ...	50.00	225.00	1677 ...	30.00	90.00	1683	Extremely rare	
1672 ...	30.00	120.00	1678 ...	45.00	175.00			

3376 — plume below bust and in centre of *rev.*

	F	VF		F	VF		F	VF
1671 ...	65.00	350.00	1675 .	75.00	400.00	1679 ...	75.00	400.00
1673 ...	75.00	400.00	1676 ...	65.00	350.00	1680 ...	150.00	550.00
1674 ...	65.00	350.00						

3377 — plume *rev.* only, 1674 .... 125.00 450.00

3378 — plume *obv.* only

	F	VF		F	VF
1677 ...	125.00	500.00	1679 ...	75.00	350.00

3379 — elephant and castle below bust, 1681/0 .... 1550 —

3380 Third (large) bust

	F	VF		F	VF
1674 ...	125.00	475.00	1675 ...	65.00	275.00

3381 Fourth (large) bust, older features

	F	VF		F	VF
1683 ...	50.00	200.00	1684 ...	45.00	175.00

3382 Sixpence

	F	VF		F	VF		F	VF
1674 ...	15.00	55.00	1678/7 .	18.00	70.00	1682/1	18.00	70.00
1675 ...	15.00	55.00	1679 ...	18.00	70.00	1683 ...	15.00	55.00
1676 ...	20.00	90.00	1680 ...	25.00	100.00	1684 ...	15.00	60.00
1677 ...	15.00	55.00	1681 ...	15.00	55.00			

3384   3386   3388   3390

3383 Fourpence. Undated. Crowned bust l. to edge of coin, value behind.
R̟. Shield 7.00 15.00

3384 Dated. *O.* As illustration. R̟. Four C's

	F	VF		F	VF		F	VF
1670 ...	4.50	10.00	1675 ...	4.00	10.00	1680 ...	3.50	9.00
1671 ...	4.50	10.50	1676 .	4.00	10.00	1681 ...	3.50	9.00
1672/1 .	4.00	10.00	1677 ...	4.00	9.50	1682 ...	4.00	9.50
1673 ...	4.00	10.00	1678 ...	4.00	9.50	1683 ...	3.50	9.00
1674 ...	4.00	10.00	1679 ...	3.50	9.00	1684/3 .	3.50	9.00

3385 Threepence. Undated. As 3383 .... 8.00 18.00

3386 Dated. As illustration

	F	VF		F	VF		F	VF
1670 ...	5.50	9.00	1675 ...	5.50	9.00	1680 ...	4.75	8.50
1671 ...	5.00	8.50	1676 ...	5.00	8.50	1681 ...	4.75	8.50
1672/1 .	5.00	8.50	1677 ...	5.00	8.50	1682 ...	4.75	8.50
1673 ...	5.00	8.50	1678 ...	5.00	8.50	1683 ...	4.75	8.50
1674 ...	5.00	8.50	1679 ...	4.25	7.50	1684 ...	4.75	8.50

Note. *Values for coins in EF (extremely fine) condition can be three or more times the value of VF (very fine) specimens.*

Milled Silver

		F £	VF £		F £	VF £		F £	VF £
3387	**Twopence.** Undated. As 3383 (double arch crown)							6.00	12.50

3388 Dated. As illustration

	F £	VF £		F £	VF £		F £	VF £
1668 ...	4.00	8.50	1675 ...	3.50	8.00	1680 ...	3.50	8.00
1670 ...	3.50	8.00	1676 ...	3.50	8.00	1681 ...	3.50	8.00
1671 ...	3.50	8.00	1677 ...	4.00	8.50	1682 ...	3.50	8.00
1672/1 .	3.50	8.00	1678 ...	3.50	8.00	1683 ...	3.50	8.00
1673 ...	4.00	8.50	1679 ...	3.50	8.00	1684 ...	4.00	8.00
1674 ...	3.50	8.00						

3389	**Penny.** Undated. As 3383 (double arch crown)	8.00	17.50

3390 Dated. As illustration

	F £	VF £		F £	VF £		F £	VF £
1670 ...	7.50	16.00	1675 ...	7.50	16.00	1680 ...	7.50	16.00
1671 ...	7.50	16.00	1676 ...	8.00	17.00	1681 ...	8.50	18.00
1672/1 .	7.50	16.00	1677	7.50	16.00	1682 .	8.00	17.00
1673 ...	7.50	16.00	1678 ...	7.50	16.00	1683 ...	7.50	16.00
1674 ...	7.50	16.00	1679 ...	13.00	25.00	1684 ...	8.00	17.00

3391	**Maundy Set.** Undated. The four coins	45.00	100.00

3392 Dated. The four coins. Uniform dates

	F £	VF £		F £	VF £		F £	VF £
1670 ...	32.50	65.00	1675 ...	30.00	60.00	1680 ...	30.00	60.00
1671 ...	30.00	60.00	1676 ...	30.00	60.00	1681 ...	35.00	70.00
1672 ...	32.50	65.00	1677 ...	30.00	60.00	1682 ...	32.50	65.00
1673 ...	30.00	60.00	1678 ...	35.00	70.00	1683 ...	30.00	60.00
1674 ...	30.00	60.00	1679 ...	32.50	65.00	1684 ...	32.50	65.00

COPPER AND TIN

3393   3394

3393 Copper **halfpenny**

	F	VF		F	VF		F	VF
1672 ...	20.00	55.00	1673 ...	20.00	55.00	1675 ...	20.00	55.00

3394 Copper **farthing.** As illustration

	F	VF		F	VF		F	VF
1672 ...	12.00	30.00	1674 ...	15.00	35.00	1679 ...	20.00	50.00
1673 ...	12.00	30.00	1675 ...	18.00	40.00			

3395 Tin **farthing.** Somewhat similar, but with copper plug, edge inscribed NUMMORVM FAMVLVS, and date on edge only

		Fair	F	VF
1684	....	20.00	45.00	125.00
1685	....		Extremely rare	

N.B. *Overstruck dates are listed only if commoner than the normal date or if no normal date is known.*

JAMES II, 1685–8

Tin halfpence and farthings provided the only base metal coinage during this short reign. All genuine tin coins of this period have a copper plug.

GOLD

	F £	VF £
3396 **Five guineas.** First bust l., sceptres misplaced, 1686	950.00	1850.00

3397 Sceptres normal. First bust

	F £	VF £		F £	VF £
1687 . . .	900.00	1750.00	1688 . . .	850.00	1600.00

3397a — second bust

1687 . . .	900.00	1750.00	1688 . . .	850.00	1600.00

3398 — first bust. Elephant and castle below bust

1687 . . .	1000.00	2250.00	1688 . . .	1000.00	2250.00

3399 **Two guineas.** Similar

1687 . . .	600.00	1750.00	1688/7 .	700.00	1850.00

3403   3404

3400 **Guinea.** First bust

1685 . . .	250.00	500.00	1686 . . .	325.00	700.00

3401 — elephant and castle below

1685 . . .	325.00	750.00	1686	*Extremely rare*	

3402 Second bust

1686 . . .	210.00	500.00	1687 . . .	210.00	500.00	1688 . . .	210.00	500.00

3403 Elephant and castle below

1686 . . .	400.00	950.00	1687 . . .	250.00	550.00	1688 . . .	250.00	550.00

3404 **Half-guinea**

1686 . . .	200.00	550.00	1687 . . .	300.00	800.00	1688 . . .	225.00	600.00

3405 Elephant and castle below, 1686	550.00	1500.00

SILVER

3406 **Crown.** First bust, 1686	55.00	250.00

3407 Second bust

1687 . . .	50.00	200.00	1688 . . .	55.00	225.00

3408 (see next page)   1st bust   2nd bust

3408   Halfcrown. First bust

	F £	VF £		F £	VF £		F £	VF £
1685 . . .	40.00	150.00	1686 . . .	40.00	150.00	1687 . . .	40.00	150.00

3409   Second bust

1687 . . .	55.00	225.00	1688 . . .	50.00	200.00

3410   Shilling

1685 . . .	35.00	135.00	1687/6 .	40.00	200.00
1686 . . .	35.00	135.00	1688 . . .	40.00	200.00

3411   Plume in centre of *rev.*, 1685 . . . . *Extremely rare*

3412   Sixpence. Early type shields

1686 . . .	20.00	70.00	1687 . . .	25.00	90.00

3413   Late type shields

1687 . . .	20.00	70.00	1688 . . .	25.00	90.00

3414   3415   3416   3417

3414   Fourpence. *O.* As illus. ℟. IIII crowned

1686 . . .	6.00	14.00	1687/6 .	6.00	13.00	1688 . . .	6.00	14.00

3415   Threepence. As illustration

1685 . . .	6.00	13.00	1687/6..	6.00	13.00
1686 . . .	6.00	13.00	1688 . . .	6.00	13.00

3416   Twopence. As illustration

1686 . . .	6.00	13.00	1687 . . .	6.00	13.00	1688 . . .	7.00	13.50

3417   Penny. As illustration

1685 . . .	10.00	20.00	1687 . . .	10.00	20.00
1686 . . .	10.00	20.00	1688 . . .	10.00	20.00

3418   Maundy Set. As last four. Uniform dates

1686 . . .	35.00	70.00	1687 . . .	35.00	70.00	1688 . . .	35.00	70.00

TIN

3419

		Fair	F	VF
3419 Halfpenny				
1685	. . . .	20.00	40.00	110.00
1686	. . . .	22.00	45.00	135.00
1687	. . . .	20.00	40.00	110.00
3420 Farthing. Cuirassed bust				
1684	. . . .	*Extremely rare*		
1685	. . . .	20.00	40.00	110.00
1686	. . . .	22.00	45.00	135.00
1687	. . . .	*Extremely rare*		
3421 Draped bust, 1687	. . . .	30.00	55.00	165.00

WILLIAM AND MARY, 1688–94

Due to the poor state of the silver coinage, much of it worn hammered coin, the guinea, which was valued at 21s. 6d. at the beginning of the reign, circulated for as much as 30s. by 1694. The tin half-pennies and farthings were replaced by copper coins in 1694. The rampant lion of Orange is now placed as an inescutcheon on the centre of the royal arms.

GOLD

3422 Five guineas. Conjoined heads r.

	F £	VF £		F £	VF £		F £	VF £
1691 ..	750.00	1750.00	1693 ...	750.00	1750.00			
1692 ..	750.00	1750.00	1694 ...	800.00	2000.00			

3423 — elephant and castle below

	F £	VF £		F £	VF £
1691 ..	850.00	1950.00	1693 ...	1100.00	2350.00
1692 ..	900.00	2000.00	1694 ...	1000.00	2250.00

3424 Two guineas. Conjoined heads r.

	F £	VF £		F £	VF £
1693 ...	500.00	1000.00	1694 ...	500.00	1000.00

3425 — elephant and castle below

	F £	VF £		F £	VF £		F £	VF £
1691 ...	*Extremely rare*		1693 ...	750.00	1500.00	1694/3 ...	750.00	1500.00

3427

3426 Guinea. Conjoined heads r.

	F £	VF £		F £	VF £		F £	VF £
1689 ...	225.00	550.00	1691 ...	300.00	675.00	1693 ...	275.00	650.00
1690 ...	250.00	625.00	1692 ...	275.00	750.00	1694 ...	225.00	600.00

3427 — elephant and castle below

	F £	VF £		F £	VF £		F £	VF £
1689 ...	250.00	600.00	1691 ...	275.00	700.00	1693	*Extremely rare*	
1690 ...	350.00	900.00	1692 ...	300.00	750.00	1694 ...	325.00	775.00

3428 — elephant only below

	F £	VF £			
1692 ...	350.00	900.00	1693	*Extremely rare*	

3429   3430

3429 Half-guinea. First heads, 1689 .... 225.00   650.00

3430 Second head, normal portraits

	F £	VF £		F £	VF £		F £	VF £
1690 ...	275.00	650.00	1692 ..	250.00	650.00	1694 ...	200.00	500.00
1691 ...	300.00	725.00	1693	*Extremely rare*				

3431 — — elephant and castle below

	F £	VF £		F £	VF £
1691 ...	225.00	550.00	1692 ...	200.00	500.00

3432 — — elephant only below 1692 *Extremely rare*

SILVER

3433 Crown. Conjoined busts, as 3436 below

	F £	VF £		F £	VF £		F £	VF £
1691 ...	135.00	400.00	1692 ...	135.00	400.00			

3434

3435

3434 Halfcrown. First busts and first shields, 1689 ....   25.00   80.00

3435 — and second shield

1689 ...	30.00	100.00	1690 ...	35.00	150.00

3436 Second busts. ℞. As illustration below

1691 ...	32.00	145.00	1692 ...	35.00	155.00	1693 ...	30.00	120.00

3436

3438

3437 Shilling. Similar

1692 ...	25.00	95.00	1693 ...	22.00	90.00

3438 Sixpence. Similar

1693 ...	20.00	65.00	1694 ...	40.00	140.00

3439 Fourpence. First busts, no tie to wreath

1689 ...	6.00	16.00	1691 ...	8.50	19.00
1690 ...	7.00	16.00	1694 ...	8.00	17.00

3440 Second busts, tie to wreath

1691 ...	8.00	20.00	1693 ...	10.00	21.00
1692 ...	7.00	18.00	1694 ...	10.00	21.00

3441 Threepence. First busts, no tie

1689 ...	6.00	14.00	1690 ...	7.00	14.00	1691 ...	12.00	28.00

3442 Second busts, tie to wreath

1691 ...	7.00	19.00	1693 ...	7.00	17.00
1692 ...	7.00	19.00	1694 ...	7.00	16.00

3443 Twopence

	F £	VF £		F £	VF £		F £	VF £
1689 ...	5.00	13.00	1692 ...	7.00	14.00	1694 ...	8.00	15.00
1691 ...	7.00	14.00	1693 ...	7.00	14.00			

3444 Penny. Legend continuous over heads, 1689 .... 110.00 250.00

3445 — legend broken by heads

1690 ...	13.00	24.00	1692 ...	13.00	24.00	1694 ...	12.00	23.00
1691 ...	12.00	23.00	1693 ...	12.00	23.00			

3446

3446 Maundy Set. As last pieces. Uniform dates

1689 ...	150.00	350.00	1692 ...	50.00	110.00	1694 ...	50.00	110.00
1691 ...	50.00	110.00	1693 ...	60.00	120.00			

TIN AND COPPER

	Fair £	F £	VF £
3447 Tin Halfpenny. Small draped busts, 1689	175.00	350.00	900.00
3448 Large cuirassed busts; date only on edge			
1690	20.00	40.00	125.00
3449 — — date in exergue and on edge			
1691	20.00	40.00	125.00
1692	20.00	40.00	125.00
3450 Tin Farthing. Small draped busts			
1689	90.00	175.00	500.00
1689, edge 1690			*Extremely rare*
3451 Large cuirassed busts			
1690, edge 1689			*Extremely rare*
1690	20.00	40.00	125.00
1691	20.00	40.00	125.00
1692	22.00	45.00	135.00

3453

3452 Copper Halfpenny, 1694		15.00	35.00
3453 Copper Farthing, 1694		20.00	45.00

N.B. *Overstruck dates are listed only if commoner than the normal date or if no normal date is known.*

Note. *Values for coins in EF (extremely fine) condition can be three or more times the value of VF (very fine) specimens.*

WILLIAM III, 1694–1702

In 1696 a great recoinage was undertaken to replace the hammered silver that made up most of the coinage in circulation, much of it being clipped and badly worn. Branch mints were set up at Bristol, Chester, Exeter, Norwich and York to help with the recoinage. For a short time before they were finally demonetized unclipped hammered coins were allowed to circulate freely providing they were officially pierced in the centre. Silver coins with roses between the coats of arms were made from silver obtained from the West of England mines.

GOLD

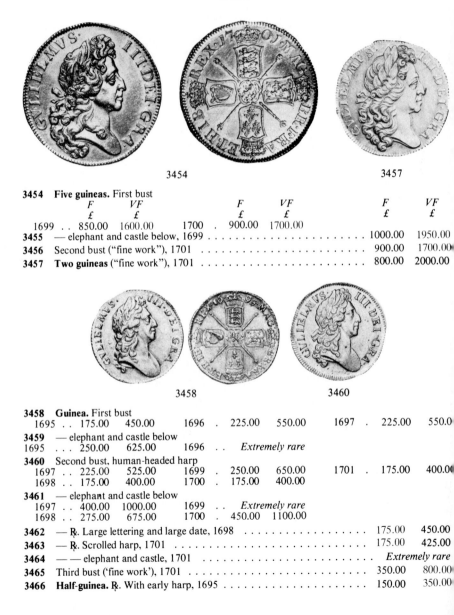

3454   3457

3454	**Five guineas.** First bust						
	F	VF		F	VF	F	VF
	£	£		£	£	£	£
	1699 . . 850.00	1600.00	1700 .	900.00	1700.00		
3455	— elephant and castle below, 1699					1000.00	1950.00
3456	Second bust ("fine work"), 1701					900.00	1700.00
3457	**Two guineas** ("fine work"), 1701					800.00	2000.00

3458   3460

3458	**Guinea.** First bust						
	1695 . . 175.00	450.00	1696 .	225.00	550.00	1697 . 225.00	550.0
3459	— elephant and castle below						
	1695 . . . 250.00	625.00	1696 . .	*Extremely rare*			
3460	Second bust, human-headed harp						
	1697 . . 225.00	525.00	1699 .	250.00	650.00	1701 . 175.00	400.00
	1698 . . 175.00	400.00	1700 .	175.00	400.00		
3461	— elephant and castle below						
	1697 . . 400.00	1000.00	1699 . .	*Extremely rare*			
	1698 . . 275.00	675.00	1700 .	450.00	1100.00		
3462	— ℞. Large lettering and large date, 1698					175.00	450.00
3463	— ℞. Scrolled harp, 1701					175.00	425.00
3464	— — elephant and castle, 1701					*Extremely rare*	
3465	Third bust ('fine work'), 1701					350.00	800.00
3466	**Half-guinea.** ℞. With early harp, 1695					150.00	350.00

3467 **Half-guinea.** Elephant and castle. ℞. With early harp.

	F	VF		F	VF		F	VF
	£	£		£	£		£	£
1695 ..	300.00	700.00	1696 .	150.00	400.00			

3468 ℞. With late harp

| 1697 .. | 200.00 | 500.00 | 1699 .. | *Extremely rare* | | 1701 | 150.00 | 350.00 |
| 1698 .. | 150.00 | 350.00 | 1700 . | 150.00 | 350.00 | | | |

3469 — elephant and castle, 1698 . . . . 250.00 600.00

SILVER

3470 **Crown.** First bust, first harp

| 1695 .. | 30.00 | 115.00 | 1696 . | 30.00 | 115.00 |

3471 Second bust (hair across breast), 1696 . . . . *Unique*

3472 Third bust, first harp, 1696 . . . . 30.00 115.00

3473 — second harp, 1697 . . . . 300.00 900.00

3474 Third bust variety, third harp, 1700 . . . . 30.00 115.00

3490

3475 **Halfcrown.** Small shields, 1696 . . . . 20.00 60.00

3476 — B (*Bristol*) below bust, 1696 . . . . 25.00 80.00

3477 — C (*Chester*) below bust, 1696 . . . . 35.00 135.00

3478 — E (*Exeter*) below bust, 1696 . . . . 50.00 200.00

3479 — N (*Norwich*) below bust, 1696 . . . . 30.00 100.00

3480 — y (*York*) below bust, 1696 . . . . 35.00 135.00

3481 Large shield, early harp, 1696 . . . . 20.00 60.00

3482 — — B (*Bristol*) below bust, 1696 . . . . 25.00 80.00

3483 — — C (*Chester*) below bust, 1696 . . . . 30.00 100.00

3484 — — E (*Exeter*) below bust, 1696 . . . . 35.00 135.00

3485 — — N (*Norwich*) below bust, 1696 . . . . 50.00 200.00

3486 — — y (*York*) below bust, 1696 . . . . 30.00 100.00

3487 Large shields, ordinary harp

| 1696 .. | 40.00 | 150.00 | 1697 . | 20.00 | 60.00 |

3488 — — B (*Bristol*) below bust, 1697 . . . . 22.00 90.00

3489 — — C (*Chester*) below bust

| 1696 .. | 40.00 | 150.00 | 1697 . | 25.00 | 80.00 |

3490 — — E (*Exeter*) below bust

| 1696 .. | 40.00 | 150.00 | 1697 . | 20.00 | 65.00 |

3491 — — N (*Norwich*) below bust

| 1696 .. | 50.00 | 200.00 | 1697 . | 25.00 | 80.00 |

3492 — — y (*York*) below bust, 1697 . . . . 20.00 65.00

3493 Second bust (hair across breast), 1696 . . . . *Unique*

3494 Half-crown. Modified large shields

	F	VF		F	VF		F	VF
	£	£		£	£		£	£
1698 ..	18.00	50.00	1700 .	20.00	65.00			
1699 ..	30.00	100.00	1701 .	20.00	65.00			

3495 Elephant and castle below bust, 1701 . . . . *Fair* £250

3496 Plumes in angles on *rev.*, 1701 . . . . 30.00 100.00

1st bust   2nd bust   3rd bust   3507

3rd bust var.   4th bust   5th bust

3497 Shilling. First bust

1695 ..	18.00	50.00	1696 .	9.00	25.00	1697 .	9.00	25.00

3498 — B (*Bristol*) below bust

1696 ..	18.00	45.00	1697 .	20.00	50.00

3499 — C (*Chester*) below bust

1696 ..	20.00	50.00	1697 .	20.00	50.00

3500 — E (*Exeter*) below bust

1696 ..	20.00	50.00	1697 .	20.00	50.00

3501 — N (*Norwich*) below bust

1696 ..	20.00	50.00	1697 .	20.00	50.00

3502 — y (*York*) below bust

1696 ..	20.00	50.00	1697 .	20.00	50.00

3503 — Y (*York*) below bust

1696 ..	.22.00	60.00	1697 .	22.00	60.00

3504 Second bust (hair across breast), 1696 . . . . *Unique*

3505 Third bust, 1697 . . . . 10.00 30.00

3506 — B (*Bristol*) below bust, 1697 . . . . 22.00 60.00

3507 — C (*Chester*) below bust

1696 ..	45.00	150.00	1697 .	20.00	50.00

3508 — E (*Exeter*) below bust, 1697 . . . . 22.00 60.00

3509 — N (*Norwich*) below bust, 1697 . . . . 22.00 60.00

3510 — y (*York*) below bust

1696 ...	*Extremely rare*	1697 .	22.00	60.00

3511 Third bust variety

1697 ..	10.00	30.00	1698 .	18.00	50.00

3512 — B (*Bristol*) below bust, 1697 . . . . 22.00 60.00

		F £	VF £		F £	VF £		F £	VF £
3513	Third bust variety C (*Chester*) below bust, 1697							55.00	150.00
3514	— ℞. Plumes in angles, 1698							65.00	175.00
3515	Fourth bust ("flaming hair")								
	1698 . . 22.00 60.00			1699 . 22.00		60.00			
3516	Fifth bust (hair high)								
	1699 . . 22.00 60.00			1700 . 16.00		35.00	1701	22.00	60.00
3517	— ℞. Plumes in angles								
	1699 . . 45.00 115.00			1701 . 45.00		115.00			
3518	— ℞. Roses in angles, 1699							55.00	150.00
3519	— plume below bust, 1700							750.00	—

3520   3542

3520	**Sixpence.** First bust, early harp								
	1695 . . 20.00 60.00			1696 . 8.00		22.00			
3521	— — B below bust, 1696							9.00	25.00
3522	— — C below bust, 1696							15.00	45.00
3523	— — E below bust, 1696							20.00	60.00
3524	— — N below bust, 1696							12.00	40.00
3525	— — y below bust, 1696							10.00	30.00
3526	— — Y below bust, 1696							20.00	60.00
3527	— later harp, large crowns, 1696							25.00	75.00
3528	— — — B below bust								
	1696 . . 25.00 75.00			1697 . 20.00		60.00			
3529	— — — C below bust, 1697							25.00	75.00
3530	— — — E below bust, 1697							22.00	70.00
3531	— — small crowns								
	1696 . . 20.00 65.00			1697 . 9.00		25.00			
3532	— — — B below bust								
	1696 . . 18.00 55.00			1697 . 12.00		40.00			
3533	— — — C below bust								
	1696 . . 35.00 100.00			1697 . 12.00		40.00			
3534	— — — E below bust, 1697							15.00	45.00
3535	— — — N below bust								
	1696 . . 30.00 90.00			1697 . 10.00		30.00			
3536	— — — y below bust, 1697							25.00	75.00
3537	Second bust								
	1696 . . . 200.00 400.00			1697 . 35.00		120.00			
3538	Third bust, large crowns								
	1697 . . 8.00 22.00			1699 . 27.00		80.00	1701	11.00	35.00
	1698 . . 9.00 25.00			1700 . 9.00		25.00			
3539	— — B below bust, 1697							15.00	45.00
3540	— — C below bust, 1697							27.00	80.00
3541	— — E below bust, 1697							27.00	80.00

		F	VF					F	VF
		£	£					£	£
3542	**Sixpence.** Third bust small crowns, 1697							12.00	40.00
3543	— — C below bust, 1697							27.00	80.00
3544	— — E below bust, 1697							16.00	50.00
3545	— — Y below bust, 1697							25.00	75.00

3546 — ℞. Plumes in angles

1698	..	12.00	40.00	1699	.	14.00	40.00

3547	— ℞. Roses in angles, 1699	25.00	75.00
3548*	— plume below bust, 1700	*Extremely rare*

* **Note.** *An extremely fine specimen sold at auction in October 1985 for £3500.*

3549	3550	3551	3552

2549 **Fourpence.** ℞. 4 crowned

1697	....	*Unique*	1699	.	11.50	22.00	1701	.	12.00	24.00
1698	..	12.00	22.00	1700	.	11.00	20.00	1702	.	11.00	20.00

3550 **Threepence.** ℞. 3 crowned

1698	..	11.00	20.00	1700	.	11.00	20.00
1699	..	12.00	22.00	1701	.	11.00	20.00

3551 **Twopence.** ℞. 2 crowned

1698	..	11.00	19.00	1700	.	10.00	19.00
1699	..	10.00	18.50	1701	.	9.50	18.00

3552 **Penny.** ℞. 1 crowned

1698	..	11.00	19.00	1700	.	12.00	20.00
1699	..	12.00	20.00	1701	.	11.00	19.00

3553 **Maundy Set.** As last four. Uniform dates

1698	..	50.00	105.00	1700	.	60.00	115.00
1699	..	60.00	115.00	1701	.	50.00	105.00

COPPER

3554 **Halfpenny.** First issue. Britannia with r. hand raised

1695	..	8.00	35.00	1697	.	7.00	30.00
1696	..	7.00	30.00	1698	.	9.00	45.00

3555 Second issue. ℞. Date in legend

1698	..	8.00	35.00	1699	.	7.00	30.00

3556 Third issue. ℞. Britannia with r. hand on knee

1699	..	7.00	30.00	1700	.	7.00	30.00	1701	.	8.00	35.00

3557	3558

3557 **Farthing.** First issue

1695	..	10.00	40.00	1697	.	8.00	35.00	1699	.	8.00	35.00
1696	..	8.00	35.00	1698	.	60.00	175.00	1700	.	8.00	35.00

3558 Second issue. ℞. Date at end of legend

1698	..	25.00	80.00	1699	.	12.00	45.00

ANNE, 1702–14

The Act of Union of 1707, which effected the unification of the ancient kingdoms of England and Scotland into a single realm, resulted in a change in the royal arms—on the after-Union coinage the English leopards and Scottish lion are emblazoned per pale on the top and bottom shields. After the Union the rose in the centre of the reverse of the gold coins is replaced by the Garter star.

Following a successful Anglo-Dutch expedition against Spain, bullion seized in Vigo Bay was sent to be minted into coin, and the coins made from this metal had the word VIGO placed below the queen's bust.

GOLD

Before Union with Scotland

3560 Five guineas

	F £	VF £		F £	VF £	F £	VF £
1705	1000.00	2250.00	1706	950.00	2000.00		

3561 VIGO below bust, 1703 . . . . 6000.00 15000.00

3562 Guinea

	F	VF		F	VF
1702	200.00	575.00	1706	300.00	750.00
1705	300.00	725.00	1707	350.00	850.00

3563 VIGO below bust, 1703 . . . . 1800.00 4250.00

3564 Half-guinea

	F	VF		F	VF
1702	250.00	600.00	1705	250.00	600.00

3565 VIGO below bust, 1703 . . . . 1600.00 3750.00

3562   3574

After Union with Scotland. The shields on the reverse are changed

3566 Five guineas. Ordinary bust, 1706 . . . . 850.00 1800.00

3567 — broader shields, 1709 . . . . 900.00 1900.00

3568 Last (coarse) bust

	F	VF		F	VF		F	VF
1711	850.00	1800.00	1713	900.00	1900.00	1714	850.00	1800.00

3569 Two guineas

	F	VF		F	VF
1709	450.00	1100.00	1713	450.00	1100.00
1711	400.00	1000.00	1714	500.00	1200.00

3570 Guinea. First bust

	F	VF		F	VF
1707	225.00	500.00	1708	*Extremely rare*	

3571 — elephant and castle below, 1707 . . . . 600.00 1250.00

3572 Second bust

	F	VF		F	VF		F	VF
1707	*Extremely rare*		1708	200.00	475.00	1709	225.00	525.00

3573 — elephant and castle below

	F	VF		F	VF
1708	450.00	1150.00	1709	375.00	850.00

3574 Third bust

	F	VF		F	VF		F	VF
1710	165.00	375.00	1712	200.00	475.00	1714	150.00	350.00
1711	165.00	375.00	1713	150.00	350.00			

3575 Half-guinea

	F	VF		F	VF		F	VF
1707	200.00	425.00	1710	150.00	350.00	1713	165.00	375.00
1708	250.00	575.00	1711	165.00	350.00	1714	165.00	375.00
1709	185.00	400.00	1712	200.00	425.00			

SILVER

Before Union with Scotland

3576

	F £	*VF* £
3576 **Crown.** VIGO below bust, 1703	80.00	275.00
3577 ℞. Plumes in angles, 1705	100.00	450.00

3578 ℞. Roses and plumes in angles

	F £	*VF* £		*F* £	*VF* £	*F* £	*VF* £
1706 . .	75.00	300.00	1707 .	65.00	225.00		

	F £	*VF* £
3579 **Halfcrown.** No marks below bust or on *rev.* (i.e. plain), 1703	275.00	750.00
3580 VIGO below bust, 1703	30.00	95.00

3581 ℞. Plumes in angles

	F	*VF*		*F*	*VF*
1704 . .	45.00	150.00	1705 .	30.00	95.00

3582 ℞. Roses and plumes in angles

	F	*VF*		*F*	*VF*
1706 . .	25.00	80.00	1707 .	20.00	70.00

3583   3589

	F £	*VF* £
3583 **Shilling.** First bust, 1702	20.00	70.00
3584 — ℞. Plumes in angles, 1702	30.00	100.00
3585 — VIGO below bust, 1702	30.00	95.00
3586 Second bust, VIGO below, 1703	20.00	70.00

3587 — plain

	F	*VF*		*F*	*VF*
1704 . .	165.00	400.00	1705 .	30.00	100.00

3588 — ℞. Plumes in angles

	F	*VF*		*F*	*VF*
1704 . . .	30.00	100.00	1705 .	25.00	80.00

3589 — ℞. Roses and plumes in angles

	F	*VF*		*F*	*VF*
1705 . .	25.00	75.00	1707 .	30.00	85.00

3593	3594	Early Shield	Late Shield

		F £	VF £
3590	**Sixpence.** VIGO below bust, 1703	12.00	35.00
3591	Plain, 1705	20.00	70.00
3592	℞. Early shields, plumes in angles, 1705	16.00	50.00
3593	℞. Late shields, plumes in angles, 1705	20.00	70.00

3594 ℞. Roses and plumes in angles

	F £	VF £		F £	VF £		F £	VF £
1705 . .	18.00	60.00	1707 .	16.00	50.00			

3595 Fourpence. ℞. Crowned 4

	F £	VF £		F £	VF £		F £	VF £
1703 . .	7.00	15.00	1706 .	6.00	14.00	1710 .	6.00	14.00
1704 . .	6.00	14.00	1708 .	6.00	14.00	1713 .	6.00	14.00
1705 . .	7.00	15.00	1709 .	6.00	14.00			

3596 Threepence. ℞. Crowned 3

	F £	VF £		F £	VF £		F £	VF £
1703 . .	7.50	15.00	1706 .	6.00	14.00	1709 .	6.00	14.00
1704 . .	6.50	12.50	1707 .	6.00	14.00	1710 .	6.00	14.00
1705 . .	6.50	12.50	1708 .	6.00	14.00	1713 .	6.00	14.00

3597 Twopence. ℞. Crowned 2

	F £	VF £		F £	VF £		F £	VF £
1703 . .	6.50	13.50	1706 .	6.50	13.50	1709 .	7.00	13.50
1704 . .	6.00	12.50	1707 .	6.50	13.50	1710 .	6.00	12.50
1705 . .	6.00	12.50	1708 .	6.00	12.50	1713 .	6.00	12.50

3598 Penny. ℞. Crowned 1

	F £	VF £		F £	VF £		F £	VF £
1703 . .	11.00	21.00	1708 .	11.00	21.00	1713 .	11.00	21.00
1705 . .	10.00	19.00	1709 .	10.00	19.00			
1706 . .	10.00	19.00	1710 .	14.00	30.00			

3599

3599 Maundy Set. As last four. Uniform dates

	F £	VF £		F £	VF £		F £	VF £
1703 . .	45.00	75.00	1708 .	45.00	75.00	1713 .	45.00	75.00
1705 . .	45.00	75.00	1709 .	45.00	75.00			
1706 . .	40.00	70.00	1710 .	50.00	80.00			

Note. *Values for coins in EF (extremely fine) condition can be three or more times the value of VF (very fine) specimens.*

After Union with Scotland

The shields on reverse are changed. The Edinburgh coins have been included here as they are now coins of Great Britain.

3600   Crown. Second bust, E (Edinburgh) below

	F	VF		F	VF		F	VF
	£	£		£	£		£	£
1707 . .	40.00	140.00	1708 .	45.00	145.00			

3601   — plain

| 1707 . . | 45.00 | 145.00 | 1708 . | 45.00 | 145.00 |

3602   ℞. Plumes in angles, 1708 . . . . 55.00   225.00

3603   Third bust. ℞. Roses and plumes, 1713 . . . . 45.00   125.00

3604

3604   Halfcrown. Plain

| 1707 . . | 22.00 | 70.00 | 1709 . | 22.00 | 70.00 |
| 1708 . . | 20.00 | 65.00 | 1713 . | 25.00 | 80.00 |

3605   Halfcrown. E below bust

| 1707 . . | 18.00 | 55.00 | 1708 . | 18.00 | 55.00 | 1709 . | 65.00 | 225.00 |

3606   ℞. Plumes in angles, 1708 . . . . 30.00   95.00

3607   ℞. Roses and plumes in angles

| 1710 . . | 25.00 | 80.00 | 1713 . | 25.00 | 80.00 |
| 1712 . . | 22.00 | 70.00 | 1714 . | 22.00 | 70.00 |

3609

3608   Shilling. Second bust, E below

| 1707 . . | 18.00 | 50.00 | 1708 . | 30.00 | 95.00 |

3609   — E* below

| 1707 . . | 35.00 | 110.00 | 1708 . | 20.00 | 60.00 |

3610   Third bust, plain

| 1707 . . | 12.00 | 35.00 | 1709 . | 12.00 | 35.00 |
| 1708 . . | 10.00 | 30.00 | 1711 . | 40.00 | 150.00 |

3611   — ℞. Plumes in angles

| 1707 . . | 22.00 | 70.00 | 1708 . | 20.00 | 55.00 |

3612   — E below

| 1707 . . | 15.00 | 40.00 | 1708 . | 25.00 | 80.00 |

			F £	VF £
3613	**Shilling.** Second bust. ℞. Roses and plumes, 1708		50.00	175.00

3614 Third bust. ℞. Roses and plumes

	F £	VF £		F £	VF £		F £	VF £
1708 ..	25.00	80.00	1710 .	12.00	35.00			

3615 "Edinburgh" bust, E* below

	F £	VF £		F £	VF £		F £	VF £
1707 ...	*Extremely rare*		1708 .	25.00	80.00	1709 .	30.00	95.00

3616	— E below, 1709	*Extremely rare*

3617 Fourth bust. ℞. Roses and plumes

	F £	VF £		F £	VF £
1710 ..	25.00	80.00	1713/2	15.00	50.00
1712 ..	12.00	35.00	1714 .	12.00	35.00

		F	VF
3618	— plain, 1711	10.00	30.00

3620

3623

3619 **Sixpence.** Normal bust. ℞. Plain

	F £	VF £		F £	VF £		F £	VF £
1707 ..	9.00	22.00	1708 .	10.00	30.00	1711 .	7.00	15.00

3620 — E below bust

	F £	VF £		F £	VF £
1707 ..	10.00	30.00	1708 .	12.00	40.00

		F	VF
3621	— E* below bust, 1708	12.00	45.00
3622	"Edinburgh" bust, E* below, 1708	15.00	55.00

3623 Normal bust. ℞. Plumes in angles

	F £	VF £		F £	VF £
1707 ..	11.00	35.00	1708 .	12.00	40.00

		F	VF
3624	℞. Roses and plumes in angles, 1710	15.00	50.00

COPPER

3625

		F £	VF £	EF £
3625	**Farthing,** 1714	90.00	175.00	325.00

N.B. *Overstruck dates are listed only if commoner than normal date or if no normal date is known.*

GEORGE I, 1714–27

The coins of the first of the Hanoverian kings have the arms of the Duchy of Brunswick and Luneberg on one of the four shields, the object in the centre of the shield being the crown of Charlemagne. The king's German titles also appear, in abbreviated form, and name him "Duke of Brunswick and Luneberg, Arch-treasurer of the Holy Roman Empire, and Elector", and on the guinea of 1714, "Prince Elector". A quarter-guinea was struck for the first time in 1718, but it was an inconvenient size and the issue was discontinued.

Silver coined from bullion supplied to the mint by the South Sea Company in 1723 shows the company's initials S.S.C.; similarly Welsh Copper Company bullion has the letters W.C.C. below the king's bust and plumes and an interlinked CC on the reverse. Roses and plumes together on the reverse indicate silver supplied by the Company for Smelting Pit Coale and Sea Coale.

GOLD

3626 Five guineas

	F £	VF £			F £	VF £			F £	VF £
1716	1000.00	2450.00	1720	.	1300.00	2850.00				
1717	1250.00	2750.00	1726	.	1000.00	2450.00				

3627 Two guineas

	F £	VF £			F £	VF £			F £	VF £
1717	575.00	1225.00	1720	.	575.00	1250.00	1726	.	475.00	1150.00

3627   3628

3628 Guinea. First head. ℞. Legend ends ET PR . EL (Prince Elector), 1714 . . — 350.00 — 850.00

3629 Second head, tie with two ends, 1715 . . . . — 200.00 — 425.00

3630 Third head, no hair below truncation

	F	VF			F	VF
1715	150.00	400.00	1716	.	200.00	500.00

3631 Fourth head, tie with loop at one end

	F	VF			F	VF			F	VF
1716	150.00	400.00	1719	.	150.00	400.00	1722	.	150.00	400.00
1717	175.00	450.00	1720	.	150.00	400.00	1723	.	200.00	500.00
1718	*Extremely rare*		1721	.	200.00	500.00				

3632 — elephant and castle below

1721	. . .	*Extremely rare*	1722	. . . .	*Extremely rare*

3633 Fifth (older) head, tie with two ends

	F	VF			F	VF			F	VF
1723	210.00	500.00	1725	.	210.00	500.00	1727	.	275.00	600.00
1724	210.00	500.00	1726	.	175.00	425.00				

3634 — elephant and castle below, 1726 . . . . — 500.00 — 1200.00

3633   3638

3635 Half-guinea. First head

	F £	VF £			F £	VF £			F £	VF £
1715	175.00	350.00	1719	.	125.00	300.00	1722	.	150.00	325.00
1717	150.00	325.00	1720	.	200.00	525.00	1723	..	*Extremely rare*	
1718	125.00	300.00	1721	..	*Extremely rare*		1724	.	200.00	425.00

3636 — elephant and castle below, 1721 . . . . *Extremely rare*

3637 Second (older) bust

	F £	VF £			F £	VF £			F £	VF £
1725	..	125.00	275.00	1726	.	135.00	300.00	1727	.	135.00	300.00

3638 Quarter-guinea, 1718 . . . . 35.00   85.00

SILVER

3639 Crown. ℞. Roses and plumes in angles

	F £	VF £			F £	VF £
1716	..	115.00	225.00	1720/18	125.00	275.00
1718/6	.	120.00	250.00	1726	.	175.00	400.00

3640 ℞. SSC (South Sea Company) in angles, 1723 . . . . 175.00   375.00

3641 Halfcrown. Plain (proof only), 1715   *FDC*   £4000

3642 ℞. Roses and plumes in angles

	F £	VF £			F £	VF £			F £	VF £
1715	..	45.00	140.00	1717	.	45.00	140.00	1720/17		45.00	140.00

3643 ℞. SSC in angles, 1723 . . . . 45.00   125.00

3644 ℞. Small roses and plumes, 1726 . . . . 500.00   1000.00

3647   3650

3645 Shilling. First bust. ℞. Roses and plumes

	F £	VF £			F £	VF £			F £	VF £
1715	..	15.00	45.00	1718	.	15.00	40.00	1721/0		18.00	55.00
1716	..	35.00	150.00	1719	.	30.00	120.00	1722	.	15.00	45.00
1717	..	15.00	45.00	1720	.	15.00	45.00	1723	.	15.00	45.00

3646 — plain (i.e. no marks either side)

	F £	VF £			F £	VF £
1720	..	15.00	45.00	1721	.	55.00	200.00

3647 ℞. SSC in angles, 1723 . . . . 9.00   25.00

3648 Second bust, bow to tie. ℞. Similar, 1723 . . . . 10.00   35.00

3649 ℞. Roses and plumes

	F £	VF £			F £	VF £			F £	VF £
1723	..	18.00	50.00	1725	.	18.00	50.00	1727	.	75.00	225.00
1724	..	18.00	50.00	1726	.	75.00	225.00				

3650 — W.C.C. (Welsh Copper Company) below

	F £	VF £			F £	VF £
1723	..	110.00	350.00	1725	.	120.00	375.00
1724	..	110.00	350.00	1726	.	110.00	350.00

3651 Sixpence. ℞. Roses and plumes in angles

	F £	VF £			F £	VF £
1717	..	15.00	45.00	1720/17	15.00	45.00

3652 ℞. SSC in angles, 1723 . . . . 5.00   20.00

3653 ℞. Small roses and plumes, 1726 . . . . 20.00   50.00

3654   3655   3656   3657

3654   Fourpence

	F £	VF £			F £	VF £			F £	VF £
1717 ..	8.00	18.00	1723	.	9.00	18.00				
1721 ..	8.00	18.00	1727	.	10.00	19.00				

3655   Threepence

1717 ..	8.00	19.00	1723	.	10.00	20.00
1721 ..	9.00	20.00	1727	.	10.00	20.00

3656   Twopence

1717 ..	5.00	10.00	1723	.	6.00	10.00	1727	.	5.00	10.00
1721 ..	5.00	9.00	1726	.	5.00	9.00				

3657   Penny

1716 ..	3.00	7.00	1723	.	5.00	7.00	1726	.	5.00	10.00
1718 ..	3.00	7.00	1725		3.00	6.00	1727	.	5.00	10.00
1720 ..	3.00	7.00								

3658   Maundy Set. As last four. Uniform dates

1723 ..	40.00	95.00	1727	.	40.00	95.00

COPPER

3661   3662

3659   Halfpenny. "Dump" issue

1717 ..	9.00	35.00	1718	.	9.00	35.00

3660   Second issue

1719 ..	6.00	35.00	1721	.	6.00	35.00	1723	.	7.00	40.00
1720 ..	6.00	35.00	1722	.	7.00	37.50	1724	.	6.00	35.00

3661   Farthing. "Dump" issue, 1717 . . . .   50.00   125.00

3662   Second issue

1719 ..	6.00	30.00	1721	.	6.00	30.00	1723	.	7.00	35.00
1720 ..	6.00	30.00	1722	.	7.00	35.00	1724	.	7.00	35.00

GEORGE II, 1727–60

Silver was only coined spasmodically by the Mint during this reign and no copper was struck after 1754. Gold coins made from bullion supplied by the East India Company bear the company's initials; some of the treasure seized by Admiral Anson during his circumnavigation of the globe, 1740–4, and by other privateers, was made into coin which had the word LIMA below the king's bust to celebrate the expedition's successful harassment of the Spanish colonies in the New World. Hammered gold was finally demonetized in 1733.

GOLD

3664

3663 Five guineas. Young head

	F £	VF £			F £	VF £			F £	VF £
1729	750.00	1650.00	1735	.	850.00	1900.00	1741	.	700.00	1500.00
1731	900.00	2000.00	1738	.	800.00	1750.00				

							F	VF
3664	— E.I.C. (East India Company) below, 1729	. . . .					750.00	1650.00
3665	Old head, LIMA below, 1746	. . . .					800.00 |	1800.00

3666 — plain

1748	. .	700.00	1550.00	1753	.	700.00	1550.00

3667* Two guineas. Young head

1734/3	.	750.00	2000.00	1738	.	200.00	400.00
1735	. .	300.00	650.00	1739	.	200.00	450.00

3668 Intermediate head

1739	. .	200.00	400.00	1740	.	200.00	400.00

3669* Old head

1748	. .	300.00	700.00	1753	.	450.00	1250.00

*N.B. *Beware recent forgeries.*

3671   3674

3670 Guinea. First young head, small lettering, 1727 . . . . 450.00   1100.00

3671 — larger lettering, smaller shield

1727	. .	300.00	700.00	1728	.	350.00	800.00

N.B. *Overstruck dates are listed only if commoner than normal date or if no normal date is known.*

3672 Guinea. Second (narrower) young head

	F £	VF £			F £	VF £			F £	VF £
1729 *proof only FDC* £3600.00			1731	.	175.00	400.00				
			1732	.	225.00	500.00				
1730	.. 275.00	600.00								

3673 — E.I.C. below

	F £	VF £			F £	VF £			F £	VF £
1729	.. 450.00	1000.00	1731	.	300.00	700.00	1732	.	300.00	675.00

3674 — larger lettering on *obv.*

	F £	VF £			F £	VF £			F £	VF £
1732	... *Extremely rare*		1735	.	175.00	400.00	1737	.	240.00	525.00
1733	.. 150.00	375.00	1736	.	200.00	475.00	1738	.	200.00	450.00
1734	.. 150.00	375.00								

3675 — — E.I.C. below, 1732 . . . . 375.00 800.00

3676 Intermediate head

	F £	VF £			
1739	.. 165.00	400.00	1741/39	*Extremely rare*	
1740	.. 180.00	450.00	1743	. . *Extremely rare*	

3677 — E.I.C. below, 1739 . . . . 350.00 750.00

3678 — larger lettering on *obv.*

	F £	VF £			F £	VF £
1745	.. 250.00	600.00	1746	.	200.00	450.00

3679 — LIMA below, 1745 . . . . 500.00 1300.00

3680 Old head

	F £	VF £			F £	VF £			F £	VF £
1747	.. 150.00	400.00	1751	.	125.00	350.00	1756	.	125.00	325.00
1748	.. 125.00	350.00	1752	.	125.00	350.00	1758	.	120.00	325.00
1749	.. 125.00	350.00	1753	.	125.00	350.00	1759	.	115.00	300.00
1750	.. 150.00	400.00	1755	.	175.00	425.00	1760	.	120.00	325.00

3681   3679   3685

3681 Half-guinea. Young head

	F £	VF £			F £	VF £			F £	VF £
1728	.. 175.00	425.00	1732	.	175.00	425.00	1736	.	150.00	400.00
1729	.. 150.00	400.00	1733	. . . . . .	*? exists*	1737	. .	*Extremely rare*	
1730	... *Extremely rare*		1734	.	140.00	350.00	1738	.	125.00	325.00
1731	.. 250.00	600.00	1735	. . . . . .	*? exists*	1739	.	125.00	325.00

3682 — E.I.C. below

	F £	VF £						
1729	.. 325.00	700.00	1731	. . *Extremely rare*		1739	. . *Extremely rare*	
1730	.. 450.00	1000.00	1732	. . *Extremely rare*				

3683 Intermediate head

	F £	VF £			F £	VF £
1740	.. 250.00	600.00	1745	.	200.00	600.00
1743	. . . . . .	*? Unique*	1746	.	140.00	350.00

3684 — LIMA below, 1745 . . . . 500.00 1250.00

3685 Old head

	F £	VF £			F £	VF £			F £	VF £
1747	.. 200.00	500.00	1751	.	150.00	350.00	1756	.	100.00	250.00
1748	.. 150.00	325.00	1752	.	150.00	350.00	1758	.	110.00	275.00
1749	... *Extremely rare*		1753	.	110.00	275.00	1759	.	90.00	225.00
1750	.. 120.00	300.00	1755	.	110.00	275.00	1760	.	90.00	225.00

Note. *Values for coins in EF (extremely fine) condition can be three or more times the value of VF (very fine) specimens.*

SILVER

3686 Crown. Young bust. ℞. Roses and plumes in angles

	F	VF			F	VF			F	VF
	£	£			£	£			£	£
1732 ..	80.00	225.00	1735	.	80.00	225.00				
1734 ..	90.00	250.00	1736	.	80.00	225.00				

3687 ℞. Roses in angles

| 1739 .. | 80.00 | 225.00 | 1741 | . | 80.00 | 225.00 |

3688 Old head. ℞. Roses in angles, 1743 . . . .   75.00 200.00

3689 — LIMA below, 1746 . . . .   75.00 200.00

3690 Plain (i.e. no marks either side)

| 1750 .. | 115.00 | 275.00 | 1751 | . | 135.00 | 350.00 |

3692

3691 Halfcrown. Young bust; plain (proof only), 1731 *EF* £1250

3692 ℞. Roses and plumes

		F	VF			F	VF			F	VF
1731	..	25.00	80.00	1734	.	27.50	90.00	1736	.	32.50	125.00
1732	..	25.00	80.00	1735	.	27.50	90.00				

3693 — ℞. Roses

| 1739 | .. | 25.00 | 80.00 | 1741 | . | 25.00 | 85.00 |

3694 Old bust. ℞. Roses

| 1743 | .. | 22.00 | 75.00 | 1745 | . | 22.00 | 75.00 |

3695 — LIMA below

| 1745 | .. | 20.00 | 50.00 | 1746 | . | 20.00 | 50.00 |

3696 — plain

| 1750 | .. | 35.00 | 150.00 | 1751 | . | 50.00 | 175.00 |

3701

3697 Shilling. Young bust. ℞. Plumes

| 1727 | .. | 30.00 | 100.00 | 1731 | . | 50.00 | 175.00 |

3698 — ℞. Roses and plumes

		F	VF			F	VF			F	VF
1727	..	20.00	50.00	1729	.	30.00	90.00	1732	.	30.00	90.00
1728	..	30.00	90.00	1731	.	20.00	50.00				

3699 Shilling. Young bust, larger lettering. ℞. Roses and plumes

	F £	VF £			F £	VF £			F £	VF £
1734 ..	15.00	40.00	1736	.	15.00	40.00				
1735 ..	15.00	40.00	1737	.	15.00	40.00				

3700 — plain, 1728 . . . . 50.00 175.00

3701 — ℞. Roses

1739 ..	15.00	40.00	1741	.	15.00	40.00				

3702 Old bust. ℞. Roses

1743 ..	12.00	35.00	1745	.	12.00	35.00	1747	.	12.00	35.00

3703 — LIMA below

1745 ..	12.00	35.00	1746		30.00	90.00				

3704 — plain

1750 ..	20.00	55.00	1751	.	30.00	90.00	1758	.	6.00	20.00

3708   3710

3705 Sixpence. Young bust, plain, 1728 . . . . 30.00 90.00

3706 — ℞. Plumes, 1728 . . . . 20.00 55.00

3707 — ℞. Roses and plumes

	F £	VF £			F £	VF £			F £	VF £
1728 ..	15.00	40.00	1732	.	15.00	40.00	1735	.	25.00	80.00
1731 ..	15.00	40.00	1734	.	25.00	80.00	1736	.	20.00	50.00

3708 — ℞. Roses

1739 ..	15.00	40.00	1741	.	15.00	40.00				

3709 — Old bust. ℞. Roses

1743 ..	15.00	40.00	1745	.	18.00	45.00				

3710 — LIMA below

1745 ..	12.50	30.00	1746	.	10.00	25.00				

3711 — plain

1750 ..	18.00	50.00	1757	.	4.00	10.00				
1751 ..	22.00	60.00	1758	.	4.00	10.00				

3712 Fourpence. Young head. ℞. Crowned 4

1729 ..	6.00	13.00	1737	.	6.00	13.00	1743	.	6.00	13.00
1731 ..	6.00	13.00	1739	.	6.00	13.00	1746	.	5.00	12.00
1732 ..	6.00	13.00	1740	.	6.00	13.00	1760	.	6.00	13.00
1735 ..	6.00	13.00								

3713 Threepence. Young head. ℞. Crowned 3

1729 ..	7.00	14.00	1737	.	6.00	14.00	1743	.	6.00	14.00
1731 ..	7.00	14.00	1739	.	6.00	14.00	1746	.	6.00	14.00
1732 ..	7.00	14.00	1740	.	6.00	14.00	1760	.	6.00	14.00
1735 ..	7.00	14.00								

3714 Twopence. Young head. ℞. Crowned 2

1729 ..	3.00	7.00	1737	.	3.00	7.00	1746	.	3.00	7.00
1731 ..	3.00	7.00	1739	.	4.00	8.00	1756	.	3.00	7.00
1732 ..	3.00	7.00	1740	.	4.00	9.00	1759	.	3.00	7.00
1735 ..	3.00	7.00	1743	.	3.00	7.00	1760	.	3.00	7.00

3715 Penny. Young head. R. Crowned 1

	F £	VF £		F £	VF £		F £	VF £
1729 ..	3.00	6.00	1743 .	3.00	5.00	1755 .	3.00	5.00
1731 ..	3.00	5.00	1746 .	3.00	5.00	1756 .	3.00	5.00
1732 ..	3.00	5.00	1750 .	3.00	5.00	1757 .	3.00	5.00
1735 ..	3.00	6.00	1752 .	3.00	5.00	1758 .	3.00	5.00
1737 ..	3.00	6.00	1753 .	3.00	5.00	1759 .	3.00	5.00
1739 ..	3.00	5.00	1754 .	3.00	5.00	1760 .	3.00	6.00
1740 ..	3.00	5.00						

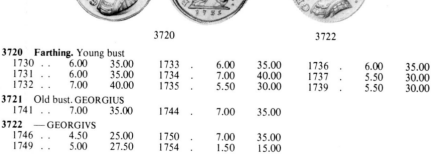

3716

3716 Maundy Set. As last four. Uniform dates

	F	VF		F	VF		F	VF
1729 ..	30.00	60.00	1737 .	28.00	55.00	1743 .	28.00	55.00
1731 ..	30.00	60.00	1739 .	28.00	55.00	1746 .	28.00	55.00
1732 ..	28.00	55.00	1740 .	28.00	55.00	1760 .	30.00	60.00
1735 ..	28.00	55.00						

COPPER

3717 Halfpenny. Young bust

	F	VF		F	VF		F	VF
1729 ..	5.50	25.00	1733 .	5.50	25.00	1737 .	5.50	25.00
1730 ..	5.50	25.00	1734 .	5.50	25.00	1738 .	5.00	22.00
1731 ..	5.50	25.00	1735 .	5.50	25.00	1739 .	5.50	25.00
1732 ..	5.50	25.00	1736 .	5.50	25.00			

3718 Old bust, GEORGIUS

	F	VF		F	VF		F	VF
1740 ..	5.50	25.00	1743 .	5.00	22.00	1745 .	5.00	22.00
1742 ..	5.50	25.00	1744 .	5.00	22.00			

3719 — GEORGIVS

	F	VF		F	VF		F	VF
1746 ..	5.50	25.00	1749 .	5.00	22.00	1752 .	5.00	22.00
1747 ..	5.50	25.00	1750 .	5.00	22.00	1753 .	5.00	22.00
1748 ..	5.00	22.00	1751 .	5.00	22.00	1754 .	5.00	22.00

3720   3722

3720 Farthing. Young bust

	F	VF		F	VF		F	VF
1730 ..	6.00	35.00	1733 .	6.00	35.00	1736 .	6.00	35.00
1731 ..	6.00	35.00	1734 .	7.00	40.00	1737 .	5.50	30.00
1732 ..	7.00	40.00	1735 .	5.50	30.00	1739 .	5.50	30.00

3721 Old bust. GEORGIUS

	F	VF		F	VF
1741 ..	7.00	35.00	1744 .	7.00	35.00

3722 — GEORGIVS

	F	VF		F	VF
1746 ..	4.50	25.00	1750 .	7.00	35.00
1749 ..	5.00	27.50	1754 .	1.50	15.00

GEORGE III, 1760–1820

During the second half of the 18th century very little silver or copper was minted. In 1797 Matthew Boulton's "cartwheels", the first copper pennies and twopences, demonstrated the improvement that could be effected as a result of the application of steam power to the coining press.

During the Napoleonic Wars bank notes came into general use when the issue of guineas was stopped between 1797 and 1813, but gold 7s. pieces were minted to help relieve the shortage of smaller money. As an emergency measure Spanish "dollars" were put into circulation for a short period after being countermarked, and in 1804 Spanish dollars were overstruck and issued as Bank of England dollars.

The transition to a "token" silver coinage began in 1811 when the Bank of England had 3s. and 1s. 6d. tokens made for general circulation. Private issues of token money in the years 1788–95 and 1811–15 helped to alleviate the shortage of regal coinage. A change over to a gold standard and a regular "token" silver coinage came in 1816 when the Mint, which was moved from its old quarters in the Tower of London to a new site on Tower Hill, began a complete recoinage. The guinea was replaced by a 20s. sovereign, and silver coins were made which had an intrinsic value lower than their face value. The St. George design used on the sovereign and crown was the work of Benedetto Pistrucci.

Early coinages

GOLD

3724

3723 Five guineas. Pattern only
  1770 *Extremely rare*   1773 *Extremely rare*   1777 *Extremely rare*
3724 Two guineas. Pattern only
  1768 *F.D.C.* £12,500.00   1773 *F.D.C.* £12,500.00   1777 *F.D.C.* £12,500.00

Note. *There are different bust varieties for 3723 and 3724, for further details see Douglas-Morris, November 1974 lots 127–132.*

		F £	VF £	EF £
3725	**Guinea.** First head, 1761	550.00	1150.00	2550.00

3725   3726   3727

3726 Second head

	F £	VF £	EF £			
1763 . .	325.00	750.00	1500.00	225.00	600.00	1250.00

3727   Guinea. Third head

	F £	VF £	EF £		F £	VF £	EF £		F £	VF £	EF £
1765 .	115	275	550	1768 .	110	250	500	1771 .	110	240	450
1766 .	100	225	425	1769 .	110	250	500	1772 .	100	225	425
1767 .	120	300	575	1770 .	120	300	575	1773 .	100	220	425

3728   Fourth head

	F	VF	EF		F	VF	EF		F	VF	EF
1774 .	80	150	325	1778 .	100	190	400	1783 .	95	175	375
1775 .	80	150	325	1779 .	85	165	375	1784 .	85	165	375
1776 .	80	150	325	1781 .	95	175	375	1785 .	80	150	325
1777 .	80	150	325	1782 .	90	160	375	1786 .	80	150	325

3728   3729

3729   Fifth head. ℞. "Spade" shaped shield

	F	VF	EF		F	VF	EF		F	VF	EF
1787 .	75	130	250	1792 .	80	135	260	1797 .	90	140	275
1788 .	75	130	250	1793 .	75	130	250	1798 .	75	130	250
1789 .	80	135	250	1794 .	75	130	250	1799 .	95	150	325
1790 .	75	130	250	1795 .	85	145	300				
1791 .	75	130	250	1796 .	105	175	400				

3730   Sixth head. ℞. Shield in Garter, known as the Military guinea, 1813   . *VF* £375 *EF* £750

3733   3734   3737

3731   Half-guinea. First head

	F	VF	EF			F	VF	EF
1762 .	175	500	1300		.	275	650	1450

3732   Second head

	F	VF	EF		F	VF	EF		F	VF	EF
1764 .	125	250	500	1768 .	150	300	600	1773 .	150	300	600
1765/4	250	600	—	1769 .	135	275	550	1774 .	250	600	—
1766 .	135	275	550	1772 . .	*Extremely rare*						

3733   Third head (less fine style)

	F	VF	EF		F	VF	EF
1774 . . .	*Extremely rare*			1775 .	200	450	1250

3734   Fourth head

	F	VF	EF		F	VF	EF		F	VF	EF
1775 .	70	135	275	1779 .	95	200	500	1784 .	70	135	275
1776 .	70	135	275	1781 .	80	140	300	1785 .	65	120	250
1777 .	65	120	250	1783 .	300	800	—	1786 .	65	120	250
1778 .	80	140	300								

3735   Fifth head. ℞. "Spade" type

	F	VF	EF		F	VF	EF		F	VF	EF
1787 .	55	115	225	1792 .	350	850	—	1797 .	55	115	225
1788 .	55	115	225	1793 .	55	115	225	1798 .	55	115	225
1789 .	65	125	250	1794 .	65	125	250	1800 .	125	350	—
1790 .	55	115	225	1795 .	80	175	300				
1791 .	65	125	250	1796 .	65	125	250				

3736 Half-guinea. Sixth head. ℞. Shield in Garter

	F £	VF £	EF £		F £	VF £	EF £		F £	VF £	EF £
1801 .	45	85	150	1802 .	45	90	160	1803 .	45	90	160

3737 Seventh head. Hd. with short hair. ℞. As last

	F	VF	EF		F	VF	EF		F	VF	EF
1804 .	45	85	150	1808 .	45	90	160	1811 .	65	150	350
1805 .	*Extremely rare*			1809 .	45	90	160	1813 .	55	135	300
1806 .	45	90	160	1810 .	45	90	160				

3738   3740   3741

3738 Third-guinea. I. First head

	F	VF	EF		F	VF	EF		F	VF	EF
1797 .	25	60	135	1799 .	35	110	225	1800 .	25	65	135
1798 .	25	60	135								

3739 II. Similar but date not in legend

	F	VF	EF		F	VF	EF		F	VF	EF
1801 .	30	70	150	1802 .	30	70	150	1803 .	30	70	150

3740 III. Second head with short hair

	F	VF	EF		F	VF	EF		F	VF	EF
1804 .	25	60	135	1809 .	30	65	135	1811 .	125	300	650
1806 .	25	60	135	1810 .	25	60	135	1813 .	50	135	275
1808 .	25	60	135								

3741 Quarter-guinea, 1762 35   85   150

N.B. *For gold of the 'new coinage', 1817–20, see page 235.*

SILVER

3742

	F £	VF £	EF £
3742 Shilling. Young bust, known as the "Northumberland" shilling 1763	125.00	250.00	425.00
3743 Older bust, no semée of hearts in the Hanoverian shield, 1787	2.00	4.00	30.00
3744 — — no stop over head, 1787	3.00	6.00	40.00
3745 — — no stops at date, 1787⌐	3.50	8.00	45.00

3746   no hearts   with hearts

	F £	VF £	EF £			F £	VF £	EF £
3746 — with semée of hearts, 1787						2.50	5.00	32.50
3747 — no stop over head 1798: known as the "Dorrien and Magens" shilling .						*UNC*	£3500.00	
3748 **Sixpence.** Without hearts, 1787						1.50	3.00	18.00
3749 — with hearts, 1787						1.50	3.00	20.00

3750 **Fourpence.** Young bust

	F	VF	EF			F	VF	EF
1763	3.00	8.00	16.00	1776	. . . . .	4.50	8.50	16.00
1765	100.00	250.00	600.00	1780	. . .˙. .	4.50	8.50	16.00
1766	5.00	9.00	17.00	1784	. . . . .	5.00	9.00	17.00
1770	5.00	9.00	17.00	1786	. . . . .	5.00	9.00	17.00
1772	5.00	9.00	17.00					

3751 — Older bust. ℞. Thin 4 ("Wire Money"), 1792 . . . . 7.00 15.00 30.00

3752 — — ℞. Normal 4

	F	VF	EF			F	VF	EF
1795	3.50	7.50	15.00	1800	. . . . .	3.50	7.50	15.00

3750   3751   3755

3753 **Threepence.** Young bust

	F	VF	EF			F	VF	EF
1762	2.00	5.00	9.00	1772	. . . . .	3.00	6.00	14.00
1763	2.00	5.00	9.00	1780	. . . . .	3.00	6.00	14.00
1765	100.00	250.00	600.00	1784	. . . . .	3.00	7.00	15.00
1766	3.00	6.00	14.00	1786	. . . . .	3.00	6.00	14.00
1770	3.00	6.00	14.00					

3754 — Older bust. ℞. Thin 3 ("Wire Money"), 1792 . . . . 7.00 15.00 30.00

3755 — — ℞. Normal 3

	F	VF	EF			F	VF	EF
1795	3.50	7.00	14.00	1800	. . . . .	3.50	7.00	14.00

3756 **Twopence.** Young bust

	F	VF	EF			F	VF	EF
1763	2.50	5.50	11.00	1776	. . . . .	2.50	5.50	11.00
1765	75.00	175.00	450.00	1780	. . . . .	2.00	5.00	11.00
1766	2.00	5.50	11.00	1784	. . . . .	2.00	5.00	11.00
1772	2.00	5.50	11.00	1786	. . . . .	2.00	5.00	11.00

3757 — Older bust. ℞. Thin 2 ("Wire Money"), 1792 . . . . 5.00 12.00 25.00

3758 — — ℞. Normal 2

	F	VF	EF			F	VF	EF
1795	2.00	4.00	7.00	1800	. . . . .	2.00	4.00	7.00

3759 **Penny.** Young bust

	F	VF	EF			F	VF	EF
1763	2.50	5.50	11.00	1779	. . . . .	2.00	5.00	10.00
1765			*? Exists*	1780	. . . . .	2.50	5.50	11.00
1766	2.00	5.00	10.00	1781	. . . . .	2.00	5.00	10.00
1770	2.00	5.00	10.00	1784	. . . . .	2.00	5.00	10.00
1772	2.00	5.00	10.00	1786	. . . . .	2.00	5.00	10.00
1776	2.50	5.50	11.00					

3760 — Older bust. ℞. Thin 1 ("Wire Money"), 1792 . . . . 2.50 5.00 8.00

3761 — — ℞. Normal 1

	F	VF	EF			F	VF	EF
1795	1.50	2.50	6.00	1800	. . . . .	1.50	2.50	6.00

3762 **Maundy Set.** Uniform dates

	F	VF	EF		F	VF	EF
	£	£	£		£	£	£
1763	26.00	45.00	130.00	1780	28.00	45.00	130.00
1766	26.00	45.00	130.00	1784	26.00	45.00	130.00
1772	26.00	45.00	130.00	1786	26.00	45.00	130.00

3763 — Older bust. ℞ Thin numerals ("Wire Money"), 1792 . . . . 50.00   90.00   200.00

3764 — ℞. Normal numerals. Uniform dates

	F	VF	EF		F	VF	EF
1795	25.00	40.00	100.00	1800	25.00	40.00	90.00

Emergency issue

3765   3767   3766

3765 **Dollar.** (current for 4s. 9d.). Spanish American 8 *reales* countermarked with head of George III in oval 60.00   125.00   275.00

3766 — — octagonal countermark 90.00   200.00   450.00

3767 **Half-dollar** with similar oval countermark 60.00   125.00   275.00

Bank of England issue

3768

3768 **Dollar.** (current for 5s.). Laureat bust of king. ℞. Britannia seated l., 1804 . . . . 35.00   75.00   200.00

These dollars were re-struck from Spanish–American 8 reales until at least 1811. Dollars that show dates of original coin are worth rather more.

3769   **Three shillings.** Draped bust in armour. ℞. BANK / TOKEN / 3 SHILL / date (in oak wreath)

	F £	VF £	EF £		F £	VF £	EF £
1811	8.00	18.00	55.00	1812	9.00	20.00	60.00

3770   — Laureate head r. ℞. As before but wreath of oak and laurel

	F	VF	EF		F	VF	EF
1812	7.00	15.00	50.00	1815	7.00	15.00	50.00
1813	7.00	15.00	50.00	1816	90.00	175.00	450.00
1814	7.00	15.00	50.00				

3771   3772

3771   **Eighteen pence.** Draped bust in armour

1811	4.00	10.00	35.00	1812	4.00	10.00	35.00

3772   — Laureate head

1812	3.00	9.00	30.00	1815	3.00	9.00	30.00
1813	3.00	9.00	30.00	1816	3.00	9.00	30.00
1814	3.00	9.00	30.00				

3773   **Ninepence.** Similar, 1812 (pattern only) . . . .   *FDC* £750

N.B. *For the last or "new coinage", 1816–20, see page 236.*

COPPER

First issue—London

3774

3774   **Halfpenny.** Cuirassed bust r. ℞. Britannia

1770	3.00	12.00	45.00	1773	2.50	10.00	40.00
1771	2.50	10.00	40.00	1774	3.00	12.00	45.00
1772	2.50	10.00	40.00	1775	3.50	15.00	50.00

3775   **Farthing**

1771	15.00	35.00	80.00	1774	3.50	12.00	45.00
1773	2.00	8.00	30.00	1775	4.00	15.00	50.00

Copper
Second issue—Soho mint. "Cartwheel" coinage

3776

	F £	VF £	EF £
3776 Twopence. Legends incuse on raised rim, 1797	6.00	18.00	90.00
3777 ʼ Penny, 1797. Similar	5.00	15.00	50.00

Halfpence and farthings of this issue are patterns.

Third issue—Soho mint

			VF £	EF £
3778 Halfpenny. Draped bust r., 1799			3.50	25.00
3779 Farthing, 1799			3.50	25.00

3778   3782

Fourth issue—Soho mint
3780   Penny. Different bust

	F £	VF £	EF £		F £	VF £	EF £
1806	1.00	5.00	40.00	1807	1.50	7.00	50.00
3781 Halfpenny							
1806		2.50	25.00	1807		3.00	35.00
3782 Farthing							
1806		2.50	25.00	1807		3.50	35.00

EIGHTEENTH CENTURY TOKENS

In 1787, the regal copper coinage being very scanty, pennies and half-pennies were struck by the Anglesey Copper Mining Company and there began a fresh token epoch. They present an immense variety of types, persons, buildings, coats of arms, local legends, political events, etc., all drawn upon for subjects of design. They were struck by many firms in most cities and towns in the country and are to be found in good condition. Circulated specimens are so common that they have little value.

For further details of 18th century tokens see *The Provincial Token-Coinage of the Eighteenth Century*, by Dalton and Hamer and Seaby's *British Tokens and their Values*.

	VF	EF
	£	£
Price of commoner pennies	5.00	14.00
Price of commoner halfpennies	4.00	11.00
— — — farthings	3.00	9.00

Bury St. Edmunds penny

Coventry halfpenny

Isaac Newton farthing

NINETEENTH CENTURY TOKENS

With the issue of the copper coinage of 1797 tokens were made illegal, but the dearth of silver currency was still felt. During the Napoleonic wars there came a small wave of prosperity in the industrial districts and the inevitable need for small change, so in 1811 tokens again made their appearance. On this occasion silver ones were made as well as copper. These, with two exceptions, were suppressed before the last coinage of George III.

For further details of 19th century silver tokens see *The Nineteenth Century Token Coinage* by W. J. Davis and *Silver Token-Coinage 1811–1812*, by R. Dalton, also Seaby's *British Tokens and Their Values*.

	VF £	EF £
Price of the commoner shillings	10.00	20.00
— — — sixpences	10.00	20.00

Newcastle Shilling   Charing Cross Sixpence

	VF £	EF £
Price of the commoner pennies	3.00	13.00
— — — halfpennies	2.00	8.00
— — — farthings	2.00	9.00

Withymoor Scythe Works Penny, 1813

London Halfpenny

GEORGE III

Last or new coinage, 1816–20

The year 1816 is a landmark in the history of our coinage. For some years at the beginning of the nineteenth century Mint production was virtually confined to small gold denominations, regular full production being resumed only after the Mint had been moved from the Tower of London to a new site on Tower Hill. Steam powered minting machinery made by Boulton and Watt replaced the old hand operated presses and these produced coins which were technically much superior to the older milled coins.

In 1816 for the first time, British silver coins were produced with an intrinsic value substantially below their face value, the first official token coinage.

Our present "silver" coins are made to the same weight standard and are still legal tender back to 1816 with the exception of the halfcrown. The old guinea was replaced by a sovereign of twenty shillings in 1817, the standard of 22 carat (.916) fineness still being retained.

Engraver's and/or designer's initials:
B. P. (Benedetto Pistrucci)

GOLD

3783

		F	VF	EF			F	VF	EF

3783* **Five pounds,** 1820 (Pattern only) . . . . *FDC* £20,000.00

3784 **Two pounds,** 1820 (Pattern only) . . . . *FDC* £8000.00

3785 **Sovereign.** ℞. St. George

	F £	VF £	EF £		F £	VF £	EF £
1817	75.00	125.00	375.00	1819		*Extremely rare*	
1818	85.00	150.00	500.00	1820	75.00	125.00	375.00

3785   3786

3786 **Half-Sovereign.** ℞. Crowned shield

1817	50.00	90.00	250.00	1820	55.00	95.00	275.00
1818	50.00	95.00	275.00				

*Beware counterfeits.

SILVER

3787

3787   Crown. Laureat head r. ℞. Pistrucci's St. George and dragon within Garter

	F £	VF £	EF £
1818, edge LVIII	9.00	30.00	115.00
— — LIX	10.00	35.00	120.00
1819 — LIX	9.00	30.00	105.00
— — LX	10.00	35.00	120.00
1820 — LX	9.00	30.00	115.00

3788

3788   Halfcrown. Large or "bull" head

	F £	VF £	EF £		F £	VF £	EF £
1816	5.00	20.00	80.00	1817	5.00	20.00	80.00

3789

3789   — Small head

1817	5.00	22.50	90.00	1819	6.00	25.00	100.00
1818	6.00	25.00	100.00	1820	9.00	35.00	150.00

3790   3791

3790 Shilling. R̶. Shield in Garter

	F £	VF £	EF £		F £	VF £	EF £
1816	1.75	5.00	30.00	1819	1.75	6.00	35.00
1817	1.75	6.00	35.00	1820	1.75	6.00	35.00
1818	5.00	20.00	95.00				

3791 Sixpence. R̶. Shield in Garter

	F £	VF £	EF £		F £	VF £	EF £
1816	1.25	4.00	25.00	1819	1.75	6.00	35.00
1817	1.50	5.00	30.00	1820	1.75	6.00	35.00
1818	1.75	6.00	35.00				

3792

3792 Maundy Set (4d., 3d., 2d and 1d.)

	EF £	FDC £		EF £	FDC £
1817	80.00	150.00	1820	80.00	150.00
1818	80.00	150.00			

		EF £	FDC £
3793	— fourpence, 1817, 1818, 1820 *from*	14.00	30.00
3794	— threepence, 1817, 1818, 1820 *from*	14.00	30.00
3795	— twopence, 1817, 1818, 1820 *from*	8.00	13.00
3796	— penny, 1817, 1818, 1820 *from*	7.00	11.00

GEORGE IV, 1820–30

The Mint resumed the coinage of copper farthings in 1821, and pennies and halfpennies in 1825. A gold two pound piece was first issued for general circulation in 1823.

Engraver's and/or designer's initials:
B. P. (Benedetto Pistrucci)
J. B. M. (Jean Baptiste Merlen)

GOLD

3797

3797 Five pounds, 1826 (Proof only). ℞. Shield . . . . *FDC*   £9000.00

3798

		VF	EF
		£	£
3798 Two pounds, 1823. Large bare head. ℞. St. George		300.00	650.00
3799 — 1826. Type as 3797 (Proof only)		*FDC*	3500.00

3800

3800 Sovereign. Laureate head. ℞. St. George

	F	VF	EF		F	VF	EF
	£	£	£		£	£	£
1821	75.00	125.00	375.00	1824	85.00	150.00	400.00
1822*	80.00	150.00	400.00	1825	110.00	310.00	1000.00
1823	125.00	350.00	1100.00				

Beware counterfeits.

3801

3801 Sovereign. Bare head. ℞. Crowned shield

	F	VF	EF		F	VF	EF
	£	£	£		£	£	£
1825	75.00	130.00	350.00	1828*	450.00	1250.00	3500.00
1826	75.00	130.00	350.00	1829	75.00	135.00	375.00
— Proof			FDC £1600	1830	80.00	135.00	375.00
1827*	85.00	135.00	375.00				

3802   3803   3804

3802 Half-sovereign. Laureate head. ℞. Ornately garnished shield.
1821	175.00	450.00	950.00

3803 — As last. ℞. Plain shield
1823	65.00	150.00	475.00	1825	60.00	140.00	425.00
1824	60.00	140.00	450.00				

3804 — Bare head. ℞. Garnished shield
1826	70.00	125.00	375.00	1827	70.00	125.00	375.00
— Proof		FDC	950.00	1828	65.00	115.00	325.00

Beware counterfeits.

SILVER

3805

3805 Crown. Laureate head. ℞. St. George
1821, edge SECUNDO	12.00	40.00	300.00
1822 — SECUNDO	15.00	50.00	375.00
— — TERTIO	14.00	45.00	325.00

3806

FDC
£

3806   Crown. Bare head. ℞. Shield with crest (Proof only), 1826 . . . .   2500.00

3807   3808

3807   Halfcrown. Laureate head. ℞. Garnished shield

	F	VF	EF		F	VF	EF
	£	£	£		£	£	£
1820	7.00	25.00	95.00	1823	225.00	650.00	1950.00
1821	7.00	25.00	95.00				

3808   — Similar. ℞. Shield in Garter and collar

	F	VF	EF		F	VF	EF
1823	7.00	30.00	120.00	1824	10.00	35.00	150.00

3809

3809   — Bare head. ℞. Shield with crest

	F	VF	EF				
1824		*Extremely rare*		1826	Proof *FDC*		£475.00
1825	7.00	25.00	90.00	1828	12.00	40.00	175.00
1826	6.50	22.00	80.00	1829	10.00	35.00	150.00

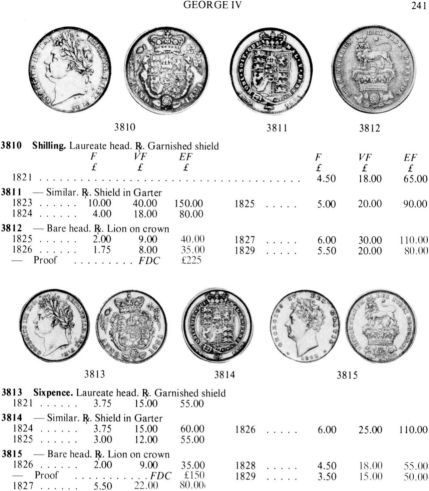

3810   3811   3812

3810 Shilling. Laureate head. ℞. Garnished shield

	F £	VF £	EF £		F £	VF £	EF £
1821					4.50	18.00	65.00

3811 — Similar. ℞. Shield in Garter

| 1823 | 10.00 | 40.00 | 150.00 | 1825 | 5.00 | 20.00 | 90.00 |
| 1824 | 4.00 | 18.00 | 80.00 | | | | |

3812 — Bare head. ℞. Lion on crown

1825	2.00	9.00	40.00	1827	6.00	30.00	110.00
1826	1.75	8.00	35.00	1829	5.50	20.00	80.00
— Proof		FDC	£225				

3813   3814   3815

3813 Sixpence. Laureate head. ℞. Garnished shield

| 1821 | 3.75 | 15.00 | 55.00 |

3814 — Similar. ℞. Shield in Garter

| 1824 | 3.75 | 15.00 | 60.00 | 1826 | 6.00 | 25.00 | 110.00 |
| 1825 | 3.00 | 12.00 | 55.00 | | | | |

3815 — Bare head. ℞. Lion on crown

1826	2.00	9.00	35.00	1828	4.50	18.00	55.00
— Proof		FDC	£150	1829	3.50	15.00	50.00
1827	5.50	22.00	80.00				

3816

3816 Maundy Set (4d., 3d., 2d. and 2d.).

	EF £	FDC £		EF £	FDC £
1822	65.00	135.00	1827	55.00	115.00
1823	55.00	115.00	1828	55.00	115.00
1824	60.00	125.00	1829	55.00	115.00
1825	55.00	115.00	1830	55.00	115.00
1826	55.00	115.00			

				EF £	FDC £
3817	**Maundy fourpence,** 1822–30		*from*	11.00	18.00
3818	**— threepence,** small head, 1822			20.00	35.00
3819	**— — normal head,** 1823–30		*from*	10.00	17.00
3820	**— twopence,** 1822–30		*from*	8.00	10.00
3821	**— penny,** 1822–30		*from*	5.00	8.00

COPPER

First issue, 1821–6

3822

3822   Farthing. Laureate bust, draped

	F £	VF £	EF £		F £	VF £	EF £
1821		3.00	20.00	1825		3.00	18.00
1822		2.75	18.00	1826	1.25	5.00	30.00
1823		3.50	22.00				

3823   3827

Second issue, 1825–30

3823   Penny. Laureate head. ℞. Britannia

1825	2.00	12.00	45.00	1826	Proof *FDC* £225		
1826	2.00	10.00	35.00	1827	25.00	80.00	900.00

3824   Halfpenny. Similar

1825	9.00	27.50	90.00	1826	Proof *FDC* £100		
1826		3.50	22.00	1827	1.00	4.50	35.00

3825   Farthing. Similar

1826		3.00	15.00	1828	3.50	20.00
— Proof *FDC* £110				1829	5.00	35.00
1827		4.50	25.00	1830	4.00	20.00

3826   Half-farthing (for use in Ceylon). Similar

1828	2.50	12.00	45.00	1830	2.50	12.00	45.00

3827   Third-farthing (for use in Malta). Similar

1827		2.50	18.00

WILLIAM IV, 1830–7

In order to prevent confusion between the sixpence and half-sovereign the size of the latter was reduced in 1834, but the smaller gold piece was not acceptable to the public and in the following year it was made to the normal size. In 1836 the silver groat was again issued for general circulation: it is the only British silver coin which has a seated Britannia as the type. Crowns were not struck during this reign for general circulation; but proofs or patterns of this denomination were made and are greatly sought after. Silver threepences and threehalfpence were minted for use in the Colonies.

Engraver's and/or designer's initials:
W. W. (William Wyon)

GOLD

3828

3828	**Two pounds,** 1831 (Proof only)					*FDC*	£6000.00

3829 **Sovereign.** ℞. Crowned shield

	F	VF	EF		F	VF	EF
	£	£	£		£	£	£
1831	90.00	165.00	550.00	1835	90.00	165.00	475.00
— Proof *FDC* £1900				1836	90.00	165.00	475.00
1832*	85.00	150.00	450.00	1837	85.00	155.00	450.00
1833	90.00	165.00	475.00				

*Beware counterfeits.

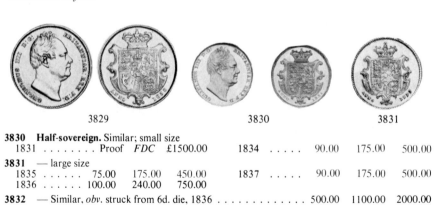

3829   3830   3831

3830 **Half-sovereign.** Similar; small size

1831 . . . . Proof *FDC* £1500.00			1834	90.00	175.00	500.00

3831 — large size

1835	75.00	175.00	450.00	1837	90.00	175.00	500.00
1836	100.00	240.00	750.00				

3832 — Similar, *obv.* struck from 6d. die, 1836 . . . . 500.00   1100.00   2000.00

3833

3833 Crown. ℞. Shield on mantle, 1831 (Proof only) . . . . *FDC* ₊£4500.00

3834

3834 Halfcrown. ℞. Shield on mantle

			F	VF	EF			F	VF	EF
			£	£	£			£	£	£
1831	Proof	*FDC*	£425			1836	. . . . .	9.00	40.00	135.00
1834	. . . . . .	9.00	35.00	120.00	1837	. . . .	12.00	50.00	200.00
1835	. . . . . .	12.00	50.00	200.00					

3835   3836

3835 Shilling. ℞. Value in wreath

			F	VF	EF			F	VF	EF
1831	Proof	*FDC*	£275			1836	. . . . .	4.00	18.00	80.00
1834	. . . . . .	4.00	18.00	80.00	1837	. . . . .	5.00	30.00	125.00
1835	. . . . . .	5.00	22.00	95.00					

3836 Sixpence. ℞. Value in wreath

			F	VF	EF			F	VF	EF
			£	£	£			£	£	£
1831	. . . . . .	2.50	10.00	40.00	1835	. . . . .	2.50	10.00	40.00
—	Proof	*FDC*	£175			1836	. . . . .	6.00	25.00	100.00
1834	. . . . . .	2.50	10.00	40.00	1837	. . . . .	4.00	20.00	80.00

3837

3837   Groat. ℞. Britannia seated

	F	VF	EF			F	VF	EF
	£	£	£			£	£	£
1836		2.00	16.00	1837			2.00	16.00

3838   Threepence (for use in the West Indies). As Maundy threepence but with a dull surface

1834	1.25	6.00	30.00	1836	1.00	5.00	28.00
1835	1.00	5.00	28.00	1837	1.75	7.00	36.00

3839

3839   Three-halfpence (for Colonial use). ℞. Value

1834		2.00	16.00	1836		3.00	20.00
1835		2.50	18.00	1837	4.00	20.00	75.00

3840

3840   Maundy Set (4d., 3d., 2d. and 1d.).

	EF	FDC			EF	FDC
	£	£			£	£
1831	80.00	150.00	1834	75.00	140.00
— Proof		250.00	1835	75.00	140.00
1832	75.00	140.00	1836	75.00	140.00
1833	75.00	140.00	1837	75.00	140.00

3841   — fourpence, 1831–7 . . . . *from* 11.00   20.00

3842   — threepence, 1831–7 . . . . *from* 20.00   30.00

3843   — twopence, 1831–7 . . . . *from* 7.50   13.00

3844   — penny, 1831–7 . . . . *from* 7.00   12.00

COPPER

3845

3845 Penny. No initials on truncation

	F £	VF £	EF £			F £	VF £	EF £
1831	5.00	25.00	90.00	1834	5.00	30.00	100.00
— Proof *FDC* £275				1837	8.00	40.00	150.00

3846   — WW on truncation, 1831 . . . .   7.00   35.00   125.00

3847 Halfpenny. As penny

1831	1.00	6.00	30.00	1834	1.00	6.50	35.00
— Proof *FDC* £100				1837		5.50	25.00

3848 Farthing. Similar

1831		2.50	17.50	1835		2.25	16.00
— Proof *FDC* £135				1836		3.00	20.00
1834		2.25	16.00	1837		2.25	16.00

3848   3849

3849 Half-farthing (for use in Ceylon). Similar
1837 . . . .   12.00   35.00   150.00

3850 Third-farthing (for use in Malta). Similar
1835 . . . .   2.00   16.00

VICTORIA, 1837–1901

In 1849, as a first step towards decimalization, a silver florin ($\frac{1}{10}$th pound) was introduced, but the coins of 1849 omitted the usual *Dei Gratia* and these so-called "Godless" florins were replaced in 1851 by the "Gothic" issue. The halfcrown was temporarily discontinued but was minted again from 1874 onwards. Between 1863 and 1880 reverse dies of the gold and silver coins were numbered in the course of Mint experiments into the wear of dies. The exception was the florin where the die number is on the obverse below the bust.

The gold and silver coins were redesigned for the Queen's Golden Jubilee in 1887. The double-florin which was then issued was abandoned after only four years; the Jubilee sixpence of 1887, known as the "withdrawn" type, was changed to avoid confusion with the half sovereign. Gold and silver were again redesigned in 1893 with an older portrait of the Queen, but the "old head" was not used on the bronze coinage until 1895. The heavy copper penny had been replaced by the lighter bronze "bun" penny in 1860. In 1874–6 and 1881–2 some of the bronze was made by Heaton in Birmingham, and these have a letter H below the date. From 1897 farthings were issued with a dark surface.

Early sovereigns had a shield type reverse, but Pistrucci's St. George design was used again from 1871. In order to increase the output of gold coinage, branches of the Royal Mint were set up in Australia at Sydney and Melbourne and, later, at Perth for coining gold of imperial type.

Engraver's and/or designer's initials:
W. W. (William Wyon)   J. E. B. (Joseph Boehm)
L. C. W. (Leonard Charles Wyon)   T. B. (Thomas Brock)

GOLD

NOTE. Over the last few years there has been substantial variation in the bullion price of gold and, as it has fluctuated, it has affected the value of British gold coins, particularly from Victorian issues onwards. The values given here were calculated at a time when the gold price was approximately $340 per fine oz. Most modern gold below EF condition sells at only a small premium above the quoted daily price for sovereigns (except scarce and rarer dates or mints).

Young head coinage, 1838–87

3851

3851   Five pounds, 1839. ℞. "Una and the lion" (proof only) . . . .   *FDC*   £15,000.00

3852   3853

3852   Sovereign, type I. R̃. Shield. London mint

	F	VF	EF		VF	EF
	£	£	£		£	£
1838	75.00	110.00	275.00	1852		135.00
1839 . . . : . . .	125.00	300.00	1000.00	1853		135.00
— Proof *FDC* £2500.00				— Proof *FDC* £4000.00		
1841	500.00	1100.00	2500.00	1854		135.00
1842			150.00	1855		135.00
1843			150.00	1856		135.00
1844			150.00	1857		135.00
1845			150.00	1858	90.00	200.00
1846			150.00	1859		150.00
1847			140.00	1860	80.00	175.00
1848			175.00	1861		135.00
1849			175.00	1862		135.00
1850			175.00	1863		135.00
1851			140.00	1872		135.00

3853   — — die number below wreath

1863		130.00	1870		135.00
1864		125.00	1871		125.00
1865		135.00	1872		125.00
1866		125.00	1873		135.00
1868		135.00	1874	1100.00	—
1869		125.00			

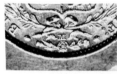

3854   3855

3854   — — M below wreath for Melbourne mint

1872 M	90.00	175.00	1883 M	130.00	600.00
1874 M		150.00	1884 M		150.00
1875 M	*? None issued*		1885 M		150.00
1880 M	250.00	1200.00	1886 M	650.00	1600.00
1881 M	125.00	400.00	1887 M	600.00	1450.00
1882 M	90.00	175.00			

3855   — — S below wreath for Sydney mint

1871 S		150.00	1881 S		170.00
1872 S		170.00	1882 S		150.00
1873 S		150.00	1883 S		150.00
1875 S		150.00	1884 S		150.00
1877 S		150.00	1885 S		150.00
1878 S		150.00	1886 S		155.00
1879 S		150.00	1887 S		175.00
1880 S		160.00			

3856

3856 — Sovereign, type II. ℞. St. George. London mint

	EF £		VF £	EF £
1871	90.00	1878		125.00
1872	90.00	1879	150.00	500.00
1873	90.00	1880		90.00
1874	90.00	1884		90.00
1876	90.00	1885		95.00

3857   3858

3857 — — M below head for Melbourne mint

1872 M	95.00	1880 M	90.00
1873 M	90.00	1881 M	90.00
1874 M	90.00	1882 M	90.00
1875 M	90.00	1883 M	90.00
1876 M	90.00	1884 M	90.00
1877 M	90.00	1885 M	90.00
1878 M	90.00	1886 M	100.00
1879 M	90.00	1887 M	100.00

3858 — — S below head for Sydney mint

1871 S	90.00	1881 S	90.00
1872 S	90.00	1882 S	90.00
1873 S	90.00	1883 S	90.00
1874 S	90.00	1884 S	90.00
1875 S	90.00	1885 S	90.00
1876 S	90.00	1886 S	100.00
1879 S	90.00	1887 S	100.00
1880 S	90.00		

Note: *Gold bullion price at the time of printing $340 per oz. at $1.50 to the £1 sterling.*
   When no values are given for sovereigns below EF condition, their price, when available, will be subject to the current gold price.

Gold

3859   3860

3859 Half-sovereign. ℞. Shield. London mint

	VF £	EF £		VF £	EF £
1838	80.00	200.00	1852	85.00	175.00
1839 Proof only *FDC*	£1100.00		1853	60.00	135.00
1841	100.00	250.00	— Proof *FDC* £2250.00		
1842	60.00	135.00	1854		*Extremely rare*
1843	100.00	250.00	1855	65.00	140.00
1844	70.00	200.00	1856	65.00	140.00
1845	250.00	800.00	1857	85.00	175.00
1846	80.00	210.00	1858	60.00	140.00
1847	80.00	210.00	1859	60.00	140.00
1848	80.00	210.00	1860	55.00	135.00
1849	70.00	175.00	1861	60.00	150.00
1850	150.00	450.00	1862	750.00	
1851	70.00	150.00	1863	65.00	135.00

3860 — — die number below shield

	VF	EF		VF	EF
1863	85.00	210.00	1873	55.00	150.00
1864	60.00	135.00	1874	65.00	150.00
1865	60.00	135.00	1875	55.00	135.00
1866	60.00	135.00	1876	55.00	130.00
1867	60.00	135.00	1877	55.00	130.00
1869	60.00	135.00	1878	55.00	130.00
1870	70.00	135.00	1879	75.00	250.00
1871	60.00	135.00	1880	55.00	130.00
1872	60.00	135.00			

3861 — — As 3859 (no die number) but head in slightly lower relief

	VF	EF		VF	EF
1880	60.00	135.00	1884	55.00	115.00
1883	55.00	115.00	1885	55.00	115.00

3862   3863

3862 — — S below shield for Sydney mint

	VF	EF		VF	EF
1871 S	90.00	275.00	1881 S	150.00	500.00
1872 S	100.00	325.00	1882 S	150.00	500.00
1875 S	95.00	300.00	1883 S	100.00	350.00
1879 S	100.00	350.00	1886 S	110.00	400.00
1880 S	100.00	350.00	1887 S	100.00	350.00

3863 — — M below shield for Melbourne mint

	VF	EF		VF	EF
1873 M	125.00	400.00	1884 M	150.00	500.00
1877 M	150.00	500.00	1885 M	250.00	900.00
1881 M	200.00	700.00	1886 M	125.00	450.00
1882 M	150.00	500.00	1887 M	170.00	600.00

Gold
Jubilee coinage, 1887–93

3864

3864 Five pounds. ℞. St. George

	VF £	EF £		VF £	EF £
1887				450.00	700.00
— Proof *FDC* £1650.00					

3865 Two pounds. Similar

1887				175.00	350.00
Proof *FDC* £850.00					

3866 Sovereign. ℞. St. George. London mint

1887	90.00	1890	90.00
— Proof *FDC* £650.00		1891	90.00
1888	90.00	1892	90.00
1889	90.00		

3866   3867   3869

3867 — — M on ground for Melbourne mint

1887 M	90.00	1891 M	90.00
1888 M	90.00	1892 M	90.00
1889 M	90.00	1893 M	90.00
1890 M	90.00		

3686 — — S on ground for Sydney mint

1887 S	90.00	1891 S	90.00
1888 S	110.00	1892 S	90.00
1889 S	90.00	1893 S	90.00
1890 S	90.00		

3869 Half-sovereign. ℞. Shield. London mint

1887 . . . . 55.00	70.00	1891 . . . . 55.00	80.00
— Proof *FDC* £375.00		1892 . . . . 55.00	75.00
1890 . . . . 55.00	70.00	1893 . . . . 55.00	80.00

3870 — — M below shield for Melbourne mint

1887 M 85.00	250.00	1893 M 85.00	250.00

3871 — — S below shield for Sydney mint

1887 S 82.50	200.00	1891 S 82.50	200.00
1889 S 85.00	225.00		

Gold

	VF	*EF*
Old head coinage, 1893–1901	£	£
3972 Five pounds. ℞. St. George		
1893	500.00	850.00
— Proof *FDC* £1800.00		

3873

3873 Two pounds. Similar

	VF	*EF*
1893	250.00	450.00
— Proof *FDC* £950.00		

3874 Sovereign. ℞. St. George. London mint

	EF £			*EF* £
1893	85.00	1898	85.00
— Proof *FDC* £600.00		1899	85.00
1894	85.00	1900	85.00
1895	85.00	1901	85.00
1896	85.00		

3876   3877

3875 Sovereign. ℞. St. George. M on ground for Melbourne mint

1893 M	85.00	1898 M	85.00
1894 M	85.00	1899 M	85.00
1895 M	85.00	1900 M	85.00
1896 M	85.00	1901 M	85.00
1897 M	85.00		

3876 — — P on ground for Perth mint

1899 P	105.00	1901 P	100.00
1900 P	95.00		

3877 — — S on ground for Sydney mint

1893 S	85.00	1898 S	85.00
1894 S	85.00	1899 S	85.00
1895 S	85.00	1900 S	85.00
1896 S	85.00	1901 S	85.00
1897 S	85.00		

3878

3878 Half-sovereign. ℞. St. George. London mint

	VF	EF			VF	EF
	£	£			£	£
1893		65.00		1897		65.00
— Proof *FDC* £450.00				1898		65.00
1894		65.00		1899		65.00
1895		65.00		1900		65.00
1896		65.00		1901		65.00

3879 — — M on ground for Melbourne mint

		VF	EF			VF	EF
1893 M		*Extremely rare*			1899 M	60.00	135.00
1896 M	60.00	150.00		1900 M	65.00	200.00

3880 — — P on ground for Perth mint

					VF	EF
1899 P	Proof *unique*			1900 P	70.00	225.00

3881 — — S on ground for Sydney mint

	VF	EF			VF	EF
1893 S	55.00	120.00		1900 S	60.00	135.00
1897 S	55.00	120.00				

SILVER

Young head coinage

3882

3882 Crown. Young head. ℞. Crowned shield

1839   Proof only   *FDC*   £2750.00

	F	VF	EF		F	VF	EF
	£	£	£		£	£	£
1844	16.50	55.00	450.00	1847	18.00	60.00	500.00
1845	16.00	45.00	425.00				

3883

	VF £	EF £	FDC £
3883* Crown. "Gothic" type, as illustration; inscribed edge, mdcccxlvii = 1847	275.00	450.00	950.00
— Proof, plain edge *FDC* £1100.00			

***N.B.** Beware of recent forgeries.*

3884   — mdcccliii = 1853. Proof   *FDC*   £3500.00

3888

	F £	VF £	EF £		F £	VF £	EF £
3885 Halfcrown, type A¹. Young head with one ornate and one plain fillet binding hair. WW in relief on truncation, 1839	250.00	600.00	2000.00				
3886 — Proof *FDC* £600.00							
3887 — type A³. Two plain fillets, WW incuse							
1839	250.00	600.00	2000.00	1840	12.00	50.00	200.00
3888 — type A⁴. Similar but no initials on truncation							
1841	25.00	75.00	350.00	1846	9.00	40.00	145.00
1842	10.00	45.00	150.00	1848/6	35.00	125.00	500.00
1843	20.00	60.00	300.00	1849	15.00	60.00	250.00
1844	9.00	40.00	120.00	1850	12.00	50.00	200.00
1845	9.00	40.00	120.00	1853 Proof *FDC* £1500.00			

3889 Halfcrown, type A[5]. As last but inferior workmanship

	F	VF	EF			F	VF	EF
	£	£	£			£	£	£
1874	5.00	20.00	75.00		1881	5.00	22.00	75.00
1875	5.50	24.00	80.00		1882	5.25	24.00	80.00
1876	5.75	25.00	85.00		1883	5.00	22.00	75.00
1877	5.50	24.00	80.00		1884	5.00	22.00	75.00
1878	5.50	24.00	80.00		1885	5.00	22.00	75.00
1879	6.00	32.50	110.00		1886	5.00	22.00	75.00
1880	5.50	24.00	80.00		1887	5.00	22.00	80.00

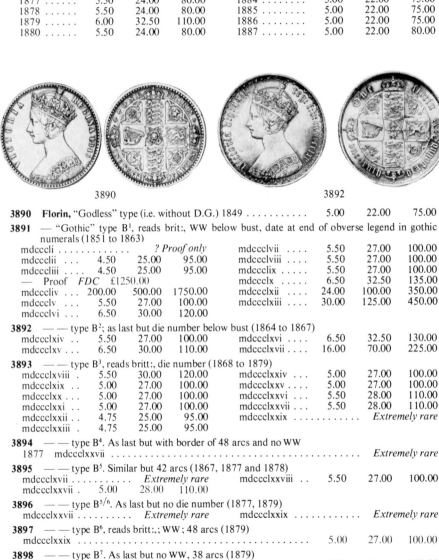

3890   3892

3890 Florin, "Godless" type (i.e. without D.G.) 1849 .... 5.00 22.00 75.00

3891 — "Gothic" type B[1], reads brit:, WW below bust, date at end of obverse legend in gothic numerals (1851 to 1863)

	F	VF	EF			F	VF	EF
mdcccli		*? Proof only*			mdccclvii	5.50	27.00	100.00
mdccclii ...	4.50	25.00	95.00		mdccclviii	5.50	27.00	100.00
mdcccliii	4.50	25.00	95.00		mdccclix	5.50	27.00	100.00
— Proof *FDC* £1250.00					mdccclx	6.50	32.50	135.00
mdcccliv ...	200.00	500.00	1750.00		mdccclxii	24.00	100.00	350.00
mdccclv ...	5.50	27.00	100.00		mdccclxiii	30.00	125.00	450.00
mdccclvi ...	6.50	30.00	120.00					

3892 — — type B[2]; as last but die number below bust (1864 to 1867)

	F	VF	EF			F	VF	EF
mdccclxiv ..	5.50	27.00	100.00		mdccclxvi	6.50	32.50	130.00
mdccclxv ...	6.50	30.00	110.00		mdccclxvii	16.00	70.00	225.00

3893 — — type B[3], reads britt:, die number (1868 to 1879)

	F	VF	EF			F	VF	EF
mdccclxviii .	5.50	30.00	120.00		mdccclxxiv ...	5.00	27.00	100.00
mdccclxix ..	5.00	27.00	100.00		mdccclxxv ...	5.00	27.00	100.00
mdccclxx ...	5.00	27.00	100.00		mdccclxxvi ...	5.50	28.00	110.00
mdccclxxi ..	5.00	27.00	100.00		mdccclxxvii ...	5.50	28.00	110.00
mdccclxxii ..	4.75	25.00	95.00		mdccclxxix		*Extremely rare*	
mdccclxxiii .	4.75	25.00	95.00					

3894 — — type B[4]. As last but with border of 48 arcs and no WW

1877   mdccclxxvii .... *Extremely rare*

3895 — — type B[5]. Similar but 42 arcs (1867, 1877 and 1878)

mdccclxvii		*Extremely rare*	mdccclxxviii ..	5.50	27.00	100.00
mdccclxxvii .	5.00	28.00	110.00			

3896 — — type B[5/6]. As last but no die number (1877, 1879)

mdccclxxvii .... *Extremely rare*   mdccclxxix .... *Extremely rare*

3897 — — type B[6], reads britt:,; WW; 48 arcs (1879)

mdccclxxix 5.00 27.00 100.00

3898 — — type B[7]. As last but no WW, 38 arcs (1879)

mdccclxxix 5.00 27.00 100.00

Silver

3899   **Florin,** "Gothic" type B$^{3/8}$. As next but younger portrait (1880)
mdccclxxx . . . .   *Extremely rare*

3900   — — type B^8. Similar but 34 arcs (1880 to 1887)

	F	VF	EF		F	VF	EF
	£	£	£		£	£	£
mdccclxxx	5.50	27.00	100.00	mdccclxxxv . . .	4.50	22.50	90.00
mdccclxxxi	4.50	22.50	90.00	mdccclxxxvi . .	4.75	25.00	95.00
mdccclxxxiii	4.50	22.50	90.00	mdccclxxxvii			*? exists*
mdccclxxxiv	4.50	22.50	90.00				

3901   — — type B^9. Similar but 46 arcs
1887   mdcclxxxvii 8.00   35.00   140.00

3906

3902   **Shilling,** type A^1. First head, WW on truncation
1838 . . . . . .   3.50   15.00   60.00   1839 . . . .   4.00   15.00   65.00

3903   — type A^2. Second head, WW (Proof only), 1839   *FDC*   £250.00

3904   — type A^3. Second head, no initials on truncation

1839	3.00	13.50	50.00	1853	3.25	14.00	55.00
1840	10.00	50.00	150.00	— Proof *FDC* £400.00			
1841	6.00	25.00	85.00	1854	40.00	135.00	450.00
1842	3.50	15.00	55.00	1855	3.00	13.50	50.00
1843	5.00	20.00	85.00	1856	3.00	13.50	50.00
1844	3.25	14.00	55.00	1857	3.00	13.50	50.00
1845	3.50	15.00	65.00	1858	3.00	13.50	50.00
1846	3.50	15.00	55.00	1859	3.00	13.50	50.00
1848 over 6 .	24.00	60.00	275.00	1860	5.00	22.00	90.00
1849	3.25	14.00	55.00	1861	5.00	22.00	90.00
1850	90.00	300.00	900.00	1862	9.00	35.00	140.00
1851	24.00	60.00	250.00	1863	9.00	45.00	175.00
1852	3.25	14.00	55.00				

3905   — type A^4. As before but die number above date

1864	3.25	14.00	55.00	1866	3.00	13.50	50.00
1865	3.00	13.50	50.00	1867	3.25	14.00	55.00

3906   — type A^6. Third head, die number above date

1867	20.00	65.00	225.00	1874	2.00	9.50	35.00
1868	3.00	13.50	50.00	1875	2.00	9.50	35.00
1869	3.50	16.00	60.00	1876	3.00	13.50	50.00
1870	3.50	16.00	60.00	1877	2.00	9.00	35.00
1871	2.00	9.00	35.00	1878	2.00	9.00	35.00
1872	2.00	9.00	35.00	1879	4.00	18.00	70.00
1873	2.00	9.00	35.00				

3907   — type A^7. Fourth head; no die number

1879	3.25	14.00	60.00	1884	2.00	7.00	27.50
1880	2.00	7.00	27.50	1885	2.00	5.50	20.00
1881	2.00	7.00	27.50	1886	2.00	5.50	20.00
1882	6.00	28.00	90.00	1887	3.00	13.50	55.00
1883	2.00	7.00	27.50				

Silver

3909   3912

3908   Sixpence, type A¹. First head

	F	VF	EF		F	VF	EF
	£	£	£		£	£	£
1838	1.50	9.00	35.00	1852	2.00	10.00	40.00
1839	1.50	9.00	35.00	1853	1.50	9.00	35.00
— Proof *FDC* £175.00				— Proof *FDC* £275.00			
1840	2.00	10.00	40.00	1854	32.50	125.00	400.00
1841	3.00	15.00	50.00	1855	1.50	9.00	35.00
1842	1.75	10.00	37.50	1856	2.00	10.00	37.50
1843	1.75	10.00	37.50	1857	2.00	10.00	40.00
1844	1.50	9.00	35.00	1858	2.00	10.00	37.50
1845	1.75	10.00	37.50	1859	1.50	9.00	35.00
1846	1.50	9.00	35.00	1860	2.00	10.00	40.00
1848	20.00	65.00	250.00	1862	12.00	45.00	200.00
1850	1.75	10.00	37.50	1863	8.00	30.00	100.00
1851	1.75	10.00	37.50	1866	20.00	80.00	250.00

3909   — type A². First head; die number above date

	F	VF	EF		F	VF	EF
1864	2.00	10.00	40.00	1866	2.00	10.00	40.00
1865	3.00	15.00	50.00				

3910   — type A³. Second head; die number above date

	F	VF	EF		F	VF	EF
1867	3.00	16.00	55.00	1874	1.50	9.00	35.00
1868	3.00	16.00	55.00	1875	1.50	9.00	35.00
1869	3.75	20.00	65.00	1876	3.00	16.00	55.00
1870	3.00	16.00	55.00	1877	1.50	9.00	35.00
1871	1.75	10.00	37.50	1878	1.50	9.00	35.00
1872	1.75	10.00	37.50	1879	3.75	20.00	65.00
1873	1.50	9.00	35.00				

3911   — type A⁴. Second head; no die number

	F	VF	EF		F	VF	EF
1871	3.00	16.00	55.00	1879	1.75	10.00	37.50
1877	1.75	10.00	37.50	1880	3.00	16.00	55.00

3912   — type A⁵. Third head

	F	VF	EF		F	VF	EF
1880	1.50	7.00	22.00	1884	1.25	6.50	20.00
1881	1.25	6.50	20.00	1885	1.25	6.50	20.00
1882	3.75	20.00	60.00	1886	1.25	6.50	20.00
1883	1.25	6.50	20.00	1887	1.25	5.50	18.00

3913   3914   3915

3913   Groat (4d.). ℞. Britannia

	F £	VF £	EF £		F £	VF £	EF £
1838		2.50	20.00	1847/6 (or 8) ..	12.00	40.00	135.00
1839		3.50	25.00	1848		2.75	22.00
— Proof *FDC* £150.00				1849		2.75	22.00
1840		2.75	22.00	1851	20.00	60.00	175.00
1841		3.75	32.50	1852	22.00	75.00	225.00
1842		3.50	27.50	1853	30.00	90.00	275.00
1843		3.50	27.50	— Proof *FDC* £275.00			
1844		3.50	30.00	1854		2.75	22.00
1845		3.50	30.00	1855		2.75	22.00
1846		3.50	27.50				

3914   Threepence. ℞. Crowned 3; as Maundy threepence but with a less prooflike surface

1838*	3.50	30.00	1864	3.50	25.00
1839*	4.75	40.00	1865	5.00	45.00
— Proof (see Maundy)			1866	3.50	25.00
1840*	4.75	40.00	1867	3.50	35.00
1841*	5.00	45.00	1868	3.50	25.00
1842*	5.50	50.00	1869*	5.50	55.00
1843*	3.50	30.00	1870	3.00	22.00
1844*	5.00	45.00	1871	3.50	30.00
1845	3.00	22.50	1872	3.00	22.00
1846	6.50	60.00	1873	2.25	18.00
1849	5.50	50.00	1874	2.25	18.00
1850	3.50	25.00	1875	2.25	18.00
1851	3.50	35.00	1876	2.25	18.00
1853	5.00	45.00	1877	2.25	18.00
1854	4.75	40.00	1878	2.25	18.00
1855	5.50	50.00	1879	2.25	18.00
1856	5.00	45.00	1880	2.75	20.00
1857	5.00	45.00	1881	2.75	20.00
1858	3.50	35.00	1882	3.50	35.00
1859	3.50	25.00	1883	1.75	15.00
1860	3.50	25.00	1884	1.75	15.00
1861	3.00	22.00	1885	1.75	15.00
1862	3.50	35.00	1886	1.75	15.00
1863	5.00	45.00	1887	1.75	15.00

*Issued for Colonial use only.

3915   Threehalfpence (For Colonial use). ℞. Value, etc.

1838	2.00	18.00	1842	2.25	25.00
1839	1.75	16.00	1843	1.50	14.00
1840	3.50	35.00	1860	3.50	35.00
1841	1.75	16.00	1862	3.50	30.00

3916

N.B. *Overstruck dates are listed only if commoner than the normal date or if no normal date is known.*

3916   Maundy Set (4d., 3d., 2d. and 1d.)

	EF	FDC			EF	FDC
	£	£			£	£
1838	45.00	70.00		1862	40.00	62.50
1839	45.00	70.00		1863	40.00	62.50
— Proof *FDC* £200.00				1864	40.00	62.50
1840	40.00	67.50		1865	40.00	62.50
1841	45.00	70.00		1866	40.00	62.50
1842	40.00	65.00		1867	40.00	62.50
1843	40.00	65.00		1868	40.00	62.50
1844	40.00	65.00		1869	45.00	62.50
1845	40.00	65.00		1870	40.00	62.50
1846	40.00	65.00		1871	40.00	62.50
1847	40.00	65.00		1872	40.00	62.50
1848	40.00	65.00		1873	40.00	62.50
1849	45.00	70.00		1874	40.00	60.00
1850	40.00	65.00		1875	40.00	60.00
1851	40.00	65.00		1876	40.00	60.00
1852	40.00	65.00		1877	40.00	60.00
1853	40.00	65.00		1878	40.00	60.00
— Proof *FDC* £300.00				1879	40.00	60.00
1854	40.00	65.00		1880	40.00	60.00
1855	45.00	70.00		1881	40.00	60.00
1856	40.00	65.00		1882	40.00	60.00
1857	40.00	65.00		1883	40.00	60.00
1858	40.00	65.00		1884	40.00	60.00
1859	40.00	65.00		1885	40.00	60.00
1860	40.00	65.00		1886	40.00	60.00
1861	40.00	65.00		1887	45.00	65.00

3917 — **fourpence,** 1838–87 .... *from*   6.00   10.00

3918 — **threepence,** 1838–87 .... *from*   12.00   20.00

3919 — **twopence,** 1838–87 .... *from*   4.00   7.00

3920 — **penny,** 1838–87 .... *from*   3.50   6.00

Maundy Sets in the original dated cases are worth approximately £5.00 more than the prices quoted.

Jubilee Coinage

3921

3921   Crown. ℞. St. George

	F	VF	EF			F	VF	EF
	£	£	£			£	£	£
1887	8.00	18.00	40.00		1890	10.00	22.00	60.00
— Proof *FDC* £400.00					1891	10.00	24.00	70.00
1888	10.00	24.00	55.00		1892	12.00	28.00	85.00
1889	8.00	18.00	40.00					

3922

3922 Double-florin (4s.). ℞. Cruciform shields. Roman I in date

	F £	VF £	EF £		F £	VF £	EF £
1887					4.50	8.00	25.00

3923 — Similar but Arabic 1 in date

1887	4.50	8.00	25.00	1889	5.00	10.00	30.00
— Proof *FDC* £225.00				1890	5.00	12.00	35.00
1888	5.00	12.00	35.00				

3924   3925

3924 Halfcrown. ℞. Shield in collar

1887	2.00	4.00	16.00	1890	2.50	12.00	50.00
— Proof *FDC* £125.00				1891	2.50	12.00	50.00
1888	2.25	7.00	30.00	1892	2.50	12.00	50.00
1889	2.25	7.00	30.00				

3925 Florin. ℞. Cruciform shields

1887	2.00	3.50	14.00	1890	4.75	22.00	70.00
— Proof *FDC* £75.00				1891	7.00	35.00	110.00
1888	2.00	5.00	20.00	1892	9.00	40.00	135.00
1889	2.00	6.00	24.00				

3926   3927

3926 Shilling. Small head. ℞. Shield in garter

1887		1.50	7.00	1888		3.00	18.00
— Proof *FDC* £55.00				1889	12.00	50.00	200.00

3927   — Large head. R̟. As before

	F	VF	EF		F	VF	EF
	£	£	£		£	£	£
1889	1.10	4.00	25.00	1891	1.25	4.50	30.00
1890	1.10	4.00	25.00	1892	1.25	4.50	30.00

| | 3928 | | 3929 | | 3930 |

3928   **Sixpence.** R̟. Shield in garter (withdrawn type)

1887		1.00	6.00
— Proof *FDC* £40.00			

3929   — R̟. Value in wreath

	VF	EF		F	VF	EF
1887	1.10	6.50	1891		3.25	20.00
1888	2.75	16.00	1892		3.25	20.00
1889	2.75	16.00	1893	95.00	300.00	750.00
1890	3.00	17.50				

3930   **Groat** (for use in British Guiana). R̟. Britannia

1888	3.00	12.00	30.00

3931   **Threepence.** As Maundy but less prooflike surface

	F	EF		F	VF	EF
1887	1.00	4.00	1890		1.50	8.00
— Proof *FDC* £27.50			1891		1.50	8.00
1888	1.75	10.00	1892		1.75	12.00
1889	1.50	8.00	1893	4.00	22.00	90.00

3932   **Maundy Set** (4d., 3d., 2d and 1d.)

	EF	FDC		EF	FDC
	£	£		£	£
1888	35.00	55.00	1891	35.00	55.00
1889	35.00	55.00	1892	35.00	55.00
1890	35.00	55.00			

Maundy Sets in the original dated cases are worth approximately £5.00 more than the prices quoted.

3933   — **fourpence,** 1888–92 .... *from*   9.00   13.00

3934   — **threepence,** 1888–92 .... *from*   11.00   21.00

3935   — **twopence,** 1888–92 .... *from*   5.00   10.00

3936   — **penny,** 1888–92 .... *from*   5.00   10.00

3932

Silver
Old head coinage

3937

3937   Crown. ℞. St. George. Regnal date on edge.

	F £	VF £	EF £
1893 — LVI	7.00	22.00	95.00
— — Proof *FDC* £425.00			
— — LVII	15.00	50.00	150.00
1894 — LVII	8.00	30.00	110.00
— — LVIII	8.00	30.00	110.00
1895 — LVIII	8.00	28.00	100.00
— — LIX	8.00	28.00	100.00
1896 — LIX	14.00	55.00	150.00
— — LX	8.00	28.00	100.00
1897 — LX	8.00	28.00	100.00
— — LXI	7.00	22.00	95.00
1898 — LXI	20.00	60.00	175.00
— — LXII	8.00	30.00	110.00
1899 — LXII	8.00	30.00	110.00
— — LXIII	8.00	30.00	110.00
1900 — LXIII	8.00	28.00	100.00
— — LXIV	7.00	22.00	95.00

3938

3938   Halfcrown. ℞. Shield in collar

	F £	VF £	EF £		F £	VF £	EF £
1893	2.25	8.00	35.00	1897	2.25	8.00	35.00
— Proof *FDC* £150				1898	2.50	10.00	40.00
1894	3.00	12.00	45.00	1899	2.50	10.00	40.00
1895	2.50	10.00	40.00	1900	2.25	8.00	35.00
1896	2.50	10.00	40.00	1901	2.25	8.00	35.00

3939 Florin. ℞. Three shields within Garter

	F	VF	EF		F	VF	EF
	£	£	£		£	£	£
1893	2.00	7.00	30.00	1897	2.00	7.00	30.00
— Proof *FDC* £90.00				1898	2.50	8.00	35.00
1894	2.75	10.00	45.00	1899	2.25	7.00	32.50
1895	2.75	10.00	45.00	1900	2.00	7.00	30.00
1896	2.50	8.00	35.00	1901	2.00	7.00	30.00

3939   3940

3940 Shilling. ℞. Three shields within Garter

1893		2.75	15.00	1897	2.75	15.00
— Proof *FDC* £70.00			1898	2.75	15.00
1894		3.25	18.00	1899	3.00	16.00
1895		3.00	16.00	1900	2.75	15.00
1896		2.75	15.00	1901	2.75	15.00

3941 Sixpence. ℞. Value in wreath

1893		2.00	12.00	1897	2.50	13.00
— Proof *FDC* £45.00			1898	2.50	13.00
1894		2.75	15.00	1899	2.50	13.00
1895		2.75	15.00	1900	2.00	12.00
1896		2.75	15.00	1901	2.00	12.00

3942 Threepence. ℞. Crowned 3. As Maundy but less prooflike surface

1893		4.50	1897	5.00
— Proof *FDC* £30.00		1898	5.00
1894		7.00	1899	4.00
1895		7.00	1900	4.00
1896		5.00	1901	4.00

3943

3943 Maundy Set (4d., 3d., 2d. and 1d.)

	EF	FDC		EF	FDC
	£	£		£	£
1893	35.00	45.00	1897	35.00	45.00
1894	35.00	45.00	1898	35.00	45.00
1895	35.00	45.00	1899	35.00	45.00
1896	35.00	45.00	1900	35.00	45.00
			1901	35.00	45.00

3944 — fourpence, 1893–1901 .... *from* 5.00   8.00

3945 — threepence, 1893–1901 .... *from* 10.00 17.00

3946 — twopence, 1893–1901 .... *from* 5.00   6.50

3947 — penny, 1893–1901 .... *from* 5.00   6.50

Maundy sets in the original dated cases are worth approximately £5.00 more than the prices quoted.

COPPER AND BRONZE

3948

Young head copper coinage, 1838–60

3948 Penny. ℞. Britannia

	F £	VF £	EF £			F £	VF £	EF £
1839	Bronzed proof	*FDC*	£200.00		1853		4.00	16.00
1841	1.00	5.00	25.00		— Proof *FDC*	£250.00		
1843	20.00	75.00	350.00		1854		4.00	16.00
1844	2.75	7.50	35.00		1855		4.00	16.00
1845	4.50	15.00	60.00		1856	6.50	20.00	70.00
1846	3.50	10.00	45.00		1857		4.50	20.00
1847	2.75	7.50	35.00		1858		4.00	18.00
1848/7	2.75	7.00	30.00		1859	1.00	5.00	22.00
1849	25.00	90.00	400.00		1860*		250.00	500.00
1851	3.50	10.00	45.00					

3949

3949 Halfpenny. ℞. Britannia

	F	VF	EF			F	VF	EF
1838		2.50	16.00		1852	1.50	5.00	24.00
1839	Bronzed proof	*FDC*	£90.00		1853		1.75	9.00
1841		2.25	14.00		— Proof *FDC*	£125.00		
1843	2.50	10.00	40.00		1854		1.75	9.00
1844	1.00	3.75	20.00		1855		1.75	9.00
1845	15.00	50.00	150.00		1856	1.00	4.50	20.00
1846	1.50	5.00	25.00		1857		2.75	14.00
1847	1.50	5.00	25.00		1858		2.50	16.00
1848	1.75	6.00	30.00		1859		3.75	18.00
1851	1.00	3.75	20.00		1860*	—	—	3500.00

N.B. Overstruck dates are listed only if commoner than normal date, or if no normal date is known.

Copper

3950

3950   Farthing. R̟. Britannia

	F	VF	EF		F	VF	EF
	£	£	£		£	£	£
1838		3.00	15.00	1850		3.00	16.50
1839		2.00	14.00	1851	3.00	10.00	37.50
— Bronzed proof *FDC* £110.00				1852	3.25	11.00	40.00
1840		2.00	14.00	1853		2.50	16.00
1841		2.00	14.00	— Proof *FDC* £250.00			
1842	1.50	6.00	35.00	1854		3.00	16.50
1843		2.00	14.00	1855		4.00	22.00
1844	15.00	40.00	150.00	1856	1.75	6.00	35.00
1845		3.00	16.50	1857		2.50	16.00
1846	1.50	6.00	32.50	1858		2.50	16.00
1847		3.00	16.50	1859	5.00	15.00	45.00
1848		3.00	16.50	1860*	—	—	2250.00
1849	7.50	25.00	90.00				

** These 1860 large copper pieces not to be confused with the smaller and commoner bronze issue
with date on reverse (nos. 3954, 3956 and 3958).*

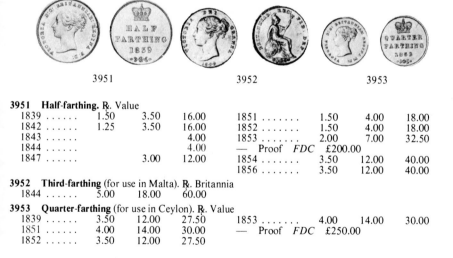

3951   3952   3953

3951   Half-farthing. R̟. Value

1839	1.50	3.50	16.00	1851	1.50	4.00	18.00
1842	1.25	3.50	16.00	1852	1.50	4.00	18.00
1843			4.00	1853	2.00	7.00	32.50
1844			4.00	— Proof *FDC* £200.00			
1847		3.00	12.00	1854	3.50	12.00	40.00
				1856	3.50	12.00	40.00

3952   Third-farthing (for use in Malta). R̟. Britannia
1844	5.00	18.00	60.00

3953   Quarter-farthing (for use in Ceylon). R̟. Value

1839	3.50	12.00	27.50	1853	4.00	14.00	30.00
1851	4.00	14.00	30.00	— Proof *FDC* £250.00			
1852	3.50	12.00	27.50				

Bronze coinage, "bun head" issue, 1860–95

3954   3955

3954   **Penny. R̝. Britannia**

	F £	VF £	EF £		F £	VF £	EF £
1860		5.00	22.00	1878	1.50	9.00	35.00
1861		5.00	22.00	1879		4.50	18.00
1862		4.50	20.00	1880	1.50	9.00	35.00
1863		4.50	20.00	1881	1.50	9.00	40.00
1864	3.00	30.00	150.00	1883	1.25	6.00	27.50
1865	1.50	9.00	35.00	1884		4.00	15.00
1866		5.00	25.00	1885		4.00	15.00
1867	1.50	9.00	40.00	1886		4.50	18.00
1868	2.50	16.00	60.00	1887		4.00	15.00
1869	20.00	75.00	250.00	1888		4.50	18.00
1870	2.00	11.00	45.00	1889		3.00	14.00
1871	7.00	35.00	125.00	1890		3.00	14.00
1872	1.25	6.00	27.50	1891		2.75	12.00
1873	1.25	6.00	27.50	1892		3.00	14.00
1874	1.50	9.00	40.00	1893		3.00	14.00
1875		5.00	20.00	1894		5.50	25.00
1877		5.00	20.00				

3955   — — H (Ralph Heaton & Sons, Birmingham) below date

	F	VF	EF		F	VF	EF
1874 H	1.50	8.00	35.00	1881 H	1.25	6.00	26.00
1875 H	9.00	50.00	175.00	1882 H		4.50	18.00
1876 H		5.00	20.00				

3956

3956 Halfpenny. Ŗ. Britannia

	F £	VF £	EF £		F £	VF £	EF £
1860		2.25	15.00	1878	2.00	7.00	40.00
1861		2.25	15.00	1879		2.25	15.00
1862		2.00	13.00	1880	1.25	5.50	25.00
1863		5.00	25.00	1881	1.25	5.50	25.00
1864	1.25	6.00	30.00	1883		4.50	22.00
1865	2.00	7.00	40.00	1884		2.00	12.00
1866	1.25	6.00	30.00	1885		2.00	12.00
1867	2.00	7.00	40.00	1886		2.00	12.00
1868	1.50	6.50	32.50	1887		1.50	10.00
1869	4.50	20.00	75.00	1888		2.00	12.00
1870	1.25	5.50	26.00	1889		2.00	12.00
1871	7.50	30.00	90.00	1890		1.50	10.00
1872	1.25	5.00	24.00	1891		1.50	10.00
1873	1.50	6.00	30.00	1892		3.00	20.00
1874	3.00	10.00	60.00	1893		2.00	12.00
1875		3.00	20.00	1894		4.50	22.00
1877		3.00	20.00				

3957 —— H below date

	F £	VF £	EF £		F £	VF £	EF £
1874 H		4.50	22.00	1881 H		3.00	20.00
1875 H	1.25	6.00	28.00	1882 H		3.00	20.00
1876 H		3.00	20.00				

3958

3960

3958 Farthing. Ŗ. Britannia

	F £	VF £	EF £		F £	VF £	EF £
1860		1.25	9.00	1880		2.00	14.00
1861		1.40	10.00	1881		1.00	8.00
1862		2.00	10.00	1883		4.00	20.00
1863	12.00	30.00	75.00	1884			5.00
1864		2.25	16.00	1885			5.00
1865		1.40	10.00	1886			5.00
1866		1.10	9.00	1887		1.20	8.00
1867		2.00	14.00	1888		1.00	7.50
1868		2.00	14.00	1890		1.00	7.00
1869	1.00	6.50	22.00	1891			5.50
1872		2.00	12.00	1892	2.50	6.50	20.00
1873		1.25	9.00	1893			5.00
1875	5.00	12.00	35.00	1894		1.00	7.00
1878			7.00	1895	3.50	8.00	30.00
1879			7.00				

3959 —— H below date

	F £	VF £	EF £		F £	VF £	EF £
1874 H		1.40	14.00	1881 H		1.50	12.00
1875 H			6.00	1882 H		1.50	12.00
1876 H	4.00	10.00	30.00				

3960 Third-farthing (for use in Malta). Ŗ. Value

	F £	VF £	EF £		F £	VF £	EF £
1866		1.25	8.00	1881		1.75	10.00
1868		1.50	9.00	1884		1.25	9.00
1876		1.75	10.00	1885		1.25	9.00
1878		1.50	9.00				

Old head issue, 1895–1901

3961

3961.   Penny. ℞. Britannia

	EF £		VF £	EF £
1895	6.50	1899		5.00
1896	5.00	1900		3.50
1897	5.00	1901		2.25
1898	10.00			

3961   "High tide"   3961A   "Low tide"

3961A   As last but "Low tide", 1895 .... 22.00   75.00

3962   Halfpenny. Type as Penny. ℞. Britannia

	EF £		EF £
1895	6.00	1899	4.50
1896	5.00	1900	3.50
1897	5.00	1901	2.25
1898	5.50		

3963   Farthing. ℞. Britannia. Bright finish

	EF £		EF £
1895	4.00	1897	5.00
1896	4.00		

3964

3964   — — Dark finish

	EF £		EF £
1897	4.00	1900	3.00
1898	4.00	1901	2.00
1899	4.00		

EDWARD VII, 1901–10

Crowns, five pound pieces and two pound pieces were only issued in 1902. A branch of the Royal Mint was opened at Ottawa and coined sovereigns of imperial type from 1908.

Unlike the coins in most other proof sets, the proofs issued for the Coronation in 1902 have a matt surface in place of the more usual brilliant finish.

Designer's initials:
De S. (G. W. de Saulles)

3965

		VF £	EF £
3965	**Five pounds.** 1902. ℞. St. George	450.00	700.00
3966	–- Proof. 1902. *Matt surface FDC* £850.00		
3967	**Two pounds.** 1902. Similar	225.00	400.00
3968	— Proof. 1902. *Matt surface FDC* £450.00		

3967   3969

3969 Sovereign.* ℞. St. George. London mint

	EF £			EF £
1902 Matt proof *FDC* £175.00		1906	....	75.00
1902	75.00	1907	....	75.00
1903	75.00	1908	....	75.00
1904	75.00	1909	....	75.00
1905	75.00	1910	....	75.00

3970 — —C on ground for Ottawa mint

1908 C(Satin proof only) *FDC* £2500.00		1910 C	175.00
1909 C	175.00		

3971 Sovereign. ℞. St. George. M on ground for Melbourne mint

1902 M	75.00	1907 M	75.00
1903 M	75.00	1908 M	75.00
1904 M	75.00	1909 M	75.00
1905 M	75.00	1910 M	75.00
1906 M	75.00		

*The price of common sovereigns in lower grades of condition is closely related to the current gold price; see also note on p. 276.

3972 Sovereign. ℞. St. George. P on ground for Perth mint

	VF £	EF £		VF £	EF £
1902 P		75.00	1907 P		75.00
1903 P		75.00	1908 P		75.00
1904 P		75.00	1909 P		75.00
1905 P		75.00	1910 P		75.00
1906 P		75.00			

3973 — — S on ground for Sydney mint

1902 S		75.00	1907 S		75.00
1903 S		75.00	1908 S		75.00
1904 S		75.00	1909 S		75.00
1905 S		75.00	1910 S		75.00
1906 S		75.00			

3974

3974 Half-sovereign. ℞. St. George. London mint

1902 Matt proof *FDC* £125.00			1906		60.00
1902		60.00	1907		60.00
1903		60.00	1908		60.00
1904		60.00	1909		60.00
1905		60.00	1910		60.00

3975 — — M on ground for Melbourne mint

1906 M	55.00	110.00	1908 M	55.00	110.00
1907 M	55.00	110.00	1909 M	55.00	110.00

3976 — — P on ground for Perth mint

1904 P	175.00	650.00	1909 P	140.00	400.00
1908 P	175.00	600.00			

3977 — — S on ground for Sydney mint

1902 S	60.00	125.00	1908 S	55.00	100.00
1903 S	55.00	100.00	1910 S	55.00	100.00
1906 S	55.00	100.00			

SILVER

3978

3978 Crown. ℞. St. George

1902	30.00	50.00	80.00

3979 — Similar, but *matt proof*   *FDC*   £165.00

3980   Halfcrown. ℞. Shield in Garter

3980

	F	VF	EF		F	VF	EF
	£	£	£		£	£	£
1902		10.00	40.00	1906		10.00	70.00
— Matt proof	*FDC*	£80.00		1907		11.00	75.00
1903	30.00	90.00	375.00	1908		16.00	100.00
1904	15.00	55.00	250.00	1909		12.00	80.00
1905*	75.00	250.00	850.00	1910		10.00	60.00

3981   Florin. ℞. Britannia standing

	F	VF	EF		F	VF	EF
1902		6.00	40.00	1906		10.00	55.00
— Matt proof	*FDC*	£60.00		1907	4.00	12.00	60.00
1903	4.00	10.00	55.00	1908	5.50	14.00	70.00
1904	4.50	14.00	65.00	1909	4.50	13.00	65.00
1905*	12.00	35.00	200.00	1910		6.00	40.00

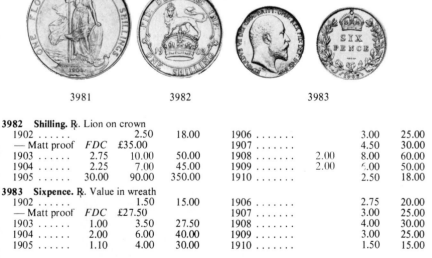

3981   3982   3983

3982   Shilling. ℞. Lion on crown

	F	VF	EF		F	VF	EF
1902		2.50	18.00	1906		3.00	25.00
— Matt proof	*FDC*	£35.00		1907		4.50	30.00
1903	2.75	10.00	50.00	1908	2.00	8.00	60.00
1904	2.25	7.00	45.00	1909	2.00	6.00	50.00
1905	30.00	90.00	350.00	1910		2.50	18.00

3983   Sixpence. ℞. Value in wreath

	F	VF	EF		F	VF	EF
1902		1.50	15.00	1906		2.75	20.00
— Matt proof	*FDC*	£27.50		1907		3.00	25.00
1903	1.00	3.50	27.50	1908		4.00	30.00
1904	2.00	6.00	40.00	1909		3.00	25.00
1905	1.10	4.00	30.00	1910		1.50	15.00

* Beware of recent forgeries.

3984 Threepence. As Maundy but dull finish

	VF £	EF £		VF £	EF £
1902	. . . .	3.75	1907	. . . .	10.00
1903	. . . .	10.00	1908	. . . .	10.00
1904	. . . . 5.00	35.00	1909	. . . .	10.00
1905	. . . . 4.00	30.00	1910	. . . .	8.00
1906	. . . . 3.00	25.00			

3985

3985 Maundy Set (4d., 3d., 2d. and 1d.)

	EF £	FDC £		EF £	FDC £
1902	. . . . 35.00	45.00	1906	. . . . 35.00	45.00
— Matt proof	. . . . . . —	45.00	1907	. . . . 35.00	45.00
1903	. . . . 35.00	45.00	1908	. . . . 35.00	45.00
1904	. . . . 35.00	45.00	1909	. . . . 40.00	55.00
1905	. . . . 35.00	45.00	1910	. . . . 45.00	60.00

3986 — **fourpence,** 1902–10 . . . . *from* 5.00 9.00

3987 — **threepence,** 1902–10 . . . . *from* 5.00 11.00

3988 — **twopence,** 1902–10 . . . . *from* 4.50 8.00

3989 — **penny,** 1902–10 . . . . *from* 4.50 8.00

Maundy sets in the original dated cases are worth approximately £5 more than the prices quoted.

BRONZE

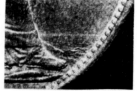

3990

3990   "High tide"   3990A   "Low tide"

3990 Penny. ℞. Britannia

	EF £			VF £	EF £
1902	4.50	1907			9.00
1903	10.00	1908			9.00
1904	14.00	1909			9.00
1905	12.00	1910			7.50
1906	9.00				

3990A As last but "Low tide", 1902 .... 5.00   25.00

3991

3991 Halfpenny. ℞. Britannia

	EF				EF
1902	4.50	1907			6.00
1903	7.50	1908			6.00
1904	10.00	1909			9.00
1905	9.00	1910			7.50
1906	7.50				

3991A As last but "Low tide", 1902 .... 12.00   30.00

3992   3993

3992 Farthing. Britannia. Dark finish

1902	3.00	1907		5.00
1903	5.00	1908		5.00
1904	7.00	1909		4.50
1905	5.00	1910		7.00
1906	4.50			

3993 Third-farthing (for use in Malta)

1902   ℞. Value 3.00

N.B. *No proofs of the bronze coins were issued in 1902.*

GEORGE V, 1910–36

Paper money issued by the Treasury during the First World War replaced gold for internal use after 1915 but the branch mints in Australia and South Africa (the main Commonwealth gold producing countries) continued striking sovereigns until 1930–2. Owing to the steep rise in the price of silver in 1919/20 the issue of standard (.925) silver was discontinued and coins of .500 silver were minted.

In 1912, 1918 and 1919 some pennies were made under contract by private mints in Birmingham. In 1918, as half-sovereigns were no longer being minted, farthings were again issued with the ordinary bright bronze finish. Crown pieces had not been issued for general circulation but they were struck in small numbers about Christmas time for people to give as presents in the years 1927–36, and in 1935 a special commemorative crown was issued in celebration of the Silver Jubilee.

As George V died in January, it is likely that all coins dated 1936 were struck during the reign of Edward VIII.

Designer's initials:
B. M. (Bertram Mackennal)
P. M. (Percy Metcalfe)
K. G. (Kruger Gray)

GOLD

3994

	FDC £
3994 **Five pounds.*** ℞. St. George, 1911 (Proof only)	1400.00
3995 **Two pounds.*** ℞. St. George, 1911 (Proof only)	600.00

Forgeries exist.

3996

3996 **Sovereign.** ℞. St. George. London mint

	EF £		VF £	EF £
1911	75.00	1915		75.00
— Proof FDC £300.00		1916		100.00
1912	75.00	1917*	3000.00	
1913	75.00	1925		75.00
1914	75.00			

Counterfeits exist of these and of most other dates and mints.

3997 Sovereign. R̟. St. George, C on ground for the Ottawa mint

	VF £	EF £		VF £	EF £
1911 C	....	95.00	1917 C	....	110.00
1913 C	.... 225.00	450.00	1918 C	....	110.00
1914 C	.... 225.00	450.00	1919 C	....	110.00
1916 C	.... *Extremely rare*				

3997   3998   4004

3998 — — I on ground for India (Bombay) mint, 1918 .... 100.00

3999 — — M on ground for Melbourne mint

1911 M	....	75.00	1920 M	.... 450.00	900.00
1912 M	....	75.00	1921 M	....	3000.00
1913 M	....	75.00	1922 M	.... 1200.00	
1914 M	....	75.00	1923 M	....	90.00
1915 M.	....	75.00	1924 M	....	90.00
1916 M	....	75.00	1925 M	....	75.00
1917 M	....	75.00	1926 M	....	75.00
1918 M	....	75.00	1927 M	....	? exists
1919 M	....	90.00	1928 M	.... 250.00	650.00

4000 — — — small head

1929 M	.... 250.00	650.00	1931 M	.... 90.00	250.00
1930 M	....	135.00			

4001   4002

4001 — — P on ground for Perth mint

1911 P	....	75.00	1920 P	....	75.00
1912 P	....	75.00	1921 P	....	75.00
1913 P	....	75.00	1922 P	....	75.00
1914 P	....	75.00	1923 P	....	75.00
1915 P	....	75.00	1924 P	....	75.00
1916 P	....	75.00	1925 P	....	85.00
1917 P	....	75.00	1926 P	....	90.00
1918 P	....	75.00	1927 P	....	100.00
1919 P	....	75.00	1928 P	....	85.00

4002 — — — small head

1929 P	....	85.00	1931 P	....	85.00
1930 P	....	85.00			

4003   **Sovereign.** ℞. St. George. S on ground for Sydney mint

	VF £	EF £		VF £	EF £
1911 S		75.00	1919 S		75.00
1912 S		75.00	1920 S		*Extremely rare*
1913 S		75.00	1921 S	450.00	900.00
1914 S		75.00	1922 S	650.00	1500.00
1915 S		75.00	1923 S	650.00	1500.00
1916 S		75.00	1924 S	200.00	450.00
1917 S		75.00	1925 S		75.00
1918 S		75.00	1926 S	750.00	2000.00

4004   — — SA on ground for Pretoria mint

1923 SA		*Extremely rare*	1926 SA		75.00
1923 SA	Proof *FDC* £750.00		1927 SA		75.00
1924 SA		2250.00	1928 SA		75.00
1925 SA		75.00			

4005   — — — small head

1929 SA		85.00	1931 SA		85.00
1930 SA		85.00	1932 SA		95.00

4006

4006   **Half-sovereign.** ℞. St. George. London mint

1911		60.00	1913	60.00
— Proof *FDC* £225.00			1914	60.00
1912		60.00	1915	60.00

4007   — — M on ground for Melbourne mint

1915 M		55.00	90.00

4008   — — P on ground for Perth mint

1911 P	55.00	100.00	1918 P	200.00	500.00
1915 P	55.00	100.00	1919 P, 1920 P (*Not circulated*)		

4009   — — S on ground for Sydney mint

1911 S	55.00	80.00	1915 S	55.00	80.00
1912 S	55.00	80.00	1916 S	55.00	80.00
1914 S	55.00	80.00			

4010   — — SA on ground for Pretoria mint

1923 SA	Proof *FDC* £475.00		1926 SA	60.00
1925 SA		60.00		

Note: *Gold bullion price at the time of printing $340 per oz. at $1.50 to the £1 sterling.*

SILVER

First coinage. Sterling silver (.925 fine)

4011   Halfcrown. R. Crowned shield in Garter

4011

	EF £			EF £
1911	30.00		1915	15.00
— Proof *FDC* £80.00			1916	15.00
1912	32.00		1917	20.00
1913	35.00		1918	15.00
1914	15.00		1919	22.00

4012

4012   Florin. R. Cruciform shields

1911	25.00		1915	15.00
— Proof *FDC* £70.00			1916	15.00
1912	30.00		1917	22.00
1913	35.00		1918	15.00
1914	15.00		1919	20.00

4013   Shilling. R. Lion on crown, inner circles

1911	12.00		1915	9.00
— Proof *FDC* £45.00			1916	9.00
1912	15.00		1917	14.00
1913	30.00		1918	9.00
1914	9.00		1919	14.00

N.B. *Prices for strictly unc. coins will be considerably higher.*

4013   4014

4014 Sixpence. ℞. Similar

	EF £			EF £
1911	10.00	1916		10.00
— Proof *FDC* £30.00		1917		16.00
1912	16.00	1918		10.00
1913	20.00	1919		12.00
1914	10.00	1920		15.00
1915	10.00			

4015 Threepences. As Maundy but dull finish

	EF £			EF £
1911	3.50	1916		3.00
1912	3.50	1917		3.00
1913	3.50	1918		3.00
1914	3.50	1919		3.00
1915	3.50	1920		4.00

4016

4016 Maundy Set (4d., 3d., 2d. and 1d.)

	EF £	FDC £		EF £	FDC £
1911	35.00	50.00	1916	35.00	47.50
— Proof *FDC* £60.00			1917	35.00	47.50
1912	35.00	47.50	1918	35.00	47.50
1913	35.00	47.50	1919	35.00	47.50
1914	35.00	47.50	1920	35.00	47.50
1915	35.00	47.50			

		EF £	FDC £
4017	— **fourpence,** 1911–20 .... *from*	5.00	9.00
4018	— **threepence,** 1911–20 .... *from*	8.00	14.00
4019	— **twopence,** 1911–20 .... *from*	5.00	8.50
4020	— **penny,** 1911–20 .... *from*	7.00	12.00

Second coinage. Debased silver (.500 fine). Types as before.

4021 Halfcrown

	EF £		VF £	EF £
1920	25.00	1924		35.00
1921	35.00	1925	20.00	125.00
1922	30.00	1926		40.00
1923	20.00			

4022 Florin

	EF £		VF £	EF £
1920	25.00	1924		35.00
1921	25.00	1925	14.00	100.00
1922	22.50	1926		35.00
1923	18.00			

4023 Shilling

	EF £			EF £
1920	18.00	1924		25.00
1921	25.00	1925		40.00
1922	17.50	1926		22.00
1923	18.00			

4024 Sixpence

	EF £			EF £
1920	12.00	1923		20.00
1921	12.00	1924		12.00
1922	13.00	1925		17.50

4025

4026

4025 — new beading and broader rim

1925	12.00	1926		14.00

4026 Threepence

1920	3.00	1925		8.00
1921	3.00	1926		12.00
1922	3.00			

4027 Maundy Set (4d., 3d., 2d. and 1d.)

	EF £	FDC £		EF £	FDC £
1921	35.00	47.50	1925	35.00	47.50
1922	35.00	47.50	1926	35.00	47.50
1923	35.00	47.50	1927	35.00	47.50
1924	35.00	47.50			

4028 — **fourpence,** 1921–7 .... *from* 7.00 10.00
4029 — **threepence,** 1921–7 .... *from* 9.00 14.00
4030 — **twopence,** 1921–7 .... *from* 7.00 11.00
4031 — **penny,** 1921–7 .... *from* 8.00 12.00

2nd coinage 3rd coinage

Third coinage. As before but **modified effigy**, with details of head more clearly defined. The BM on truncation is nearer to the back of the neck and without stops; beading is more pronounced.

	VF £	EF £		EF £
4032 Halfcrown				
1926	6.00	40.00	1927	20.00
4033 Shilling				
1926		18.00	1927	22.00
4034 Sixpence				
1926		10.00	1927	11.00
4035 Threepence				
1926				3.00

N.B. *Prices for strictly unc. coins will be considerably higher.*

Fourth coinage. New types, 1927–35

4036

4036 Crown. ℞. Crown in wreath

			VF £	EF £			VF £	EF £
1927	Proof only	FDC	£150.00		1932	....	90.00	225.00
1928	....		55.00	135.00	1933	....	65.00	165.00
1929	....		65.00	165.00	1934	....	500.00	850.00
1930	....		65.00	165.00	1936	....	110.00	250.00
1931	....		80.00	200.00				

4037   4038

4037 Halfcrown. ℞. Shield

1927	Proof only	FDC	£30.00		1932	....		25.00
1928	....			9.00	1933	....		10.00
1929	....			9.00	1934	....		35.00
1930	....		10.00	90.00	1935	....		10.00
1931	....			10.00	1936	....		8.00

4038 Florin. ℞. Cruciform sceptres, shield in each angle

1927	Proof only	FDC	£50.00		1932	....	8.00	80.00
1928	....			8.00	1933	....		10.00
1929	....			8.00	1935	....		9.00
1930	....			10.00	1936	....		7.50
1931	....			9.00				

4039   4040

4039 Shilling. ℞. Lion on crown, no inner circles

		EF £			EF £
1927	. . . .	14.00	1932	. . . .	9.00
—	Proof *FDC* £25.00		1933	. . . .	8.00
1928	. . . .	8.00	1934	. . . .	16.00
1929	. . . .	8.00	1935	. . . .	8.00
1930	. . . .	20.00	1936	. . . .	7.50
1931	. . . .	9.00			

4040 Sixpence. ℞. Three oak sprigs with six acorns

1927	Proof only *FDC* £18.00		1929	. . . .	4.00
1928	. . . .	5.00	1930	. . . .	6.00

4041 — — closer milling

1931	. . . .	9.00	1934	. . . .	10.00
1932	. . . .	15.00	1935	. . . .	8.00
1933	. . . .	8.00	1936	. . . .	4.00

4042

4042 Threepence. ℞. Three oak sprigs with three acorns

1927	Proof only *FDC* £35.00				
1928	. . . .	10.00	1933	. . . .	1.20
1930	. . . .	8.00	1934	. . . .	1.20
1931	. . . .	1.35	1935	. . . .	1.20
1932	. . . .	1.25	1936	. . . .	1.20

4043 Maundy Set. As earlier sets

	EF £	FDC £		EF £	FDC £
1928	40.00	50.00	1933	38.00	50.00
1929	38.00	50.00	1934	38.00	50.00
1930	38.00	50.00	1935	40.00	50.00
1931	38.00	50.00	1936	46.00	55.00
1932	38.00	50.00			

4044 — **fourpence,** 1928–36 . . . . *from* 6.00 10.00

4045 — **threepence,** 1928–36 . . . . *from* 7.00 12.00

4046 — **twopence,** 1928–36 . . . . *from* 6.00 9.00

4047 — **penny,** 1928–36 . . . . *from* 8.00 13.00

Silver Jubilee Commemorative issue

4048

	VF	EF
	£	£
4048 **Crown,** 1935. ℞. St. George, incuse lettering on edge	5.00	12.50
4049 — Similar. Specimen striking issued in box	*Unc.*	£30.00
4050 — — Raised lettering on edge. Proof (.925 ℞) *FDC* £275.00		

BRONZE

4051

4051 **Penny.** ℞. Britannia

	F	VF	EF		F	VF	EF
	£	£	£		£	£	£
1911	. . . .		4.75	1918	. . . .		4.75
1912	. . . .		5.00	1919	. . . .		4.25
1913	. . . .		4.75	1920	. . . .		3.50
1914	. . . .		5.50	1921	. . . .		3.50
1915	. . . .		6.50	1922	. . . .		12.00
1916	. . . .		4.75	1926	. . . .		15.00
1917	. . . .		4.25				

4052   — — H (The Mint, Birmingham, Ltd.) to l. of date

1912 H	. . . .	2.00	25.00	1919 H	. . . .	8.00	80.00
1918 H	. . . .	10.00	90.00				

4053   — — KN (King's Norton Metal Co.) to l. of date

1918 KN	. . . .	2.00	12.50	125.00	1919 KN	. . . .	2.25	16.00	150.00

4054   — — modified effigy

1926	. . . .	4.00	30.00	300.00	1927	. . . .		3.00

4055   — — small head

1928	. . . .	2.50	1933*	. . . .	*Extremely rare*
1929	. . . .	2.50	1934	. . . .	10.00
1930	. . . .	4.00	1935	. . . .	2.00
1931	. . . .	5.50	1936	. . . .	1.25
1932	. . . .	14.00			

* **Note.** *An extremely fine specimen sold at auction for £15,000 in November 1985.*

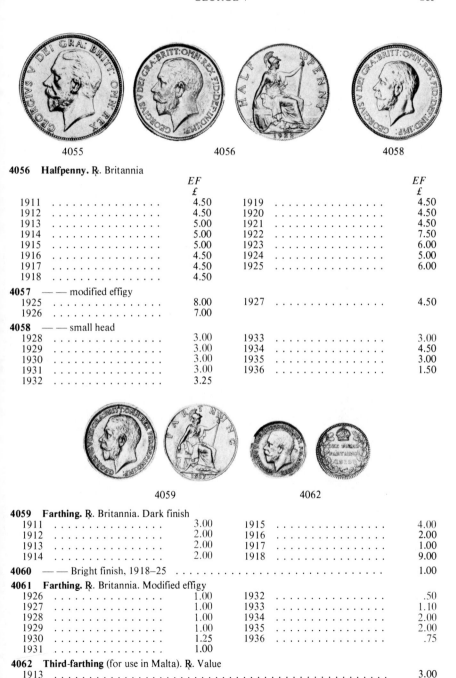

4055   4056   4058

4056   Halfpenny. ℞. Britannia

		EF £			EF £
1911	...	4.50	1919	...	4.50
1912	...	4.50	1920	...	4.50
1913	...	5.00	1921	...	4.50
1914	...	5.00	1922	...	7.50
1915	...	5.00	1923	...	6.00
1916	...	4.50	1924	...	5.00
1917	...	4.50	1925	...	6.00
1918	...	4.50			

4057 — — modified effigy

1925	...	8.00	1927	...	4.50
1926	...	7.00			

4058 — — small head

1928	...	3.00	1933	...	3.00
1929	...	3.00	1934	...	4.50
1930	...	3.00	1935	...	3.00
1931	...	3.00	1936	...	1.50
1932	...	3.25			

4059   4062

4059   Farthing. ℞. Britannia. Dark finish

1911	...	3.00	1915	...	4.00
1912	...	2.00	1916	...	2.00
1913	...	2.00	1917	...	1.00
1914	...	2.00	1918	...	9.00

4060 — — Bright finish, 1918–25 . . . . 1.00

4061   Farthing. ℞. Britannia. Modified effigy

1926	...	1.00	1932	...	.50
1927	...	1.00	1933	...	1.10
1928	...	1.00	1934	...	2.00
1929	...	1.00	1935	...	2.00
1930	...	1.25	1936	...	.75
1931	...	1.00			

4062   Third-farthing (for use in Malta). ℞. Value

1913 . . . . 3.00

EDWARD VIII, Jan.–Dec. 1936

Abdicated 10 December. Created Duke of Windsor (1936–72)

No coins of Edward VIII were issued for currency within the United Kingdom bearing his name and portrait. The mint had commenced work on a new coinage prior to the Abdication, and various patterns were made. No proof sets were issued for sale and only a small number of sets were struck.

Coins bearing Edward's name, but not his portrait, were issued for the colonial territories of British East Africa, British West Africa, Fiji and New Guinea. The projected U.K. coins were to include a shilling of essentially "Scottish" type and a nickel brass threepence with twelve sides which might supplement and possibly supersede the inconveniently small silver threepence.

Designer's initials:
H. P. (T. Humphrey Paget)
K. G. (Kruger Gray)

4063

4063* Proof Set
Gold. £5, £2 and £1, 1937 . . . . *not issued*

Silver Crown, Halfcrown, Florin, Scottish shilling, sixpence and threepence, 1937

not issued

Note: *The following coins were sold at auction in December 1984 & October 1985.*
Sovereign, brilliant, with some hair lines in field *£40,000*
Halfcrown, brilliant mint state *£16,000*
Shilling, brilliant mint state *£12,000*
Sixpence, brilliant mint state *£9,500*

Nickel brass. Threepence, 1937 .... *not issued*
Bronze. Penny, Halfpenny and Farthing, 1937 .... *not issued*

Pattern

4064   Nickel brass dodecagonal, threepence, 1937. ℞. Thrift plant   *Extremely rare*
of more naturalistic style than the modified proof coin.
A small number of these coins were produced for experimental
purposes and a few did get into circulation

Colonial issues

4068   4071

		EF £	Unc. £
4065	**British East Africa.** Bronze 10 cents, 1936		2.00
4066	—— 5 cents, 1936		2.00
4067	**British West Africa.** Cupro-nickel penny, 1936		2.00
4068	—— Halfpenny, 1936		2.00
4069	—— One-tenth penny, 1936		1.00
4070	**Fiji.** Cupro-nickel penny, 1936		3.00
4071	**New Guinea.** Bronze penny, 1936		3.00

NB: The coins of East Africa and West Africa occur without mm. (London) and with H (Heaton)
Birmingham and KN (Kings Norton) Birmingham. The prices quoted are for the commonest of each
type, regardless of mm.

GEORGE VI, 1936–52

Though they were at first issued concurrently, the twelve-sided nickel-brass threepence superseded the small silver threepence in 1942. Those dated 1943–4 were not issued for circulation in the U.K. In addition to the usual English 'lion' shilling a shilling of Scottish type was issued concurrently. This depicts the Scottish lion and crown flanked by the shield of St. Andrew and a thistle. In 1947, as silver was needed to repay the bullion lent by the U.S.A. during the war, silver coins were replaced by coins of the same type and weight made of cupro-nickel. In 1949, after India had attained independence, the title *Indiae Imperator* was dropped from the coinage. Commemorative crown pieces were issued for the Coronation and the 1951 Festival of Britain.

Designer's initials:
K. G. (Kruger Gray)
H. P. (T. Humphrey Paget)
W. P. (Wilson Parker)

GOLD

4074

		FDC £
4074	**Five pounds.** ℞. St. George, 1937. Proof only	700.00
4075	**Two pounds.** Similar, 1937. Proof	425.00
4076	**Sovereign.** Similar, 1937. Proof	375.00
4077	**Half-sovereign.** Similar, 1937. Proof	200.00

SILVER

First coinage. Silver, .500 fine, with title IND : IMP

4078

		VF £	EF £
4078	**Crown.** Coronation commemorative, 1937. ℞. Arms and supporters ...	6.50	16.00
4079	— — Proof *FDC* £40.00		

4080   4081

4080 Halfcrown. ℞. Shield

	EF £	Unc. £		EF £	Unc. £
1937		6.50	1942		4.50
— Proof *FDC* £12.00			1943		6.00
1938	3.25	16.00	1944		4.00
1939		6.50	1945		4.00
1940		6.00	1946		4.00
1941		6.00			

4081 Florin. ℞. Crowned rose, etc.

	EF £	Unc. £		EF £	Unc. £
1937		6.00	1942		4.00
— Proof *FDC* £9.00			1943		4.00
1938	3.00	15.00	1944		4.00
1939		5.50	1945		4.00
1940		5.00	1946		4.00
1941		4.50			

4082   4083

4082 Shilling. "English". ℞. Lion on large crown

	EF £	Unc. £		EF £	Unc. £
1937		6.50	1942		4.00
— Proof *FDC* £7.00			1943		4.00
1938	2.50	15.00	1944		4.00
1939		5.00	1945		3.00
1940		5.50	1946		3.00
1941		5.50			

4083 — "Scottish". ℞. Lion seated facing on crown, etc.

	EF £	Unc. £		EF £	Unc. £
1937		6.00	1942		5.50
— Proof *FDC* £6.50			1943		5.50
1938	2.50	15.00	1944		5.00
1939		5.50	1945		3.00
1940		5.50	1946		3.00
1941		6.00			

4084   4085

4084 Sixpence. ℞. GRI crowned

	EF	Unc.		VF	EF	Unc.
	£	£		£	£	£
1937		3.50	1942			2.25
— Proof *FDC* £4.50			1943			2.25
1938	1.25	7.00	1944			2.00
1939		4.25	1945			2.00
1940		4.25	1946			2.00
1941		4.00				

4085 Threepence. ℞. Shield on rose

	EF	Unc.		VF	EF	Unc.
1937		2.00	1941	1.00		3.00
— Proof *FDC* £4.50			1942*	2.00	8.00	17.50
1938		2.00	1943*	2.25	10.00	20.00
1939	3.00	9.00	1944*	4.00	15.00	30.00
1940		3.00	*For colonial use only.*			

4086

4086 Maundy Set. Silver, .500 fine. Uniform dates

	FDC		FDC
	£		£
1937	50.00	1942	50.00
— Proof *FDC* £50.00		1943	50.00
1938	50.00	1944	50.00
1939	50.00	1945	50.00
1940	50.00	1946	50.00
1941	50.00		

4087 — fourpence, 1937–46 . . . . *from*   8.50

4088 — threepence, 1937–46 . . . . *from*   8.50

4089 — twopence, 1937–46 . . . . *from*   8.50

4090 — penny, 1937–46 . . . . *from* 12.00

Second coinage. Silver, .925 fine, with title IND . IMP (Maundy only)

4091 Maundy Set (4d., 3d., 2d. and 1d.). Uniform dates

1947	50.00	1948	50.00

4092 — fourpence, 1947–8 . . . .   9.00

4093 — threepence, 1947–8 . . . .   9.50

4094 — twopence, 1947–8 . . . .   9.00

4095 — penny, 1947–8 . . . . 12.00

Third coinage. Silver, .925 fine, but omitting IND . IMP. (Maundy only)

4096 **Maundy Set** (4d., 3d., 2d. and 1d.). Uniform dates

	FDC £		FDC £
1949	50.00	1951	50.00
1950	50.00	1952	52.00

The 1952 Maundy was distributed by Queen Elizabeth II.

4097 **— fourpence**, 1949–52	*from*	9.00
4098 **— threepence**, 1949–52	*from*	9.00
4099 **— twopence**, 1949–52	*from*	9.00
4100 **— penny**, 1949–52	*from*	12.00

CUPRO-NICKEL

Second coinage. Types as first (silver) coinage, IND . IMP.

4101 **Halfcrown.** ℞. Shield

	Unc. £		Unc. £
1947	4.00	1948	4.00

4102 **Florin.** ℞. Crowned rose

1947	4.00	1948	3.25

4103 **Shilling.** "English" type

1947	5.00	1948	3.00

4104 **— "Scottish" type**

1947	4.00	1948	3.00

4105 **Sixpence.** GRI crowned

1947	3.00	1948	2.00

Third coinage. Types as before but title IND . IMP . omitted

4106   4110

4106 **Halfcrown**

1949	6.50	1951	8.00
1950	7.00	— Proof *FDC* £10.00	
— Proof *FDC* £10.00		1952	*Extremely rare*

4107 **Florin**

1949	8.50	1951	8.50
1950	8.00	— Proof *FDC* £7.50	
— Proof *FDC* £8.50			

4108 **Shilling.** "English" type

1949	6.00	1951	6.50
1950	6.50	— Proof *FDC* £6.50	
— Proof *FDC* £6.50			

4109 **— "Scottish" type**

1949	8.00	1951	7.00
1950	7.00	— Proof *FDC* £6.50	
— Proof *FDC* £6.50			

Cupro-nickel

4110 Sixpence. As illustration on page 289

	EF £	Unc. £		VF £	EF £	Unc. £
1949		4.00	1951			4.00
1950		4.00	— Proof *FDC* £5.00			
— Proof *FDC* £5.50			1952	2.50	12.50	35.00

Festival of Britain issue

4111

4111 Crown. ℞. St. George, 1951. *Proof-like* 3.50 6.50

NICKEL BRASS

4112 4113

First issue, with title IND . IMP.

4112 Threepence (dodecagonal). ℞. Thrift

1937		2.00	1942		2.25
— Proof *FDC* £4.25			1943		2.25
1938	2.00	6.50	1944		3.00
1939	3.50	15.00	1945		6.00
1940		5.00	1946	3.00	30.00	125.00
1941		3.50	1948	3.50	15.00

Second issue, omitting IND . IMP.

4113 Threepence

	VF £	EF £	Unc. £		VF £	EF £	Unc. £
1949	3.50	35.00	135.00	1951	1.00	9.00	35.00
1950		8.00	30.00	— Proof *FDC* £25.00			
— Proof *FDC* £30.00				1952			4.00

BRONZE

First issue, with title IND . IMP.

4114 Penny. ℞. Britannia

4114

	Unc. £		Unc. £
1937	2.25	1944	7.00
— Proof *FDC* £6.50		1945	5.00
1938	2.25	1946	2.00
1939	5.00	1947	2.00
1940	6.50	1948	2.00

4115 Halfpenny. ℞. Ship

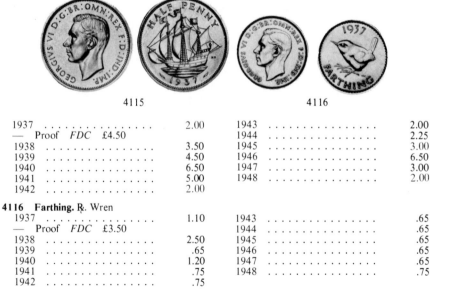

4115   4116

1937	2.00	1943	2.00
— Proof *FDC* £4.50		1944	2.25
1938	3.50	1945	3.00
1939	4.50	1946	6.50
1940	6.50	1947	3.00
1941	5.00	1948	2.00
1942	2.00		

4116 Farthing. ℞. Wren

1937	1.10	1943	.65
— Proof *FDC* £3.50		1944	.65
1938	2.50	1945	.65
1939	.65	1946	.65
1940	1.20	1947	.65
1941	.75	1948	.75
1942	.75		

Bronze

Second issue, without IND . IMP. Types as before

4117   Penny

	VF £	EF £	Unc. £		VF £	EF £	Unc. £
1949			2.00	1951 . . . . .6.00		12.00	18.00
1950	4.00	10.00	25.00	— Proof *FDC* £16.00			
— Proof *FDC* £18.00							

4118   4119

4118   Halfpenny

1949		5.50	1951		5.50
1950		4.50	— Proof *FDC* £4.50		
— Proof *FDC* £4.50			1952		3.00

4119   Farthing

1949		1.25	1951		.70
1950		.70	— Proof *FDC* £3.00		
— Proof *FDC* £4.00			1952		.80

The coins dated 1952 were issued during the reign of Elizabeth II.

ELIZABETH II, acc. 1952

The earliest coins of this reign have the title BRITT · OMN, but in 1954 this was omitted from the Queen's titles owing to the changing status of so many Commonwealth territories. The minting of "English" and "Scottish" shillings was continued. A Coronation commemorative crown was issued in 1953, another crown was struck on the occasion of the 1960 British Exhibition in New York and a third was issued in honour of Sir Winston Churchill in 1965. A very small number of proof gold coins were struck in 1953 for the national museum collections, but between 1957 and 1968 gold sovereigns were minted again in quantity for sale in the international bullion market and to counteract the activities of counterfeiters.

Owing to inflation the farthing had now become practically valueless; production of these coins ceased after 1956 and the coins were demonetized at the end of 1960. In 1965 it was decided to change to a decimal system of coinage in the year 1971. As part of the transition to decimal coinage the halfpenny was demonetized in August 1969 and the halfcrown in January 1970. (See also introduction to Decimal Coinage on p. 299.)

Designer's initials:	Other designers whose initials
G. L. (Gilbert Ledward)	do not appear on the coins:
W. P. (Wilson Parker)	Christopher Ironside
M. G. (Mary Gillick)	Arnold Machin
W. G. (William Gardner)	David Wynne
E. F. (Edgar Fuller)	Professor Richard Guyatt
C. T. (Cecil Thomas)	Eric Sewell
P. N. (Philip Nathan)	Leslie Durbin
R. D. M. (Raphael David Maklouf)	
N. S. (Norman Sillman)	

PRE DECIMAL ISSUES
GOLD

First coinage, with title BRITT · OMN, 1953. *Proof only*

4120	**Five pounds.** ℞. St. George	*None issued for collectors*
4121	**Two pounds.** Similar	*None issued for collectors*
4122*	**Sovereign.** Similar	*None issued for collectors*

* **Note:** *A brilliant mint state specimen sold at auction for £24,000 in June 1985.*

4123	**Half-sovereign.** Similar	*None issued for collectors*

Second issue, BRITT · OMN omitted

4125

	Unc. £
4124 Sovereign. ℞. St. George	
1957	70.00

4125 — Similar, but coarser graining on edge

	Unc. £		Unc. £
1958	70.00	1965	70.00
1959	70.00	1966	70.00
1962	70.00	1967	70.00
1963	70.00	1968	70.00
1964	70.00		

Note: *Gold bullion price at the time of printing $340 per oz. at $1.50 to the £1 sterling.*

SILVER

The Queen's Maundy are now the only coins struck regularly in silver.
The location of the Maundy ceremony is given for each year.

First issue, with title BRITT · OMN.

		FDC £
4126	**Maundy Set** (4d., 3d., 2d. and 1d.), 1953. *St. Paul's*	250.00
4127	— **fourpence,** 1953	40.00
4128	— **threepence,** 1953	40.00
4129	— **twopence,** 1953	40.00
4130	— **penny,** 1953	50.00

Second issue, with BRITT · OMN omitted

4131

4131 Maundy Set (4d., 3d., 2d. and 1d.). Uniform dates

		FDC £			FDC £
1954	*Westminster*	55.00	1963	*Chelmsford*	55.00
1955	*Southwark*	55.00	1964	*Westminster*	55.00
1956	*Westminster*	55.00	1965	*Canterbury*	55.00
1957	*St. Albans*	55.00	1966	*Westminster*	55.00
1958	*Westminster*	55.00	1967	*Durham*	55.00
1959	*Windsor*	55.00	1968	*Westminster*	55.00
1960	*Westminster*	55.00	1969	*Selby*	55.00
1961	*Rochester*	55.00	1970	*Westminster*	55.00
1962	*Westminster*	55.00		*See also p. 300.*	

4132	— **fourpence,** 1954–70 .... *from*		10.00
4133	— **threepence,** 1954–70 .... *from*		10.00
4134	— **twopence,** 1954–70 .... *from*		10.00
4135	— **penny,** 1954–70 .... *from*		11.00

CUPRO-NICKEL

First issue, 1953, with title BRITT · OMN.

4136

		EF £	Unc. £	Proof FDC £
4136	**Crown.** Queen on horseback. ℞. Crown in centre of cross, shield in each angle, 1953	1.50	3.75	30.00

4137   4138

4137	**Halfcrown,** with title BRITT · OMN. ℞. Arms, 1953	3.25	10.00
4138	**Florin.** ℞. Double rose, 1953	3.00	8.00

4139   4140   4141

4139	**Shilling.** "English". ℞. Three lions, 1953	1.00	4.00
4140	— "Scottish". ℞. Lion rampant in shield, 1953	1.00	4.00
4141	**Sixpence.** ℞. Interlaced rose, thistle, shamrock and leek, 1953	.70	3.00
4142	Set of 9 uncirculated cu-ni, ni-br and Æ coins (2/6 to $\frac{1}{4}$d.) in Royal Mint plastic envelope	8.00	

Cupro-nickel
Second issue, similar types but omitting BRITT · OMN.

4143   4144

		EF £	Unc. £
4143	**Crown,** 1960. Bust r. ℞. As 4136	3.50	6.50
	— — Similar, from polished dies (New York Exhibition issue)	5.00	20.00
4144	— Churchill commemorative, 1965. As illustration. ℞. Bust of Winston Churchill r..		.75
	— — Similar, satin-finish. *Specimen*		375.00

4145   Halfcrown. ℞. As 4137

	EF £	Unc. £		
1954	2.00	15.00	1961	1.00
1955		4.50	1962	1.00
1956		5.00	1963	1.25
1957		2.25	1964	3.50
1958	2.00	15.00	1965	1.00
1959	2.00	15.00	1966	.60
1960		3.50	1967	.60

4146

4146   Florin. ℞. As 4138

	EF £	Unc. £		
1954	3.00	35.00	1961	2.00
1955		3.00	1962	1.10
1956		3.00	1963	.75
1957	2.25	25.00	1964	.60
1958	1.00	12.00	1965	.50
1959	2.50	30.00	1966	.45
1960		2.25	1967	.40

4147 Shilling. "English" type. ℞. As 4139

	EF £	Unc. £		Unc. £
1954		2.50	1961	.75
1955		2.00	1962	.50
1956		7.50	1963	.25
1957		1.50	1964	.30
1958	2.00	18.00	1965	.30
1959		1.00	1966	.30
1960		1.00		

4148 Shilling. "Scottish" type. ℞. As 4140.

	EF £	Unc. £		Unc. £
1954		2.00	1961	6.00
1955		3.00	1962	1.00
1956		7.50	1963	.25
1957	2.00	17.50	1964	.50
1958		1.00	1965	.50
1959	2.00	17.50	1966	.30
1960		1.00		

4149 Sixpence. ℞. As 4141

	Unc. £		Unc. £
1954	3.25	1961	3.25
1955	1.00	1962	.30
1956	1.00	1963	.25
1957	.65	1964	.20
1958	4.00	1965	.15
1959	.35	1966	.15
1960	4.25	1967	.15

NICKEL BRASS

4152   4153

First issue, with title BRITT . OMN.

4152 Threepence (dodecagonal). ℞. Crowned portcullis, 1953 . . . .   1.50
— Proof   *FDC*   £3.50

Second issue (omitting BRIT . OMN)

4153 Threepence. Similar type

	Unc. £		Unc. £
1954	4.00	1961	.35
1955	5.00	1962	.30
1956	5.00	1963	.20
1957	3.50	1964	.20
1958	6.00	1965	.20
1959	3.50	1966	.15
1960	3.00	1967	.15

BRONZE

First issue, with title BRITT . OMN.

4154   4158

		VF £	EF £	Unc. £	Proof FDC £
4154	**Penny.** ℞. Britannia (only issued with Royal Mint set in plastic envelope), 1953	.60	1.75	5.00	6.00
4155	**Halfpenny.** ℞. Ship, 1953			1.75	4.00
4156	**Farthing.** ℞. Wren, 1953			.75	2.25

Second issue, omitting BRITT . OMN.

4157   **Penny.** ℞. Britannia (1954–60 *not issued*)

	Unc. £		Unc. £
1954	*Extremely rare*	1964	.15
1961	.60	1965	.15
1962	.20	1966	.15
1963	.20	1967	.15

4158   **Halfpenny.** ℞. Ship (1961 *not issued*)

	Unc. £		Unc. £
1954	4.50	1962	.15
1955	4.00	1963	.15
1956	4.25	1964	.15
1957	.75	1965	.15
1958	.40	1966	.15
1959	.25	1967	.15
1960	.25		

4156   4159

4159   **Farthing.** ℞. Wren

	Unc. £			EF £	Unc. £
1954	.80	1956		.55	1.75
1955	.75				

DECIMAL COINAGE

In December 1967 a decision to build a new mint at Llantrisant in South Wales was announced. The first phase was completed by December 1968 when H.M. The Queen struck the first coins at the official opening. The second phase was completed during late 1975 at which time all coin production at Tower Hill ceased.

Though the official change-over to a decimal currency did not take place until 15th February 1971, three decimal denominations were circulated prior to this date. The 10 and 5 *new pence*, equivalent to the former florin and shilling, were introduced in 1968 and the seven-sided 50 *new pence* (equal to 10 shillings) was issued during October 1969. The old halfpenny was demonetized on 1st August 1969, and the halfcrown was withdrawn on 1st January 1970.

In 1968 bronze 2, 1 and ½ *new pence* dated 1971 were issued, together with the 1968 10 and 5 *new pence*, as specimens of the new coinage, but these bronze coins were not legalized for current use until 1971.

Britain's accession to the E.E.C. was commemorated by a special 50 pence piece in 1973. A crown-sized 25 pence has been issued to celebrate the Silver Wedding of H.M. The Queen and Prince Philip in 1972, the Queen's Silver Jubilee in 1977, the 80th birthday of Queen Elizabeth, the Queen Mother and for the Royal Wedding in 1981.

Britain's first 20 pence piece appeared in 1982 and 1983 saw the first circulating non-precious metal £1 coin. In 1986 the Royal Mint has introduced a nickel-brass £2 piece only available in proof or UNC sets. This coin has been specially struck in honour of the XIII Commonwealth Games to be held in Scotland (see illus. 4279). The word 'NEW' was omitted from the 1982 cupro-nickel coins which now bear the denomination in words and figures. The ½ pence was demonetized in December 1984.

In 1979 the first proof sovereign since 1937 was issued and 1980 saw a proof five pound, two pound and half sovereign.

GOLD

| 4160 | 4161 | 4164 |

	Unc. £					*Unc.* £
4160 Five pounds. As illustration						
1980. Proof *FDC* £550.00		1982. Proof *FDC* £550.00				
1981. Proof *FDC* £500.00		1984. Proof *FDC* £550.00				
4161 Five pounds. As illustration.						
1984	£400.00					
4162 Two pounds.						
1980. Proof *FDC* £325.00		1983. Proof *FDC* £325.00				
1982. Proof *FDC* £350.00						
4164 Sovereign. As illustration						
1974	£70.00	1981				£70.00
1976	£70.00	— Proof *FDC* £90.00				
1978	£70.00	1982				£70.00
1979	£70.00	— Proof *FDC* £90.00				
— Proof *FDC* £90.00		1983 Proof *FDC* £90.00				
1980	£70.00	1984 Proof *FDC* £110.00				
— Proof *FDC* £80.00						
4166 Half-sovereign.						
1980 Proof *FDC* £60.00		1983 Proof *FDC* £60.00				
1982	£45.00	1984 Proof *FDC* £65.00				
— Proof *FDC* £60.00						

(For proof sets which include some or all of the above coins, see the list on pages 307–8.)

SILVER

4170 Maundy Set (4p, 3p, 2p and 1p). Uniform dates. Types as 4131

		FDC £			FDC £
1971	*Tewkesbury Abbey*	55.00	1979	*Winchester Cathedral*	55.00
1972	*York Minster*	55.00	1980	*Worcester Cathedral*	55.00
1973	*Westminster Abbey*	55.00	1981	*Westminster Abbey*	55.00
1974	*Salisbury Cathedral*	55.00	1982	*St. David's Cathedral*	55.00
1975	*Peterborough Cathedral* ...	55.00	1983	*Exeter Cathedral*	55.00
1976	*Hereford Cathedral*	55.00	1984	*Southwell Minster*	75.00
1977	*Westminster Abbey*	65.00	1985	*Ripon Cathedral*	75.00
1978	*Carlisle Cathedral*	55.00	1986	*Chichester Cathedral*	90.00

4180 — **fourpence,** 1971–85 .... *from* 13.00

4181 — **threepence,** 1971–85 .... *from* 13.00

4182 — **twopence,** 1971–85 .... *from* 13.00

4183 — **penny,** 1971–85 .... *from* 15.00

N.B. *The Queen's Maundy are now the only coins struck regularly in .925 silver. The place of distribution is shown after each date.*

NICKEL-BRASS

4185   4186

		Unc. £
4185	**One pound** (U.K. type). Edge DECUS ET TUTAMEN	
	1983	1.50
	—Specimen in presentation folder	2.50
	—Proof in Ʀ	30.00
	—Proof piedfort in Ʀ	85.00
4186	**One pound** (Scottish type). Edge NEMO ME IMPUNE LACESSIT	
	1984	1.50
	—Specimen in presentation folder	2.50
	—Proof in Ʀ	20.00
	—Proof piedfort in Ʀ	55.00

CUPRO-NICKEL

4190   4191

4190 Fifty new pence (seven sided). Ʀ. Britannia r.

	Unc. £		Unc. £
1969	2.00	1978	.75
1970	4.00	1979	.75
1976	1.10	1980	.75
1977	1.10	1981	.75

4195

		Unc.
		£

4191 **Fifty (50) pence.** 'New' omitted. As illustration (on previous page)

1982 . . . .   1984* (*See note on p. 303*) 75

1983 . . . .

4195 Accession to European Economic Community. ℞. Clasped hands, 1973 . . . .   1.10

—— (Proof in case) . . . .   *FDC*   £4.00

4200

4200 **Twenty-five new pence** (crown). Silver Wedding Commemorative, 1972 90

—— (Ӕ proof in case) . . . .   *FDC*   £15.00

4201

4201 Silver Jubilee Commemorative, 1977 60

—— (Ӕ proof in case) . . . .   *FDC*   £10.00

—— (Cu. ni. proof). Only issued in 1977/Mint set. See PS27 on p. 304

—— (Cu. ni. Specimen striking). Issued in Royal Mint folder 1.75

4202

<table>
<tr><td></td><td align="right">Unc.
£</td></tr>
</table>

4202 Queen Mother 80th Birthday commemorative, 1980 45
— — (*R* proof in case) . . . . *FDC* £25.00
— — (Cu. ni. Specimen striking). Issued in Royal Mint folder 1.75

4203

4203 Royal Wedding Commemorative, 1981 45
— — (*R* proof in case) . . . . *FDC* £25.00
— — (Cu. ni Specimen striking. Issued in Royal Mint folder) 1.75

4208

4208 **Twenty (20) pence.** As illustration

1982 40	1983	.40
— *R* Proof piedfort *FDC* £20.00	1984	.40

4210   4211

4210   Ten new pence. ℞. Lion passant guardant .

	Unc.		Unc.
	£		£
1968	.25	1975	.25
1969	.30	1976	.25
1970	.30	1977	.25
1971	.30	1979	.25
1973	.25	1980	.25
1974	.25	1981	.25

4211   Ten (10) pence. As illustration

| 1982* .... | | 1984* .... | |
| 1983* .... | | | |

4220   4221

4220   Five new pence. ℞. Crowned thistle

1968	.15	1977	.15
1969	.18	1978	.15
1970	.18	1979	.15
1971	.15	1980	.15
1975	.15	1981 Proof only	

4221   Five (5) pence. As illustration

| 1982* .... | | 1984* .... | |
| 1983* .... | | | |

BRONZE

4230   4231

4230   Two new pence. ℞. Plumes

1971	.07	1978	.10
1975	.10	1979	.10
1976	.10	1980	.10
1977	.10	1981	.10

4231   Two (2) pence. As illustration

| 1982* .... | | 1984* .... | |
| 1983* .... | | | |

* Note. Coins marked with a * by the date occur in the Royal Mint specimen or proof sets, there being none made for general circulation at the time of going to press.

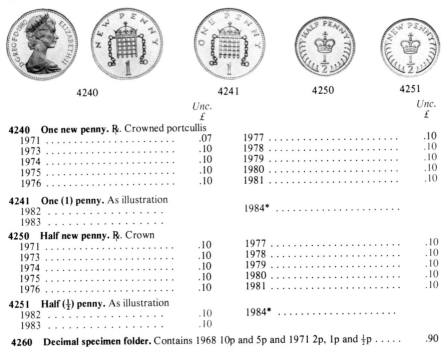

| 4240 | 4241 | 4250 | 4251 |

	Unc. £		Unc. £

4240   One new penny. ℞. Crowned portcullis

1971	.07	1977	.10
1973	.10	1978	.10
1974	.10	1979	.10
1975	.10	1980	.10
1976	.10	1981	.10

4241   One (1) penny. As illustration

1982		1984*	
1983			

4250   Half new penny. ℞. Crown

1971	.10	1977	.10
1973	.10	1978	.10
1974	.10	1979	.10
1975	.10	1980	.10
1976	.10	1981	.10

4251   Half (½) penny. As illustration

1982	.10	1984*	
1983	.10		

4260   Decimal specimen folder. Contains 1968 10p and 5p and 1971 2p, 1p and ½p 90

NEW PORTRAIT

The new effigy is designed by Raphael David Maklouf, FRSA. It is only the third portrait of the Queen to be used on U.K. coinage, the previous change of portrait being in 1968 with the introduction of decimal coins. The designer's initials R.D.M. appear on the truncation. There is no portrait change on the Maundy coins.

GOLD

| 4261 | 4266 | 4271 | 4276 |

4261 Five pounds. ℞. St. George
1985 Proof . . . . *FDC*   £550.00

4262 Five pounds. ℞. St. George, 'U' in a circle to left of date
1985 . . . . *UNC*   £400.00

4266 Two pounds. ℞. St. George
1985 Proof . . . . *FDC*   £325.00

4267 Two pounds. ℞. St. Andrew's cross surmounted by a thistle of Scotland. Edge XIII
COMMONWEALTH GAMES SCOTLAND 1986.
1986 Proof . . . . *FDC*   £300

4271 Sovereign. ℞. St. George
1985 Proof . . . . *FDC*   £135
1986 Proof . . . . *FDC*   £150

4276 Half-sovereign. ℞. St. George
1985 Proof . . . . *FDC*   £70
1986 Proof . . . . *FDC*   £80

NICKEL-BRASS

4279

4279 Two pounds. ℞. St. Andrew's cross surmounted by a thistle of Scotland. Edge XIII
COMMONWEALTH GAMES SCOTLAND 1986.
1986* . . . .

4281

	Unc. £
4281 One pound (Welsh type). Edge PLEIDIOL WYF I'M GWLAD	
1985	1.50
— Specimen in presentation folder	2.75
— Proof in Ꝛ	20.00
— Proof piedfort in Ꝛ	55.00

4282

4282 One pound. (Northern Ireland). Edge DECUS ET TUTAMEN.
1986 . . . .
— Specimen in presentation folder . . . .
— Proof in Ꝛ . . . .
— Proof piedfort in Ꝛ 55.00

* These coins occur in the Royal Mint specimen or proof sets. There were none for general circulation

CUPRO-NICKEL

4286

4286　Fifty pence. ℞. Britannia r.
　1985 . . . .
　1986* . . . .

4291

4291　Twenty pence. ℞. Crowned double rose
　1985 . . . .
　1986* . . . .

4301

4301　Ten pence. ℞. Lion passant guardant
　1985* . . . .
　1986* . . . .

4306

4306　Five pence. ℞. Crowned thistle
　1985* . . . .
　1986* . . . .

4311

4311   Two pence. ℞. Plumes

1985 . . . .
1986* . . . .

4316

4316   One penny. ℞. Portcullis with chains

1985 . . . .
1986* . . . .

* These coins occur in the Royal Mint specimen or proof sets. There were none made for general circulation at the time of going to press.

PROOF or SPECIMEN SETS

Issued by the Royal Mint in official case from 1887 onwards, but earlier sets were issued privately by the engraver.

All pieces have a finish superior to that of the current coins.

		No. of coins	FDC £
PS1	**George IV.** New issue, **1826.** Five pounds to farthing	11	18,000.00
PS2	**William IV.** Coronation, **1831.** Two pounds to farthing	14	17,000.00
PS3	**Victoria,** young head, **1839.** "Una and the Lion" five pounds, and sovereign to farthing	15	21,000.00
PS4	— **1853.** Sovereign to quarter-farthing, including Gothic type crown . .	16	19,500.00
PS5	Jubilee head. Golden Jubilee, **1887.** Five pounds to threepence	11	5,000.00
PS6	— — Crown to threepence	7	950.00
PS7	Old head, **1893.** Five pounds to threepence	10	5,250.00
PS8	— — Crown to threepence	6	1,000.00
PS9	**Edward VII.** Coronation, **1902.** Five pounds to Maundy penny. Matt surface	13	1,500.00
PS10	— — Sovereign to Maundy penny. Matt surface	11	500.00
PS11	**George V.** Coronation, **1911.** Five pounds to Maundy penny	12	2,750.00
PS12	— — Sovereign to Maundy penny	10	750.00
PS13	— — Halfcrown to Maundy penny	8	300.00
PS14	New types, **1927.** Crown to threepence	6	225.00
PS15	**George VI.** Coronation, **1937.** Gold. Five pounds to half-sovereign . . .	4	1,450.00
PS16	— — — Silver, etc. Crown to farthing, including Maundy	15	120.00
PS17	Mid-Century, **1950.** Halfcrown to farthing		35.00
PS18	Festival of Britain, **1951.** Crown to farthing	10	55.00
PS19	**Elizabeth II.** Coronation, **1953.** Crown to farthing	10	35.00
PS20	"Last Sterling" set, **1970.** Halfcrown to halfpenny plus medallion	8	12.00
PS21	Decimal coinage set, **1971.** 50 new pence ("Britannia") to $\frac{1}{2}$ penny, plus medallion	6	12.00
PS22	— **1972.** As last, but includes the cu.-ni. Silver Wedding crown	7	12.00
PS23	— **1973.** As PS21 but "EEC" 50p	6	10.00
PS24	— **1974.** As PS21	6	10.00
PS25	— **1975.** As last	6	10.00
PS26	— **1976.** As last	6	10.00
PS27	— **1977.** As PS21 but including the proof Silver Jubilee crown struck in cupro-nickel	7	13.00
PS28	— **1978.** As PS21	6	13.00
PS29	— **1979.** As last	6	16.00
PS30	— **1980.** As last	6	10.00
PS31	— — Five pounds to half sovereign	4	800.00
PS32	— **1981.** U.K. Proof coin Commemorative collection. (Consists of £5, £1, Royal Wedding crown (25p) in Æ, plus base metal proofs as PS21.)	9	600.00
PS33	— — As PS21	6	10.00
PS34	**Elizabeth II, 1982.** U.K. Uncirculated (specimen) set in Royal Mint folder. New reverse types, including 20 pence	7	3.50
PS35	— — As last but proofs in Royal Mint sealed plastic case, plus medallion	7	14.00
PS36	— Æ Five pounds to half-sovereign	4	900.00
PS37	— **1983.** As PS34, includes 'U.K.' £1	8	5.00
PS38	— — As PS35, includes 'U.K.' £1	8	18.00

		No. of coins	
PS39	— — *N* £2, £1, £½ in case	3	450.00
PS40	— **1984** As PS37 but with 'Scottish' £1	8	5.00
PS41	— — As PS38 but with 'Scottish' £1	8	19.00
PS42	— — *N* £5, £1, £½ in case	3	650.00
PS43	— **1985.** As PS37 but with new portrait, also includes 'Welsh' £1. The set does not contain the now discontinued halfpenny	7	5.00
PS44	— — As last but proofs in Royal Mint sealed plastic case, plus medallion	7	18.00
PS45	— — As last but within a deluxe red leather case	7	25.75
PS46	— — *N* £5, £2, £1, £½ in case	4	900.00
PS47	—**1986.** As PS43 but with a new two pounds and the Northern Ireland £1	8	9.95
PS48	— — As PS44 but with two pounds and Northern Ireland £1	8	20.00
PS49	— — As last but within a deluxe red leather case	8	30.00
PS50	— — *N* £2 (as 4267), £1, £½ in a deluxe red leather case	3	500.00

Note. *The prices given are for absolutely perfect sets with uncleaned, brilliant or matt surfaces. Sets are often seen with one or more coins showing imperfections such as scratches, bumps on the edge, etc. Any flaws will substantially affect the value of a set.*

APPENDIX I

A SELECT NUMISMATIC BIBLIOGRAPHY

A list of Seaby publications and other new books is advertised at the end of this catalogue. Listed below is a selection of general books on British numismatics and other works that the specialist collector will need to consult.

General Books:

NORTH, J. J. *English Hammered Coins,* Vol. I, *c. 650–1272*; Vol. II, *1272–1662.*
BROOKE, G. C. *English Coins.* (3rd Ed., 1951).
SUTHERLAND, C. H. V. *English Coinage, 600–1900.*
KENYON, R. Ll. *Gold Coins of England.*
GRUEBER, H. A. *Handbook of the Coins of Great Britain and Ireland.*

Specialist Works:

MACK, R. P. *The Coinage of Ancient Britain.*
ALLEN, D. *The Origins of Coinage in Britain: A Reappraisal.*
DOLLEY, R. H. M. (Ed.). *Anglo-Saxon Coins; studies presented to Sir Frank Stenton.*
KEARY, C. & GREUBER, H. *English Coins in the British Museum: Anglo-Saxon Series.*
BROOKE, G. C. *English Coins in the British Museum: The Norman Kings.*
ALLEN, D. F. *English Coins in the British Museum: The Cross-and-Crosslets ('Tealby') type of Henry II.*
LAWRENCE, L. A. *The Coinage of Edward III from 1351.*
WHITTON, C. A. *The Heavy Coinage of Henry VI.*
BLUNT, C. E. and WHITTON, C. A. *The Coinages of Edward IV and of Henry VI (Restored).*
MORRIESON, LT.-COL. H. W. *The Coinages of Thomas Bushell, 1636–1648.*
SEABY, H. A. *The English Silver Coinage from 1649.*
SPINK & SON, LTD. *The Milled Coinage of England, 1662–1946.*
PECK, C. W. *English Copper, Tin and Bronze Coins in the British Museum, 1558–1958.*
LINECAR, H. W. A. *British Coin Designs and Designers.*
COPE, G. M. & RAYNER, P. A. *English Milled Coinage 1662–1972.*

and other authoritative papers published in the *Numismatic Chronicle* and *British Numismatic Journal.*

APPENDIX II

LATIN LEGENDS ON ENGLISH COINS

A DOMINO FACTUM EST ISTUD ET EST MIRABILE IN OCULIS NOSTRIS. (This is the Lord's doing and it is marvellous in our eyes: *Psalm* 118, 23). First used on "fine" sovereign of Mary.

AMOR POPULI PRAESIDIUM REGIS. (The love of the people is the King's protection). Reverse legend on angels of Charles I.

ANNO REGNI PRIMO, etc. (In the first year of the reign, etc.). Used around the edge of many of the larger milled denominations.

CHRISTO AUSPICE REGNO. (I reign under the auspice of Christ). Used extensively in the reign of Charles I.

CIVIUM INDUSTRIA FLORET CIVITAS. (By the industry of its people the State flourishes). On the 1951 Festival crown of George VI.

CULTORES SUI DEUS PROTEGIT. (God protects His worshippers). On gold double crowns and crowns of Charles I.

DECUS ET TUTAMEN. (An ornament and a safeguard). This inscription on the edge of all early large milled silver was suggested by Evelyn, he having seen it on the vignette in Card. Richelieu's Greek Testament, and of course refers to the device as a means to prevent clipping. (Virgil, *Aenid* v.262). This legend also appears on the edge of U.K. and Northern Ireland one pound coins.

DIRIGE DEUS GRESSUS MEOS. (May the Lord direct my steps). On the "Una" 5 pounds of Queen Victoria.

DOMINE NE IN FURORE TUO ARGUAS ME. (O Lord, rebuke me not in Thine anger: *Psalm* 6, 1). First used on the half-florin of Edward III and then on all half-nobles.

DomiNuS DeuS Omnipotens REX. (Lord God, Almighty King). (Viking coins).

DUM SPIRO SPERO. (Whilst I live, I hope). On the coins struck at Pontefract Castle during the Civil War after Charles I had been imprisoned.

EXALTABITUR IN GLORIA. (He shall be exalted in glory). On all quarter-nobles.

EXURGAT DEUS ET DISSIPENTUR INIMICI EIUS. (Let God arise and let His enemies be scattered: *Psalm* 68, 1). On the Scottish ducat and early English coins of James I (VI) and was chosen by the King himself.

FACIAM EOS IN GENTEM UNAM. (I will make them one nation: *Ezek.* 37, 22). On unites and laurels of James I.

FLORENT CONCORDIA REGNA. (Through concord kingdoms flourish). On gold unite of Charles I and broad of Charles II.

HANC DEUS DEDIT. (God has given this, *i.e. crown*). On siege-pieces of Pontefract struck in the name of Charles II.

HAS NISI PERITURUS MIHI ADIMAT NEMO. (Let no one remove these [letters] from me under penalty of death). On the edge of crowns and half-crowns of Cromwell.

HENRICUS ROSAS REGNA JACOBUS. (Henry *united* the roses, James the kingdoms). On English and Scottish gold coins of James I (VI).

INIMICOS EJUS INDUAM CONFUSIONE. (As for his enemies I shall clothe them with shame: *Psalm* 132, 18). On shillings of Edward VI struck at Durham House, Strand.

JESUS AUTEM TRANSIENS PER MEDIUM ILLORUM IBAT. (But Jesus, passing through the midst of them, went His way: *Luke* iv. 30). The usual reverse legend on English nobles, ryals and hammered sovereigns before James I; also on the very rare Scotch noble of David II of Scotland and the unique Anglo-Gallic noble of Edward the Black Prince.

JUSTITIA THRONUM FIRMAT. (Justice strengthens the throne). On Charles I half-groats and pennies and Scottish twenty-penny pieces.

LUCERNA PEDIBUS MEIS VERBUM EST. (Thy word is a lamp unto my feet: *Psalm* 119, 105). Obverse legend on a rare half-sovereign of Edward VI struck at Durham House, Strand.

MIRABILIA FECIT. (He made marvellously). On the Viking coins of (?) York.

NEMO ME IMPUNE LACESSIT. (No one provokes me with impunity). On the 1984 Scottish one pound.

NUMMORUM FAMULUS. (The servant of the coinage). The legend on the edge of the English tin coinage at the end of the seventeenth century.

O CRUX AVE SPES UNICA. (Hail! O Cross, our only hope). On the reverse of all half-angels.

PAX MISSA PER ORBEM. (Peace sent throughout the world). The reverse legend of a pattern farthing of Anne.

PAX QUÆRITUR BELLO. (Peace is sought by war). The reverse legend of the Cromwell broad.

PER CRUCEM TUAM SALVA NOS CHRISTE REDEMPTOR. (By Thy cross, save us, O Christ, our Redeemer). The normal reverse of English angels.

PLEIDIOL WYF I·M GWLAD. (True am I to my country). Taken from the Welsh National Anthem. Used on the 1985 Welsh one pound.

POST MORTEM PATRIS PRO FILIO. (For the son after the death of the father). On seige pieces struck at Pontefract in 1648 (old style) after the execution of Charles I.

POSUI DEUM ADJUTOREM MEUM. (I have made God my Helper: *comp. Psalm* 54, 4). Used on many English and Irish silver coins from Edward III until 1603. Altered to POSUIMUS and NOSTRUM on the coins of Philip and Mary.

PROTECTOR LITERIS LITERÆ NUMMIS CORONA ET SALUS. (A protection to the letters [on the face of the coin], the letters [on the edge] are a garland and a safeguard to the coinage). On the edge of the rare fifty-shilling piece of Cromwell.

QUÆ DEUS CONJUNXIT NEMO SEPARET. (What God hath joined together let no man put asunder: *Matt.* 19, 6). On the larger silver English and Scottish coins of James I after he succeeded to the English throne.

REDDE CUIQUE QUOD SUUM EST. (Render to each that which is his own). On a Henry VIII type groat of Edward VI struck by Sir Martin Bowes at Durham House, Strand.

RELIGIO PROTESTANTIVM LEGES ANGLIÆ LIBERTAS PARLIAMENTI. (The religion of the Protestants, the laws of England, the liberty of the Parliament). This is known as the "Declaration" and refers to Charles I's declaration to the Privy Council at Wellington, 19th Sept., 1642; it is found on many of his coins struck at the provincial mints during the Civil War. Usually abbreviated to REL : PROT : LEG : ANG : LIB : PAR :

ROSA SINE SPINA. (A rose without a thorn). Found on some gold and small coins of Henry VIII and later reigns.

RUTILANS ROSA SINE SPINA. (A dazzling rose without a thorn). As last but on small gold only.

SCUTUM FIDEI PROTEGET EUM *or* EAM. (The shield of faith shall protect him *or* her). On much of the gold of Edward VI and Elizabeth.

TALI DICATA SIGNO MENS FLUCTUARI NEQUIT. (Consecrated by such a sign the mind cannot waver: from a hymn by Prudentius written in the 4th cent., entitled "Hymnus ante Somnum"). Only on the gold "George noble" of Henry VIII.

TIMOR DOMINI FONS VITÆ. (The fear of the Lord is a fountain of life: *Prov.* 14, 27). On many shillings of Edward VI.

TUEATUR UNITA DEUS. (May God guard these united, i.e. kingdoms). On many English, Scottish and Irish coins of James I.

VERITAS TEMPORIS FILIA. (Truth, the daughter of Time). On English and Irish coins of Mary Tudor.

Some Royal Titles:

REX ANGLorum—King of the English.

REX SAXONUM OCCIDENTALIUM—King of the West Saxons.

DEI GRAtia ANGLiae ET FRANCiae Dominus HYBerniae ET AQVITaniae—By the Grace of God, King of England and France, Lord of Ireland and Aquitaine.

Dei Gratia Magnae Britanniae, FRanciae ET Hiberniae REX Fidei Defensor BRunsviciensis ET Luneburgensis Dux, Sacri Romani Imperii Archi-THesaurarius ET ELector = By the Grace of God, King of Great Britain, France and Ireland, Defender of the Faith, Duke of Brunswick and Luneburg, High Treasurer and Elector of the Holy Roman Empire.

BRITANNIARUM REX—King of the Britains (i.e. Britain and British territories overseas).

BRITT : OMN : REX : FID : DEF : IND : IMP—King of all the Britains, Defender of the Faith, Emperor of India.

Although not *Latin* legends, the following Norman-French mottos might usefully be added here:

DIEU ET MON DROIT. (God and my right). On halfcrowns of George IV and later monarchs.

HONI SOIT QUI MAL Y PENSE. (Evil to him who evil thinks). The Motto of the Order of the Garter, first used on the Hereford (?) halfcrowns of Charles I. It also occurs on the Garter Star in the centre of the reverse of the silver coins of Charles II, but being so small it is usually illegible; it is more prominent on the coinage of George III.

Seaby's Coin and Medal Bulletin
This is a magazine published for all interested in numismatics. It contains articles and notes on coins and medals; details of numismatic society meetings; answers to questions; letters to the Editor; cuttings from the press, etc., etc.; also many pages of coins and medals of all kinds offered for sale. These are well catalogued and act as a good guide to help collectors to catalogue and classify their own coins. Please send for a specimen copy and current subscription rates. Bound Bulletins for some previous years are available (prices upon request).

Numismatic Clubs and Societies
There are well over one hundred numismatic societies and clubs in the British Isles, a number of which form part of the social and cultural activities of scholastic institutions or commercial industrial concerns.

The two principal learned societies are the Royal Numismatic Society and the British Numismatic Society, both of which publish an annual journal.

Many local clubs and societies are affiliated to the British Association of Numismatic Societies (the B.A.N.S., which holds an annual conference). Details of your nearest local club may be obtained from: The Hon. Sec., B.A.N.S., K. F. Sugden, Dept. of Numismatics, Manchester Museum, The University, Oxford Road, Manchester.

APPENDIX III

MINTMARKS AND OTHER SYMBOLS ON ENGLISH COINS

A MINTMARK (*mm.*), a term borrowed from Roman and Greek numismatics where it showed the place of mintage, was generally used on English coins to show (and a religious age preferred a cross for the purpose) where the legend began. Later, this mark, since the dating of coins was not usual, had a periodic significance, changing from time to time. Hence it was of a secret or "privy" nature; other privy marks on a coin might be the code-mark of a particular workshop or workman. Thus a privy mark (including the *mm.*) might show when a coin was made, or who made it. In the use of precious metals this knowledge was necessary to guard against fraud and counterfeiting.

Mintmarks are sometimes termed "initial marks" as they are normally placed at the commencement of the inscription. Some of the symbols chosen were personal badges of the ruling monarch, such as the rose and sun of York, the boar's head of Richard III, the dragon of Henry Tudor or the thistle of James I; others are heraldic symbols or may allude to the mint master responsible for the coinage, e.g. the *mm.* bow used on the Durham House coins struck under John Bowes and the WS mark of William Sharrington of Bristol.

A table of mintmarks is given on the next page. Where mintmarks appear in the catalogue they are sometimes referred to only by the reference number, in order to save space, i.e. *mm.* 28 (= mintmark Sun), *mm.* 28/74 (= *mm.* Sun on obverse, *mm.* Coronet on reverse), *mm.* 28/- (= *mm.* Sun on obverse only).

MINTMARKS AND OTHER SYMBOLS

1 Edward III, Cross 1 (Class B + C).
2 Edward III, broken Cross 1 (Class D).
3 Edward III, Cross 2 (Class E).
4 Edward III, Cross 3 (Class G).
5 Cross Potent (Edw. III Treaty).
6 Cross Pattée (Edw. III Post Treaty Rich. III).
7 (a) Plain or Greek Cross.
  (b) Cross Moline.
8 Cross Patonce.
9 Cross Fleurée.
10 Cross Calvary (Cross on steps).
11 Long Cross Fitchée.
12 Short Cross Fitchée.
13 Restoration Cross (Hen. VI).
14 Latin Cross.
15 Voided Cross (Henry VI).
16 Saltire Cross.
17 Cross and 4 pellets.
18 Pierced Cross.
19 Pierced Cross & pellet.
20 Pierced Cross & central pellet.
21 Cross Crosslet.
22 Curved Star (rayant).
23 Star.
24 Spur Rowel.
25 Mullet.
26 Pierced Mullet.
27 Eglantine.
28 Sun (Edw. IV).
29 Mullet (Henry V).
30 Pansy.
31 Heraldic Cinquefoil (Edw. IV).
32 Heraldic Cinquefoil (James I).
33 Rose (Edw. IV).
34 Rosette (Edw. IV).
35 Rose (Chas. I).
36 Catherine Wheel.
37 Cross in circle.
38 Halved Sun (6 rays) & Rose.
39 Halved Sun (4 rays) & Rose.
40 Lis-upon-Half-Rose.
41 Lis-upon-Sun & Rose.
42 Lis-Rose dimidiated.
43 Lis-issuant-from-Rose.
44 Trefoil.
45 Slipped Trefoil, James I (1).
46 Slipped Trefoil, James I (2).
47 Quatrefoil.
48 Saltire.
49 Pinecone.
50 Leaf (-mascle, Hen. VI).
51 Leaf (-trefoil, Hen. VI).
52 Arrow.
53 Pheon.
54 A.
55 Annulet.
56 Annulet-with-pellet.
57 Anchor.
58 Anchor & B.
59 Flower & B.
60 Bell.
61 Book.
62 Boar's Head (early Richard III).
63 Boar's Head (later Richard III).
64 Boar's Head, Charles I.
65 Acorn (a) Hen. VIII (b) Elizabeth.
66 Bow.
67 Br. (Bristol, Chas. I).
68 Cardinal's Hat.
69 Castle (Henry VIII).
70 Castle with H.
71 Castle (Chas. I).
72 Crescent (a) Henry VIII (b) Elizabeth.
73 Pomegranate. (Mary; Henry VIII's is broader).
74 Coronet.
75 Crown.
76 Crozier (a) Edw. III (b) Hen. VIII.
77 Ermine.
78 Escallop (Hen. VII).
79 Escallop (James I).
80 Eye (in legend Edw. IV).
81 Eye (Parliament).
82 Radiate Eye (Hen. VII).
83 Gerb.
84 Grapes.
85 Greyhound's Head.
86 Hand.
87 Harp.
88 Heart.
89 Helmet.
90 Key.
91 Leopard's Head.
91A Crowned Leopard's Head with collar (Edw. VI).
92 Lion.
93 Lion rampant.
94 Martlet.
95 Mascle.
96 Negro's Head.
97 Ostrich's Head.
98 P in brackets.
99 Pall.
100 Pear.
101 Plume.
102 Plume. Aberystwyth and Bristol.
103 Plume. Oxford.
104 Plume. Shrewsbury.
105 Lis.
106 Lis.
107 Portcullis.
108 Portcullis. Crowned.
109 Sceptre.
110 Sunburst.
111 Swan.
112 R in brackets.
113 Sword.
114 T (Henry VIII).
115 TC monogram.
116 WS monogram.
117 y or Y.
118 Dragon (Henry VII).
119 (a) Triangle (b) Triangle in Circle.
120 Sun (Parliament).
121 Uncertain mark.
122 Grapple.
123 Tun.
124 Woolpack.
125 Thistle.
126 Figure 6. (Edw. VI).
127 Floriated cross.
128 Lozenge.
129 Billet.
130 Plume. Lundy Is.
131 Two lions.
132 Clasped book.
133 Cross pommee.
134 Bugle.

N.B. *The reign after a mintmark indicates that from which the drawing is taken. A similar* mm. *may have been used in another reign and will be found in the chronological list at the beginning of each reign.*

1	2	3	4	5	6	7a	7b	8	
10	11	12	13	14	15	16	17	18	
20	21	22	23	24	25	26	27	28	2
30	31	32	33	34	35	36	37	38	
40	41	42	43	44	45	46	47	48	
50	51	52	53	54	55	56	57	58	B 5
60	61	62	63	64	65a	65b	66	67	6
69	70	71	72a	72b	73	74	75	76	
78	79	80	81	82	83	84	85	86	
88	89	90a	90b	90c	91	92	93	94	9
96	97	98	99	100	101	102	103	104	10
106	107	108	109	110	111	112	113	114	11
116	117a	117b	118	119a	119b	120	121	122	12
124	125	126	127	128	129	130	131	132	13
134									

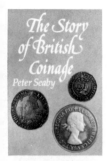

THE STORY OF BRITISH COINAGE

by Peter J. Seaby

£25.00

A comprehensive history of British coinage, examined chronologically by the reigns of the British monarchs. Over 300 coins are illustrated in fine detail at actual size.

COLLECTING COINS

by P. Frank Purvey

£7.95

This very readable work is the perfect introduction to the fascinating hobby of coin collecting. The enormous variety of coins open to the collector at any level is shown in more than 150 illustrations.

ENGLISH COINS

in the British Museum:
Anglo-Saxon Coins
by Charles Keary & Herbert Grueber

£35.00

A reprint in 2 volumes of the widely quoted reference work on Anglo-Saxon Coins.

822 pages, 62 plates.

THE ENGLISH SILVER COINAGE FROM 1649

by H. A. Seaby & P. A. Rayner

£9.95

The fourth edition of this standard work of reference on English milled silver coinage, giving comparative rarity of all varieties, also patterns and proofs.

238 pages, over 625 illustrations.

SEVENTEENTH CENTURY TOKENS
of the British Isles
and their values

by Michael Dickinson

£35.00

Based on J. G. Williamson's classic work *Trade Tokens Issued in the Seventeenth Century*, this catalogue lists all known major types, with valuations.

Seaby's Standard Catalogue of British Coins   volume 2

COINS OF SCOTLAND, IRELAND AND THE ISLANDS

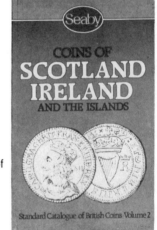

by Peter Seaby and P. Frank Purvey

£9.75

A detailed listing in one volume of all the coins of Scotland, Ireland, and the Islands.

Every major type and date listed with current valuations.

238 pages, over 650 illustrations.

BRITISH TOKENS
AND THEIR VALUES
(revised 1984)

Edited by Peter Seaby and Monica Bussell. Revised by Michael Dickinson and P. Frank Purvey

£6.75

The only compact collector's guide to British Tokens with a good representative selection of the 17th, 18th and 19th century copper and silver tokens of England, Scotland, Ireland and Wales.

200 pages, 172 illustrations.

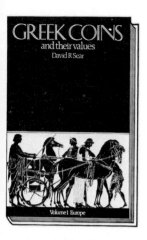

GREEK COINS
and Their Values

by D. R. Sear

Vol I. **Europe**
£17.50
Vol II. **Asia & Africa,**
including the Hellenistic Monarchies.
£17.50

The most comprehensive priced guide to Greek coins ever published. The average collector should be able to locate all the types he is likely to encounter in one denomination or another. Useful historical notes and illustrated preface. Altogether 7956 coins listed with 3356 photographs of coins in the British Museum.

GREEK COIN TYPES AND THEIR IDENTIFICATION

by Richard Plant

£14.95

Nearly 3000 Greek coins are listed and illustrated, concentrating on types not immediately identifiable from their inscriptions or subjects represented. Place of issue, date, denomination, metal and size are given. An invaluable aid to the identification of Greek and 'Greek Imperial' coins.

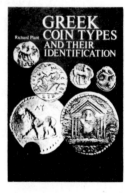

GREEK IMPERIAL COINS AND THEIR VALUES

The Local Coinages of the Roman Empire

by David R. Sear

This catalogue is unique in providing the collector with the only comprehensive and authoritative guide devoted specifically to the local coinages of the Roman Empire. The chronological arrangement aids the collector in identification and emphasises the true importance of these coins as a complement to the Empire-wide Roman state coinage. Over 6000 coins catalogued and valued, 1750 illustrations, 10 maps, 672 pages.

Price £35.00

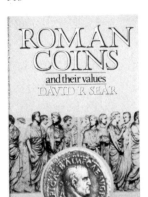

ROMAN COINS
and Their Values

by D. R. Sear
3rd Revised Edition 1981

£14.95

A general catalogue of Roman coins, with
values, containing biographical and historical
details, and descriptions of over 4300 coins.
376 pages, with chronological tables, twelve
plates and many half tone illustrations in text.

THE COINAGE OF
ROMAN BRITAIN

by Gilbert Askew

£4.75

Second edition with new Introduction and
listing of the Governors of Roman Britain
by Peter Clayton. The most compact listing
of the Roman coins relating to the Province
of Britannia.

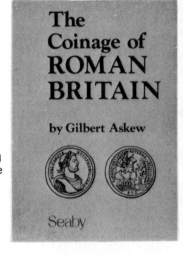

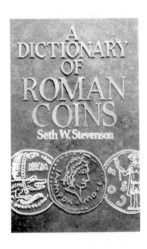

A DICTIONARY OF
ROMAN COINS

by S. W. Stevenson

£30.00

First published in 1889, this is a reprint of the
most comprehensive dictionary of Roman
coin types, legends, emperors, etc., ever
published in a single volume and contains
much information for students of Roman
coinage not assembled elsewhere.
929 pages, several hundred illustrations.

ROMAN SILVER COINS

by H. A. Seaby

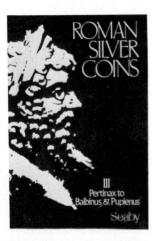

Volume I. **The Republic to Augustus,** 3rd edition, 1978
Revised by D. R. Sear and Robert Loosley.   **£12.50**

Volume II. **Tiberius to Commodus,** 3rd edition, 1979
Revised by D. R. Sear and Robert Loosley.   **£12.50**

Volume III. **Pertinax to Balbinus and Pupienus,** 2nd edition, 1982
Revised by D. R. Sear.   **£12.50**

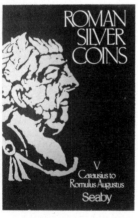

Volume IV. **Gordian III to Postumus,** 2nd edition, 1982
Revised by D. R. Sear.   **£12.50**

Volume V. **Carausius to Romulus Augustus,**
by C. E. King, publish 1987

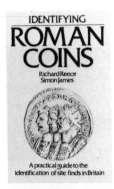

IDENTIFYING ROMAN COINS

by Richard Reece

£5.95

An easily usable, visual recognition guide to Roman coins. All major reverse types from the first to the late fourth century AD are illustrated with explanatory notes and useful background information is included.

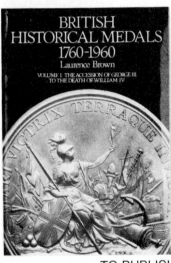

BRITISH HISTORICAL MEDALS 1760–1960

by Laurence Brown

Vol. I. The Accession of George III to the death of William IV. £50.00

The authoritative continuation of *Medallic Illustrations.* Full numismatic description of each piece is given, its designer where known, its size, metal in which specimens are known (together with an indication of their rarity), and locations of specimens in the principal British collections. Full indexes of inscriptions, artists, engravers, medallists, publishers and provenances of illustrated medals. 1755 medals listed, 406 illustrations, 496 pages, cloth bound.

TO PUBLISH 1987. **Vol. II. The Reign of Queen Victoria**

MEDALLIC ILLUSTRATIONS OF THE HISTORY OF GREAT BRITAIN AND IRELAND TO THE DEATH OF GEORGE II

The first ever reprint of the plates of this major work on British historical medallions. Contains 183 superb plates, information to enable correct identification and a certain amount of historical data.

In addition there are indices covering inscriptions, engravers and artists, engraver's initials and a general subject index.

Size $16\frac{1}{2}''$ x $11\frac{1}{2}''$. Heavy library binding **£75.00**
Deluxe half-leather limited edition **£125.00**

All Seaby publications together with a wide range of numismatic books may be ordered from:

B.A. Seaby Ltd.
8 Cavendish Square
London W1M 0AJ